More praise for *A Chosen Few*

"This book is a fascinating review of the changing life of Jews and Judaism and Europeans in general since the Second World War."
— *Rocky Mountain News*

"Kurlansky does an astonishingly informative job here, covering a vast array of individuals and communities throughout Europe, chronicling the economic, political, and cultural trends that re-shaped and often played havoc with their lives and destinies. His descriptions of life in Antwerp, Paris, Budapest, and Amsterdam are superb, while his chapters on Poland are among the best I've read."
— SUSAN MIRON
Forward

"A richly descriptive and insightful survey of post-Holocaust European Jewry . . . With a novelist's eye for irony and description, [Kurlansky] offers many moments of transcendence and humor; entertaining culture clashes between communists and capitalists, religious and secular, Zionists and diasporists. . . . A lively, penetrating follow-up to Holocaust readings that speaks volumes about the resiliency of the Jewish people."
— *Kirkus Reviews*

"Kurlansky's collection of case histories unfolds like a novel."
— *The Jewish Advocate*

Please turn the page for more reviews. . . .

Other Books by Mark Kurlansky

Salt: A World History
The Basque History of the World
Cod: A Biography of the Fish that Changed the World
A Continent of Islands: Searching for the Caribbean Destiny

The White Man in the Tree and Other Stories (fiction)
The Cod's Tale (for children)

A CHOSEN FEW

====

The
Resurrection
of European Jewry

====

MARK KURLANSKY

Ballantine Books • New York

A Ballantine Book
Published by The Ballantine Publishing Group

Portions of this book have appeared, in somewhat different form, in *Partisan
Review* and *Harper's*.

www.ballantinebooks.com

Library of Congress Catalog Card Number is
2001012345

ISBN 0-345-44814-6

Cover photo © Frederic Brenner

Manufactured in the United States of America

First Ballantine Books Edition: April 2002

10 9 8 7 6 5 4 3 2 1

TO LISA BETH

"If God lets me live, I shall achieve more than my mother ever did, I shall not remain insignificant, I shall work in the world for people."
—ANNE FRANK's diary, April 11, 1944

"Solange ed Juden gibt, wird es immer Nazis geben." (As long as there are Jews there will always be Nazis.)

"A Jew is a citizen of no country except Israel."

"Waarom leef ik?" (Why am I alive?)

—three of the comments written in the guest book at the Anne Frank house in Amsterdam

CONTENTS

x | C O N T E N T S

INTRODUCTION, 2002

if they do it for no reason
there's no motive
if they all do it
no one knows who has done it.
—HENRYK GRYNBERG,
"The Perfect Crime," 1989

Anti-Semitism has proven to be one of the most enduring concepts in European civilization. In a 1927 book called *The Wandering Jew*, about the struggles of poor eastern European Jews, Viennese Jewish novelist Joseph Roth concluded that anti-Semitism would vanish from the world, ended by the Soviet Union. He wrote of anti-Semitism, "In the new Russia, it remains a disgrace. What will ultimately kill it off is public shame." He noted virulent outbursts in Russia but dismissed them as the death struggles of dinosaurs resisting the inevitable future.

Roth even speculated that "If this process continues, the age of Zionism will have passed, along with the age of anti-Semitism—and perhaps even that of Judaism itself."

Today the Soviet Union has been gone for a decade but anti-Semitism is still here. So for that matter, is Judaism. "The Jewish question"—I have never been certain what the question is—that Roth predicted would be put to rest with Russian leadership, has endured.

The lesson to be learned from Roth, aside from a warning to writers not to publish predictions in books, is that both Judaism and anti-Semitism have deep and permanent roots in Europe. Though Judaism is a less European idea than anti-Semitism, for many Jews, Jewish culture is European—or was.

Because of the Holocaust, Europe is no longer the most Jewish continent. It may have remained the most anti-Semitic, though Africa and Asia, with their Muslim populations are certainly vying for the title. It is difficult to be certain because anti-Semitism is more difficult to quantify than Judaism. As the nations of the former Soviet bloc struggle for acceptance in the West—admission into Western clubs such as NATO and the European Union— Jewish organizations such as the World Jewish Congress have urged that progress towards democracy in these nations be measured by the way they are treating their Jews. This is not as skewed a perspective as it at first sounds. Anti-Semitism, whether in Hungary, Germany, or France, has usually been tied to undemocratic movements. The growth of anti-Semitism in France, from the Dreyfus case to World War II collaboration, was tied to monarchists, fascists, and other groups that did not support republicanism. The Soviet Union was in principle opposed to anti-Semitism, and even outlawed its outward manifestations. But as that nation grew increasingly repressive, it also became increasingly anti-Semitic. The "anti-zionist campaign" in Poland in the late 1960s was the precursor to general repression.

But a more subtle anti-Semitism is allowed to breathe and grow even in the setting of democracy. Now in the early twenty-first century when so much urgency is given to fighting international terrorism, it is useful to remember that in the late twentieth century Jews feared Arab gunmen and bombs in Paris, Antwerp, Munich—much of western Europe. No European Jew went to a Jewish restaurant or a synagogue without calculating the risk of attack. These attacks against social organizations, restaurants, schools and synagogues were met with official statements of outrage and very little else. Almost no effort was made to capture or punish the perpetrators, even when Israeli intelligence offered information that could lead to their capture. Today when wondering how international Arab terrorism could have become so brazen, we should note that twenty years ago they were allowed to kill Jews in western Europe with impunity.

In the decade that has passed since I researched A Chosen Few, the standing in Europe of both Judaism and anti-Semitism has barely changed. This is not surprising, but what is surprising is that none of the countries about which I wrote in this book has moved one step further away from World War II. Europe, sixty years after the Holocaust, has achieved no more closure than had Europe fifty years after. Dariusz Stola, a historian of the twentieth century at the Polish Academy of Sciences, said in a lecture delivered in June 2001 at the University of Warsaw, "The Holocaust is not a problem of the past. It is a problem of the present. I can hardly find a European country without a World War II problem from Germany, French collaboration, Swiss banks, the role of the Vatican. If you do not have problems with World War II, you are not European."

The World War II problem, the Jewish question—these are distinctly European debates. It would have been logical to imagine that these issues had to be resolved, before the Jews would return. But in fact they returned before there was any resolution and now children, grandchildren, and even great grandchildren of survivors, live their lives half citizen and half metaphor.

The Jews have an irrefutable claim on what all Europeans want—standing as World War II victims. Everyone was either—in the words of Holocaust historian Raul Hilberg—a victim, a bystander, or a perpetrator. The worst fate has become the best status. Just as Jews have always been envied and resented for whatever they had, they are envied today for their victim status. Europeans need to show that they too, not just Jews, were the victims of World War II. The French and Dutch accomplish this with some difficulty. The Poles stubbornly fight for their victim status. Even the Germans hope that somehow Dresden gives them a chance for victim status.

The Jews of Dresden in the former East Germany have recently found their real life in Germany and their metaphorical one at cross purposes. Across the wide and curving Elbe, in the Baroque historic city center, where blackened sandstone fairies cavort from ancient rooftops, workers waddle by, clearing debris with wheelbarrows. The city is finally digging out from the famous February 13, 1945, British RAF bombing run followed the next morning with an attack by the U.S. Army Air Force. Initially, the German police claimed 18,000 dead. But in subsequent years the count has wavered between 30,000 and 130,000.

Germany fell, and with little chance for recrimination against the rest of the world, Germans have, for a half century, denounced the bombing of Dresden as cruel and unnecessary.

Before it was bombed into a ruin, Dresden, the capital of Saxony, had been one of the prized centers of Germany. The old walled medieval town reached its golden age in the eighteenth century. A Protestant church with a huge dome defining the city skyline, the Frauenkirche, became the symbol of Dresden—like an Eiffel

Tower or an Empire State building. Bach gave the Frauenkirche's first organ concert.

But for forty-five years after the 1945 bombing, the view across the Elbe was of the piles of stone, staircases overgrown with bushes, wall fragments silhouetted against the sky, the skeleton of one burned-out dome sticking out above overgrown rubble piles amid a huge vacant lot that had been cleared with bulldozers.

In 1949, when the Cold War began with Germany splitting into West and East, East Germany, the German Democratic Republic, found a perfect convergence of political rhetoric and economic reality. They did not have the money to completely rebuild their cities, but in leaving central Berlin with bullet holes and crumbling walls and Dresden with its charred remains, they were creating monuments to the horror the fascists had brought on the German people. Fascists were the perpetrators and Germans were the victims.

In the new East Germany, history might be rewritten, but it was never to be forgotten. Every February 13, Dresden school children were gathered in a remembrance of the bombing. Townspeople went to the remaining charred tower facing the pile of rocks that was once the Frauenkirche, and lit candles.

All this ended in 1990 along with East Germany. The West Germans, unlovingly known in the East as the Wessies, arrived with their own brand of Wiedergutmachung, making it good again. It was all so nice before the Communists and the Nazis, they said, couldn't we just put it back the way it was.

Since the reunification of Germany—that is the term always used because it has been unified before—the Wessies have been rushing into the bombed-out parts of the East such as Dresden and the center of Berlin and rebuilding, making Germany historic and lovely again and, in so doing, removing those East German reminders of unlovely history.

In Dresden alone, in the ten years following the reunification of Germany in October 1990, about $47 billion, some private and some government funds, was spent on reconstruction. Dresden's new tourist literature, in giving the history of the city, seldom offers a date between 1918, when the Saxon monarchy was abolished, and the 1945 bombing. "The Friends of Dresden" brochure to raise money for the rebuilding of the Frauenkirche, offers no date between an 1843 Wagner debut and the 1945 bombing. Photographs of the blackened rubble, some of it untouched until very recently, are readily available. More difficult to find is the 1934 picture of little Nazi boys in brown shirts, all at attention for the visit of Nazi Propaganda Minister Josef Goebbels to the city, or the 1944 photo of thousands of Dresdeners cheering flags of the Third Reich, the graceful arches of the fourteenth-century Augustus Bridge in the background.

A decade after reunification, Ossies and Wessies still look and think so differently that they are immediately distinguishable in a bar or on a street corner. The Ossies look defeated and the Wessies strut like conquerors. The demeanor, the body language, would betray them if the clothes and words didn't. The Ossie Jews who went back to build Communism and the Wessie Jews, who went back to earn money, along with their children, have remained even farther apart than non-Jewish Germans.

The local Ossies, even the non-Jewish ones, showed little enthusiasm for the Wessies and their billions spent rebuilding the Frauenkirche. Many viewed the project as the destruction of their anti-war and anti-fascism monument.

Other curious controversies have arisen. The Dresden castle was to be restored to its 1733 condition. But as stone fragments are fitted together and missing parts resculpted and a fresh bright layer of gilding laid on, an argument has emerged. Should it all look bright and shiny the way it did in 1733, or antique and historic the way it did in 1945 before the bombing? Should the Frauenkirche be furnished with a baroque organ, the kind of light, crisp, harpsicord-like instrument for which Bach and the other baroque composer wrote, an organ like the original installed when the church was completed in 1743, or should they install a large, grumbling nineteenth-century organ like the one that was destroyed in the 1945 bombing?

Are they restoring the eighteenth-century splendor of Dresden's golden age or simply undoing the 1945 bombing? Are they trying to remember the eighteenth century or forget the twentieth century? Are there to be no traces left of World War II?

The Dresden debate becomes more tense when discussing one of the last baroque buildings on the restoration list. In 1838, Gottfried Semper, the man who designed the Dresden Opera house and the adjacent Old Masters Picture Gallery, also designed a synagogue. The Jews prayed in Semper's baroque palace that looked like the Christians' baroque palaces, holding services that resembled those of the Protestants, in German instead of Hebrew, on Sundays rather than Saturdays. They believed in fitting into Dresden life.

Most Dresdeners remember the synagogue being bombed in 1945 along with everything else in the center. The tourist board even noted that it could not be rebuilt like the Frauenkirche but would have to be completely reconstructed from new materials because the destruction from the bombing was so total. But in fact the reason that no wall, not even stones, remain from the synagogue is that it was not destroyed in 1945. On the night of November 9, 1938, Kristallnacht, when Jewish stores and synagogues throughout Germany were attacked, the Dresden synagogue was burned. After the mob burned the synagogue, a "civic group" cleared the ruins, an operation for which the Jewish community was forced to pay. Heinz-Joachim Aris, the current director of the Dresden Jewish Community, then a small boy, remembers his father being forced to wear a yellow star as he and other Jews were made to gather the remaining stones from the synagogue and use them to pave streets.

Of the nearly 5,000 Jews who had lived in Dresden when Hitler came to power, by 1945 all but 198 had fled or been killed or were dying in concentration camps. With the Reich rapidly disintegrating, the German government was desperate to kill the last of the Jews. On Tuesday morning, February 13, the remaining Jews received orders to report for deportation to the camps on Friday. But that evening when Dresden was destroyed, the roaring wall of fire that collapsed the beautiful Frauenkirche also destroyed Gestapo headquarters and deportation from Dresden came to an end. Aris and his family were among the 198 who survived because of the bombing.

Herbert Lappe, a Jewish engineer whose parents survived in England and returned when he was three in 1949, said, "When the Dresden people remember the bombing, some of the Jews remember how they survived." On February 13, when the city bells would ring to signal the gathering at the Frauenkirche rubble for the annual bombing memorial, Lappe's mother always refused to go.

A group of Protestants raising money for the Frauenkirche felt strongly that it would be wrong to rebuild their church and not the synagogue. They formed a "Christian-Jewish friendship group," Lappe said. "As always happens with such groups, they were entirely Christian." Once again the question was not what kind of synagogue the Jews of Dresden wanted but what would be the proper symbolic gesture toward this metaphoric people. The Germans wanted the Jews to have back their synagogue, even though the Jews did not want it. To the Dresden Jews, the baroque palace was a symbol of their parents' failed experiment at assimilation. The few who still want to pray do not want to pray in German on Sunday or in a synagogue that looks like a church.

The Jews want to add something different to the cityscape, something that was not there before the bombing, and so the Jewish community commissioned a concrete block, slightly twisted, straining toward Jerusalem, with a courtyard that marks the outline of the original synagogue. This was not what the Wessies had in mind for the new Dresden.

"It is friction," said Lappe. "It should be a needle in the town. Nothing aggressive. But people should see it and say, 'What is this?' " At the insistence of the Jewish community, the relatively inexpensive $9.5 million building was financed mostly by the city of Dresden and the regional government of Saxony rather than by Jewish contributions. The building was dedicated on November 9, 2001, the sixty-third anniversary of Kristallnacht.

The day after the new synagogue opened, someone had drawn a swastika on one of the walls. This kind of attack on Jewish monuments and buildings by right wing extremists has steadily increased in Germany over the past decade.

In France, though dialogue about the Nazi occupation has been fairly open for a long time—if not since the death of De Gaulle in 1970, certainly since the return of the Socialists in 1981—books, television, film and commentary continue to expose the shameful French collaboration, as though it had never been exposed before. For all its sorrow and pity, France did not have one of the worst records of Nazi-occupied countries. The Belgians and the Dutch did worse. But no one wants to write about Belgium. Understandably, the French love to write about France. So do Americans. And so they continue to expose the already well-documented French collaboration.

While France still struggles with its history of Nazi collaboration, the majority of both Jews and non-Jews there were born since the Liberation. More than half of French Jews are either from North Africa or related to North African Jews who did not directly experience the Holocaust. Today French Jews feel secure enough to do what Jews do, fight among themselves—angry arguments over such subjects as the future of Israel.

While the large French Jewish population debates endlessly, the tiny surviving Polish Jewish population remains a topic of endless debate—the Jewish question, which, in reality, is the Polish question.

Almost six decades after the Holocaust, in which three million Polish Jews were murdered, mostly on Polish soil, Poles continue to see themselves as a heroic and suffering people who have fought for freedom and endured the brutality of their neighbors—in other words, they are the victims. The Poles are undeterred by the fact that virtually no one outside of Poland sees them that way.

It is true that three million non-Jewish Poles also died in the war. The Polish three million was ten percent of the population. The Jewish three million was more than ninety percent. According to the Polish version of history, the Jews were murdered by the Germans not by the Poles and when Poles participated they were forced at gunpoint. Poles, when not victims, were bystanders, never perpetrators. This does not explain why Jews were massacred in Poland before the Germans came or after they left, nor why anti-Semitism has remained part of Polish life.

Curiously, the difference in viewpoint inside and outside Poland has created an important rift between the Jews of Poland and the Jews of America. Poles both Jewish and Christian resent the American Jewish tendency to indulge in hatred of Poles. After all, the few Jews who have remained have done so because they feel that Poland is their home and non-Jewish Poles are their friends and colleagues.

It is interesting to compare the attitude of world Jewry toward the Netherlands and Poland. Both countries were occupied by the Nazis. Both countries had organized resistance but a general population that cooperated in the removal of more than ninety percent of its Jewish population. One difference was that in Holland the Nazis could count on the help of a home-grown Nazi movement whereas there was no such movement in Poland.

And yet the few remaining Jews in Holland do not have to constantly justify their existence in their own country. Holland is not filled with Jewish tourists openly displaying contempt for the Dutch. Dutch Jewry do not have to be on a constant vigil to keep their art treasures from being removed by the world Jewish community. But the Jews of Poland must explain why they are living in their native country. The Jews of Poland, the Czech Republic, and elsewhere in central Europe must constantly fight American and Israeli Jews wishing to take their art treasures to Israel.

Poland suffers from the chronic outbreak of history. In one

sense, these debates are healthy. They were never allowed until the late 1980s, when the Communist regime was losing its control of the national dialogue. In 1987, the first such national debate erupted when the Catholic press suggested that the Jews were owed some sort of compensation by the Poles for the Polish role as bystanders in the German Holocaust. Since then, at least nine other crises have occurred, including fights over the operation of Auschwitz as a historic site, and the memory of the post-war Kielce pogrom. The most recent such battle began in May 2000 when the Polish press reported that Jan Gross, a Polish Jew who had emigrated during the 1968 wave of anti-Semitism, was about to publish a book in Polish on Jedwabne.

Jedwabne was one of those pieces of Polish history that Jews knew about but of which Poles somehow had no memory. The entire Jewish community of this town, some 1,600 Jews according to Gross, were locked in a barn and massacred, not by Germans but by the local townspeople. There were not even Germans present giving orders. What happened was completely on the initiative of Poles—Poles as perpetrators.

This came as no shock to Polish Jews. Jedwabne was one of several such Polish massacres. Another took place in the nearby schtetl of Radzilow. And there may have been ten or more similar incidents, all in the same area. No one, including Jews, knows of this happening anywhere else in Poland. This was an infamously anti-Semitic area. Before the war it was the only rural stronghold of the Jew-hating National Democratic Party.

The Jews and non-Jews of Poland are well aware that there were Poles who saved Jews and resisted Nazis. There was an armed resistance, the first prisoners sent to Auschwitz were anti-Nazi Poles. Several hundred Poles were executed by the Germans for trying to help Jews. Even in Jedwabne, one of the local women, Antonina Wyrzykowska, saved seven Jews by hiding them. Rather than becoming a national hero, she was so abused that she immigrated to the U.S. She is still hated in the town because not only is she a witness to what they did but she is proof that individuals could have done something to stop it.

Poles through the debates of the 1980s and 1990s have come to accept that not all Poles were heroes. Many were bystanders. Some turned Jews in and cooperated in other ways with the German plan of genocide. But, by the year 2000, most Poles were still not ready to accept the fact that Poles had actively participated in the Holocaust, that they had been perpetrators. Dariusz Stola, searching through only what he regarded as the major dailies and weeklies of Poland, counted 270 articles on Jedwabne during the twelve months following the first news of the Gross book.

Gross's book was greeted by disturbing defenses. It was only a few hundred Jews, some said. Gross is a Jew who wrote the book at the behest of the American Jewish community that hates Poland, said others. Or why should Poles apologize for the killing of Jews when the Jews don't apologize for the killing of Poles.

Some who gave testimony for the book have been driven out of town. These witnesses said they have been waiting all these years to tell someone but no one ever asked. Konstanty Gebert, now a well-known journalist, went to the town and reported, "It is a village seething with hatred."

After more than a year of debate, on July 10, 2001, Aleksander Kwasniewski, the Polish President, went to Jedwabne and in a ceremony that was broadcast on national television, apologized for the way Poles had acted there. He said, "It was justified by nothing. The victims were helpless and defenseless." He asked forgiveness "in my own name and in the name of the Polish people whose consciences are shocked by this crime."

Unfortunately he was not apologizing for the majority of Poles. Many were angered by his apology and an earlier poll had shown that only thirty-two percent of Poles were in favor of an apology. But Polish Jews see progress in their chosen homeland. Even ten years ago, it would have been unlikely to have gotten thirty-two percent in favor of an apology. "That's a third, that's huge!" said Konstanty Gebert.

At the time *A Chosen Few* was being researched, Gebert had taken to wearing a yarmulke when at home in his central Warsaw apartment. In those days he would not wear it on the street. Now he does. Occasionally Poles come up to him, not to abuse him, but to say how pleased they are that today a Jew is free to wear a yarmulke on the streets of Poland.

Polish Jewish writer Julian Stryjkowski in a recent speech described how when growing up in Galicia he spoke only Yiddish. When he was sent off to school he was told to say when he heard his name, *jestem*, a Polish word meaning literally "I am." It was the Polish way of saying "here." This being the only Polish he knew, he would answer any question on any subject, *"jestem."* The other children would laugh. Today there are some four million Jews in Europe, not quite a third of the 1935 population but a million more than in 1945. They do not always want to be symbols. Not all of them even want to live Jewish lives. But they all wish to live their lives, in what they see as their own countries, just like other Europeans. Yet they must constantly assert, *jestem*—here.

Breaking my own rule about making predictions, I suspect that there will always be Jews in Europe.

New York, November 2001

INTRODUCTION, 1994

In the final days of the Soviet empire, when there was little left but humor, a story circulated about two men who on a cold winter's day put up a sign, "Fish for Sale." Immediately a huge line formed. The two fish vendors, realizing that there were far more customers than fish, angrily marched outside and shouted, "There will be no fish for Jews. All Jews go home."

After the Jews left, the line was only a little smaller. The two men had to think of something else. The customers were stamping their feet to stay warm, but they were keeping their places. The two sheepishly emerged from their storefront forty minutes later. "I'm sorry, but we only have enough fish for party members. Everyone else go home."

This time about two thirds of the line left. The rest continued to stand with their hats pulled down and their collars tugged up. When after another hour the fish vendors saw that no one had given up, they came out again and said, "Sorry but there will be fish only for recipients of the Order of Lenin."

There were two Order of Lenin winners in the line. Everyone else left. The two stood there in the cold for another hour, wondering when they would get their fish. Finally the fish vendors came out and said, "I'm sorry, we really don't have any fish at all."

The one frozen Order of Lenin winner turned to the other

frozen Order of Lenin winner and said, "You see—the Jews always get the best deal."

For all its unbelievably destructive wars, its weaponry, and its genocide—to use a word invented in this century—the end of the twentieth century is bearing some remarkable similarities to its beginning. At the turn of the century, just as stability and prosperity seemed to be within Europe's grasp, the future was menaced by the crumbling of the Russian empire and the emerging nationalism of small Balkan states. Through unification, Germany, the economic giant of Europe, had created an affluent internal market far larger than that of its neighbors.

So striking are the similarities that German chancellor Helmut Kohl angrily declared to his country's neighbors, who were nervous in the face of a newly reunited Germany, "We are in the year 1992, not 1902."

Another similarity is that the world's Jewish population will finish the century at about the same size as it began. In the 1930s Hitler promised that after the next war, there would be no Jews in Europe. He came extraordinarily close to achieving his goal. Before the Holocaust, Judaism was predominantly a European culture. The character of Jewish culture had become essentially European, and Jews were a significant part of Europe. This all changed with the Final Solution.

A half century later, the global Jewish population is still some three million fewer than the eighteen million Jews in 1933 when the Nazis came to power. What was once a population of almost nine million European Jews—half of world Jewry—is today four million, little more than a quarter of world Jewry. But at last it can be said with some confidence that European Jewry will continue, that the remaining Jews of Europe will not all move to the United States or Israel, as had often been suggested. There are only one million more Jews in Europe today than there were when the camps were liberated, but Paris has become a major Jewish center, traditional Jewish life is thriving in Antwerp, and Budapest has the makings of a large and diverse Jewish center. Communites in Berlin, Prague, and Amsterdam are struggling, but there are reasons for optimism. Poland, on the other hand, which started the century with one out of every five Jews in the world, seems today almost devoid of Jewish life—an historical reversal of Jewish demography comparable only to the Spanish expulsion in 1492 and the final Roman conquest of Judaea in A.D. 135.

I grew up in immigrant America. The Poles, Italians, and Irish had relatives in "the old country," but Jews did not. No Jew I knew did. I certainly didn't. All the relatives I knew of had either left or been killed. No one really gave much thought to the fact that American Jews lacked European relatives. It was just one of those things that made Jews different, like Saturday instead of Sunday. Jews are accustomed to the idea of being different. But while no one said it, it was generally understood that Jews did not have relatives in Europe because there were no longer Jews in Europe. People seeing my name would ask me if I had relatives in Poland. "No, I'm Jewish," I would say as an unemotional and readily understood explanation.

But even in Poland, a few Jews are trying to breathe life into the remnants of Jewry. The question arises—is often rudely asked— why a Jew would want to live in Poland. More than three million Jews were massacred there, the survivors were subjected to pogroms and attacked on trains, and finally a new regime that had promised to end racism unleashed its "anti-Zionist" campaigns. Not only in Poland but everywhere in Europe Jews are faced with the question, often from Jewish visitors, "Why are you still here?"

I wanted to know the answer to that rude question. I also wanted to know what price had been paid and what struggles waged over the past fifty years to stay and rebuild. Not surprisingly, I found no single answer to the question. People stayed because, in spite of what anti-Semitic countrymen might claim, they were indeed Poles or Frenchmen or even Germans. Some stayed because they did not want to see the history of their Jewish community come to an end. Some stayed to build a new society. Some never intended to stay but couldn't get their relatives to move. Some hated the thought of moving anywhere. Some always meant to move but could not get organized to leave, and some just got too involved with their careers.

What *has* emerged is a half-century of European history seen through the eyes of Jews—a traumatized and damaged people's experience in rebuilding their lives in the postwar, cold war, and post-Communist eras.

The Jews who were committed to rebuilding their communities sometimes found themselves at cross-purposes with their local Zionist movement. In much the same way, this book too is in conflict with Zionism, a conflict that is inevitable but in neither case specifically intended. I have never believed that all Jews should move to Israel, and I have always been bemused by Zionists who themselves had no plans to move there. I like the idea that there are still Jews in Europe, that Amsterdam's Esnoga and Prague's Old-New Synagogue are still working synagogues and not museums. Perhaps it is just that I do not want Hitler to posthumously attain his goal.

On the other hand, I understand that many Jews and non-Jews alike view Europe's future with foreboding. This is not an optimistic moment in Europe, a continent long given to pessimism. Eastern Europe's borders are tense and the Balkans are embroiled in a shooting war. Western Europe's slowly nurtured trading bloc is suffering from rising unemployment and feels outmaneuvered by deals in the Americas and Asia. Europe is turning inward, becoming obsessed with its own internal relations, problems, and battles.

As I write this introduction, during the week leading up to the 5754th year of recorded Jewish history, the French government has moved to rewrite its constitution to facilitate laws harassing immigrants; a statue of Kaiser Wilhelm I, a symbol of German military aggression, has been installed in Koblenz; while in the south, yet another of Germany's almost daily attacks resulted in the death of four immigrants in a burned-out hostel. This incident was not uniquely German—a week later a Bangladesh man lay in critical condition after being beaten and kicked in East London. The remains of Admiral Miklós Horthy—who, although less bloody than his successor, allied Hungary with the Third Reich and initiated the persecution and massacre of thousands of Jews—were reburied in his hometown with honors. Several government ministers attended the ceremony. The Hungarian prime minister asserted that Horthy had been a great patriot who had gained back Hungarian land, which angered the prime minister of the Slovak Republic, Vladimir Meciar—not because of Horthy's war record but because some of that regained land had been at Slovak expense. The same week, Meciar made an interesting observation of his own. Gypsies, the prime minister explained, are "socially unadaptable and mentally backward." Later, he denied the quote but rephrased the same thought in more polite language. While these things were happening, Bosnians were openly slaughtering each other for being Croats or Serbs or Muslims.

This is what European news is like these days. Although the style of this nationalism may be particularly European, the racism and racist attacks are not. The United States, too, has seen an increase in extreme right-wing facist violence groups like the Ku Klux Klan find willing shock troops in young skinheads. What is especially worrisome about Europe, however, is that the political establishment there reacts to such activities by pandering to the extremists. Rather than ostracizing the extremists, the establishment treats them as mainstream and goes on to ostracize the victims of extremist violence by discussing the "immigrant problem." In reality, the problem is not immigrants but the fact that immigrants are being attacked.

Germany, whose culture I have always admired—its music, its demanding and expressive language—is a country with which I have been trying to come to terms during twenty years of visits. While I am awed by its brilliance, there is something undefinable that I fear. Germans themselves fear it as well. Today, Germany's best writers are consumed with a dread of their own country. But it is too tempting to make simplistic assumptions about Germany. One time in Cologne, while I was trying to catch a soon-departing express train to Berlin, I cut into the only moving line. As I ordered my ticket in German, I heard a British couple behind me saying, "They're still like that. They'll never learn."

This book is not intended as an argument about where Jews ought to live. It is the story of brave and tenacious people who have rebuilt their lives in the face of incomprehensible horror and refused to be pushed out of their homes by bigots.

The Jews I write about here are an eclectic group, selected in as arbitrary a fashion as possible. My only criterion for choosing a particular community was that it had previously been decimated by the Holocaust. In those communities I sought out Jews of any kind—the more varied, the better. I spoke with tailors, bakers, and butchers—I did not want only prominent people. But two people I interviewed are well-known political activists: one has an international literary reputation. A few are well-known leaders in their communities, because such people, after all, are highly representative of European Jews. There are atheists, Yom Kippur Jews, and Hasids. Any Jew in Europe is a representative of European Jewry.

Wherever possible, I have tried to verify facts, and while most of the stories seemed truthful, there were a few rare interviews that I eliminated because the stories did not check out. Though some of the material in this book is derived from my own eyewitnessing in the late 1970s, 1980s and 1990s, most of the stories here are of people's lives as they told them to me. It is true that all people tend to remember their lives in selective and self-serving ways; nevertheless, I have confidence in their essential truth.

Where there is dialogue, I was either present or I reproduced it as it was related to me by a participant. Scenes that I did not witness were described to me by those who did.

I avoided people who would not let me use their names, although I respected some requests to leave out the names of or information about certain relatives.

Verifying stories and probing for truth was particularly difficult with camp survivors, who often went into tremendous but selective detail about their camp experiences, even though I did not ask them. Survivors often have a despairing sense that no one can possibly understand them, and I think that to some extent they are right. The more I learn about the Holocaust, the less I understand it. When radio correspondent Edward R. Murrow was reporting on the liberation of Buchenwald, one of the emaciated survivors went up to him and asked him if he intended to write about what he saw. The survivor, a Frenchman who had formerly worked for the news agency Havas, told him, "To write about this, you must have been here at least two years, and after that . . . you don't want to write anymore."

But people did continue with their lives—damaged people whose psyches were wounded in ways that go beyond the comprehension of the rest of us had the strength and courage to rebuild, remarry, and raise children. Because of them, Jewry today has a future in Europe, and Hitler, at last, has been defeated.

Paris, October 1994

A CHOSEN FEW

PROLOGUE

===

The Fifth Son in Berlin

"Afterward Moses and Aaron went and said to Pharaoh,
Thus says the Lord, the God of Israel: Let my people go
that they may celebrate a festival for me in the wilderness."
— Exodus 5:1

===

A loud thumping noise at the head table shook the plastic wine cups but failed to silence the die-hard old Communists. It was a rabbinical gesture — a long fluid arm motion resembling the straightening of an egret's neck, ending in a palm-down whack on the table. Orthodox rabbis do this at the reading stand when they want to silence the synagogue. Irene Runge had been accused of numerous things in the past year, but being an Orthodox rabbi was not one of them. Still, having seen the gesture, she thought she would give it a try. As former East Berlin drifted in the post-Communist era, there was something enviable about the authority wielded by an Orthodox rabbi.

In East Berlin the Passover dinner, the seder, was being offered in a government-subsidized cultural center off the Oranienburgerstrasse for fifteen marks per person — a bargain, considering that the official Jewish Community over in West Berlin was charging fifty marks. The East Berlin seder was strictly kosher — to the satisfaction of Irene, the hostess. A lifelong Communist, she had lost her position at Humboldt University after the collapse of the Communist state for having ties to the East German secret police, the infamous Stasi. The seder was to be supervised by a religious leader, long-bearded and behatted, a virulent anti-Communist religious traditionalist from the ultra-Orthodox Lubavitcher sect. He was to bring together fifty atheists — a blend of committed German Communists and Russian immigrants who had never been exposed to any religion—in the recitation of praise to God, while outside in the cool spring night, a dozen prostitutes stood in tights and glittery string bikinis, plying their trade in the newly capitalist East Berlin.

The prostitutes were happy to see the neighborhood getting more foot traffic and the Communist thought it was a "lovely evening," although a few of the Russians wished there was more singing. To the English Lubavitcher, just the fact that Jews were still having seders in Berlin was a victory.

This was Berlin almost a half-century after it was bombed into rubble. Berlin, the haunted city, still had a wall running through it. But it was no longer white concrete covered with colorful graffiti. The wall had become invisible. There was still never any doubt here or anywhere else in Berlin as to whether you were in the East or the West.

This seder was held in East Berlin, in an old central Berlin neighborhood that had once been the home of impoverished *Ostjuden*, with synagogues, kosher shops, brothels, and cabarets. The neighborhood—the buildings, but not the residents—had survived the war. Now it seemed earmarked for gentrification. Slightly chic little bars with a West Berlin slickness were starting to open. The prostitutes had come out on the street. The Oranienburgerstrasse, famous for its large synagogue that was just now being repaired from Allied bombings, had long been a red-light district, but since prostitution does not exist in a Communist state, it was kept judiciously indoors. Now the prostitutes stood off the curb every night dressed in oddly colored tights, sequined strings, and blond wigs that looked like doll hair. Here, West Berliners in BMWs could cruise for prostitutes more discreetly than they could by walking the clean modern Ku'damm in the West, where all their friends and colleagues coming back from the movies might see them.

East Berliners called West Berliners *Wessis*, and the *Wessis* called the East Berliners *Ossis*, and neither term was meant to express fondness. At this point there still wasn't much question of the East Berlin Jews mixing with the West Berlin Jews, whom they referred to as "the millionaires." There were only a few hundred East Berlin Jews, and there were a few thousand in West Berlin. Both groups' ranks were being swollen by Russian Jews. The new unified Germany had opened its gates to welcome—even help finance—any Soviet Jews who wanted to immigrate, a fact that many Russians discovered when they came to Germany to buy goods for the black market in Russia. Thousands of Jews, along with half-Jews and would-be Jews, were now coming to Germany to escape anti-Semitism.

In Germany they received housing and a living allowance. Between 1991 and 1993, Germany had given permission for 25,000 Soviet Jews to immigrate, and with less than half arrived, the Berlin Jewish Community was already 70 percent Russian. For the first time in half a century, there were more than just a small handful of Jews in Berlin.

Many of these Russian Jews would have preferred to go to the United States, but Germany welcomed them and the United States didn't. They spoke little English or German but, in the presence of Americans, they would sporadically blurt out geographical information on the northeastern United States. "Ocean Parkway," a man from Leningrad who spoke no other words of English asserted for no apparent reason, to which a Muscovite woman responded with the well-pronounced but not entirely accurate assertion, "New Haven, Connecticut—250 kilometers from New York City." A woman from Odessa smiled approvingly, though she had no geographical data to add.

The East Germans were still groping around, looking for a place in the new unified Germany. "New unified Germany" was a *Wessi* concept. To many *Ossis*, it was simply the newly expanded West Germany. The change was particularly difficult for people who felt that they had had a place in the old German Democratic Republic. Irene Runge felt certain enough of her place to freely acknowledge her vague links to the Stasi; for this act of candor she had been fired from her university post.

Sympathetic East Berliners would now say to Irene, "I understand. You had to cooperate. They tried to blackmail you, didn't they?" Over and over again she would explain that no one blackmailed her—"I thought it was the right thing to do."

After the fall of East Germany, it was discovered that about a half-million East Germans had contributed to Stasi files. These Stasi revelations had cost people like Irene not only their jobs but some of their friends. Still, the old-line Communists understood. Mia Lehmann, 84, said, "If you believed in your country and a government agent said, 'This is for the good of the country,' wouldn't you cooperate?" Many people might answer negatively to that question, but among Irene's circle were many who had said yes. In the last years of the German Democratic Republic, Irene had grown increasingly disenchanted with the government and, at the same time, increasingly interested in Judaism. After the GDR collapsed, she had no job, no party, no country really, but she did have the Jewish Cultural Association, or Jüdische Kulturverein, which she had created. She was also a paid member of the Jewish Community, but that was mainly *Wessis*. If not for the American movies and her unshakable determination that "*Wessis* make better popcorn," she wouldn't go over there at all. At her Kulturverein she gathered a small group of the kind of people she had always been around, Jewish Communists.

Unlike the Jewish Community, the Kulturverein was something she could run herself. She liked running things, holding them together with her own wild charisma and whimsy, shouting in her harsh Berlin German or her harsh New York English. She had been born in Washington Heights, New York, where many leftist Jewish families had taken refuge from the Third Reich. Most of the Jews at her Berlin Kulturverein had lived part of their life somewhere else. That was how they or their parents had survived.

These days, Irene's lifetime beliefs earned her only the contempt of the *Wessis*. There was no more party, no more Stasi, no more inside line. But she did have an ultra-Orthodox rabbi in Jerusalem who called her every Friday and before every Jewish holiday and gave her religious instructions and holiday wishes. Then there were the Lubavitch Hasidim, who had been quick to come to the aid of this little East Berlin community. Lubavitchers are a sect of the Hasidic movement, a more-than-two-hundred-year-old current from Eastern Europe that takes a more spiritual, less intellectual approach to strict observance of Jewish laws and customs. Unlike other Jews, the Lubavitchers have a missionary zeal of near Christian proportions for searching out secular Jews and bringing them back to religion. This has made them unpopular in some Jewish communities, but since the collapse of Communism, they have found fertile ground in Eastern Europe, where Jews for the first time in their lives are trying to learn about Judaism. A West German journalist who happened to be Jewish telephoned Irene to ask about her Passover plans, and as she started describing the event, he asked, "What is your thing for Lubavitchers?"

She explained, "They are poor people without pretension, and they are easy to relate to." In other words, they act like *Ossis*, not *Wessis*.

In 1989, Irene had gone to Brooklyn to see Menachem Mendel Schneerson, the white-bearded Rebbe who at almost 90 was leader of the Lubavitchers. Schneerson, who regularly predicted the coming of the Messiah and according to some of his followers was himself the Messiah, told Irene to get money and help from the official West German Jewish Community. Irene patiently pointed out that he was talking about West Germany, but she was in East Germany. What did this New York rabbi know about Germany? She patiently explained, "But Rebbe, I am in *East* Berlin, you know. I mean, there's the wall."

"Yes, yes, yes. I know," replied the Rebbe in his Yiddish-inflected English. "But this will not stay. It will change. Everything will change." Seven months later, to the amazement of almost everyone but Schneerson, the wall came down.

Now, for several weeks before Passover, Irene, who had never kept a kosher kitchen in her life, boasted to everyone she could find, in and out of the press, that her seder would be extremely Orthodox and strictly kosher. She took to wishing everyone she saw a "kosher Passover." Only a few years before, she had thought that keeping kosher meant not eating pork. But she had recently learned a great deal about not mixing meat and dairy, eating only fish with scales, looking for the right seals on kosher meat that guaranteed the animal had been properly slaughtered, not eating eggs with blood spots, and even more obscure things, such as cutting off pieces of apple rather than biting into the fruit whole.

She was not going to give up the Japanese sushi restaurants she looked forward to on her visits abroad, but she loved the mystique of orthodoxy. She had been an orthodox Communist, and now she would have Orthodox Judaism. Except for one thing: She was an atheist. She took up a ritual but not a religion. Even her son Stefan, who had himself circumcised and started going to synagogue, said that he had no religious feelings.

Most of the events held at the Kulturverein were not religious. A week before Passover, Irene provided an evening for a group of non-Jewish party organizers from various local Social Democrat offices around West Germany. These dozen or so *Wessis* at the Kulturverein made the difference between east and west apparent. They were expensively dressed, with a clear preference for the color gray, which befitted their reserved gestures and soft voices — in dramatic contrast to Irene, with her multicolored oval eyeglasses, her close-cropped blond hair, her perennial oversized plaid jacket on her small feisty frame, and her enthusiastic voice never much softer than a shout. And to Mia Lehmann, whose kind and interested face revealed something determined around the lips and jawline, and whose aged and quivering voice shook with passion for her beliefs. Before the evening started, Mia had sat down to talk to a woman who had been helping with the food. Mia, who had a radar that always led her to people with troubles, noticed that the woman looked depressed, and she found out that like two million other people in the former GDR, her job had been eliminated. It had happened only the day before, and the woman was very upset.

Mia, slightly stooped with age, stood up at the Social Democrats' meeting and in simple language told them that these were bad times for Germany. She had seen bad times before, she said, but she had never doubted that a better society could be built. Now if they all worked together, a better Germany could still be built.

Her directness and emotion left the West Germans awkwardly examining the toes of their shoes. They suffered from the uneasiness that progressive Germans often feel when they are around Jews. A thin Social Democrat with gray glasses and a gray suit stood up and made a speech in which he called Jews "a certain group" and referred to the Holocaust only as "a special experience."

Meanwhile, two young Orthodox Jews from Switzerland had arrived. They were hard to ignore because they were both very tall and one of them was enormously fat. These days, Jews from the West were forever dropping by the Kulturverein to help out. The contribution that these two made was to point out that a mezuzah marking the front doorway was not enough. They would send Irene enough mezuzahs for every doorway in the Kulturverein. "Fine, fine," Irene told them, slightly harried but glad to take in whatever orthodoxy came her way.

The evening was saved by Mark Aizikovitch, a burly black-bearded Ukrainian Jew. With his rich baritone voice and large comic black eyes, he worked the crowd with robust Yiddish and Russian songs until they twitched. Then here and there fingers and toes started tapping. Aizikovitch did not stop trilling, dipping, mugging, and growling until the guests were actually out-and-out clapping to the music.

Aizikovitch was finding life difficult in Germany, where everyone acted as though the name Mark Aizikovitch meant nothing. But Mark Aizikovitch had built a reputation in the Soviet Union for singing everything from electric rock to opera. The Germans were definitely not interested in Soviet rock. What seemed to sell best here were the old Yiddish songs he had learned in his childhood in the Ukrainian town of Poltava. Yiddish singing had become a fad in Germany, and Aizikovitch had an edge over the non-Yiddish-speaking German non-Jews who were doing it. Everything Jewish was hot in Germany these days. When the Jewish Community over in West Berlin offered courses in Hebrew, more non-Jews signed up than Jews. The Hebrew course that the Kulturverein offered had a higher ratio of Jews, but a large number of gentiles regularly participated in events.

Mia Lehmann was still struggling with her own relationship to Jewishness. Seventy-three years earlier, in a small Romanian town in the Bucovina region, she had gone to visit her mother at Yom Kippur services and had found her sitting on the ground outside the synagogue. Supporting Mia on her own, the mother could not afford to pay for her synagogue membership and so was not let in for Yom Kippur. "I don't understand this," said eleven-year-old Mia, and she resolved to have no more to do with religion. A few years later, she learned of the kibbutz movement—people all working together in the middle of Palestine. She thought it sounded very "romantic." Traveling to Belgium, she trained in agricultural techniques with a group that would soon leave for Palestine. But her habit of wandering off and talking to people and listening to their troubles led her to Antwerp's diamond district, where she met very poor Polish Jews. They told her their troubles. They were Communists, and they told her about the party. She fell in love with a German Jewish organizer, and joined the Communist party. In 1932, instead of being on a ship to Palestine, she was on a train to Berlin with her German Communist lover and a very different destiny.

Three-quarters of a century later, a few weeks before the seder, a small group of Communists from the old Antifa—the Antifascist Resistance Fighters, loyal East German Communists who had opposed the Nazis—took a tour of Israel. Since 1967, the East German Communist state they supported had vilified Israel, compared Israelis to Nazis, and actively backed violent Palestinian groups. Since the demise of the GDR, many of these East Berlin Jews had gone on trips to Israel to at last see what it was about.

Traveling by bus from northern Israel to Jerusalem, they decided they must get the Palestinian point of view, and they insisted that

the driver take them to an Arab village. As their bus approached
the village, two teenagers ran up and threw rocks at the windows.
The glass shattered into small sparkling kernels, landing in the hair
and clothes of the old Communists. One rock barely missed a
man's head. Hunching over protectively, Mia Lehmann thought,
"I can't understand this."

DAVID MARLOWE, a London-based Lubavitcher, came to Berlin
to kosher the Kulturverein and lead the Passover seder. A hefty
man with a graying scraggly beard and a rolling mumble of British
English, he was an introvert who did not know four words of German and, as both Englishman and Jew, didn't like Germany very
much. In addition, he hated Communism. "The Communists
were worse than the Nazis," he asserted. "The Nazis killed bodies,
but the Communists killed souls. That was worse. They turned
men from God."

He was shocked to discover that Irene and other Jews at the
Kulturverein were unrepentant Communists. "I don't understand,"
he said to Irene one day while they were koshering the kitchen. "I
thought everyone was cheering and celebrating and happy to be rid
of Communism."

"Right," said Irene in her blunt New York English. "Then they
found out they didn't have jobs anymore. They didn't like *that* too
much."

David, not an arguing man, gathered up the frizzy blond ex-
tremities of his beard, thought for an instant, then examined the
ingredients listed on an apple juice label. To no one's surprise, he
pronounced it unclean. Koshering the Kulturverein was a major
undertaking. The dark prewar building consisted of several bright
rooms that served a variety of functions—office, lounge, library,
meeting room, dining room—with simple modern furniture.

While David Marlowe was koshering the kitchen, Mark
Aizikovitch was wandering around the Kulturverein learning new
songs. He had agreed to sing at the seder, but he was perplexed to
find that his repertoire was not satisfactory. He had to learn seder
songs, Hebrew songs like "Dayenu," which means "It would have
been enough" and recounts all the miracles God performed so that
Moses could lead the Jews from Egyptian slavery. Aizikovitch
didn't know such songs, and he didn't understand why he could
not do his usual performance—something like the one he had

done for the Social Democrats. In spite of his Yiddish background, he didn't really know what a seder was.

While Aizikovitch paced around the Kulturverein singing "Dayenu" with a confused expression on his animate face, the search for chametz was on. *Chametz* is a Hebrew word meaning "leavening," which is strictly forbidden during the Passover period. It is not enough to eat matzoh, the cracker-like unleavened Passover substitute for bread. Not only must there be no bread in the house, there must be no trace of chametz, not even a barely visible bread crumb. The day before Passover, the house must be completely cleaned of chametz before there are three stars in the sky (or would be if Berlin ever had a clear April night). Although few households are scattered with bread crumbs or bits of mold and yeast, the Orthodox so extensively clean for Passover that chametz seems to be an imaginary creature that only they can see. Everything had to be scrubbed. Appliances and shelves had to be lined with foil or paper. Pots and utensils had to be boiled. Wooden tools could not be used, because chametz could be lurking in the grain.

Irene Runge loved it all. Mia Lehmann found it amusing. She walked around the Kulturverein imitating a rabbi, periodically raising an index finger skyward and mockingly asking, "But is it kosher?" and then breaking into a mischievous grin. A woman volunteer with a slight Australian accent muttered, "I will never be a Lubavitcher." Then she added, "Of course, I never thought I would be doing some of the things I've been doing in the past few years."

German television crews were making the most of the search for chametz, since they were forbidden to film an actual seder. They seemed to find great visual material at the Kulturverein, zooming in on David Marlowe as he sealed off a room with tape because it was not yet kosherized. The German press loves Jewish stories as an affirmation—something positive to say about the new Germany. Yes, neo-Nazis and adolescent skinheads were roaming the streets attacking foreigners, but there were also Jews, and they were doing some kind of Jewish holiday.

The press attention was annoying to David Marlowe, in part because he was shy and did not appreciate attention, but also because German history weighed heavily on his thoughts. He felt that a new generation of Germans was trying to document the few Jews their parents had failed to kill. "What do they want with us?" he muttered. Irene Runge, on the other hand, was not shy, and she very much appreciated the media attention. She had an instinct for the snappy quote and soon learned that such one-liners are to journalists what cookies are to bears.

One German journalist who had failed to make arrangements to cover this year's preparations asked Irene if she would do another seder next year. "Since Jews have been doing this for about three thousand years," she said with irritation, "we will probably do it next year." Then she added impishly, "Unless the Mashiach comes." One of her favorite things about the Orthodox was their adherence to the ancient belief that one day the Mashiach, the Messiah, would come. This expectation of the Messiah is at the heart of a debate about the State of Israel. Some Orthodox, even some of those living in Israel, believe that a state of Israel should not be declared until the Messiah comes. When He does come, the temple that the Romans destroyed will descend rebuilt in Jerusalem, and all Jews from around the world will return there. But in the meantime, Irene loved to joke with the Orthodox about His coming. "I hope He comes tonight so I don't have to go to work tomorrow," she would say at the end of a particularly hard day.

Being a Lubavitcher, imbued with the missionary spirit, David cornered whatever men were around and tried to persuade them to tie *tefillin*—two small leather boxes containing four biblical passages. The boxes have leather straps, and one box is tied tightly to one arm, while the other is tied to the forehead. Short morning prayers are recited. The strange spectacle confused Mia Lehmann's radar for people in trouble, and with a look of real concern, as though the leather straps were a kind of desperate tourniquet, she walked up to a volunteer onto whom David had lashed the little boxes. "What's happened to you?" she asked in a sympathetic voice.

After the cleaning was completed, five pieces of chametz, which in this case came from a cookie Marlowe had brought with him, were placed around the Kulturverein and the veteran Communists, equipped with a feather for sweeping and a lit candle, as is tradition, began the final purge, searching for the hidden pieces. Once found, the chametz was burned out on the courtyard balcony, leaving the Latin American women at the multicultural women's group across the way to wonder what could possibly be going on.

Irene Runge and David Marlowe differed in more than their politics and personalities. Marlowe was a religious Jew, and Judaism is a deeply intellectual religion. Never is this more apparent than in the Passover seder, where various food items are presented as symbols, each discussed, and then eaten. Questions are asked, and answers pressed for. "Why is this night different from all other nights?" has the simple response that on this night only bread without leavening is eaten. But the prescribed questions and answers are intended as only a point of departure for a discussion on the Book of Exodus, the story of Moses leading the Jews from Egypt. Among the issues to be discussed are the relationship between God and man, what it means to be a Jew, and what freedom is.

This was David Marlowe's idea of a Passover seder. To Irene Runge, it was fun to be kosher and fun to be Orthodox, but above all it had to be a good evening in which things kept moving. None of her guests at this seder were religious. She was trying to build up a Jewish nucleus and did not want to alienate these people with religious discussions; for many of them, it would be their first seder. If a law was inconvenient, she felt, it should be dropped. The ritual washing of the hands in the middle of the seder was to be skipped. "We can't have fifty people running to the washroom!" said Irene.

"We could carry a basin to them," David suggested.

"There's no room!" she shouted, as though from an uptown New York window.

"It's not optional," David mumbled softly. But in the end he gave in.

In addition to the difficulties involved in getting a group of volunteers with little experience in large-scale cooking to turn out a kosher meal for fifty, Irene faced the problem that David Marlowe was not only schooled in Jewish dietary laws but had once been in the catering business and had taken a course in hygiene. He searched for invisible salmonella with the same zeal with which he pursued unseen chametz. With the combined forces of science and religion at work, it was not certain that any food was edible, but somehow an odd and inelegant meal of salads, chicken soup, and prepackaged gefilte fish was produced.

The guests arrived at eightish, which seemed to Irene a reasonable hour to invite people for dinner. But David would not start until the official sunset, which was at 8:45. In the meantime he locked himself in a room dressed in his dark suit and hat and prayed, while the guests were left to roam the Kulturverein wondering what was wrong. A heavy-set woman who had survived the entire Nazi epoch in Berlin by hiding, furtively unwrapped a hard

candy and popped it into her granddaughter's mouth, whispering
in German, "Eat it quickly, it's not kosher."

Finally the Haggadahs, the books containing the seder ritual
and the story of the flight from Egypt, were passed out to the guests
in German, English, Russian, and French with accompanying Hebrew. David Marlowe took his place at the head table in front of a
bay window, from which the women in tights and sequin strings
could be seen taking their work positions on the street one story
below. Irene sat next to David so that she could translate into
German as he read through the Haggadah, pausing to explain and
invite questions. "We say 'Next year in Jerusalem,' but there is a
Jerusalem we could go to this year,"—and he explained that the
current State of Israel did not follow strict religious practices and so
Jews must wait for the Messiah.

The seder crowd on the first night of Passover included many
old-line Communists like Mia Lehmann and an East German authority on Sartre who had been born in France while his father was
fighting with the Resistance. These people were strangers to religion, but they understood intellectualism and were prepared to
listen to David's explanations. The first night went fairly smoothly,
in part because there were a number of German Jews present who
had lived in Israel, and being fluent in Hebrew, they could lead in
the singing of songs and reciting of prayers. There were some minor language problems, as when David told the participants that
they should feel free to schmooze, which in Yiddish means "to
chat" but in German means "to neck or make out."

The second night, the crowd was largely Russian, including
many sophisticated Muscovites such as Stanislava Mikhalskaia, an
attractive young architect who could get no architectural work in
Germany, and Kima Gredina, a doctor and novelist who had
traded partial censorship of her books in Russia for no publication
of them at all in Germany.

David carefully explained each step of the seder, while the Russians expectantly stared at their wine glasses. He recounted the
Passover legend of the four sons who ask the questions—the wise,
the wicked, the simple, and the unquestioning. Explaining that
these were the different types of Jews, he added his own Lubavitch
doctrine of a fifth son who didn't come at all because he didn't
know this was Passover. Most of the Jews these people had ever
known were of the fifth son type. But David was quick to add that
"it is none of you, because you are all here."

Irene muttered, "He's talking too much," fearing that people would start leaving. Unlike the first night, there were no Israelis to lead in the songs tonight—but that well-known Ukrainian actor-singer and irrepressible ham, Mark Aizikovitch, was there. He had spent the first night at a special Russian seder at Alexanderplatz, where he did not have to stick to "Dayenu" and the other Hebrew songs that he didn't really know. The people there had been thrilled to get his standard repertoire. Tonight, with the first part of the seder over and everyone merrily eating their kosher dinner, David agreed that Aizikovitch could sing whatever he wanted. After teasing David with the opening bars of "Hello, Dolly," Aizikovitch did a series of comic Yiddish songs. A few of the old Communists remembered the words and sang along. This music was popular in Germany.

Then David resumed reading the last stretch of the Haggadah in Hebrew.

Suddenly Aizikovitch got an idea. As an intuitive entertainer, he could see that the crowd's interest in all this Hebrew recitation was waning. But he knew a Hebrew song that always pleased. The Russians had requested it the night before, and it had been the perfect grand finale. With no warning, Mark Aizikovitch, in his deep baritone, broke into "Hatikvah," "The Hope," once the anthem of Zionism and now the Israeli national anthem. How could he have known how taboo this song was to ultra-Orthodox Jews like David Marlowe? But instead of cutting Aizikovitch off, Marlowe simply burst out laughing and declared the seder finished. It was the only way to avoid the sacrilege of singing the national anthem in the middle of a seder. He was not unhappy. Given the twentieth-century history of this city, it was enough that there were Jews having a seder here at all.

PART ONE

THE
BREAD
YEARS

"Der Tod ist ein Meister aus Deutschland." (Death is a master from Germany.)

PAUL CELAN, Todesfuge

1

From Łódź
to Paris

THE THUD OF AN ORANGE STARTLED MOISHE WAKS.
After hearing stories about Poland all his life from his parents,
he was not surprised that the Poles were throwing things at him.
What was surprising was that they would waste an orange. Oranges
were expensive in post-Communist Poland. Then he picked it up,
and the Waks family laughed. It was only the peel, so there really
wasn't anything to be amazed about.

The Waks family always did a lot of laughing when they got
together, which was not that often. Moishe lived in Berlin, a
plump and successful Berlin businessman, and he was the one
leader in the West Berlin Jewish Community who took an interest
in Irene Runge and the *Ossis* at the Kulturverein. His older brother
Ruwen, taller and less plump but otherwise looking very much like
his brother, lived in Israel. Their mother, Lea, a strong-willed
woman with a crisp, ironic sense of humor and a proud, straight
posture, still stubbornly lived in Düsseldorf, all the while preaching Zionism.

By the time Poland opened up for visitors and the Wakses could
go back to look around, Moishe's father, Aaron Waks, a dogmatic
but loving man, had died in Düsseldorf. Moishe and his brother
had gotten the idea of having their mother show them Łódź, where
she and Aaron had grown up. But the trip was making her visibly
ill. She was showing her sons things she had never even been able

to talk about. Still, like many Jews with Polish roots, in recent years her sons felt that they had to see Poland.

Families from Łódź were part of almost every Jewish community in the world, but in Łódź itself there was only one usable synagogue left. The Wakses knew better than to look for Jews there. They went directly to the cemetery. The few Jews left in Łódź knew that the best chance of meeting foreign Jewish visitors was to wait around the cemetery. When Jews came to Łódź now, they were looking for the dead. On Saturday mornings, Shabbat, Jews went to the cemetery and waited for weekend visitors like the Waks family.

Piotrkowska Street was being cleaned up and transformed into a commercial pedestrian mall to greet the new capitalism. But most of Łódź was chipped and peeling, its bygone affluence revealed in the richly decorative architecture. The wood-paneled mansions with long sweeping stairways that used to belong to the mill owners were now museums. Some of the old mills were still operating, like the colossal red brick gothic cottonworks of Poltex, and a few two-story wooden houses with outdoor staircases, where mill workers' families crowded together, were still standing.

With the collapse of the Soviet Union and its trade bloc, Łódź was again without a local economy. It had lost its Russian market. Between 1990 and 1993, forty thousand Łódź textile workers were laid off. Almost half of the 285 factories had closed.

The same thing had happened at the beginning of the century. In 1918, when Poland received its independence, Łódź had also lost its Russian market. The Poles started getting their wish, that often-proposed answer to "the Jewish question": The Jews, on the bottom of the crumbling economy, were leaving Poland, not by the hundreds but by the hundreds of thousands. In the seventeenth century, three-quarters of the world's Jews had lived in Poland, after fleeing anti-Semitism in Western Europe but stopped from going further by anti-Semitism in Russia. But over the next four centuries Poland became an increasingly unfavorable place for Jews to live. By the 1920s, only one out of every five Jews in the world still lived there. Even so, it had the second-largest Jewish population in the world. Only the United States had more, and that was because so many Polish Jews had moved there.

ICCHOK FINKELSZTAJN'S CERTAINTY about his decision to move from Łódź to Paris was a little shaken when he finally arrived at the

Gare du Nord. After days of bumping across Europe, as he made his way from the high-roofed ironwork railroad station and out into his first Parisian day, his first thought was, "*This* is what they call the city of light?"

There had been more light back in Łódź, with its wide streets and ornate buildings. Even in the smaller ghetto streets there had been more light. It was 1931, and the buildings of Paris had not been cleaned for centuries. Everywhere he walked he looked up at blackened buildings.

Still, Finkelsztajn had not had many choices. He was a cabinet-maker, but there was no more work in Łódź. No one had money anymore. Paris was alive, even if it was coated with the color of mourning. The markets were full of food—fruit and vegetables and meat. In Paris, when a man wanted to smoke a cigarette, he reached into his pocket and pulled out a pack and took one out. When the pack was empty, he would go to any corner store and buy another. In Poland, if a man wanted a cigarette and he had the money for one, he would go to the store and buy a single cigarette to smoke. Sometimes he might buy two or three cigarettes.

As Poland got poorer, moves were made to exclude Jews from universities and to force shops to stay open on Saturdays, which meant that practicing Jews could no longer be shopkeepers. Finkelsztajn had had no intention of going to a university: nor did he observe the Sabbath—or for that matter, any other religious practice. He did not really believe in religion. He believed that the future was socialism, a kind of social justice that would do more to improve the lives of working Jewish people than religion ever had. But he had also heard about an increasing number of Jews who for no apparent reason could not get a license to operate a shop. The old nightmare of Russian times returned—pogroms, those sudden unexplainable violent attacks against whole Jewish communities. Shortly before he left Poland, Kielce, the town of his girlfriend, Dwojra Zylbersztajn, had a pogrom.

Icchok was a small sturdy man, with black hair that was combed back from his square forehead and handsome Semitic features that made him look almost debonair, despite his thick worker's build. Dwojra had a soft fleshy look, a kind of generous maternal bearing, and a warm melon-shaped face and thick hair that strained in waves and frizzes against the pulled-back style of the period. They decided that before they got married, they would leave Poland, The Hasidim were offering vocational training in preparation for *aliyah*—the return to Israel—and many were moving to Palestine. David Ben-Gurion had visited Poland—under heavy armed guard—in 1933. But Palestine was not for Icchok and Dwojra. They had come from a leftist tradition that considered France the home of liberty. True, France had also been the home of Dreyfus; all Jews knew that. But they also knew that in the end Dreyfus had won, had been returned from Devil's Island and reinstated in the French army.

The plan was for Icchok to go to France first and for Dwojra to follow once he had secured an income. Icchok's sister, Leah, had already moved to Paris and was married to a baker, Korcarz, who was also from Poland. In 1932 the Korcarzes had opened their own bakery. But Icchok rejoiced in hard physical work, fresh air—and light. He did not want to be cooped up in a bakery.

He decided to leave Paris, this dark "city of light," and went south to the Alps region of France, where there was work even during the Depression. He got a job in an aluminum foundry, applied for his work papers, and thrived on hard labor in the mountain air. He liked the French workers, not only for their way of smoking and their lunch breaks of sour red wine and crusty bread, but also for their camaraderie. If you were a worker, you were one of them and you could talk and joke with them and feel that you belonged. It was the kind of working-class life he believed in.

But after three months, the foundry management told him he could not work there anymore because the French government had rejected his application for working papers. Reluctantly, he returned to Paris and learned to be a baker in Korcarz's shop, mixing huge vats of dough and kneading and braiding the challah for Friday night. What he most hated was having to be in a basement. Bakers stripped nearly naked to bear the heat, working with coal- or wood-burning ovens in closed basements. After a few hours' work, the entire room would feel like an oven—with no light, no scenery, no jovial French comrades.

The bakery was located in the Pletzl, a Yiddish word meaning "settlement" that was also the local name for most of Paris's fourth arrondissement, in the center of the city. The buildings there looked even worse than the sooty nineteenth-century facades that had so depressed Icchok at the Gare du Nord. They were smaller and several centuries old, cracked, sometimes even tilting, and the apartments inside were small and getting smaller as they were subdivided to make room for more and more immigrants. The neighborhood had been dominated by Alsatian Jews, who had moved to Paris in the 1870s after the Germans took Alsace. The Alsatians of the Pletzl were working-class Jews in sturdy crude clothing, but they were noticeably better off than the new arrivals—strange, bearded, scruffy-looking Yiddish-speakers without education or even hygiene. Finkelsztajn was one of thousands of Polish Jews who had turned up in the Pletzl in the past ten years. Entire families had arrived, carrying their belongings, looking for a room. Many were leftists like Finkelsztajn. The ones who were religious would have nothing to do with the Grand Rabbi of Paris; they set up their own little one-room synagogues—what are called *shtibls* in Yiddish—where they could murmur their ancient five-tone Hebrew chants. In 1934 the president of the Consistoire, the official Jewish establishment, complained that the influx of all these immigrants would slow down the process of assimilation.

While there had been little possibility for Jews to assimilate in Poland, in France it was expected of Jews. When the French Revolution addressed "the Jewish question," it was said that "there cannot be a nation within a nation." Therefore, it was decreed, Jews were free Frenchmen and would henceforth have the same rights as all other Frenchmen. But in exchange, Jews had agreed to act like all other Frenchmen. In order to make Jews more like Catholics and therefore easier to understand and regulate, Napoleon had the Jews reorganize their community into a hierarchy like that of the Catholic Church, with a central authority, the Consistoire Israélite, and a central synagogue with a head rabbi known as the Grand Rabbi of France.

One hundred years after the French Revolution, there were 85,000 Jews in France. Of these, some 500 were thought to be traditional, but the rest were not very different from Catholics. Rabbis wore priestlike robes. Jewish children had little celebrations at the appropriate age that corresponded to baptism and first communion. The adults offered flowers to the dead instead of the traditional stones, and they played organ music in synagogues instead of the traditional five-tone Hebrew chants. There were even discussions about shifting the Sabbath from Saturday to Sunday.

THE KORCARZ BAKERY was on a corner in a narrow, dark, and particularly dirty street named Rue des Rosiers, "Rosebush Street," not out of irony but because in the early thirteenth century it had led to a royal rose garden. The corner was sunny, though, and the Korcarzes decorated the building's facade with cheerful bits of blue-glazed tile in a bright modern mosaic. In 1933, back in Poland, Dwojra said good-bye to her parents, her sister Bella, and her baby brother Sacha in their little village outside Kielce, and moved to Paris to join Icchok. They found a little apartment at 14 rue des Ecouffes, just around the corner from the bakery.

In 1937 their son, Henri, was born. When he was three years old, the Wehrmacht took Paris. One of Henri's earliest memories was a train trip with his mother, for which they carried big packages. They were going to see his father. He can't remember much more. It was 1941. That year, concentration camps were built in Poland. In September all Jews were ordered to wear yellow stars. But even before that, on May 14, when the nationality of French Jews was still more or less respected, there had been a roundup of four thousand foreign Jews. Icchok Finkelsztajn had been caught on the street. Even if he had had the right papers, he had the wrong accent. He was sent to a prison—or, as it was officially labeled, a "lodging camp," in Pithiviers, just a little south of Paris.

Soon after Dwojra and Henri went to visit him, Icchok escaped. The family hid in the town of Tarbes, in the Pyrenees. The Korcarzes fled to a neighboring town. Since they had been forced to flee in 1941, the Finkelsztajns and the Korcarzes were not among the Jews who were rounded up the following year on Rue des Rosiers and Rue des Ecouffes and shipped off to gas chambers in Poland.

Icchok found work in the Pyrenees. A group of Republicanos— Spanish leftists who had fought Franco and had taken refuge across the border in 1939—hired him, knowing he was Jewish and knowing he needed work. His job was chopping firewood in the mountains, sometimes for weeks at a time. Dwojra and Henri tried to stay indoors as much as possible. Only Icchok would venture out on his bicycle to shop for food or go off to work in the mountains.

Many of Henri Finkelsztajn's memories of Tarbes are glimpses from behind curtains. Henri would go to the window and lift up the bottom of the curtain about two inches, just enough for his eyes, and watch the Gestapo search the building across the street. Dark uniforms would move through the building. Suddenly one would appear on a balcony and then disappear, and then the same man would pop up a few minutes later at another window or on another balcony. It was fun to try to guess who would pop up where next. But he could sense his parents' fear.

In 1943, Dwojra gave birth to another son, Willy. Icchok, the leftist atheist, surrounded by Gestapo, was adamant that his son must be circumcised. In 1943 nobody wanted to be circumcised, let alone have a circumcision performed on someone they loved. The greater part of that generation of European Jewry simply skipped this biblical demand. But somehow Icchok found a *mohel*, a ritual circumciser, some twenty miles from Tarbes in the Catholic shrine town of Lourdes. He brought this terrified elderly Jew to the apartment. The infant Willy was placed with the mohel in the living room, and a curtain was stretched across the corner for privacy. Little Henri of course peeked under curtains, but what he saw this time was in a way more terrifying than the Gestapo. The *mohel* had a knife in his hand and was leaning over Willy. Henri couldn't tell if it was his old age or just simple fear, but the hand with the knife never stopped shaking, causing the knife to wave in little abrupt spasms.

In the summer of 1944, young Henri Finkelsztajn was staying with the Korcarzes in their neighboring village. He was surprised one day to see his father coming for him, not on a bicycle but in a car. They rode back to Tarbes and saw all the Germans being held as prisoners. The townspeople, ordinary civilians, were walking up to them and spitting in their faces. Henri, still only seven years old, immediately understood this extraordinary scene.

"For me," he said later, "this was the end of fear."

2

Liberated
Paris

O N AUGUST 22, 1944, WHILE ALMOST FIVE THOUSAND
Parisians were being killed or wounded in the liberation of
the capital, Grenoble fell calmly. Townspeople shouted "They're
here!" and an irregular army of resistance fighters walked, drove,
and bicycled into town looking tired from days of fighting in the
mountains. The Germans had left during the night, first emptying
the Bank of France of 185 million francs and burning the Gestapo
records.

Emmanuel Ewenczyk had one thought upon liberation—to go
back to Paris and reopen the family business on Rue Bleue. His
father, Yankel, said, "You are crazy. Wait awhile. You can't go there
now."

"I've waited almost four years already," said Emmanuel. "I want
to get to work."

Emmanuel and Yankel had many arguments like that. Emmanuel had not wanted to leave the shop in Paris in the first place.

Rue Bleue is a commercial Parisian street of unremarkable nineteenth-century buildings, long and not particularly wide, angling
off in a slight curve as the blocks wind across the ninth into the
tenth arrondissement. Before the war, the Ewenczyks lived there in
a five-room apartment on the third floor. The two floors below
were occupied by the family sweater-making business.

Before sweaters, the family business had been lumber. In the

early twentieth century, the lumber business had boomed. Western
Europe needed wood for new railroad lines, and Eastern Europe,
Poland, and Russia, had the forests. Yankel Ewenczyk had been in
the lumber trade in White Russia, Byelorussia, in an area that was
largely populated by Jews. Jews even sat on the municipal coun-
cil—which meant that after the Russian Revolution they were tar-
geted by the Red Army. As a result, Yankel, his wife Syma, and
their three young sons—Samuel, Oscar, and Emmanuel—moved a
little west to Poland. The family continued to prosper in lumber,
and in 1930, the oldest son, Sam, decided he wanted to become an
engineer. He debated between going to a university in Haifa, in
Palestine, where there were numerous Jews from Poland, or to one
in Grenoble in the French Alps. He chose Grenoble, and for two
years he studied there while Yankel sent him money. But in 1932
there was not much more money to send. The lumber business
had collapsed, and the Poles were making it increasingly difficult
for Jews to do anything in Poland.

In 1932 the Ewenczyks moved to Paris and found an apartment
in the heart of a right-bank wholesale district on Rue Poissonière.
Sweater-making was an emerging trade in the neighborhood. The
entire family worked together in a sweater shop, and with Yankel's
instinct for trade and all five of them working, the little business
prospered even in the difficult 1930s.

In 1940 all three sons, having become naturalized French citizens, were called into service in the French army for what would
be a forty-six-day war with Germany. Oscar was among the thousands of prisoners of war taken near the Belgian border and deported to a prisoner-of-war camp in Germany. Emmanuel's unit
was captured in Orleans. The rest of the family fled to Grenoble.

Even then, as a prisoner of war, Emmanuel thought only of
getting back to the shop on Rue Bleue which would now be full of
fall merchandise. In all the chaos, he realized, other shops would
not be producing goods. Emmanuel reasoned that the market
would be hungry for his family's stock. It could all be liquidated at
top prices—if only he could get back.

There were more prisoners than the Germans could handle.
Emmanuel found himself in a column of two thousand French
prisoners, guarded by a handful of Germans, being marched one
hundred miles to Beauvais, north of Paris. There they would be
questioned and sent to a distribution camp at Drancy and from
there to Germany. Later, Drancy was to become a central transit

point for shipping Jews to Auschwitz, but this was 1940, long before Emmanuel ever heard the word *Auschwitz*. He was just one of
thousands of French prisoners of war.

At one point, a truck with a French crew came to distribute food
to the prisoners. Emmanuel took off his army coat and, looking
remarkably like a civilian, started helping the French crew distribute the food as if he were one of them. After everyone had eaten,
the crew — including Emmanuel — got back on the truck and drove
off. Simply by trying to get back to his shop, Emmanuel had probably saved his life.

Paris had been left undefended and possessed by what was
called "the great fear." Shops and apartments were abandoned, and
the banks stripped of deposits. The streets were littered with jetti-
soned belongings. The main boulevards were crammed with cars,
trucks, hand carts, and bicycles — and scared people clutching the
most precious belongings that were portable and heading south.
On June 14 the German Eighteenth Army entered the city and
hoisted a red swastika on the Eiffel Tower.

But while other Parisians, especially Jews, were fleeing, Emmanuel wanted to go home to Rue Bleue. By the time he got there, the
exodus was over. The shop and apartment were deserted except for
one non-Jewish employee. Nobody in the neighborhood seemed
even to realize that Emmanuel had been away. Things were not
bad. People talked about how the *métro* was working well again.
The big fear had ended. The German soldiers didn't seem as bad
as everyone had expected. In fact, some people were starting to
come back. Jews were coming back. Nothing had happened, and
perhaps they had fled too hastily.

Yankel sent word from Grenoble: "You must leave Paris immediately!"

"But we have merchandise," Emmanuel pleaded.

"It's nothing," Yankel insisted. "Come right away!"

"I'll come as soon as I liquidate," Emmanuel answered.

On September 27, 1940, an item appeared in the newspapers:
"All Jews must report by October 20 to the *sous-préfet* of the arron-
dissement in which they live to be registered on a special list." A
Jew was defined as "anyone who belonged or used to belong to the
Jewish religion, or has more than two Jewish grandparents." Em-
manuel went, as did 149,733 other Parisian Jews. The French
police put a stamp on his identity papers indicating that he was
Jewish. Then he went home.

Confined to their buildings by a nighttime curfew, Parisians passed their evenings talking to neighbors. One neighbor on Rue Bleue was a French pilot who kept warning Emmanuel to get out of Paris. The pilot knew he was Jewish. Everyone knew that a man named Emmanuel Ewenczyk was Jewish.

But it took months for Emmanuel to unload all the stock at good prices, even with the high demand. Then there were taxes to pay. And rent on the apartment. How long would he be away? Finally, he paid several months' rent in advance and joined his family in Grenoble.

WHEN PARIS WAS LIBERATED, Emmanuel got on the first train available and went directly from the Gare de Lyon to Rue Bleue. He climbed the stairs to the third floor. The concierge, who had seen him come in from her perch behind the curtain at her glass door, followed him up the stairs trying to call him back, whispering, "Monsieur, Monsieur!"

Emmanuel knocked on the door on the third floor. A man answered and explained in a meek voice that he was a refugee. "And," he added, his voice growing less meek, "I have a lease." He waved the document.

Emmanuel went downstairs to the lower shop floor. Where sweaters had once been stacked, there now stood a neatly arranged pile of wooden legs. A full staff of craftsmen were working on artificial limbs. Then Emmanuel climbed up the shop stairs to the upper floor and discovered that a gendarme was living there.

True, he had signed the paper releasing the apartment, but with collaborationists being chased through the streets, beaten, arrested, and put on trial, no one would want to go to court and explain that they had forced a Jew in hiding to relinquish his property.

Before he went into "hiding," Emmanuel had left a forwarding address with the concierge. While in Grenoble, the Ewenczyks had received a letter from the manager of the building on Rue Bleue, saying that it was apparent that they had left the building, and could they therefore write a letter agreeing to let the apartment go? The Ewenczyks wondered if non-Jews got such requests. Yankel reasoned that it would be better to avoid trouble and write the letter.

But Emmanuel thought differently. "I paid three months' rent in advance!" he argued.

"But they have our address," Yankel said gravely.

"But the rent is not that much! We can afford to keep paying—a few months at a time, if they want. This is a good set-up. We don't want to lose it."

With a grim face, Yankel told him, "Listen, Emmanuel. We haven't left much there. We don't want to do anything—risky. They have our address." The family finally sent the letter. Then they lost contact with Paris.

When Emmanuel returned to Paris and found all three floors occupied, he went to see the owner of the building—a pleasant, polite man who explained sympathetically that he had given the man and his family the apartment because they were refugees. Their own home had been destroyed, the owner explained as he reached into a drawer and retrieved a folded piece of paper. It was an official city document clearly stating that this man and his family had lived at 19 rue Rodier until it had been destroyed.

Emmanuel had trafficked in false documents for the Resistance in Grenoble and knew better than to take official documents at face value just because they had the right form with the right stamps. He went to Rue Rodier, which was not far from Rue Bleue, and found number 19—standing whole and undamaged. These people were not refugees at all. They had simply wanted a better apartment.

All over Paris, Jewish property had been taken over. *Nobody had expected the Jews ever to come back.* When Emmanuel asked friends for advice they repeatedly told him not to pursue his claim. Even though he seemed to have a good case, it would take years in the French legal system to win it. He would be better off finding another place so he could start working. He could not apply to reopen his business until he had an address, and with all the shortages, if he could get into production at a new place soon, his business would boom. But still, Rue Bleue was his home. . . .

He went to see the gendarme who was living in the upper story of what had been the sweater shop. "Monsieur," the gendarme told him icily, "I am here because the gendarmerie gave me this apartment, because I have a wife and child. I do not have the slightest intention of leaving."

Emmanuel went back to the owner and said the "refugee" family on the third floor had false papers—the building on Rue Rodier had never been destroyed. The owner nodded in agreement and said with a polite smile, "But what can I do?"

"And what about this gendarme? What right does he have to be there?"

The building owner answered with seemingly irrefutable logic, "But he is there, and there is nothing I can do about that. You will have to take it up with him."

Emmanuel went to the gendarmerie in the neighborhood, where he was told, "Well, he is living in the apartment. If he doesn't want to leave, there is nothing we can do."

Emmanuel went to the building manager who had so courteously extracted the letter from him when he was in hiding. The manager said he would make it up to him and offered another apartment in a different neighborhood. "And why is this apartment available?" Emmanuel wanted to know.

"Ah, because the tenants left."

"Were they Jews?"

The manager said he thought they were—"but they have not come back." Everyone was confident that the Jews weren't coming back. But Emmanuel was not eager to grab this place. And in a few weeks, although the tenants themselves did not come back, one of their parents claimed the apartment. Then the embarrassed manager offered Emmanuel two little rooms on the sixth floor of the building on Rue Bleue. Six flights of stairs to bring merchandise in, six to take it out? Emmanuel thought. But still, it was an address, and he could apply for a permit with an address.

Emmanuel set up the sweater business there. Everything in Paris was rationed and tightly controlled after the war, but the Ewenczyks had bought large orders of wool for their business before the war, and everyone was permitted to acquire materials now based on their 1940 purchases. The same distributors were back in business, and the demand for sweaters, cloth, and even sacks was at a level that Emmanuel had never seen before.

How could the pig-headed Emmanuel Ewenczyk ever have resisted the equally strong-willed Fania Elbinger? Fania was a nervy, outspoken twenty-year-old who had immigrated to Paris with her mother and sister from Poland in 1930. Having met in the Resistance in Grenoble, Fania and Emmanuel seemed destined to love and argue. While they were living in Grenoble, about once a month Fania would travel to nearby Chambéry with money and clothes and sometimes even a little meat that the Jewish Resistance had smuggled into the district to feed Jewish families. Sometimes she was able to save their children by taking them to the Swiss border with false papers. The Germans would let children pass the border, provided their papers showed that they were not Jewish. In the Resistance, men were of limited use in this kind of work. Although there was no problem in providing them with top-quality Christian identification papers, the Germans would sometimes stop men on the road and make them show that they were uncircumcised. When the Germans moved into the formerly Italian-occupied zone of France, they decreed that any circumcised male was a Jew, regardless of what his papers said. For this reason, much of the underground work was done by women.

Wartime life was relatively easy for Jews in Grenoble, at first. The entire southeastern border area, from Grenoble to Nice, had been occupied by Italian troops instead of Germans. Not only did the Italians not harass the Jews, but on several occasions, when French police arrested Jews, the Italians had them released. But in September 1943 the Italians surrendered, and the Germans moved into Grenoble. One night Emmanuel brought Fania home with him to try to persuade his parents to assume a false identity and leave the town. Fania could get them the papers they needed.

"Why should I leave?" said Yankel Ewenczyk.

"Your name is Yankel. Yankel and Syma. You can't stay like this."

"Why not? Why should I fear the Germans? Let them take me—I have nothing to hide. I've never done anything wrong in my life. But if they catch me with false papers, then what do I do?"

"Papa, you don't understand. Just listen to your accent."

"What can I do about my accent?" He shrugged.

Emmanuel went to the library in Grenoble and spent an entire day leafing through the pages of the official journal that published names of people who had been naturalized, looking for ideas. Finally he found an Armenian couple from Turkey.

"You can be from Armenia," he told his father. "Armenians have accents. A lot of people in Turkey are circumcised because they are Moslem. If the Germans see that you are circumcised, that is more or less explained—"

"What's to explain?" Yankel protested. But they got him the papers.

After the Liberation, Fania returned to Paris with her mother and sister. But when the three arrived at the family leather goods shop, they found that it had been rented to someone else, as was their seven-room apartment. The new tenant was a refugee, but unlike the family at Rue Bleue, this tenant was a real refugee. The Elbingers decided to fight, but the years of futile legal battles that they spent trying to recuperate their spaces only proved to Emmanuel that he had received good advice when he had been told not to pursue it.

AROUND THE CORNER from Rue Bleue on Rue Cadet was a club for diamond merchants. Diamonds, a traditional Jewish trade, was a fast business in 1945, because so many people were selling off their jewels in order to survive. In times of crisis, gold and diamonds flourish, and in 1945, in the diamond and jewel districts of the ninth arrondissement, near the garment district, people had money. But they still had trouble getting food.

Icchok and Dwojra Finkelsztajn, on the other hand, had food, but they needed money. There were shortages of almost everything in Paris, especially food, which was tightly rationed. But it was different in the Pletzl, where numerous Polish peasants lived among the Jews who had moved there from Poland before the war. When food became scarce during the war, these peasants, gravitating toward what they knew best, had moved out of the city and grew food on small plots. By chance, Dwojra ran into a family she had known in Poland, and they offered to sell her their produce. This was, as the French like to say, not altogether legal. In fact, it was a black market that circumvented the rationing system. But Paris was full of black markets. Dollars and silver were traded illegally on the narrow Rue des Rosiers sidewalks. Everyone wanted food, and Dwojra now had access to it. The problem was that nobody in the Pletzl had very much money. Then Dwojra found a diamond merchant.

Icchok and Dwojra would regularly get on the *métro* with large net bags full of black market food and go to the diamond traders' club on Rue Cadet. In a thickly carpeted room, they would lay out fruit, vegetables, meat, and butter from Polish farmers, on the waxed dark wood furniture. The Finkelsztajn family supported itself and even saved a little money from this.

The Finkelsztajns had returned to Paris from the Pyrenees in December 1944, during one of the coldest winters on record, a winter that further toughened the bitter battle that was under way in the Ardennes. Some winters, Parisians do not see a single snow-flake. But this winter, the streets were encrusted with a thick layer of snow. Icchok, Dwojra, Henri, and their baby had gone to 14 rue des Ecouffes, where they had left their apartment fully furnished with most of their possessions. When they opened the door, a woman holding a child stared at them, and several more pairs of young eyes peered out at them from inside.

"Excuse me," said Dwojra. She closed the door, and the Finkelsztajns went back down the stairs and left.

Other apartments were available on Rue des Ecouffes. In the summer of 1942 the police, using the lists they had made in the fall of 1940, had sealed off Jewish neighborhoods. In the middle of the night they had pulled whole families from their apartments and put them in a sports stadium, where they wallowed in squalor until they could be deported for extermination. In this citywide opera-tion—which yielded only 12,884 Jews, not even half of the number hoped, based on the lists—Rue des Ecouffes was one of the richer veins of the motherlode. Number 22 alone, with the work of forty policemen, had yielded five whole families and a total of fifteen children. In the winter of 1945 there were still empty apartments at number 22, and the Finkelsztajns rented one of them, a two-room apartment with a bathroom. In the Pletzl, two rooms for four peo-ple was considered a good apartment and a bathroom was a notable luxury.

Icchok, who did not want to go back to day and night labor in the hot basement of the Korcarzes' bakery, learned of a pleasant little space that was available on Rue des Rosiers. Started by Alsa-tian Jews, it had been a Jewish bakery for almost a hundred years. The ovens were still in the basement, but the ground floor was big enough that the ovens could be moved up there, and the floor above had a large four-room apartment. The apartment even had enough space to build a bathroom.

The owner of the bakery was a Romanian Jew. During the war his shop had been "Aryanized." All over Paris—in fact, all over Nazi-occupied Europe—Jewish commercial property had been Aryan-ized, or given to non-Jews. When the policy was instituted in 1941, more than twenty thousand Jewish-owned businesses had immedi-ately been confiscated and handed over to those who were willing to call themselves "Aryan" in exchange for the gift of someone else's shop. But this Romanian had surprised the new "Aryan" owners of his bakery by surviving the war. He demanded back his bakery after

Liberation. Since most of these "Aryans" had received their property as a reward for their collaboration, they were lucky to escape the Liberation with their lives. Yet in late 1944 there were still more collaborators than Jews living in the Pletzl. Little by little they were losing their property, but not their arrogance. They had numbers on their side, and there was little in the way of police or any kind of law to oppose them. The war was still going on, and Hitler was still in Germany and still had a fighting army—and who could be sure that the Nazis would not come back to Paris? Collaborators in the Pletzl regularly shouted from their windows, "*Vive* the Nazis! Down with the Jews!" A group of these so-called Aryans were so arrogant that they actually staged a demonstration protesting the return of the shops to Jews.

The Romanian, however, fought until he got back his bakery. But at the end of 1945 he decided to sell it to a Jew from the Pletzl. He liked Icchok, but the amount Icchok and Dwojra had saved was not even close to the price he wanted. The Romanian agreed to hold the bakery for Icchok and gave him a deadline for raising the rest of the money. Their fundraising became a Pletzl-wide project. Most of the merchants on Rue des Rosiers donated, and soon the Finkelsztajns had their own new bakery.

If Icchok had to be a baker and spend his life working alone and indoors, at least he would do it the right way in his own shop. He was not going to spend his days laboring in a dark basement. After moving the ovens to the back of the ground floor, he permanently sealed up the basement, proclaiming that working in a basement was slavery.

Their first customer was the diamond merchant who had taken them to the club on Rue Cadet.

IT WAS NOT ONLY small businesses that "Aryans" had taken. René Lévy lost a huge enterprise. At the outbreak of the war, he had been the sixty-two-year-old retiring president of the textile association. He had foreseen that he would lose his extremely profitable factory, which produced men's handkerchiefs, those huge rectangles of fine material that were a stylish accessory in the 1930s. Smart "Aryan" businessmen knew that they didn't have to offer Jews good prices for their businesses, since the Jews were going to have to sell anyway. Lévy, with little choice, sold to the association secretary, a man named Boussac.

The Lévy family's fortunes had risen and fallen with a half-century of French history. In 1895 the Lévys had been an established French textile family, part of the solid upper-middle class of eastern France. In January of that year, Captain Alfred Dreyfus was publicly degraded, his buttons removed, and his sword broken, as an angry crowd shouted "Death to Jews!" Dreyfus was of a background similar to the Lévys', and, like them, he made the mistake of thinking that he totally blended into French society. Now suddenly he was being convicted of passing information to the Germans, based on erroneous evidence and supported by the notion that "Jews are like that." Anti-Semitism became so virulent at workplaces, in schools, and on streets, that the Lévys were forced to leave France, where their family had lived since before the Revolution, and relocate their textile business to Belgium.

After a decade had passed, the anti-Semites became quiet again, except for a few radical-right newspapers. The Lévys moved back to France. Their son René married a woman who, also like Dreyfus, was from an affluent Alsatian Jewish industrial family. Her family had built a textile factory in northern France. In 1912, René Lévy and his wife settled into the grand bourgeois life of western Paris. He became the president of the textile association and was well-known to important politicians between the wars. Religion was of little concern to him. On Rosh Hashanah, the Jewish New Year, he would eat an apple. On Passover, always known in France as "Jewish Easter," he would eat matzoh, not because of any religious belief but because matzoh was the holiday food. More basic to the Lévys' lives were the rounds of opera once a week and dinner parties in their elegant apartment, where they brought in musicians for small performances.

In 1940 the Lévys once again had to leave Paris. This time they went south and became non-Jews. In Klaus Barbie's Lyons, the Lévys—now the Picards—lived a quiet life. They bought a nearby plot of land and hired a peasant to work it, assuring themselves of a good food supply throughout the war. In the summers they vacationed in Argenton-sur-Creuse, a short drive away from Oradour-sur-Gland, where 642 Jews were massacred by the SS.

One of René's daughters lost her husband, Georges Caen. Caen was not from the Norman city of the same name; he was a Kohen, a name that implied he was descended from the priestly line of Aaron. Georges Kohen was now trying to survive in Lyons as Caen, the name that his father had chosen years earlier to better blend

into French society. The Germans never found out that this bourgeois Caen was no Norman. But someone informed on him for
possessing a revolver, and so the Germans came to the Caens'
comfortable home and demanded Georges. The family, instead of
hiding him or denying that he was there, ushered the Germans in,
like confident Frenchmen who knew their rights. Georges Caen
was taken away, never to be seen again.

Another of René's daughters was attending art school in 1944,
and there she met Robert Altmann, the brother of a fellow student.
Altmann had been born in Düsseldorf in 1922. His father came
from a religious family but had moved away from religion as he
became a successful businessman. He bought and sold steel, and
after the Russian Revolution he did a lucrative business with the
new struggling Soviet nation. The Russians had no cash, but they
had a wealth of lumber that, as the Ewenczyks had also found, was
in great demand in Western Europe. Altmann was able to work out
barter arrangements with them—trading steel for wood.

After Liberation, René Lévy and his family went back to Paris.
He was unable to get back his business, which under Boussac went
on to become one of the textile giants of postwar France. The
Altmanns settled in Lyons, but Robert, who spoke flawless French,
German, and English, went north and served as a translator for the
U.S. Army until the end of the war. In 1947 he married René
Lévy's daughter, resumed his family's steel trading business, and
started raising a family. Once again, they were simply affluent,
assimilated Parisians living in an expensive neighborhood, eating
an apple for Rosh Hashanah and matzoh for Passover so their three
children would know that they were Jewish. Otherwise, they could
live like other Frenchmen. The Germans were gone, and France
was once again a liberal country where Jews did not have to mark
themselves.

THE EAGERNESS OF ROBERT ALTMANN to pick up the old life
he had left off was not characteristic of all French Jewry. Perhaps
they would have felt differently if it had been only the Germans
who had tried to destroy them. But it had also been the French.
Many French Jews remembered that French police had rounded
up French Jews for deportation. A widely reported Nazi expression
attributed to number-two Nazi Hermann Goering was, *"Wer Jude
ist, bestimme Ich,"*—"I decide who is a Jew." Assimilation had

meant nothing to Goering and other Nazis. After the war, to many French Jews, the French ideal of assimilation seemed a fantasy of the foolish.

Most people do not have neighbors whose humanity has been tested. But in France, Jews now had such neighbors. The Nazis had proven throughout Europe that most people, when threatened, act badly. It is difficult to live in a society in which it has already been proven to you that your neighbors will pretend not to notice that your children have been murdered. Many French Jews preferred to go to an untested society and hope that Israeli or American neighbors would not be like this. In any case it would be better not to know for certain, as it now was known of European neighbors.

Zionism, the longing for a Jewish state, was first popularized by Theodor Herzl, an Austrian journalist who had covered the Dreyfus case. He had principally argued for Zionism in London, where the colonial administration of Palestine was controlled. But Zionism had found some of its strongest adherents in Poland. Even in the 1920s, Jewish communities in Poland had already been preparing for the *aliyah*, the historical return to Israel. Both Fania Elbinger and Emmanuel Ewenczyk had been raised in Polish Zionism.

Now, after the Nazi butchery, many Jews felt that surely no one could refuse them their state. The wartime Jewish Resistance was falling apart—at least half of Fania and Emmanuel's group from Grenoble were going to Palestine. Even before the war ended, some Jews had made it to neutral Spain and from there to the Middle East. At the end of the war the Jewish neighborhoods of Paris were filled with Jewish refugees from throughout Europe looking for contacts to help them get to Palestine.

Fania, too, wanted to go, and she told her mother so. Her mother looked at Fania with moist eyes and said, "So you are going to leave us all alone—just the two of us."

It was true. Fania's mother had only her two daughters. Fania's father had died before the war, and there had been no word from any surviving relative back in Poland. Fania Elbinger's *aliyah* ended when she looked into her mother's eyes.

Yankel and Syma Ewenczyk stayed in Grenoble with their oldest son, Sam, who could at last finish his studies, after which he would remain at the university and work in nuclear energy research. Emmanuel's brother Oscar returned to Paris from Germany, where he had torn up his identity papers, concealed his Jewish identity, and spent the war in forced labor as a prisoner of war on a farm. At least on a farm he had had enough food to eat.

Oscar and Emmanuel kept the sweater business in Paris, and as Emmanuel had predicted, it was an instant success. As soon as they secured the supplies and their designers came out with a new line, the wholesalers started selling sweaters at top prices, as fast as they could produce them. France was hungry for consumer goods.

Fania and Emmanuel were married on December 30, 1945, in a just-restored synagogue on Rue Notre-Dame-de-Nazareth, one of several synagogues the Germans had blown up in October 1941. Two years later, Oscar married Fania's sister Georgette.

It took a long time to sort out the missing people. Many of them were never found. For some, like Fania's mother, it took time just to comprehend what had happened. Back in Grenoble during the war, Fania had shown her mother a flyer from the Jewish Resistance saying that hundreds of thousands of Jews who had been taken to camps in Poland were being gassed to death. Her mother had left parents, a brother, a sister, and a niece in Baronovitchi, in eastern Poland. Tossing the flyer down, her mother told Fania, "Don't believe that. It can't be true. It's not possible." In fact, most of the Jews Fania talked to in the Grenoble area had not believed the flyer. How could you take hundreds of thousands of people and gas them to death? Perhaps some had been gassed, maybe even a few hundred, but more likely they had been shot. Rumors run wild in time of war.

After the Liberation, Fania tried without success to find a trace of her mother's family in Baronovitchi. She wrote letters. She went to special offices. She discovered that huge extended Jewish families had entirely vanished without a trace. Whole communities were gone, with no precise explanation. Europe was full of individuals who did not have a single friend or relative in the world. Some of them found each other and married quickly. Many went to Israel, at least to be with other Jews.

In early 1945 the elegant turn-of-the-century Hotel Lutetia, located at an expensive Left Bank Parisian intersection, was set up to receive concentration camp survivors. The original idea was to establish a reception center at the train station, the Gare d'Orsay. Liberated prisoners of war and labor camp inmates had already been coming in, a little thinner but happy to be home, and the staff at the center imagined that the liberated concentration camp inmates would be similar. But in April, when the first of them started returning—skeletal ghosts with glazed, sunken eyes—Parisians could see that something very different had happened to them. Some of the staff who worked in the Hotel Lutetia center openly expressed distaste for their work. The people were frightening to look at and terrible to listen to, with their tales of horror or, as one staff member put it, their "complaining." This did not fit well with the myth that General De Gaulle was carefully constructing, of a military victory over the Germans, a repeat of 1918. Although survivors marched in their striped uniforms in victory celebrations in 1945, that practice was soon barred.

The hotel functioned as a missing-persons center. A list was established where returning survivors put their names. Most people who went to the hotel searching for survivors did not find the names they were looking for and anxiously canvassed the hotel with photographs and wedding portraits, hoping to find someone who had seen their loved ones alive. Walls became bulletin boards, layered with snapshots and notes. Every day, people came and waited. It was becoming clear that the flyers that the Resistance had circulated during the war had been true. In fact, it was even worse than the flyers had said—not hundreds of thousands, but millions had been murdered. Long after the Hotel Lutetia ran out of survivors to process, relatives still turned up there every day, hoping for news. Since displaced Jews were moving all over the world, they clung to the hope that the ones they were seeking would turn up somewhere. They clung to that hope for years.

When Dwojra Finkelsztajn got back to the Pletzl, she learned that her sister Bella, who had moved to Paris before the war, had been deported to Auschwitz. Bella was not among the few who passed through the Hotel Lutetia. Nor was there any trace of Dwojra's parents, another sister, or a little brother, Sacha, who had stayed in the village outside Kielce. Unlike Bella, these family members had simply vanished without explanation. They could still be alive. It was only after years of looking for relatives that Dwojra finally located a cousin in Canada. He provided the ending of the Zylbersztajn story. He had seen the Germans march the entire Jewish population of their village down a road. Then they shot them all.

The ninety thousand Jews of France who had been murdered represented a quarter of France's Jewish population, but the percentage of people missing from the Pletzl was much higher.

The Nazis had started with foreign-born Jews, and the Pletzl had been one of the places to find them.

But although so many familiar faces were missing, the Pletzl was now crowded with gaunt survivors, most of them young, many from Eastern Europe. The neighborhood itself became a transit center. The young people who had lost everyone they knew and who wanted to restart their lives would come for a few months and mill around the neighborhood, until they made the connections to arrange passage to Palestine. A few went to the United States, Canada, and Australia, but most wanted to go to Palestine. Only a few stayed in Paris. The ones who stayed were called *"les griners,"* from the Yiddish word for green—young men and women who had seen the unimaginable depths but were nevertheless considered green, because they didn't know the neighborhood.

3

Liberated
Antwerp

"YOU HAVE TO LAUGH AT THIS," THOUGHT SAM PERL AS pain tightened his face and forced up the corners of his mouth. Antwerp's monumental Central Station was still there, with its lacy ironworks. All the little stone turrets were still sticking up from the elevated tracks that ran through the Jewish section of Antwerp, a neighborhood that seemed to cling to rail lines as though it were contemplating a fast exit. The dark tunnels where streets passed under the raised tracks were still there, with the curly ironwork around and even under the bridges. And all the fine high-ceilinged, tall-windowed homes were still there. As he came through the underpass from the broad Belgielei, Perl could see that the Van Den Nestlei Synagogue was still a charred shell, as it had been since that day in 1941. But the other synagogues—though torn up, burned, and vandalized—still stood. In the fall of 1945, when Perl came back to Antwerp, the only thing missing was most of the people he knew. His parents and his brother and wife and two children and a sister and friends were all gone. There were only a few hundred Jews left.

But look who had survived! Sam Perl could not help but be amazed. So many of the strong young people were gone. There seemed to be almost no teenagers at all. But there were old people, even elderly people who had seemed weak even before the war. Great leaders, like the Chief Rabbi, Mordechai Rottenberg, were gone. And yet people Perl had always thought of as "complete *shlimazels*," the kind of people to whom everything always happened, had survived. "Who in a million years would have thought it?" he asked himself.

He would always remember this moment when Darwin's theory of natural selection did not apply, when survival had its own random force. "Life is selfish. It can't end. It's not a matter of what is driving you," he thought. "There have to be some people who survive." There was also the remarkable fact that he was one of them. A few people he knew had come back, like Rabbi Rottenberg's sons, Chaim and Jozef, whom he had not seen since the transit camp, when their sister got them South American papers. Sam Perl was put on a train to Auschwitz. He jumped off, but it took the Germans only a few months to find him again. Before they put him on a second train to Auschwitz, the chief of the Gestapo had had him brought to an office where they spent several hours applying the lit end of cigarettes and cigars to the sensitive areas of his body. The second time Sam Perl was deported, he jumped off the train again, and this time he had been able to find a network of Flemish Catholics in the town of Namur, who hid him until the Liberation.

Slowly, more Jews returned. It was not going to be like before the war, but a few hundred were turning up from the safe corners they had found in France and Switzerland and New York, where in the intervening years they had built up the diamond business on Forty-seventh Street.

ANTWERP BECAME an important Jewish center in the late nineteenth century, when pogroms had driven Jews out of Eastern Europe. As major diamond deposits were discovered in the Belgian Congo, the diamond trade flourished in Antwerp, predominantly in the hands of Jews from what was then the Austro-Hungarian Empire and is now Poland, Ukraine, Hungary, and Romania. During the First World War most of the trade had been lost to Amsterdam, since Belgium was at war while Holland was neutral. But in the 1920s and 1930s Antwerp, the Belgian port on the Dutch border, started getting back its diamond trade, fed by a steady Jewish immigration from the east.

Jews were coming to Belgium not only because of its liberal immigration laws, but also because Antwerp had a port with ships bound for America and Palestine. Mia Lehmann had gone there to leave for Palestine. But once they arrived, many Jews in transit decided to stay, because there was work available in diamonds. You could become a sawer, someone who cut rough diamonds in two. Or you could become a cleaver, who cut the basic facets that determine a diamond's shape. Or if you were not good with your hands but gifted at commerce, you could become a broker, buying and selling rough stones. None of these jobs required a great deal of knowledge or education. A cleaver, one of the standard entry jobs in the diamond business, apprenticed for one year, then earned more money than many doctors.

By the outbreak of World War II, the great majority of Antwerp's more than fifty thousand Jews were earning their living in the diamond trade. It was a religious community dominated by devout Orthodox Jews from the east, many of them members of the emotional and flamboyant Hasidic movement. In the early twentieth century the Orthodox community in Antwerp was modifying and modernizing—not drastically, but enough to worry some of the traditionalists from Poland. So to maintain the old ways, they sent for a Hasidic rabbi from Katowice who had a reputation for unerring orthodoxy. The rabbi, Mordechai Rottenberg, arrived in 1912 with his wife, six sons, and three daughters.

Rottenberg was a rabbi of considerable energy and charisma, and he kept the religious community not only together but unusually traditional for a Western community. One of his last official acts was to marry Dwora and Hershl Silberman in 1941. Dwora's family was also from Łódź, having left for Antwerp in 1927, when she was eight years old. Like many immigrants with no particular knowledge of diamonds, Dwora's father had become a broker. Dwora's brother, having the advantage of growing up around diamonds, became a dealer, which required an eye for and a depth of knowledge about gems.

Hershl Silberman's family had·also prospered in Antwerp. They owned a three-story house on Simonsstraat in the heart of the diamond district. This street, which farther up changes its name to Pelikaanstraat, is long and straight and runs along the elevated train tracks to the station.

By the time Mordechai Rottenberg married Dwora and Hershl on October 29, 1941, the Germans had occupied Antwerp for almost a year and a half. Every week, Jewish life was becoming more restricted. Banks could not accept Jewish deposits. Jews could not operate stores. The traditional Orthodox wedding at night under the stars was now impossible, because Jews were not allowed outside after seven o'clock in the evening. Rabbi Rottenberg had to make one of his rare compromises and perform the wedding ceremony during the day, inside the synagogue. Then lists of Jews who were to report to the train station for deportation to "work camps" started appearing. Dwora's parents feared for their children, because they thought that labor camps would be looking for young people. So they persuaded the newlyweds to flee to France. Tens of thousands of Belgian Jews had already gone there, including Dwora's brother and his wife, who were now in Lyons. The Jewish underground could get them through the occupied zone to southern France.

But just as Hershl and Dwora were about to cross the French border, Dwora declared that she could not leave her parents, she had to go back to Antwerp, this was all a mistake. But the underground responded that they had already taken too many risks to move them and there was no turning back; she would have to wait until the war was over to return. Among the last Jews to escape Belgium, the decision was out of her hands. Yet it would torment her for the rest of her life.

Lyons was not safe, either. Dwora's brother and his wife were caught in one of the French police roundups and deported to Auschwitz. Dwora and Hershl spent the war years moving across southern France, from the Swiss to the Spanish border, looking for a place to hide.

At the time of the Liberation of France, they were in a rural area in central France. When they saw men from the FFI Resistance group take three Germans prisoner, they realized the Nazi occupation of France had ended. One of the Germans, an officer, was arguing his case to the Resistance fighters. Dwora heard him say in clear German, "What we did, everybody else wanted to have done. But we were the fools who got the job done."

Seven months pregnant, Dwora immediately tried to get back to her family—she did not want to wait for the war to be over. But the Belgium border was closed, as the war moved to the Ardennes. Hershl and Dwora stood by the side of a muddy road outside Lille while the Allied army slogged toward its next rendezvous. After talking a British Army driver into giving them a ride, they arrived in Belgium in the back of his canvas-covered truck. The driver even gave them chocolate. Their first sight of Antwerp was with an orange flash across the sky, followed by an earth-shaking boom.

Although forced to retreat, the Germans had not been able to destroy the city's harbor, which was now the best undamaged port across the channel from England. They were trying to hit the city with V-1 and V-2 rockets. The V1 would make a tremendous noise as it streaked over the city; The V2 was silent. The anti-aircraft battery outside of town was heard, then nothing until suddenly a building blew up. The Germans never hit the port, but one day, as though guided by vengeful fate, a rocket hit the Rex Cinema while it was showing a matinee, and hundreds were killed. Decades later, this incident remained one of those defining differences between Jews and non-Jews who had lived through the war. Mention the Rex to a non-Jew, and he would talk about the day the rocket hit. Mention the Rex to one of the few surviving Jews, and he would talk of another day, April 14, 1941, when the Rex had offered a special matinee showing of a Nazi movie called *Jud Süss*, or *Süss, the Jew*. It presented the story of a Jew in the Middle Ages who had risen to a high position in Frankfurt am Main and squeezed taxes out of the good Christian people until they were ruined. After the screening the local people marched down the Pelikaanstraat, smashing Jewish shop windows. When they got to the Van Den Nestlei synagogue, they broke into the building and carried the Torahs out onto the street. For a short time they seemed content simply to throw the scrolls around and unwind and abuse them. But they finally burned the synagogue and then marched on to lay siege to two other principal synagogues in the city.

WHEN HERSHL and the very pregnant Dwora arrived in Antwerp, they went to the Silberman family house on Simonsstraat, across from the elaborate masonry of the elevated tracks. The strangers who were living there assured them that there were no Silbermans in the house.

On December 28, 1944, Dwora gave birth to their first child, a girl. Knowing nothing about babies, she turned to the flourishing black market to buy as much food as she could. To Dwora, Antwerp looked almost prosperous. There was trade and busy shops, and she bitterly reflected that the Flemish seemed to have thrived on selling to the Germans. She bought food as though she expected it to vanish from the markets. Soon her parents would come back from somewhere. Her brother and his wife would be coming back from Auschwitz. They would need a lot of good food. They would be so hungry.

To the disappointment of the people living in the Simonsstraat house, Hershl's family did return, and after a court battle the Silbermans got their house back. But no one in Dwora's family was among the returning survivors. Now Dwora was certain that her instinct had been right: She should never have left them in Antwerp and gone off with Hershl.

In March 1942, when the Germans had begun deporting Belgian Jews to Auschwitz, they had not taken only young people who would be good laborers, as Dwora's parents had expected. The deportation was not, in fact, about labor at all. Her parents had been taken, and so had the aging Rabbi Mordechai Rottenberg, along with his wife and children. But the Rottenbergs' daughter, Recha, had married a Swiss Hasid, Yitzchak Sternbuch, and during the war the couple lived at the Lake Geneva resort of Montreux. From this position of relative safety, they had smuggled Jews into Switzerland and had then gone on to ever wilder schemes, such as swapping Jews for money and equipment. In her search for niches of safety in the Final Solution, Recha had discovered that the Germans would not hurt Jews who had South American passports. The Germans had a vague idea that at some point they could swap these South American Jews for Germans living in South America. The Paraguayan government was delighted that its passports were worth something to people with hard currency, and it made the documents available for a handsome fee.

Among the hundreds for whom Recha obtained these papers were her two brothers, Chaim and Jozef. As a result, they were sent to a labor camp in Germany instead of a death camp. Both brothers had inherited some of their father's charisma, and Jozef in particular had an easy charm and an impish wit. Before the war, he had taken to Antwerp's commercial world, becoming an entrepreneur who understood the role of money in getting things done. After their sister got them South American papers, it was Jozef who tried to get money to Sam Perl and the others in the transit camp, so that if they were sent to Auschwitz and could jump off the train, as many were talking of doing, they would have some cash.

Jozef's brother Chaim was a man whom most people immediately liked. All his life and even for years after his death, mentioning the name Chaim Rottenberg to anyone who knew him would elicit a warm smile and a shake of the head, accompanied by a statement like, "Chaim—he was a personality!" Chaim was not an entrepreneur like Jozef. He was more like a biblical prophet, perhaps an Isaiah, declaring, "Set thy house in order." Tall and lean, with precise elongated features, his peering eyes made it clear at one glance that nothing would deter this man once he had made up his mind. His mind was usually focused, as in the oldest of Jewish traditions, on the law.

While Chaim and Jozef were in the labor camp, Recha managed to get them a shipment of matzoh for Passover through the Red Cross. Since there was a general shortage of food, religious and nonreligious Jews alike were grateful for this package. Chaim distributed the matzoh, but before getting a piece, each prisoner had to sign a written statement that he would never eat bread with leavening on Passover.

Recha was able to get both her brothers and hundreds of other Jews to Switzerland. But in 1944 the Paraguayan scheme collapsed, and the remaining Jews with South American passports were sent to Auschwitz, where only three survived. Among those who did not survive were Recha's parents.

After the war, Recha continued her work. The DPs—displaced persons, thousands of homeless Jews in Allied-supervised refugee camps in Germany—needed help. As she traveled to these camps in the charred remains of the Third Reich, Recha tried, although not always successfully, to observe traditional religious practices, which meant that all work activity had to stop on Friday evening until Saturday evening.

One Friday afternoon in late 1945, she was traveling in Germany and came upon a house for young Orthodox women in Landsberg am Lech. This was the same beautiful Bavarian mountain village where Hitler had been imprisoned in 1923 following the failed putsch; he had passed his time there dictating *Mein Kampf*. The Orthodox women were all survivors who were trying to make contacts to get out of Europe and into Palestine. Among them were a young woman named Rifka Melchior and her younger sister Frankel. In January they had been among two thousand Jewish women forced to march from labor camps in central Germany, away from the Americans and the Russians. Once a day, the Germans had fed them each a piece of bread, but first they had taken the ones that were too weak to go on and shot them by the side of the road. When the women arrived in Czechoslovakia in

May, only two hundred of them were left. Rifka weighed less than seventy-five pounds.

Recha spent the Sabbath with the survivors in the house at Landsberg am Lech. She later returned on another Sabbath and found that Rifka, who was now working for a Jewish charity, was about to leave for the Jewish holidays. As Rifka started to say good-bye to Recha, Recha informed her that she could not leave. Rifka had to come with her to Brussels instead. "I have work for you in Brussels," Recha told Rifka, with a smile and a peculiar wink.

Rifka, whose only dream was to get to Palestine, followed Recha to Belgium anyway. Recha was a woman who had once talked her way across the Swiss border, badgered the Gestapo into releasing twelve Jewish prisoners, then taken them back across to Switzerland. Few people could say no to her. It was a Rottenberg family trait.

Her brother, Rabbi Chaim Rottenberg, was the work she had in mind for Rifka. Among the strictly Orthodox, arranged marriages are commonplace at about the age of eighteen. Rifka was already twenty-one when she married Chaim under a canopy beneath the stars, as prescribed by law, on the terrace of a hotel set against the background of dark, glittering Lake Geneva and the silhouette of the Swiss Alps. But even in this setting it was hard to feel romantic. Maybe it was hard to feel anything at all. So many of the people in their lives had died terrible deaths. They were still just learning of it—of Rifka's four sisters and mother gassed at Auschwitz, of her two brothers who had been shot, of her father who had lain down and died in Poland. Her sister Frankel was her only relative at the wedding. After the wedding, the Rottenbergs went to Antwerp, and Frankel went alone to Palestine.

JEWS CENTERED their lives on checking Red Cross lists, sometimes more than once a day. The Red Cross list of known survivors was easy to scan because it was never very long. But it wasn't infallible, and you never knew who you would run into on the Belgielei or Pelikaanstraat. Survivors would sight each other by chance from across a street and run up to each other and trade horror stories. Where were you? And one would tell the other, and then ask the same. Then would come the real questions: "Is your brother back? Have you seen my cousin?" Everyone had a few people for whom they were still looking.

Simple events took on tremendous significance. The birth of a child, such as the Silberman girl, or the first wedding, which was Sam Perl's marriage to Anna Baum, who had also hidden in Namur, became a major community event. As late as 1951, people were hugging each other in the street over news that a new Rottenberg had been born—Jozef's first child, Mordechai. Hundreds attended his circumcision. Later, Chaim and Rifka would also name their first son Mordechai.

Chaim Rottenberg performed the Perl–Baum wedding in a synagogue on Terliststraat, near the diamond district. Of the five main synagogues, it was the only one still in good enough condition to use. What was left of the Jewish community came to celebrate, along with Christians from Namur who had saved Anna and Sam.

For hundreds of thousands of Jews, Antwerp, like Paris, was just a place where they could try to find passage to Palestine or North America. But because of those who stayed to work in the diamond industry, the Antwerp Jewish community grew after the war from a few hundred to a few thousand. It became even more dependent on the diamond industry than before. Jozef Rottenberg—no bearded prophet like his brother, but an amiable, clean-shaven businessman—was one of the few who did not go into diamonds. Seeing that credit lines had opened up for new businesses, he started a small pharmaceutical manufacturing company with a few employees.

Sam Perl, whose entire family had been in diamonds ever since they had emigrated to Antwerp from Transylvania when he was a small boy, now in his early twenties became a sawer. It takes ninety minutes, more or less, depending on the stone, for a rotating diamond saw to bisect a rough diamond, a preliminary step in the gems' manufacture. As he got more work, he hired a few sawers to work under him, until the payroll reached fifteen, which in diamonds is a factory.

Another man from a diamond family who had also jumped off the transport train to Auschwitz was Israel Kornfeld. He too had been captured and put on a second train. And he too had jumped again. The second time, he managed to get to Switzerland, where he and his wife, son, and two daughters were able to live quietly throughout the war. When they got back to Antwerp, they found a small old house to rent on the other side of the train tracks from the Pelikaanstraat. Israel had had to reinforce the banisters and doorjambs in the shaky little house to enable it to withstand three wild children, who had managed to break almost everything in their sturdier Swiss home.

Israel had learned diamond cleaving in the 1930s, after he had emigrated to Antwerp from Poland. His wife had come from Poland, too, and had worked slavish garment jobs to earn money to send back to her family. But once Israel started cleaving, he earned enough money for both of them. After the war they returned to Antwerp from Switzerland, confident that he could again bring in a comfortable income from cleaving. At least, it would have been a comfortable income, if it were only three children—or four, since they soon had another daughter—who were supported by it. But Israel Kornfeld was that rare kind of religious man who believed that ultimately what matters to God is how you treat other people. And so in his small house he used his diamond cleaver's earnings to support anywhere from ten to thirty people at a time. If he saw somebody on the street who looked hungry, he would ask them if they needed a meal or a place to stay.

He had done this before the war too. But after the war, with Antwerp awash in camp survivors—this was his moment. He had his children gather flour sacks and stuff them with straw for beds, then run over to the medieval city center to buy olive drab U.S. Army surplus blankets. Survivors would come and stay for a week or a month or several months. There was always floor space for another stuffed sack. They ate potatoes. The children would peel potatoes for two dozen or more people every day. On special days there might be a piece of meat in the potatoes, but the basic diet was just potatoes.

The gaunt strangers, mostly men, would sit around on their sacks and trade spectacularly horrifying stories about brutality and degradation in places called Auschwitz, Bergen-Belsen, and Buchenwald. Israel Kornfeld understood that they needed to talk about it. They would talk to each other or to his wife, but mainly they talked to him. Not only was he a good listener, but he had the perfect job for it, because he cleaved at home. As he listened, Israel, bent over a small wooden box, would carefully place a knife along grooves in the diamond he was working on, and with experienced fingers he would split off pieces along the grain of the crystal. To an outsider, it looked like whittling. He had done it for years, and it was easy for him to listen to people talk while he worked.

The children listened, too, especially the Kornfelds' son Pinchas. Pinchas was eight years old and curious about everything—about the hole in the floor of the upstairs *shul* in the big

Orthodox synagogue, and about the blackened ruins of the Van Den Nestlei synagogue. He would stand on the sidewalk at Van Den Nestlei and stare at a surviving red-colored wall where a slogan had been written in Yiddish by angry Jewish leftists before the war: "Down with Passover. Long live May Day!" Pinchas wondered about those May Day Jews. He had never heard Jews talk like that. What really aroused his curiosity was the fact that they had misspelled the word for Passover, *Pesach*. What kind of school had they gone to, misspelling *Pesach*?

This wide-eyed skinny boy was barely noticed in post-Holocaust Antwerp, but he stole glimpses at a world that was so dark and so twisted, it was beyond all imagining. No monster story, no horror fiction, was like this. At night, in his parents' small house, everyone had their sleeping place. Pinchas's place was in the big front room on a couch. The room was always full of survivors, and rather than sleep, he lay still and listened to their terrifying stories of how they had lost their parents, their children, their wives. The survivors could not stop talking—and Pinchas could not stop listening. He read books with first-hand accounts of survivors—there was an explosion of such books in Yiddish after the war.

The survivors shared more than their stories. Many of them were ill with contagious diseases, which spread through the little house. All three children developed a skin disease, an itchy rash that plagued them for months. Finally they were taken to the hospital and placed in a sulphurous solution and scrubbed with wire brushes while they screamed in pain. Sometimes the Kornfeld children had to miss a few weeks of school because of these diseases, but they were still ahead of most of the Jewish children because unlike most surviving children, they had gone to school throughout the entire war. Not many Jewish children were left. The first postwar Jewish school had started with only seventeen pupils.

Even with their diseases, it was inconceivable that Israel Kornfeld would close his door to survivors. It was what he believed in doing. Later on, when there were no longer needy survivors, he found other people who needed help. There is always someone who needs help.

4

Liberated Budapest

"Autumn and Buda were born of the same mother," wrote Gyula Krúdy, a turn-of-the-century Hungarian novelist. On one bank are the hills of Buda, the last foothills of the lower Carpathian range. On the other side is the cramped urban flatland of Pest, the beginning of the Great Hungarian Plains that were once Europe's wheat fields. For a few weeks in the fall, when the horse chestnuts start dropping from the trees, and the hills turn amber and coral, and a sweet smell of rot rises, people succumb to the beauty of Buda with a kind of drunken emotionalism. A porous light, the color of raspberry cream, appears on the horizon and filters the view of the curvaceous green steeples over in Pest. Between Buda and Pest flows the wide Danube. If rivers had voices, in the fall of 1944 the Danube would have screamed.

In March of that year the Germans, no longer trusting their ally, Miklós Horthy, had invaded. Jews were herded into a small neighborhood around the huge synagogue on Dohány Street. The streets were walled off, and guarded gates installed. About 130,000 Jews were trapped inside this ghetto. A few months later, on October 14, Horthy was overthrown by Hungarian fascists. Goon squads called Arrow Cross, after their emblem, a Hungarian version of the swastika, took over Budapest. Vicious, uneducated young men, some only teenagers, ruled the streets by force of arms. If they felt like shooting someone, they shot. But their favored activity was rounding up Jews in Pest, marching them to the banks of the Danube, standing behind them, opening fire, and simply letting the bodies crumple into the river, to be swept south by the current.

Zsuzsa, a nurse, went to visit her mother in the ghetto at the end of her hospital shift and found her walking down a street toward the river with a group of Jews, carrying their belongings in bundles as though they were leaving on a trip. Teenagers wearing armbands pointed the way with machine guns and pistols. Zsuzsa was able to grab her mother, pull her away, and hide her in the hospital until the Liberation.

György Konrád was one of eighteen people living in a house in Pest that was under the protection of the Swiss government. One of the others was an eighteen-year-old girl, with whom eleven-year-old György had fallen into the throes of quivery young love. When she ventured out onto the street one day, the Arrow Cross found her, threw her in with a group they had already gathered, and marched them to the Danube. The group stood on the riverbank in a line, with the Arrow Cross behind them. She was at one end and could hear the gunshots and the splash of falling bodies as they worked down the line. And then—nothing. They had used their last bullet on the man next to her. Out of ammunition, they let her go.

In another house near the ghetto Erzsébet Falk, a non-Jewish woman with a Jewish husband had given shelter to eighty-seven people, including sixty-four Jews. In January 1945 the artillery at night was getting closer. On the night of the seventeenth, the refugees in the Falk house hid in the basement, listening to the bursts and explosions as the world's largest army blasted the world's second-largest army off the streets of Pest one block at a time.

As they huddled in the basement speculating on where each ever-closer explosion had landed, they heard a young voice shout, "All right, line up!" Seven young men in brown and green with Arrow Cross armbands, machine guns, and pistols had broken into the basement, looking wild with panic and fury.

"Come on!" they shouted. "Everybody has to go! You are all Jews. We are going to the Danube. Now!"

Erzsébet Falk went over to them, and in a soft, gracious voice said, "Please. There is plenty of time to line everyone up. But first, we have a very nice dinner here. What I suggest is that you have a little dinner. It is past seven. We have some good wine. Whatever we do, we should do after dinner. Let's have some wine now."

The seven teenagers had some wine, and as they gulped it by
the glassful over the course of an hour, their speech grew sloppy,
their voices louder. Soon they rolled up their jacket sleeves, exposing arms that were covered with watches and bracelets, from wrist
to elbow, like displays in a pawnshop. "Know where we got these?"
one of them called out. "Jews! We got them from Jews like you!
Two hours ago at the river." One of them mimed machine-
gunning. All seven burst into laughter.

One glass later, they were again ordering everyone to line up,
shouting, "Come on! We're going to the damned river!" But at that
moment a shell exploded nearby, and two of the Arrow Cross pan-
icked and ran out of the cellar toward the gate. As they crossed the
courtyard, another explosion shook the building, and when the
hidden people looked out into the courtyard through the settling
cloud of dust and smoke, they saw one of the Arrow Cross lying in
a half-inch of blood, with his right leg missing from the midthigh.

The other six Arrow Cross, pale and trembling, returned to the
basement and the wine bottles. For hours, the people of the house
sat and watched these young men grow drunker and drunker. Finally, when a lookout at the gate reported that the Red Army was
only a few blocks away, the Arrow Cross took off their brown shirts
and replaced them with red ones, preparing to cheer the Red
Army. Their logic was uncomplicated: If Brown Shirts wore brown
shirts, surely the Reds liked people in red. But one of them could
not bring himself to be a Red. "I'm not going to wear that. Never,"
he declared. Then they ran chaotically into the street. A burst of
gunfire was heard, and the Arrow Cross who had not changed his
shirt was dead. One who had changed into civilian clothes went up
to the fifth floor and was shooting down at the Soviets. They
charged into the house, climbed the stairs, and killed him.

After the Soviets finished off the Arrow Cross at the Falk house,
they returned with bread and supplies. It was January 18, and it
had been a cold snowy winter, made harsher by the fact that there
was hardly an unbroken window left in Pest. The streets were
blocked with the carbonized chassis of trucks and tanks and the
corpses of soldiers and civilians. In the distance, explosions were
heard. The Germans, having retreated to Buda, were blowing up
all the bridges on the Danube.

There were two different vantage points from which one could
view the arrival of the Red Army—another one of those defining rifts
between Jews and non-Jews. Non-Jews were not hiding in basements

waiting for a band of adolescent maniacs to march them to the river and shoot them. Nor had they seen their relatives shipped off by train to Polish death camps. Recently the trains had stopped, because someone had mysteriously blown up the tracks. But the Germans, ever resourceful, were working on a new idea. They had wired the ghetto, where seventy thousand Jews were still walled in, and they intended to blow up the entire ten blocks. Had the Red Army not arrived, they certainly would have flipped the switch.

One of the men with the Red Army was Béla Gadó, a Hungarian Jew who had been shipped off to forced labor in a Serbian mine. His wife had been deported to the Ravensbrück concentration camp. After the Soviets took Serbia in October, Gadó used his limited Russian to talk them into taking him with them through Romania and the Hungarian plain and into Pest. Just north of Pest, in the suburb of Újpest—New Pest—his two sons were being hidden by Catholic priests in a Silesian brothers' school. The boys thought it was only a matter of time before the Arrow Cross found them. Then suddenly the Red Army was blasting its way through the streets, and their father was there. György Gadó, Béla's fourteen-year-old son, did not remember the Liberation as festive. "A part of the population feared this change and the Liberation. A part had felt it was an occupation. . . . As for me, all the Jews felt they were liberated. For if the Russians had not come, all the Jewish population of Budapest would have been exterminated, without any doubt."

Historian John Lukacs later wrote about what he saw of the Red Army on that day: "Immediately behind the fighting patrols appeared a flood of soldiers in the street, some of them caracoling on horseback." He described them robbing and raping their way through Pest.

Ilona, Erzsébet Falk's niece who was hiding in the Falk house, recalled it differently: "They came by horses, and they brought colored telephone wire. And I was so happy to see the young soldiers with the red star here." She pointed to her forehead. "And the people came out with yellow stars. And the young soldiers went down from the tanks, and there was very great happiness."

György Konrád, who had been living in the Swiss house, was a little less euphoric. "There was some stealing and not too many rapes," he recalled. But with his parents being held in some unknown place abroad, he had been waiting in his "safe" house wondering how long the Swiss protection would be respected. He had already worked out a desperate plan of action for running from the Arrow Cross when they tried to drag him to the river. For him, the Soviets could not have come too soon. What he most remembered about those first days was Soviet soldiers going to pharmacies and searching for bottles of a brand of eau de cologne called Chat Noir, which they would drink in hearty gulpfuls.

One infantryman, Moritz Mebel, remembered Budapest as giving a notably cool reception to the liberators. Mebel was not a Soviet. He had been born in Erfurt in the Thüringer region of central Germany, in a kosher Jewish household. When he was seven years old, his religious grandmother died and the household's dietary laws were dropped, although the family still occasionally went to synagogue. Other children would shout "dirty Jew" at him as he walked down the street. When he was ten years old, Hitler came to power, and his parents fled with him to Moscow. His cousins and their family stayed behind and were killed by the Nazis, while Moritz was safely studying, attending a German-language international school for leftist refugee families. When the war came, he joined the Red Army and stood with thousands of other infantrymen at a line that in 1941 was virtually the gateway to the city, although it is now within the Moscow city limits and marked with a monument that people pass on their way into town from the airport. It was there that Mebel's infantry unit began their journey. They drove the Germans back across Russia, Romania, and the Ukraine. But Budapest stood out in Mebel's memory as a particularly tough fight. The unit had to liberate Pest house by house, fighting not Germans but Hungarians, while the Germans in Buda held the high ground and shot down on them at will.

In Mebel's mind, there were two kinds of people in Budapest. "A part of the population was glad we were liberating them—but of course, not the ones who were fighting us." After Pest fell, some welcomed them, but others hoped—the great fear of Pest's Jews— that the Germans who were just across the river in Buda with its commanding heights, would come back.

ALTHOUGH THE GERMANS did not come back, ghetto survivors were still dying from hunger and disease at a rate of hundreds every week. The American Jewish Joint Distribution Committee, an amalgam of American Jewish organizations, cooked for 3,500 people each day. Synagogues, which had been used as stables, and other community buildings were in ruins. It would take several years to restore them.

Erzsébet Falk's niece Ilona, born in 1921 to an old middle-class Jewish Budapest family, had not been able to finish her high school education because in the late 1930s the Hungarian government, as a good faith gesture to its German friends, passed laws restricting Jews from schools. After Liberation, Ilona's father rebuilt his soda water factory, where she had had to spend her teens instead of in school. Now she realized that the extra chairs and tables in the factory could be used to furnish a new Jewish kindergarten that the Joint was funding. When the kindergarten was opened, Géza Seifert, the lawyer in charge of the project, took her by the hand and said, "I would like to thank you for the beautiful work that you have done." Ilona looked back with her soft eyes and elegantly featured face. She could see the effect she was having on him. As Géza Seifert took her hand, she had only one thought: "Is he married?" He was not, and soon after their meeting, he married Ilona.

As the Third Reich collapsed, the men who had been deported to labor camps started to return to Budapest. But often they found that their women and children were gone, murdered in Polish death camps. Gyula Lippner was one of them. He made it back to the family china shop in Újpest, but he came back alone. His mother, his three sisters, his wife, and his daughter were all killed at Auschwitz. He reopened the shop that his father had inherited from his grandfather, who had first opened it in 1908. A friend who had survived the labor camp with him had two sisters who had survived Auschwitz. In 1946 Gyula Lippner married one of his friend's sisters. A year later, they had their first son, George.

Now with a child to support, Lippner had to supplement his small income from the china shop. Fortunately, he had experience in one of the most useful trades of 1945 — installing windows. Anyone in Pest who could install windows had work.

GYÖRGY KONRÁD's parents both survived, and once they were reunited, the family returned to their town, Berettyó Ujfalu, near the Romanian border, only to discover that they were virtually the only intact Jewish family left. Almost all of György's schoolmates were dead. While Budapest still had a sizable Jewish population, there were few left in the rest of Hungary. Jews who did return to towns and villages found it difficult to get their property back. In Miskolc hostility became so violent that it turned into a small pogrom.

Before the war, about one in every ten people in Berettyó was Jewish—a total of about a thousand Jews. The Konrád name was originally Kahn, one of the many names borne by Kohenim, the descendants of Aaron. For more than three thousand years, the male descendants of Moses's brother Aaron have been recognized for a priestly role in Judaism. Names such as Cohen, Kahn, Cowen, Kahane often indicate this line. Just as Georges Caen's father had slightly changed the name to sound more French, György's father had changed it to Konrád to sound more Hungarian. It hadn't spared either of them.

The Konrád family had kept a fairly traditional Jewish life in Berettyó. György hated having to wear the religious vest under his clothes. The only way anyone could tell that he was wearing it, though, was by its four fringes that appear on the outside. Finally, he took to carrying four strings around. When he saw the rabbi coming, he would stand with his mop of curly black hair and his mischievous off-center grin, and arrange his hand with the strings unfurled at his hip so that it looked as if he were wearing the undergarment.

Under Horthy, Jewish men in provincial Hungary had been sent off to forced labor camps. Later, the Jews who had been left behind, women and children, had been sent to death camps. Now most of the survivors were men. Every time György caught a glimpse of one of them looking at his own family, he imagined seeing in their sad, sunken eyes what they were thinking: "Why did you survive and not my wife and children?" György was certain that that was their thought. It was his too. "Why were we the lucky ones?" György wondered.

Berettyó was an interesting place for an inquisitive twelve-year-old to live. Soviet troops were stationed there, and a corporal served as translator for the officers. György had to speak to these Russians because he had to speak to everyone, and this corporal was the only one who spoke his language. They would make trades, striking bargains that always tremendously satisfied György but on occasion greatly displeased his mother, such as when he traded her watch for a bayonet.

The soldiers tried to maintain good relations with the townspeople. Occasionally, soldiers would rob someone's home. When the locals complained, the guilty soldiers were arrested and jailed in the headquarters. Sometimes an extremely fat and good-natured colonel, who drove a Mercedes too big and shiny for the town, would personally kick a soldier down stairs into a cellar, which made a good impression on the townspeople. Soldiers bought things in the Konráds' hardware store and became acquainted with the family. Sometimes they would come over to the Konráds' house. On those occasions György's parents would always get his sister out of sight—these Russians could be unpredictable. They drank vodka and ate raw onions, taking crunching bites off them as though they were apples, and slurped tremendous amounts of raw eggs, sucking them noisily out of the top of the shells. György thought these Russians were a funny people.

5

Liberated Prague

JUST NORTH OF BERLIN, IN THE TOWN OF ORANIENBURG, not hidden in the woods but in the town, was the Sachsenhausen concentration camp. For twelve years, people living in gray Prussian houses with high-pitched roofs, neat little gardens, and painted metal gates watched emaciated prisoners march by. Then in 1945 the Germans marched forty thousand prisoners away to nowhere. They did not have the capacity to kill them all and they did not want them to fall into Allied hands, so they marched them. Hundreds dropped dead. Hundreds more were shot. But three hundred were left behind in the hospital, a long, one-story barrack on the edge of the camp.

When the Germans gave the order for the march out of the camp, there was disagreement among the prisoners in the hospital. Should they drag themselves out, or should they claim to be too weak to stand up? Their survival had turned on such decisions for years. Some of the hospital inmates expected that the people who went on the march would be shot. Then, too, they might really be too weak to survive it. How far would they be marched? Others thought that anyone who said he was too weak to march would be shot. Some thought the hospital had been wired and that the Germans would blow it up with them in it.

The three hundred hospital inmates watched the SS march the last survivors off. Some waited for the explosion. There was none.

They waited longer—nothing happened. There was no point in leaving, nowhere to go, and no use in turning to the people who lived in the neat gray houses along the road from the main gate. The hospital had shelter and a little food, and so they stayed there.

The Sachsenhausen concentration camp was liberated one week later by three heavily armed Red Army soldiers who burst into the hospital. They had mongolian features and said something quickly in Russian. Then they left, and the group was alone again. Karol Wassermann, a Slovak Jew, understood enough Russian to know that what they had said was, "You are free."

ONCE THE THREE HUNDRED Sachsenhausen inmates were pronounced free, they were alone—free at last, free to eat and die. And that was what they did. First they looked around the camp for food. Then they slipped out, nervously avoiding the town, going out to the woods, where they caught rabbits and birds and found plants and fruits. Returning to the camp, they cooked rich stews and roasted meats. And they died. These people had been living— some of them for years—on a slice of bread and thin soup that was little more than flour and water. You could never get enough. "I could have eaten—or rather drunk—ten liters of that soup. There was nothing in it," said Karol Wassermann.

Now they had real food, and they died from it. In all the liberated camps of Europe in the spring of 1945, some survivors dropped over from exhaustion, some succumbed to epidemics— tuberculosis and typhoid—and thousands died from overeating. Survivors hoarded sausages, meat, bread, clothing, blankets—the things that had made the difference between life and death in the camps. Who knew how long this "liberation" phase would last? When the Holocaust started again, they would be ready. Or they would be ready for the next one. Even in the early 1950s orphanages for camp survivors found that some of the children were still hoarding food from the dining hall.

Karol Wassermann, a pharmacist who knew something about medicine, was not going to eat himself to death. The first few days, he barely allowed himself to eat at all. He tried to warn the others as well. But Wassermann was a difficult man; he always went against the grain and was not well liked. When he had first been admitted to the hospital in a fever-driven delirium, he had repeatedly talked about death and—worse—the smell of death. By then, a small crematorium had been built on the edge of the camp, and

the smell from it drifted throughout the triangular-shaped Sachsenhausen compound and into the little town of Oranienburg. But
in the camp, as in the town, you didn't talk about the smell. The
inmates did not like people who talked about these things. After
the Liberation, when Wassermann tried to tell people that they
would die from eating, it was just Wassermann talking about death
again. For now, there was food. They should try to get a few
pounds back on their bodies before the Germans returned.

They spent their first week completely on their own. Then the
Soviets, not the Germans, came back and tried to help them. By
then, half of them were dead or dying from overeating.

Two days after the war ended, Wassermann was able to get a bus
to Prague. When he arrived, he saw that the city's stone bridges,
spires, and dark passageways were still undamaged. Moritz Mebel
remembered the Prague Liberation very differently from the one in
Budapest. "Oh, Prague! It was a huge party. I have never again
seen anything like that. We were hosted by people. You felt that
Liberation was really celebrated with their hearts!"

Once Wassermann was in Prague, he looked for his aunt, who
he hoped would not have been deported because she was married
to a Christian. He recognized a few other survivors wandering the
cobblestone streets. They looked like him, like most people he had
known in recent years. The stare, the body that looked as if it were
held together by strings. They too were looking for a relative or
friend who was still alive. After days, Wassermann did find his aunt
alive. She had a place where he could stay and begin to reorganize
his life.

He was a Slovak and did not plan to stay in Prague. Czechoslovakia, which had been put together at the end of World War I, had
been separated by Hitler. He had kept the western part—Bohemia
and Moravia, including Prague—because he considered it to be
German. The eastern Slovak region had been handed over to the
pro-Nazi Slovak nationalist Father Jozef Tiso. Now that the Slovak
nationalists had been defeated and disgraced, Czechoslovakia was
a single country again. For a few weeks, Wassermann and his aunt
waited in Prague in the hope that his brother Tybor would turn up
on one of the trains of returning survivors, just as he had. But after
some weeks of vainly checking the arriving trains, Karol and his
aunt returned to their native central Slovak mining town of Banska
Stiavrica.

With a list of family possessions that had been hidden in various
non-Jewish homes in town, they went from door to door asking for

their belongings. And at each doorway they heard the same claim: Their possessions had been stolen by the Russians. In the end, all they managed to collect was the one item of no monetary value—a portrait of Karol's father.

Karol went to see a woman he had known before the war to tell her that he had been with her husband in Sachsenhausen. So many people were missing, and if you knew someone's story, you had to tell the family. Wassermann had seen the husband "go to the other side." Everyone was learning this phrase. When a train had arrived at the camp, some of the passengers had been sent off to work and others had been pointed in a different direction—"to the other side," for extermination. The woman explained to Karol that he was mistaken, that she had been to a clairvoyant who had seen him in Siberia. "He will be coming back from Siberia," she kept insisting.

"He is not coming back," Wassermann repeated. "I was there. He is not coming back."

"I saw him in Siberia. You'll see."

Wassermann shook his head. He had no patience for this nonsense. But she also had news for him. She had found her brother on a train of survivors from Poland. He was weak and had died within days, but he had spent those last days telling her about things he had seen, including the death of Wassermann's brother Tybor. His death had been so horrible that Wassermann was never able to retell that story.

It took one more stop for Karol Wassermann to decide that he was through with the Slovaks. He went to the Jewish cemetery to visit the graves of his mother and father, who had died before the war. The cemetery was now just an empty field, littered with fragments of stone. Slovak fascists had destroyed it. Standing over the shattered stones where his parents' graves used to be, Wassermann asked himself, "How can I live in this town ever again? Whenever I shake someone's hand, I will wonder if these are the hands that knocked over my parents' gravestones."

THE CZECH LIBERATION ARMY of Ludvik Svoboda was still in Prague. With it was a newspaper correspondent, František Kraus. Before the war, Kraus had been a well-known Prague journalist living with his wife Alice on Kozi Street in the old Jewish ghetto that dated back to the Middle Ages. After 1848, Jews had been allowed to live outside the ghetto, and as they became prosperous citizens, they moved out of the cramped old neighborhood. Whoever was poorest took their place, and the Jewish town eventually became the rat-infested Prague slum. In 1893 slum clearance began, and when it was over, the ancient Jewish neighborhood had been converted into a fashionable art nouveau neighborhood. Only six synagogues, the cemetery, and the Jewish town hall were preserved. By 1938, Prague Jews had become indistinguishable from gentiles. Prague remained, as it had been for centuries, one of the important Jewish centers in the world, but it was more famous for its writers and composers than for its Torah and Talmud scholars. The Kraus family was typical of sophisticated, well-educated modern Prague Jewry. František, a fourth-generation Praguer, would go to synagogue for Sabbath, but instead of walking there as required by religious law, he would take a streetcar.

When the Germans came, they did not seem to have many problems finding the Jews, even the most assimilated. Shortly after the Nazi invasion on March 15, 1939, twenty-six thousand Jews emigrated to Palestine. Of the ninety thousand who remained in the Czech lands, only twelve thousand survived the war.

František and Alice were sent to Theresienstadt and from there, because they were young and strong, to labor camps. While František's forced labor detail was repairing rail lines in Germany, he escaped and resumed his profession: He traveled with Svoboda as a war correspondent. After the war, when he got back to Prague, he discovered that the apartment on Kozi Street was taken. During the war Germans had lived there, and once they fled, a Czech family had found it abandoned and moved in. They told Kraus that it was now their apartment and that they intended to stay.

Not only did he have no home, but he found no trace of Alice, who had been sent to a women's labor camp. The Allied military operated an office for camp survivors who were looking for their relatives, but he could learn nothing from them. But unknown to him, the war had not yet ended for Alice.

She was in southern Poland, just across the Bohemian border in Kudowa, where the Germans had used almost three hundred women prisoners for a small airplane parts factory. Almost every night during the last three months of the war, she had seen zips of light, followed by the deep booms of Katyushas, Soviet rockets. On the evening of May 7, 1945, with Hitler already dead for a week, the Germans signed an unconditional surrender. On the same day, a man from Nachod, a Bohemian town a mile and a half away from Kudowa, walked across the Czech-Polish border to Kudowa to negotiate with the woman SS commandant. His offer was simple: Let these women go, and we will give you civilian clothes. On the morning of May 8 there were no more uniformed SS in the camp. The people of Nachod took the freed prisoners into their homes, fed them, and looked after them. But on May 11, only a few days after the end of World War II, a large SS division came through Nachod, desperately fleeing the Red Army and trying to reach the nearby U.S. Third Army. The townspeople tried to stop the division, holding it up just long enough for the Red Army to arrive. Once there the army forced a final stand in the Nachod town square as the locals and work camp refugees hid in the nearby woods listening to more Katyushas.

Alice got back to Prague and found František, and they resolved to start life again the way it had been. They would go on being Prague Jews as they had always been—not very religious, but active and clear in their Jewish identity. She would try to forget everything that had just happened.

But not all survivors felt that way. One woman who had been with Alice in Kudowa and Theresienstadt left for America, vowing never again to even tell anyone she was Jewish. She settled in California, and there she discovered something strange about America: Everybody was something. They were Jewish, or they were Italian, or they were Mexican. They all talked about it. You apparently had to be something, and so she and her family called themselves Jewish. It was a distant and safer world, where Jews always talked about Jewishness. One day years later, she saw a book in a shopping mall bookstore about Rudolf Höss, the Auschwitz commander. In one of the pictures inside she saw an emaciated girl who she recognized as herself in that far away nightmare.

6

Liberated
Poland

B Y THE TIME MARIAN TURSKI WAS 18 YEARS OLD, HE HAD survived the Łódź ghetto, two winter forced marches across Central Europe, and three concentration camps. Finally, on May 8, 1945, the last day of the war, the Germans ran out of places to move their prisoners. Turski, exhausted from the marches and already cheated out of two camp liberations, was able to stay in Theresienstadt until the Soviet Third Guard Tank Army rolled up to the fortress town. But his struggle to survive was not yet over. Suffering from typhoid, he lay in a Soviet field hospital too weak to move until the following September.

The first sealed-off ghetto had been in his native Łódź. In 1941, ten years after Icchok Finkelsztajn fled the depression, the Germans had walled off a section of the city in which they trapped 163,177 Jews from all over Europe, forcing them to operate more than a hundred factories for the Nazi war effort. Those who survived the squalor had been shipped to death camps.

Turski's mother, father, and younger brother and most of the people he knew were among the missing 160,000. It seemed certain that his father and brother had been gassed at Auschwitz. A woman he had worked with in the ghetto's Communist underground told him she had seen his mother in Bergen-Belsen. That was something he could try to hold onto—the fact that the last time his mother had been seen, she was still alive. But he was still too weak to look for her. He had to rest and try to put on some weight and get some strength or, after all he had lived through, he would not survive.

After a few weeks, Turski went to the Silesian town of Waldenberg, a displaced persons center. There he befriended a man in his midthirties who was eager to meet a ghetto and camp survivor like Turski. The man was full of questions. He was not sure what he wanted to do, he told Turski, but he was certain that he wanted to leave Poland. They talked and pondered the future together. Turski also did not know what he would do once he got back his strength. His friend—this stranger who was his only friend at the moment—decided to search Jewish clubs and organizations for other DPs and to find a way to get to Palestine. Before he left, he asked Turski for a photo by which to remember him.

After the man left, he drifted to camps and clubs, talking to as many other refugees as he could. One night, he ran into a group of DPs who had not seen Poland since they were deported to camps. How is Warsaw? How is Łódź? They wanted to know everything he had seen while wandering Poland. The man had pictures to show them—photos of the piles of rubble that had been Warsaw, of Łódź, of his friend Marian Turski who had survived the Łódź ghetto.

One of the DPs, a woman, suddenly grabbed the photo of Turski. She was his mother. Marian Turski was not alone.

BEFORE THE WAR had even ended, Jakub Gutenbaum, only a teenager, already knew that he had lost almost everything. He had last heard from his father in the summer of 1940, when he was 11 years old. The father had escaped into the Soviet Union, and the family could only guess about how he had vanished.

Gutenbaum, his mother, and his younger brother were among the almost 400,000 Jews who had been forced into the Warsaw ghetto. The 80,000 non-Jewish residents of that neighborhood had been ordered to leave, and Jews had been packed into the three-and-a-half-mile area. Walls were built to close it off, and the Jewish third of Warsaw's population was left inside to starve.

Impatient with the death rate from hunger and disease, the Germans rounded up six thousand Jews each day and took them to an area by one of the gates, the Umschlagplatz. From there they would be shipped to camps for extermination. In 1943, when there were only about 40,000 Jews left in the ghetto, a thousand young people decided to fight to the death with smuggled arms. The Gutenbaums went to their hiding place in the ghetto, a basement, with about forty other people. The hatchway was concealed by a pile of coal. As they hid, they could hear the Germans enter the house overhead, could hear them fire off their weapons. But the Germans didn't seem to find the hatchway under the coal. Then smoke started to snake its way through cracks in the ceiling. The Germans were burning down the house. The hidden Jews rushed to stuff rags in all the cracks. As the basement grew hot and then hotter, the forty, naked on the floor with their mouths open, gasped for air, and it still got hotter.

At night the Germans retreated and the basement cooled off. The Jews could go upstairs into the burned-out shell of the house to breathe. But the next day they went back into the basement, and the Germans burned again. They existed like this from April 19 until May 3. Then they heard a banging on the hatchway. Germans armed with machine guns ordered them all out. As they were marched through the ghetto with their hands behind their heads, they could see that the ghetto was now a charcoal-colored world in which nothing was alive, as though swept by a storm of fire.

The Gutenbaums and the other Jews spent three days in the Umschlagplatz, during which more and more groups with hands behind their heads were brought in. Finally, they were all stuffed into freight trains and taken to Maidanek. When they got out of the train, Germans with clubs in their hands, leading growling dogs that strained at their leashes, inspected them. Jakub was pushed away from his mother and younger brother. Soon they were in two different groups. Now 14, Jakub was taken to room number four with the men. His mother and brother were taken to room number five with the women and children.

While he was in the ghetto Jakub had heard from the Resistance that all the Jews were being taken to camps and killed. He wasn't sure if this was true, or if it was, how they were going to be killed. The first thing he had to do was get to his mother and brother. The next day, he managed to get to room five, but he found no sign that they had ever been there. He had no illusions now. He was certain that the Resistance had been right and that his mother and brother were already dead.

Two years and several camps later, Gutenbaum, like Marian Turski, was a teenage orphan liberated at Theresienstadt. When he returned to the crumbled black remains of what had been Warsaw, he found an orphanage where he could stay. And then, unexpectedly, he discovered that he was not alone. An uncle came to the orphanage looking for relatives and Jakub moved into his uncle's one-room apartment.

BY THE TIME the war ended, thirteen-year-old Barbara Góra, her mother, her father, and her sister had all gone by a variety of names. When she was ten in 1942, she had been Barbara Englisz. A German who checked her papers on a Warsaw street thought Englisz was a droll name in wartime Warsaw, and he laughed. He would not have laughed if he had known that her real name was Irene Hochberg and that she had been smuggled out of the ghetto.

She had come from a comfortable Jewish household on Urabia Street, in the old center of Warsaw. Her mother had grown up in a devout Orthodox home, where she had hated the rigid religious life with its dietary laws, special clothing, and constant rules about what to do each day and at different times of the day. She married a Jew from a nonreligious home, and they had raised their two daughters like Poles. They spoke Polish at home, reserving Yiddish for times when they wanted to keep secrets from Irene and her sister.

Irene was sent to a new school in the center of Warsaw where many of the students were children of people in powerful positions and where she was the only Jew. Relative to the experiences she would soon have, being the only Jew in this Polish school in the 1930s was a minor trauma. Yet it shaped her as much as any of her later experiences. The school had a compulsory religion class, but her parents told her she did not have to go if she did not want to, so she did not attend. The school, even the religion teacher, were very agreeable about it. They gave her a comfortable place to sit and wait, to study, play, and do whatever she wanted while the other children were in religion class. But because she was absent from the class, the children were merciless in their attacks on "the dirty little Jew." They battered her with phrases they had learned from their parents. They didn't know what these things meant, and Irene didn't know either. But most days she left school crying.

When she was eight years old, the Hochberg family was forced to move to the ghetto, which was not far from their home. Irene's father, Wiktor, knew a non-Jew who lived in the neighborhood that was becoming the ghetto. Since the non-Jewish family had to move too, the two families simply swapped apartments. Irene was happy that she did not have to go to school anymore.

Once the Germans began their roundups at the Umschlagplatz, her father used his contacts in the city to smuggle the entire family and himself out one by one. They all got new birth certificates with new names—authentic documents of deceased people who had been born in Warsaw. Only Irene's mother hid. Even though she was blonde and not particularly Jewish-looking, her Orthodox background had fixed such a strong Jewish identity in her mind that she imagined that anyone at a glance could see she was Jewish. Irene's sister was placed in the old part of Warsaw, where she lived openly and worked in a factory. Irene, now called Barbara, was moved from family to family. She would stay for a time in one Christian home, and then her father, now calling himself Witold Góra, would suddenly show up and take her to a new Christian home. The Germans were killing more and more people, and it was getting harder and harder to find families with the courage to take her. Finally, he placed her with what was called a *Treuhander*, a collaborator.

The *Treuhander* knew the war was going badly and that when the Germans were gone, he was going to be in trouble with his fellow Poles. Now at least he could say he had saved someone. Besides, it was a perfect cover for his smuggling business to have this little girl riding in a wagon with him as he brought black market goods into Warsaw. She worked very hard at the business while her "uncle"—a lanky man with round little glasses and a hard, bitter face—spent most of his time drinking and smoking cigarettes. Sometimes Barbara would even bring the goods into Warsaw by herself.

Her "uncle's" family and friends were mostly *Volksdeutsche*, Poles whom the German Reich had officially recognized as being ethnically German and not of the inferior Slavic race. Once the "uncle" took her to visit his cousins. They had a daughter who was Barbara's age, a little Nazi in a Hitler Youth uniform. The two girls played together. Most people were kind to Barbara. She was a pretty blond girl with smart and cautious eyes in a handsome rounded face. She looked like a cute little Pole, but though her "good look" gave her a certain confidence, she was never sure if people knew about her or not. Sometimes other children would ask her to cross herself, and it seemed that this was a test. She thought it would look suspicious if she did it—it would look as if she were afraid. So she would just tell them it was stupid to cross yourself when you weren't even in church. And that seemed to sound good.

When she was selling smuggled goods in Warsaw, there was one man she met who worried her. Whenever she referred to her aunt and uncle, he would say, "They aren't your family." She didn't know what he knew about her. But he was always very kind to her, this poor hard-working little girl.

At home with her false family, she cleaned house obsessively. When she had first moved there, she had seen that the apartment was not particularly clean. Now eleven-year-old Barbara scrubbed everything. She scrubbed places where no one had ever looked. She scrubbed the floor under the beds. She washed the walls behind the furniture. The taunt from her school days—"dirty Jew"—still stung. No one was ever going to call her dirty.

By the time Warsaw was liberated, little remained of the city. According to official history, it was 80 percent destroyed. The Polish Home Army had risen up against the Germans, assuming that the rapidly approaching Red Army would finish the revolt for them. But the Soviets—according to some versions, they were unexpectedly held up by German resistance, and according to others, they wanted the Polish army to be destroyed—did not enter Warsaw until the Germans had annihilated the Polish Home Army and most of the city. Since 1943, the site of the ghetto had been a large blackened lot. Most of the rest of Warsaw was now tall hills of debris. Witold Góra at last reunited his family, but he could not return to Urabia Street, where they had lived when he had been Wiktor Hochberg. Now the street was not even there, except for part of a path through the piles of rubble. Warsaw was nothing but mountains and valleys. On Marszałkowska, one of the longest main streets, only four buildings were left standing.

Barbara Góra had a friend who lived near where the ghetto had been. She lived on the second floor of a building that had no first floor anymore—only the stairway. It scared Barbara even to look at the building, let alone go up to the apartment. But soon she learned that many people lived in buildings like this. She gingerly entered and exited them every day and grew accustomed to the fact that none of them ever fell over.

One of the few remaining buildings in the center of the city was the turn-of-the-century Polonia Hotel, with its ornate white exte-

rior, its glass art nouveau awnings over the doors, its grand interior
with sweeping staircase, and its two-tier rococo dining room. In its
new status as one of the few intact structures in town, the hotel
building now housed all of the embassies and was teeming with
reporters. Poland was one of the big news stories of 1945 because of
what had been found in the death camps there. The six main
camps of Poland had killed 5,400,000 people. The world had never
seen anything like it.

The Polonia Hotel became an exciting place to visit. Barbara
Góra, now 13, was drawn to all the colorful flags draped on the
building. Inside were Russians, Americans, French, and English.
And there were journalists from all over the world—anxious aggressive people speaking dozens of languages, running up and down
the stairs. She was particularly interested in the British and the
Americans because she was going to school again and was studying
English from a Polish teacher. But at the Polonia, there were foreigners speaking real English.

Barbara's father had been an active member of the Communist
underground. The man who had worried Barbara during the war
because he always said that her "uncle" wasn't really her family,
also turned out to be a member of the underground, a friend of her
father. Because the Communist party wanted to remember people's wartime records, all the underground activists were asked to
keep their wartime names. Barbara was happy to be Barbara Góra,
daughter of Witold Góra. *Góra* was a good Polish name that meant
the same thing in Polish as the old Jewish name *Hochberg* meant
in German—"high mountain." The entire family was happy to
keep their Polish names and continue their wartime identities,
never mentioning that they were Jewish. They had all had enough
of being Jewish.

Witold Góra was made chief of police in a small town in Lublin
province. Barbara was once again the only Jew in school. But now
she was a Góra, not a Hochberg, and she went regularly to the
Catholic church. The priest knew that her father was a Communist and was very pleased that he was sending his daughter to
church. In 1946 the family moved back to Warsaw, and Barbara
went to a high school with required religion classes. This time she
wasn't the only Jew in the school, but all of the Jews quietly took
the course and never talked even among themselves about being
Jewish. Barbara was far happier than she had been years before,
when she had been Irene and wouldn't take the class. When the

teachers in her school asked the class who had gone to mass on Sunday, Barbara always raised her hand.

At first it was easy to sit through the religion classes, but then there was a change in teachers. The new teacher was a fanatical priest who taught that Darwin was evil, that the world was created in seven days, and that anything else was heresy. Barbara was growing tired of religion, and she transferred to a new school that she had learned of, a socialist school that did not teach religion. It was a long way from where she lived, and she had to pack into an overcrowded streetcar to get there. But it was worth the trouble. Communism, her father had told her, was bringing about a new society, free of religion. For a Jew in Poland, at last, here was an answer to the Jewish question: No religion at all, for anyone.

NOW THAT HIS FATHER was dead, Marian Turski reflected sadly on how hurt his father had been in the Łódź ghetto when Marian had joined the Communist underground and turned his back on Judaism. But to Marian, Communism was the future. His family had been more Zionist than religious, and many of his cousins had survived by going to Palestine before the war. Now an office in Łódź was helping to arrange for emigration to Palestine, and many of the survivors were leaving.

But Marian thought he had a stake in the new Poland that was emerging. People who had missed school could now get degrees and good positions very quickly. Poland had never before offered such opportunities, and certainly never before to Jews. Barbara Góra helped her father with mathematics, and soon he earned an engineering degree. After she finished her basic education, she herself was able to study in Moscow for an advanced agricultural degree. Jakub Gutenbaum, living in his uncle's small room, could make up all the schooling he had missed. He had his diploma in two years and then got a scholarship to study electrical engineering in Moscow. Although 3.1 million Polish Jews had been murdered, somehow Jewish life was returning to Poland. Wrocław, which before the war had been Breslau and had had the third largest Jewish community in Germany, now reopened its Yiddish theater, in spite of heavy damage inflicted on the historic center of the city. Later, Warsaw and Łódź did the same. Once again, there were synagogues and Jewish schools. Yiddish newspapers such as *Dos Nahe Lebn*, "The New Life," started up. In Cracow, where the buildings had not been touched, Jews embraced as they met each other on the street. Kazimierz, the old Jewish quarter with its run-down charm, was now inhabited by non-Jews, but two of the synagogues there were reopened, and Hasids even started their own prayer rooms. On Friday nights, men from each group scouted the streets for the requisite ten men, the minyan, to hold a service.

About 40,000 Polish Jews returned from concentration camps, and another 55,000 turned up from hiding in Poland or other countries. And then 180,000 came back from the Soviet Union. By June 1945, there were already more than 10,000 Jews in Cracow, almost 8,000 in Wrocław, 135,000 in Warsaw, and 41,000 in the Łódź area. These were only small fractions of the prewar population, but they were enough for Jewish communities to function with schools and synagogues.

The Central Committee of Polish Jews established an office in Lublin to disseminate information about who was living and who was dead. Slowly, the incomprehensible figures were compiled and published in press releases. The Committee started to establish orphanages, and by the end of 1945, they already housed seven hundred orphans. By the middle of 1946, they had established forty-four secondary schools for 3,400 children and thirty-six primary schools for another 3,300 children. Miraculously, Polish Jewry was back.

But it was not welcomed. Returning Jews expected to get their property back, and the Poles who had taken over their homes, businesses, and possessions had not counted on this. The Poles grew increasingly hostile to the returning Jews. Polish fascists were still armed and operating in the east and southeast. In Cracow on May 3, 1945, a youthful mob smashed windows in Jewish homes and shouted anti-Semitic slogans until the Red Army moved in to control the disturbance. In August "blood libel" reemerged in Cracow—the old claim, dating back to the Middle Ages, that Jews murdered Christian children to use their blood in satanic rituals.

An extreme right-wing group called Narodowe Siły Zbrojne, the National Defense Force, pulled Jewish survivors off trains and murdered them. They even attacked Jewish orphanages. The Central Committee of Polish Jews listed four hundred Jews murdered in such attacks between February and September 1945. In 1946 things got even worse. As hostility grew toward the Communists, a new anti-Semitic stereotype gained currency—żydokomuna, a Jewish Commie. There had been Jews/the usurers, Jews/the bloodsuckers, and Jews/the baby-snatchers, and now there were Jews/the Communists plotting to undermine the Polish national destiny.

Although Jews represented only a minority of the Communists, it was frequently said that they were the Communist movement. Hadn't they cheered the entry of the Soviets? Poles hadn't cheered the Red Army—only the Jews. The fact that the Jews were being saved from total extinction never entered this argument.

Jewish leaders tried in vain to solicit the help of the Catholic Church hierarchy. They were repeatedly refused audiences with cardinals and bishops. In June 1946 the Bishop of Kielce refused to issue a pastoral letter against the spread of anti-Semitic violence. On July 4 a nine-year-old Polish boy, Henryk Blaszczyk, was reported missing in Kielce. A crowd quickly grew, claiming he had been murdered by Jews who wanted his blood. The crowd marched into the Jewish area and went on a violent rampage. While they were laying siege to the building of the Jewish Committee, the Jewish leaders inside desperately tried to telephone the bishop, but his office refused to put through the call. Forty-two Jews, mostly camp survivors, were killed.

A similar pogrom was averted in Częstochowa because there the local bishop, Teodor Kubin, denounced the accusations of blood ritual. But Bishop Stefan Wyszynśki of Lublin, who later became Cardinal Primate, explained to the Jews that they were resented because "they took an active part in the political life of the country." The statement went on to explain, "The Germans murdered the Jewish nation because the Jews were the propagators of Communism." When the Lublin Jews asked him for his position on the accusations of ritual murder, he said, "The use of blood by Jews was never completely clarified."

The role of Jews in the Polish Communist movement was greatly exaggerated. In 1938 some five thousand out of 3.3 million Jews had been active Communists. About one-quarter of Polish Communists were Jews. But there was an element of self-fulfilling prophecy in all this. The Jews were now marked as Communists because they had depended on the Red Army to protect them from Poles. Between Liberation and 1947, fifteen hundred Jews were murdered. The percentage of Jews in Poland who were Communists dramatically increased simply because most Jews who were not Communists decided to leave. Soon Polish Jewry had dropped down to about 90,000. A Jewish woman from a Warsaw Communist family said, "Primarily Communists stayed. Everybody else in their right mind took off."

7

Liberated Amsterdam

AMSTERDAM WAS LIBERATED ON THE LAST DAY OF WORLD War II, freeing the Dutch at last to restore their vaunted orderliness. A Red Cross office was organized to help people who were looking for vanished relatives by offering a series of forms, which they then tried to process with a maximum of efficiency. The office had to contend with long lines; it gave each applicant one card to fill out for each missing relative. Once the applicant got to the front of the line, someone would say, "How many, please?" and hand over the correct number of cards.

Sal Meijer, the kosher butcher, waited his turn patiently. "How many please?"

"One hundred, please," he said in his husky voice.

"Just one card for each missing relative, please."

"One hundred, please," Sal Meijer repeated, trying to look straight ahead with no particular emotion.

They gave him ten cards. Coming from a large Amsterdam family, he actually did have one hundred missing relatives, including his mother, six brothers, their wives, and children. They could not all be gone. But he could find none of them.

The Dutch are a methodical people. An obsession with lists, registration, and carefully filled-out and catalogued forms was one of the Dutch traditions that the Germans had found helpful in the deportation and murder of 78 percent of the Jewish population of the Netherlands. In 1944 the SS in France had complained about the troublesome French character that was preventing the Paris SS from matching the deportation rate in Holland.

Sal Meijer went home to the room he was renting because a Christian family had taken over his apartment while he had been in hiding. He had not been surprised when strangers answered his door. "Excuse me," he said as he pushed past them. "I just wanted to get something." He walked over to a doorway, reached up, and removed a concealed panel that the new residents had never noticed. From it he pulled out a twelve-inch oil-burning brass menorah that had been in his family for two hundred years, as well as a few other valuables that he had hidden there before he left in 1940. "Excuse me," he said again, then left.

Meijer's grandfather had been mayor of Amsterdam. His father, like Sal, was a kosher butcher. The Meijers never would have hidden their Jewishness. There was no need to, and besides, Sal had always assumed that his prominent Semitic nose and strong features left no doubt as to his identity. If the Germans had wanted to know that he was Jewish they would not have needed a yellow star. Nevertheless, the Germans made him and the other 140,000 Dutch Jews wear them. One day when he was riding on a train, a German saw his yellow star and ordered him to stand up. Struck that the German had looked at the star first, Meijer realized that this German would not have known that he was Jewish except for the label. After that Meijer stopped wearing the star. He and his wife-to-be moved to Hillegom, in the heart of Holland's tulip-farming region.

There they lived as Catholics, regularly attending mass. No one in Hillegom had ever seen a Jew, and it never occurred to any of them to doubt that their new neighbors were what they said they were. Many people had left the cities for the countryside, where there was more food. Few villagers even thought about his typically Jewish name. They didn't know what a Jewish name was. Occasionally it would come up, and he would explain that his family came from near the Meijerei River, in the Brabant region. There was nothing suspicious about them, although it took some practice for them to become convincing Catholics. When he had been there only a month, he took a handkerchief out of his pocket to blow his nose during a mass, and one of his removed and forgotten yellow stars fell out of his pocket. He stuffed it back in his pocket before anyone saw it.

In their home the Meijers tried to keep Jewish law. He fasted for the Yom Kippur holiday each year, telling his neighbors that he was ill and could not eat. But news of his sickness always concerned them, and they would bring him food. Toward the end of the war food was scarce even in this farm district. By 1944, famine was widespread in Holland. When people later asked Meijer how he had kept kosher during the occupation, he always shrugged and said, "Tulip bulbs are kosher."

In the winter of 1944–45 many Dutch were eating tulip bulbs. It was called the hunger winter—an almost total breakdown in the economy because the Dutch were sealed off from Allied help, farming was not producing enough, and the occupiers had grabbed everything from food to bicycles and shipped it to besieged and desperate Germany. Southern Holland, like Belgium, was liberated in the early fall of 1944. But the Germans tenaciously held on to central and northern Holland, including Amsterdam. At the end of September the Allied airborne assault on Arnhem was driven off by German troops. Through that record cold winter, Amsterdamers struggled to survive. Wood was stripped from everything for heat— the ties in the tram tracks, the benches in the abandoned synagogues, any wood that could be found.

After the Liberation, Sal Meijer, eager to look for his family, pedaled from Hillegom back to Amsterdam on the rims of a bike that no longer had tires. There were almost no tires in Holland for either bicycles or cars. Amsterdam was a shock to Meijer. The city seemed empty. The old Jewish areas had been almost totally depopulated. Everywhere, iron rails—tram tracks that had been stripped of their ties—were lying uprooted. Ditches had been dug for latrines. Most of the synagogues had been completely gutted. Benches, arks, balconies—if they were made out of wood, they were gone. The old Jewish neighborhood around Jodenbreestraat—an area like Paris's Pletzl, where working-class Jews lived in crowded, narrow streets that led to five major synagogues—was destroyed. The residents had all been deported, and Amsterdamers had gotten through the hunger winter by stripping not only synagogues but abandoned houses of furniture and even beams and floorboards. Buildings were still collapsing from missing beams.

Every day, Jews would go to the Central Station to see who got off the trains. They would go to the Red Cross office and fill out cards. The Red Cross started to compile a list of those known to have been killed in the camps and another of known survivors. But it made mistakes. Some who survived and came back were listed as dead. So people who saw their wife or son on the death list could still hope it was a mistake.

The Moppes diamond factory became a shelter for camp survivors. Sal Meijer and other Jews went regularly, searching for relatives, but not a single one of his missing hundred relatives ever turned up there. Then one day he saw a newspaper article about a ship from Odessa that was landing in Tilburg. The article said that four Jewish camp survivors were on board the ship. Sal went back to the diamond factory the day after the ship landed and found his brother. Jaap was alone. His wife and child had been killed, and among the bodies Jaap had seen removed from the gas chamber were those of three of their brothers.

WHEN VICTOR WATERMAN got back to Amsterdam from the safety of Switzerland, he was shocked by the condition of Jews. Not only were they sickly looking, they were in rags. Some of the women were wearing dresses they had made from men's prayer shawls. He saw these people walking in the streets as though they were lost. Sometimes he would recognize people he knew, but they wouldn't talk to him. He would run up to someone and say "How are you?" and they would stare at him, and he would look into their vacant eyes and say, "It's me, Victor Waterman, from Jodenbreestraat. Waterman, remember—the matzoh bakers. I had the chicken place. . . . "

But the only response he would get was, "Leave me alone." Sometimes they would walk away without saying anything at all.

Waterman had been born on the Jodenbreestraat in 1896, when ten percent of Amsterdam was Jewish. He had grown up in a world of diamond workers and matzoh bakers. He and his eight brothers were all matzoh bakers at a time when Amsterdam was a matzoh center, exporting to Jewish communities all over the world every spring. His parents were organizers in the early days of the city's labor movement, which began with diamond cutters and matzoh bakers. But unlike the diamond cutters, the matzoh bakers would not strike, because they only worked thirty-two weeks a year. If they ever talked about striking, the rabbi would say, "But we have to have the matzoh ready for Passover," and they would go back to work.

In 1920, Victor married Heinje Hamerslac, and they had three sons. He started a kosher chicken business and exported the feathers, which were used in quilts and pillows. There was a tremendous demand for feathers in Switzerland and the United States. Poor Jewish children who lived around the Jodenbreestraat could always earn money as Waterman's pluckers.

He stayed in Amsterdam when the Germans came, and when they decreed that all Jews must register, and when they banned Jewish children from schools. Then in 1942, when they started rounding up Jews for labor camps, Victor Waterman decided that it was time to take his family to America. For many Jews, it would have been too late to get out. If he had waited a month or two longer, it would have been too late for him too. But his business had given him connections in Switzerland and the United States. His Swiss contacts were able to get him to Montreux, and from there they were supposed to arrange the trip to America. But they were never able to arrange it, and instead of America, the family spent the rest of the war in Montreux.

By the time Victor Waterman was able to return to the three handsome canalside houses where much of his family had lived, they had all been sold, and all his relatives and their families had been deported. Out of eight brothers and two sisters, only one brother and one sister returned. They told him about the camps, about how their mother, an eighty-three-year-old widow, had been forced onto a train, been found unfit at Auschwitz, and killed in a gas chamber. Victor's brother told him how their sister had died and how their seven brothers had died, story after story, and he was in the middle of telling him about a starving man who had killed his son for a piece of bread when Victor put his hands to his ears and shouted, "Enough! I don't want to know anymore!" He never again listened to stories about the camps.

A LITTLE RECEPTION CENTER was set up at the Central Station for returning camp survivors. Each was handed ten guilders and a pack of cigarettes. This was the only program that the Dutch government had set up for survivors. After the Liberation, with that peculiar sense of fairness, the government had decided that nothing special should be done for Jews. The Nazis had singled out Jews, set them apart. Now the Dutch government would not be like the Nazis—it would treat their Jews exactly like everyone else.

When Sieg Biedermann returned from Auschwitz, he talked the

reception office into giving him sixty guilders instead of ten. It would be enough for several meals. But he had no family, and no place to go. His wife had been among those rescued from the camps by Swedish diplomacy, but her rescue had come too late, and four days later she had died. He had found no trace of his sister and seven brothers who had been deported from Vienna. Sieg was Viennese, but he had lived with his uncle in Amsterdam since he was a small child. Now, with sixty guilders in his pocket, he went back to his uncle's house. The people who were living there had no idea what had happened to his uncle or his uncle's family—and they made it clear that they had no intention of giving back the house.

Biedermann had to start life again. Like many survivors, he had lost everything he had known, and because he was a true survivor, he understood that to keep going he had to begin a new life as quickly as possible. He married Evelyne, a nurse who had looked after his wife in the camp and been with her when she died in Sweden. Evelyne also needed to begin a new life. Her entire family was dead. When her father was deported to Auschwitz, he had confidently boarded the freight car they were being stuffed into, saying, "I've never been afraid of good, hard manual labor." When Evelyne returned to Amsterdam she found that her father's millinery business was still in the hands of the elderly man, a member of the Dutch Nazi party, the NSB, who had been given the business through the "Aryanization" program. As a known Nazi, the man was convicted, ordered to pay damages, and sentenced to prison. But he was 87 and too ill to serve out his term. In 1947 he died without having paid back anything.

But she and Sieg now had their marriage and the millinery business, and life could begin again.

IN AUGUST 1944, when the Red Army entered Bucharest, four Russians tore into a night club that Germans were known to frequent. Most of the Germans had left, but the Russians grabbed the piano player. He was a small thin man in his midthirties who spoke both German and Romanian, with an accent. He had been popular with the Germans, picking out tunes on the keyboard while booted Germans stood around him staring tearfully at the ceiling, singing, " . . . *wie einst Lili Marleen,*" or whatever else they wanted to hear. If you could give him a few bars, he could play the song.

As the Russians pulled this collaborator piano player out of the club, he shouted to them in awkward Russian. They didn't really understand him, and it didn't matter to them—these Romanians were going to pay for their Nazi alliance. But the wiry piano player wrestled one arm free and called out in German, *"aus das Lager!"*—something about "escaping camp." He cried, "Auschwitz!" and held out a bony forearm belly up, so they could see the numbers tattooed on it.

His name was Mauritz Auerhaan, from a diamond-polishing family on a small street off the Jodenbreestraat, the crowded old Jewish section of Amsterdam. He had spent two years in Auschwitz and was then shipped to Birkenau, the death factory down the road. One day he found himself in a group of prisoners who were being marched past the tracks, past the crematoriums, past the fields where they dumped the ashes, and into a woods of tall straight Polish pines. He started to hear the pop of the German weapons and saw prisoners down the line falling—and he ran. Struggling through Eastern Europe at the height of the war, he managed to survive from place to place, working at odd jobs, looking for people who would help him, running from people who would turn him in. He worked for Poles, Russians, Germans, Ukrainians, and Romanians, always hiding the telltale tattoo on the inside of his arm. Eventually, he had found safety as a club pianist in Bucharest.

When he returned to Amsterdam and got his pack of cigarettes and his ten guilders, he found little sympathy for camp survivors among the general population. The people in the Netherlands felt that they had suffered tremendously during the hunger winter. They were and have remained full of tales of deprivation—eating pets to survive, burning their furniture to try to stay warm, suffering through a terrible diphtheria epidemic just before the Liberation. They did not regard the suffering of these gaunt sickly people—some still in striped clothes—as anything remarkable.

The survivors felt that nobody cared about them, and even if they had cared, they could never understand. "People would say it isn't true," said Mauritz Auerhaan. "I would tell them I have seen the gas chambers. I have seen them. I know what they did. I stayed alive because I could engrave SS on the cigarette cases they stole from the Jews. They did everything. I tried to stay alive." But he quickly learned that people did not want to hear all this. They had survived the hunger winter.

Auerhaan had survived the Holocaust through his array of skills. Now he could survive postwar Holland. What could he do in a city that had been stripped bare? Sell tires. Nothing could move for lack of tires. Bicycles were on rims. Rusting prewar cars and trucks stood idle on their wheel drums. He could not get enough shiploads of tires—used tires to retread. Any kind of tire he could get, he could sell.

ONE OF THE FEW undamaged synagogues in Amsterdam was the huge Portuguese-Israelite, popularly known as the Esnoga. This was the synagogue of the Sephardic community, the direct descendants of the Spanish Jews whom Ferdinand and Isabella had expelled in 1492. These Jews had lived in Portugal for more than a generation, then moved to Morocco, and from there the grandchildren of the Spanish exiles had moved to Amsterdam. Their first Amsterdam religious service had been held in the Palache house in 1590. They flourished in Amsterdam without persecution for four centuries, marrying within their subgroup and keeping their unique customs, the language and music of the Portuguese Sephardic rite.

For several years the Nazis exempted the Amsterdam Sephardic Jews from the Final Solution, partly because of their vague tie to Portugal, which was a neutral country. There were protracted negotiations to try to get all 5,500 of them Portuguese nationality, which would have ensured their safe passage to Portugal. In the meantime, the SS thought that since the Esnoga was such a large space, it would make an excellent gathering place for Jews awaiting deportation. Throughout Europe, the SS created such centers, like the sports stadium in Paris and the Umschlagplatz in Warsaw, where Jews waited for days until enough of them had been collected to fill a transport train to a camp. The SS informed the leaders of the Sephardic Community that someone would be coming around to look over the space. Since refusing the SS did not seem a realistic possibility, the Jewish leaders decided that the best approach would be to have an innocent-looking teenager who could not answer any questions show them around. They chose seventeen-year-old Leo Palache, a direct descendant of the Palache who had hosted the first service in 1590.

Leo politely answered all the SS's questions as they walked around the synagogue. The SS discussed where would be the best spot for the first-aid unit, how the balcony could be used, what could go up on the raised reading area. Then there was the question of the windows. It was wartime, and any building used at night had to be blacked out. "There are seventy-two windows," Leo, their young guide, informed them. The SS looked up at the ornate decor with the rows of arched decorative windows.

After this tour, the Germans never came back, and the Esnoga got through the entire occupation without damage. The SS chose a theater for their transit spot instead. Exactly why this happened is unknown. But the Sephardic-Portuguese community ran out of luck in early 1944, when the Germans lost interest in their negotiations with Portugal. They deported the Sephardim to the camps, including the Palaches—father, mother, older brother and sister, and Leo. They were able to stay together in Theresienstadt, but Leo was separated from the family when he was sent to Auschwitz. Then, as the Red Army approached southern Poland, he was sent to Buchenwald, where he was liberated by the Americans.

Thousands of the 5,500 from the old Sephardic-Portuguese community were missing without a trace. About 600 returned. But these few were determined to preserve their traditions. Shortly after the Liberation, they reopened their historic synagogue, the Esnoga, and held a service to which they invited all the Jewish community. Hundreds came. Some came for the service, to thank God for saving them. Some made speeches about showing the world that Jews were back. But it soon became clear that many had come in the hope of seeing their missing relatives. As they milled around, as Jews often do during the chanting of the service, the search grew increasingly frantic, some completely abandoning all pretense of doing anything but sifting through the faces in the crowd.

Leo Palache never did find his relatives, or even most of his friends. One woman whom he had known all his life, like himself a direct descendant of the original Sephardim, had made it back. They were even very distantly related. She too had survived Buchenwald, although she was so ill that upon her return she spent the next two years in the hospital. They chose April 10, 1949, the fourth anniversary of the liberation of Buchenwald, as their wedding date.

Since Jews had been banned from schools under German occupation, most of the returning teenagers and young adults had not been to school for five years. When Leo Palache got back, he was almost twenty and had never finished high school, which was deeply troubling for a man who had come from a scholarly household. His father had been a distinguished Old Testament professor whose name had been given to one of the schools in the university, the Judah Palache Institute. Leo had wanted to be a lawyer.

A program of adult education was established for cases like his, but Leo had no one to advise him to go there. Instead, he simply went back to high school. There he sat, a twenty-year-old man who had survived the death camps, in a class with fourteen-year-olds. "I felt that emotionally, it was absolutely impossible," he said. He never did get an education, and all his life, with a mixture of humor and sadness, he would call himself "*am ha-arez*," the biblical word for one of the ignorant masses.

ON THE TRAIN going into Amsterdam, Leo Palache had vowed that he would immediately return to a strictly kosher diet and strict observance of the Sabbath. Others, like Jaap Meijer, could never again believe in God and his commandments. For those who wanted to be kosher after Liberation, it was difficult because there was still little food. Sal Meijer wanted to return to his trade as a kosher butcher, but no meat was available, let alone kosher meat. Instead, he opened a coffee shop on the Jodenbree-straat, next to a Sephardic butcher. Sal suspected that the meat next door was not really kosher, and it certainly wasn't legal, since the import of meat was not allowed. Some meat did come from London and Antwerp on the black market. A small scandal erupted when one kosher steer arrived and two kosher tongues were sold.

Meijer rented a room in the Transvaalbuurt, an area so named because before the war it had been largely populated by diamond workers. Once meat became available, Meijer re-opened his kosher butcher shop on the Jodenbreestraat, but the area was still in ruins.

For years, the Dutch government held fast to the policy of not giving Jews special treatment. German Jewish refugees and fleeing Nazi war criminals were thrown into the same prison camp for illegal German aliens. Immediately after the Liberation, the tax office billed the Jewish Community of the Hague—most of whom were dead—for several years of back taxes on the plot of land under the unused synagogue. Nor did the government offer Jews much help in recuperating private property that had been stolen from them. Jewish property that Dutch Nazis had taken over was repossessed by the government, and survivors like Sieg and Evelyne Biedermann had to sue to get theirs returned to them.

The Biedermanns got their millinery business back, and after it was starting to prosper by the mid-1950s, a sheepish-looking man appeared at the Biedermann door. "I'm very sorry," he began. "But you understand—I was sent. This is not my idea." Sieg slowly came to understand he was from the government. But what did he want?

"Well, you understand, this is not my idea. And you don't have to do it. Other people have said no, and nothing has happened to them."

Biedermann was losing patience. "What do you want?"

"Well, in fact, the sixty guilders."

"What?"

"At the train station in 1945. Ten guilders were allotted, but you got sixty guilders. That was a loan. But, as I say . . . "

Biedermann paid back the sixty guilders and demanded a receipt.

The Netherlands wanted to remember its Resistance, but it did not want to remember what it had let happen to Jews. A pension was offered for Resistance veterans but not to Jewish victims. An equivalent pension for Jewish victims was not passed until 1973.

Not only was there little sympathy for Jews, but books and newspapers published in the Netherlands after the war revealed a certain anti-Semitism in comments about the cowardice of Jews, how they had to depend on other people to save them, how Jews in hiding stole things and couldn't be trusted.

More than 150,000 Dutch people were denounced as collaborators and arrested. A few were sentenced to death for war crimes, but most of the executions were never carried out. Dutch retribution fell far short of that of France, which prosecuted 170,000 cases of collaborators, sentenced 120,000, executed some 2,000, and lynched another 4,500. Belgium, with a population of only eight million, investigated 634,000 cases of collaboration, though only 87,000 were actually prosecuted, most of which led to convictions. It wasn't that the Dutch hadn't had collaborators. Dutch collaborators enabled the Germans to kill a far higher percentage of Jews there than in France or Belgium. Major SS operations, such as Westerbork camp, were operated by Dutch, not by Germans. Thirty thousand Dutchmen had volunteered to fight for Germany. The Germans paid seven guilders for a tip on a Jew in hiding, and

one-third of the Jews hidden by Christians were betrayed to the
Nazis, the best-known example being the family of Anne Frank.

But now the Dutch government seemed to lack either the will
or the means to process all the cases that were being reported.
Complaints were often investigated by amateurs. After a few years
the government decided to release all but the most flagrant cases. It
sent a letter to the Jewish Community saying that it had decided to
release the others into society and hoped that the Jewish Community would understand and receive these people "in a Christian
manner." It was a form letter that went to all religious groups.

JEWISH LIFE RESUMED in Amsterdam. But the scale of it was
different. Amsterdam had been a city like New York, where Jewish
life was a basic component of the culture. Like New York, the local
slang in Amsterdam was heavily laced with Yiddish. The slang
continued, but with few Jews. Slowly, the figures were tabulated.
Of the 110,000 Dutch Jews who had been sent to the camps, 5,000
had survived. More than three-quarters of Dutch Jewry had been
murdered, the worst rate of genocide in all of Western Europe. In
1945, Victor Waterman was walking on an Amsterdam street wearing a good suit, when he heard a voice from somewhere behind
him say, "Look, they missed one."

PART TWO

BROYGEZ IN THE COLD WAR

"And what did our Eternal Father have to say on the subject? If he had no part in this, then what did he have a part in? Was he looking at life as you look at a newsreel? Was he shaking his head, and then wondering whether the survivors still loved him? And what did Jesus do about Hitler, Himmler and the Waffen SS? Turn the other cheek? And what did the pope do, and the Allies, and the Jews? God and man, old and young, wise and foolish, this race and that religion—who did not take part in this obscenity?"

GYÖRGY (GEORGE) KONRÁD, A Feast in the Garden

8

From Łódź
to Düsseldorf

I⟨T DID NOT TAKE A POGROM IN KIELCE TO CONVINCE LEA⟩ Lesser or Aaron Waks that this burned-out cemetery called Poland was no longer their home. The Lessers had survived by fleeing to the Soviet Union. Aaron Waks had done the same, but he had failed to convince a single member of his family to come with him. They had all believed that their home was in Łódź, and they were just not people for moving. There were even optimists among them who thought everything would be all right in Poland—now every one of them was dead. Aaron Waks was not going to forgive or forget anything. The Poles were murderers, and the Germans were murderers. Europe was a slaughterhouse of racist butchers, and a Jew was a fool to trust any of them.

Immediately after the war Aaron Waks left Łódź for an American-run camp in central Germany near Kassel, to get his connection to Palestine. Soon after, the Lesser family—Lea, her parents, three sisters, and a brother—left for the same camp. They arrived to find Aaron Waks in charge of relations with the Americans. Aaron and Lea had known each other since their childhood in the little town of Nowy Miasto, "New Town," which had its shtetl—a little Jewish village—on the far side of the hill. They had grown up together in the Jewish part of Łódź. The few Jews who remained in their Łódź neighborhood were mostly preparing to leave, and nobody lived on the far side of the hill in Nowy Miasto anymore. But when Aaron went to Germany, he reasoned that there was more to all of this than just getting himself out. He thought there should be no Jews at all in Europe. After two thousand years of abuse, this was the end of it. When the next pogrom was launched, there should be no Jews to be found.

The DP camps were established in Allied-occupied Germany for the 45,000 Jews who had been liberated from concentration camps in Germany and were awaiting passage out of the country. That population increased by hundreds of thousands as people like Aaron and Lea came in from the east. After the pogrom in Kielce, Polish Jews packed into the DP camps in Germany.

In 1946, Aaron and Lea were married, and one year later their first son, Ruwen, was born in the DP camp. The following year, after the State of Israel was established, Lea's entire family emigrated. The DPs who had been kept out of Palestine when it was British-controlled could now enter Israel and become citizens. This should have meant the end of the DP camps, with people like Aaron Waks getting everyone out in an orderly fashion and then closing up the camps and leaving. But not everyone went and so the camps did not close down, and Aaron Waks did not see his job as finished. There were still thousands of DPs. First run by the Allied military, the camps were then turned over to the United Nations Relief and Rehabilitation Administration, then to the International Refugee Organization. As they were passed from one organization to the next, each expected it to be a short-term project.

Many of these camps had originally been German prisoner-of-war camps. Future French President François Mitterrand had been among the French prisoners held in the camp where Ruwen Waks was born. But as the camps became increasingly settled by DPs, they were turned into very livable villages. Ruwen remembers his childhood there fondly. "It wasn't like being in a camp," he recalled. Families lived in houses, sometimes two-family houses, and conditions were pleasant, even privileged. The Allies saw to it that the DPs lived considerably better than most of the Germans who were suffering from shortages in their bombed-out cities.

The camps became Jewish villages, with their own autonomous governments. DPs wanted no relations with Germany, recognized no German authority over their territory, and they dealt only with the occupying powers and their own Jewish police and courts within the camps. They became in effect an Israel in Europe. Simply wanting to be in a place for Jews that was run by Jews, many of the camp inhabitants had no real desire to leave in order to live in the underdeveloped, politically destabilized Middle East. Aaron Waks, perhaps without ever thinking about it in this way, became a municipal official in a European Jewish village. His was a life of responsibilities, with the satisfaction of a sense of mission.

But something was beginning to trouble Aaron and other camp leaders: Many of the DPs were slowly settling into Germany. Germany was out there, not in their village. Living in Germany was exactly what Aaron did not want Jews to do.

Because the camps were supplied with many goods that were not available in the Germany outside the camps, black marketeering was an easy temptation for DPs. Near each DP camp, a German community sprang up from its economic activity. Some DPs were making substantial profits in the German economy. DP Jewish communities started to appear outside of the camps. In Bavaria, Lower Saxony, and Hesse, Jewish communities were founded in places that had had no Jews before the war. Among the DPs who settled in Germany, there was a strong tendency toward disreputable or even criminal activity. They hated Germany and the Germans, and anything was fair. What didn't the Germans deserve?

By 1949, excluding the Soviet sector, which had no DPs, more than half the Jews in Germany outside the DP camps were former DPs. Only about fifteen thousand German Jews had survived in Germany, most because of mixed marriages. Few among the German survivors had a strong Jewish identity. Of the 4,378 married Jews remaining in Berlin after May 1945, 94 percent were married to non-Jews. For these few survivors, most of whom had lost all property and livelihood, there was no help. A generation later, Germans would express their guilt in an eagerness to be seen helping and working with Jews. But directly after the war, German guilt worked very differently. Germans were reluctant to hire Jews because Jews made them feel bad. The survivors went hungry until foreign Jewish agencies provided them with assistance.

Slowly, in urban centers around occupied Germany, minuscule Jewish communities began to reappear. DPs were not always seen as an opportunity to enlarge these communities. Some communities put out flyers warning their members against "DP panhandlers" who might be working the area. The unscrupulous and lawless attitude of these new arrivals aggravated the old German Jewish prejudices against Eastern Jews, *Ostjuden*. In a harsh echo of traditional German citizenship law, some communities passed laws stating that only a German-born Jew could become Community president. In spite of everything, German Jews were Germans.

DPs settled in the larger cities like Frankfurt, where sleazy bars and beer halls that catered to soldiers and prostitutes became stereotypical DP businesses. They drifted aimlessly from one city to another. Their only moral principle was that doing anything to help Germany rebuild was wrong.

When Aaron Waks's camp was closed in 1949, it was at last time for him, Lea, and their baby to make *aliyah* to Israel. They had learned from Lea's family and others that it was difficult to get consumer goods in Israel. Everything that would be needed in their new home, even furniture, was bought in Germany and shipped. But the Israeli port authorities, for incomprehensible bureaucratic reasons, would not let Lea's parents pick up their goods, and the crates remained on the Israeli dock until everything in them was ruined. This became part of the Waks family mythology. Decades later, the family still insisted that Aaron and Lea did not go to Israel because the Israelis let all their goods rot on a dock. "A country that would do that? They must be criminals," Lea said in Yiddish.

Moishe Waks, who was not born until three years later, grew up firmly believing that his family did not move to Israel because the British blockade had captured the ship with their goods and his parents had lost everything. "The ship was taken by the British, and therefore my parents stayed still in Germany," he explained erroneously, more than forty years later in Berlin. Asked why they had not tried again, he speculated that "all their money must have been gone."

The more complicated truth was that Aaron and Lea had become involved in a different kind of life in Germany. They had become German Zionists—Jews who lived among Jews in Germany and campaigned to get them to move to Israel. It was becoming clear that this was not a finite task but a permanent struggle. Some Jews were going to stay in Germany for some time, and it would be Aaron's job to try to convince them to leave. At the same time, Israel, "the land of milk and honey," was turning out to be the land of war and deprivation. Many refugees, including Lea's parents, returned to Germany.

Instead of going to Israel, the Wakses moved to another DP camp, Förenwald, near Munich, where Lea's parents joined them. It was the only camp that hadn't yet been closed down. All the remaining refugees from around Germany were sent to Förenwald. Moishe was born there in 1952. That year, with twelve thousand DPs still in Germany, the International Refugee Organization announced that its DP activities had come to an end. Lea's parents went back to Israel to give it another try. But two thousand Jews refused to leave Förenwald, and Aaron Waks decided to stay with them.

Finally in 1955, the American Jewish Joint Distribution Committee—the Joint—agreed to support the remaining one thousand camp DPs. At this point Aaron had finished his Zionist camp work, even though many of the DPs were still in Germany, and he was free to make *aliyah*. But instead, he decided to move to Düsseldorf. The Jewish Community leader from Düsseldorf had visited him at Förenwald and urged him to come there. In Düsseldorf Waks came across a German-language Jewish newsletter that told its readers in boldface type, "Learn Hebrew!" Their community meetings, like those in many other German cities at the time, were under the influence of the Eastern European Zionists who had settled there and therefore always ended with singing "Hatikvah," the Israeli anthem.

It was a small community, and Aaron Waks thought he could work with Zionist organizations and help Jews leave. This had become his way of working for Israel, and Germany was where he did it. It offered familiar comforts and certainties after twenty years of upheavals. Israel, the war-torn impoverished dream, would remain a goal for some time in the future.

9

From
the Lowlands
to Palestine

IMMEDIATELY AFTER THE WAR, RELATIONS AMONG THE various Jewish groups in Antwerp were so harmonious that it almost seemed un-Jewish. Working with international Jewish organizations, they quickly established a system of kosher food, two Jewish schools, an orphanage, and a working synagogue. Jewish leaders began to hope they could stay united in a single organization. But as Sam Perl said, "When things got better, everybody started acting like Jews again."

One of the most divisive issues was the movement to establish an Israeli state. The British, who still controlled Palestine, had promised to reverse their 1939 policy of tightly restricting Jewish immigration. The policy reversal had been a campaign promise of the Labour party. But once in power, Labour enforced the old policy with even harsher measures against illegal immigrants. The British hold on its Middle Eastern oil fields concerned the Labour government far more than the party's historical commitment to Zionism.

After the Kielce pogrom, when the population of the DP camps surged into the hundreds of thousands, pressure on the British to let Jews into Palestine increased. The British and American governments formed the Anglo-American Committee of Inquiry, which recommended that a hundred thousand refugees from DP camps be quickly let in. But again, even in the face of recommendations from its own committee, the British Labour government refused.

In Palestine the Haganah decided that it would undertake a massive smuggling of Jewish refugees. The Haganah, whose name means "defense," had been founded by Vladimir Jabotinsky, a Jew from Odessa who had organized a Jewish Legion in the Middle East to fight with the British in World War I. When the British attempted to disband it after the war, Jabotinsky held it together as a clandestine Jewish defense militia. Now the Haganah set up a network of agents throughout Europe who helped move Jewish refugees across borders onto rusting ships docked in Mediterranean ports and through British blockades to Palestine. More ships were intercepted than made it through, and their cargoes of concentration camp survivors were placed in a British camp on Cyprus.

The tough measures of the British Labour government did not prove to be much of a deterrent to people who had survived the worst of the Third Reich. They walked or rode across Europe to wherever they could link up with the Haganah. Many of the refugees were drawn to the lowlands, Belgium and Holland, because of their busy ports and liberal immigration policies. The Belgian government allowed Jewish organizations to bring in thirty thousand Jewish refugees at a time. If they re-emigrated, another thirty thousand could be brought in.

One of the Haganah operatives in Antwerp was Sam Perl, the diamond sawer. Between 1945 and 1948 he helped move thousands of refugees clandestinely to Palestine. It was not a systematic operation. With a seemingly inexhaustible demand, they took as many refugees as they could whenever it was possible. They used two houses to hide and prepare Palestine-bound immigrants until the night when a Haganah agent would come and take them by train to the town of Kortrijk, in southern Belgium, then across the French border through France to a ship in Marseilles. Sometimes they would instead be taken across the Italian border and down the peninsula to Bari.

Meanwhile, a nagging theological debate was inflamed. A strictly religious Jew prays three times a day, and each time, among the prayers recited is the hope to someday return to Israel. When a religious Jew dies, a small sachet of soil from Israel is placed under the corpse's head. Every Passover, Jews pray that they will be next year in Jerusalem. This had been a central part of diaspora culture for nineteen hundred years, ever since the Romans conquered

Jerusalem and destroyed the temple. Someday a Messiah would appear and all the Jews throughout the world would return to Israel. In seventeenth-century Amsterdam the building of the Esnoga had been delayed a number of years because the community was convinced that the Messiah was about to appear and that they would all be momentarily leaving for Israel. Now, after the Second World War, the real possibility was being raised that they could be "next year in Jerusalem." The problem was that—in Europe—it was quite clear that the Messiah had not come, and thus by strict interpretation, it was not yet time for Jerusalem. Moreover, the Zionist movement was not particularly religious. Many of the Jews who were now building the new nation were from a secular leftist tradition—the same tradition as the unknown angry Jew who in the late 1930s had scribbled "Down with Passover. Long live May Day!" on Antwerp's Van Den Nestlei synagogue. Some Orthodox felt that it was better to have no Israel than to have one that did not follow the laws.

Antwerp was a center for the Haganah, but it also had a higher percentage of traditional religious Jews than any other Jewish community in the world. The subject of Israel's nationhood became particularly tense in Antwerp. A small number of the Jews there were actively opposed to the creation of the State of Israel. Not all of them were Orthodox. This was not a conflict between religious and non-religious Jews. There were all kinds of Jews on both sides of the issue for a variety of reasons. The sight of homeless Jewish refugees made some religious opponents accept the idea of the Jewish state in spite of their misgivings. Sam Perl, for all his Haganah activity, was a deeply religious Orthodox Jew.

Struggling to hold together their new, fragile postwar unity, the Antwerp Jewish leaders tried to get all the rabbis to agree not to talk about Israel at all. It was a political issue and should just be left alone. But it is not in Jewish tradition to avoid debate, and the agreement did not last long. Rabbi Chaim Rottenberg, for one, could never resist criticizing Zionists, and after Israel was created in 1948, he extended his attacks to the government of Israel. "Stop—it's not your business. Don't mix with it," Sam Perl told him.

"You couldn't get to him. He wouldn't stop," said Perl. The community finally fractured into two groups, both of them Orthodox, both of them traditional, but with separate Chief Rabbis and separate central synagogues. Rottenberg, who otherwise might have been a Chief Rabbi like his father, was kept away from the important rabbinical posts.

AT THE LE-EZRATH HA-JELED ORPHANAGE in Amsterdam, Isaac Lipschits, a small teenage boy from Rotterdam, found his new family of fellow orphans, the people he would always think of as his brothers. Near the diamond exchange, across the street from a home for the elderly that had been reopened as a home for ill camp survivors, le-Ezrath Ha-jeled, which in Hebrew means "help for children," was home to twenty-three boys who had no home and no family but each other. They became their own family, and bonded together in both sadness and secrecy, they worked for the Haganah. In fact, the top floor of the orphanage became the Dutch headquarters of the Haganah.

The family that Isaac Lipschits had lost had been in Holland since at least the eighteenth century. Like many Jewish families in Rotterdam before the war, they had worked in the central market, in their case selling bananas. Like many poor people they were concerned about being buried well and they had taken out a policy to insure their funeral and burial. Once a week, an insurance man came to collect a few cents in payment. The six Lipschits children always called the man Uncle Pete. Not much was known about Uncle Pete other than that he was some kind of Communist. When the Germans occupied Holland, Uncle Pete hid the Lipschitses with their three younger children.

Uncle Pete, his wife, and daughter were not as poor as the Lipschitses, but they did not live so well that they had space for five extra people. Uncle Pete would come home late at night with a few other men to his crowded apartment. They would arrive breathless and excited, armed with machine guns, grenades, and large quantities of the kind of fresh, well-stacked money found in banks. But his little group took orders from a Communist organization that told him it was foolish to be hiding Jews while doing this work, and the Lipschitses were sent away. Isaac went to a childless Rotterdam couple who pretended he was their son. But they were extremely nervous and would panic if he walked near a window. Then suddenly one day a stranger came, stared at him grimly, and without explanation moved Isaac to another house. In the next two weeks the boy was moved by strangers to twelve different homes. The strangers were always whispering to each other, and Isaac would catch a few words such as "orphan" and "poor thing." He realized that the Germans must have found his parents.

In the flat north region of Friesland, the city boy had his name changed and lived the life of a rural Dutch boy going to school in a two-room schoolhouse and ice skating after school. He never even noticed a sign on the village café that said "Jews forbidden."

When the war was over, Isaac returned to bombed-out Rotterdam. The tiny two-bedroom house where his family had lived was still standing, but none of the family possessions were in it and other people now lived there. Isaac went to see Uncle Pete, who told him what he already knew: His parents had been caught, and killed at Auschwitz. His oldest brother and his family were also deported and killed, as were his sister and her husband. "I am one hundred percent sure they are not alive now," said Uncle Pete. "The same thing for your brothers Maurits and Jacob."

Isaac was stunned. He had been braced for almost all of this, but not Jacob. Jacob was supposed to be safely hiding in Amsterdam but he had been caught on a train while trying to visit Rotterdam and had been deported to Sobibór, where the entire train of people had been unloaded and immediately killed.

Isaac had one relative left—his baby brother Alex. Uncle Pete gave him an address on one of the little islands in Zeeland, in southern Holland. When Isaac went to this flat polder farming region, he found a working-class Dutch family, followers of the Dutch Reformed Church—tidy, hard-working, and very religious. And there he found little Alex, now six years old, without much of an idea who Isaac was and with little memory of any other life. "Look," he said to Isaac, pulling out a small color print of Christ on a cross. "It is Jesus, the Messiah. He died to save us."

Alex explained the story he had learned in his Christian Bible school. He was very proud of the print because he had won it for doing well in arithmetic. Isaac, not knowing what he should do, returned to Rotterdam and settled in with Uncle Pete and his wife. Peacetime was very hard on Uncle Pete. He drank a lot of beer, argued a great deal with his wife, and reminisced with his old gang. All the beer and reminiscing led to an idea—to hit one last bank. They had gotten good at their work, but had neglected to ever keep any of the money for themselves. Why not do just one last job for themselves? The idea grew until it became irresistible. The robbery went as smoothly as it always had in wartime, and they would have gotten away with it had the government not decided to change the currency. Wartime money, it was announced, would no longer be legal tender but was redeemable at a portion of its value for new guilders. Uncle Pete, sitting on a fortune in stolen wartime guilders, thought it was worth some risk, and he turned the cash in for new guilders. But the stolen money had registered serial numbers. He was sentenced to a year in prison and lost his job with the insurance company.

Isaac moved to the le-Ezrath Ha-jeled Orphanage and found the boys who would be his family for the rest of his life. His one blood relative, Alex, could have joined them, and then he would truly have had a family and a home. But Alex's foster parents would not let him go.

Child custody cases like Alex's were being fought throughout Western Europe. The most famous of them was the Finaly case in France. The directress of a Grenoble municipal nursery had sheltered ten Jewish children during the war, then decided to keep two boys whose parents had been deported and killed, in spite of the fact that a surviving aunt wanted them back. When the Grenoble court ruled in favor of the family, the nursery directress enlisted the help of a Basque priest in kidnapping the boys and taking them to Spain. The case became what is known in France as "an affair"— an issue argued daily in the press. Some thought the Jews were being ungrateful after Catholics had risked their lives to save Jewish children. The Catholic Church asserted that the boys had been baptized and were therefore under Church authority. The Cardinal Primate and the Grand Rabbi entered into negotiations, and the children were eventually returned from Spain. But the debate never really stopped until the aunt finally took the two boys and moved them to her home in Israel.

In Antwerp a committee that included Sam Perl and Jozef Rottenberg had a list of forty Jewish Holocaust orphans who were being held in Belgian Catholic institutions that would not release them. Many of these children were like Alex Lipschits in that they were so young that they had little memory of being Jewish or of having another family. Some of them were older, such as two teenage girls in a Catholic convent whom Sam Perl tried to relocate. He helped one to move in with relatives in the United States. The other girl refused to leave. She was 19, her entire family had been killed in concentration camps, and she now considered herself a Christian. "I have nothing to do with Jews," she angrily told Perl. He left her his address in Antwerp in case she ever changed her mind.

One afternoon six months later, Perl was surprised to see the girl walk into the Jewish agency with tear-shined eyes and a small suitcase in one hand. He asked her what was wrong. She and a Flemish boy had decided to get married, she told him, and he had taken her to meet his family. The parents had smiled at the girl icily, but at the first possible moment the father put his arm around the son, led him to a far corner, and whispered too loudly, "I did not work my whole life to have a Jew in my home." Perl helped the girl connect with the Haganah, and she moved to Palestine.

In 1945 the Dutch government asked all non-Jews with Jewish children to report them to the Committee for War Orphans. Reports came in from 3,942 homes. In 1950 the Dutch, still passionate for lists, published the outcome: 1,902 had been reunited with their parents, 199 were placed with Jewish guardians immediately, another 1,004 were given Jewish guardians by a judge later, 11 died, 151 emigrated to Israel, 316 came of age . . . the list continued. When the items were carefully tabulated, one could see that 368 Jewish orphans had remained with Christian families. This was only among those who were reported. Logically, people who did not want to give up their children would not have reported them, but in that Dutch tradition of filling in forms and registering, 368 non-Jewish families who had Jewish wards whom they refused to give up still obligingly registered with the government.

Isaac Lipschits wanted his only relative back, but at 15 he did not have much of an idea of what to do about it. He went to the Committee for War Orphans, but they seemed to feel that in such cases the child was better off with the new Christian family than with an uncle, aunt, or grandparent, much less a teenage orphan brother. Isaac continued to try to persuade the family in Zeeland, but they seemed to regard Alex as their own little Christian boy. Isaac did not know exactly how to respond to these religious and well-meaning people who were stealing his only surviving relative.

Then there was a change. Isaac received a letter from them in which they suddenly agreed to turn over Alex—on condition that the Jewish community pay back every cent the family had spent on him. Now Isaac got very upset. It had been disturbing enough to him to hear his little brother talking about Jesus. But he had thought that the family was trying to teach him what they thought was right, according to their beliefs. Suddenly it was all looking

very different. Isaac took the letter to the Committee for War Orphans, which sent him to a social worker, who told him to come
back in a week. At last, Isaac thought, he would get some help. But
when he went back, the social worker informed him that the committee had examined the letter and found it to be "a primitive
expression of love."

At this point young Isaac's expressions of love were also getting
primitive. He went to Zeeland and asked the family if he could
take Alex for a walk. Alex was now seven and had gotten to like
very much the attention that this fifteen-year-old who said he was
his brother was giving him. As they went walking into the countryside, Isaac said, "Alex, guess what. I've planned a trip. You want to
come with me?"

Alex's eyes widened. He had never been on a trip to anywhere.

"I'm going away forever," Isaac said with breathless excitement.
"You want to come?"

Alex nodded his head eagerly and said "Yes!" and fifteen-year-old
Isaac Lipschits took off with little Alex to join the Haganah and
fight for a Jewish state.

Their first stop was Putte, a Dutch town on the Belgian border
that has a Jewish cemetery for the Antwerp community. The Belgians dig up graves when enough years have gone by and the
relatives have all died off, whereas the Dutch don't. Because Jewish
law requires that graves remain undisturbed, the Antwerp Jews bury
their dead across the Dutch border in Putte. Between 1945 and
1948 the Haganah led recruits into a house in Putte, through the
house, and out another door, and then they were in Belgium, from
where they took a tram to Antwerp. Isaac and Alex stayed overnight
in Antwerp's Jewish orphanage, which was also a Haganah center.
They spent the next day there as well, too excited to do anything
but talk. That night, they were taken by train to Kortrijk. On the
way they passed through Brussels, where Alex, full of curiosity on
his great adventure, pointed at a pile of yellow tubular things someone was selling. "What's that?" he asked his brother. Alex could not
remember having ever before seen a banana.

A car was waiting at the Kortrijk train station to drive them over
the French border. A pre-arranged hand signal was flashed at the
French customs agent, and they drove through without being asked
a question. The car drove the boys to Lille, where they boarded a
train to Paris. A taxi at the Gare du Nord took them to another
orphanage, where they slept. The next night, they were put on

another train for Marseilles, and from there they went to the nearby town of Cassis, where there was a Jewish sports camp. What would a Jewish sports camp be doing on the Mediterranean coast in late 1946? There Isaac and three hundred others received their first military training. Then they boarded a ship for Palestine. At the port a French official was handed a stack of fifteen passports for the entire group of three hundred. The official did not seem troubled by this discrepancy, and with an appropriately bored expression he stamped the passports one at a time until he had been through the pile about a dozen times and decided that was enough stamps. The French had never liked the British Mandate for Palestine and did little to obstruct either Jewish Zionists or Arab anti-Zionists from operating in the area.

A few months later, the British agreed to give up the Mandate, and on November 29, 1947, the United Nations voted by a margin of three votes for a partitioning of the area, thereby creating the State of Israel. It was a small state that lacked defendable borders, and the Arabs vowed to drive the Jews out by force of arms. Azzam Pasha, secretary general of the Arab League, promised to wage "a war of extermination." As has so often happened since, his words, perfectly chosen to arouse his Arab constituency, also served to better mobilize his adversaries. Young European Jews like Isaac Lipschits were not going to sit tight and hope for the best in another war of extermination. That had been their parents' mistake. The Haganah was frantically bringing in survivors from Europe. By the end of 1947, about forty thousand recruits were ready or in training, although they had only rifles, Sten guns, and machine guns. After the British abandoned the Mandate, the Haganah could bring in thousands more. It needed fighters. The Arabs had also recruited a Liberation Army, but in addition had almost thirty thousand regular army troops from Arab states.

Isaac, along with seventeen others from the Amsterdam orphanage, was assigned to a Dutch-speaking border unit. Its commander, who came from the northern Dutch town of Groningen, had served as a demolitions expert in the British Army during the war. Alex was left in the hands of an organization called the Youth Aliyah, which was placing children in homes and even operating entire villages. Aaron Waks was working for this same organization in DP camps.

While fighting on the border, Isaac lost track of his brother. When the Arab-Israeli war was over, he and a friend traveled

through Israel looking for Alex. Now Isaac began to reflect on what
he had done. The Germans had forced Alex to separate from his
father and mother when he was two years old. Then when he was
seven and had another father and mother, Isaac had done the same
thing to him. Isaac was starting to feel guilty when he thought of
Alex alone in this ungentle new country. You ask a seven-year-old if
he wants to take a trip with you and leave forever. What a question.
It was crazy. Along with guilt came panic: What if something had
happened to him? More than a thousand Jews had already been
killed.

Isaac served on the Israeli border for thirteen months. Then,
unaccustomed to the lack of water in the desert, his kidneys gave
out. This young survivors' country intended to keep its forces at a
lean fighting weight. Isaac was told that Israel did not need kidney
cases, and he was sent back to Holland to recuperate.

But before he left, he learned of a Dutch-speaking kibbutz and
there he found Alex. Now he realized that he had no home to offer
him. Alex could have a home in Israel. Isaac went back to Holland
without him, and Alex, the little Jewish boy from Rotterdam who
had become the little Christian boy from south Holland, was now
called David, part of a new generation of Israeli citizens.

ANTWERP WAS ABOUT TO LOSE its first postwar Jewish couple.
After more than a year of traveling between Israel and Antwerp,
Sam Perl and Anna had bought an apartment in Tel Aviv. In 1950
they shipped their furniture and prepared to move there. But they
never went. Sam wanted to raise his children in a traditional Jewish
world. He didn't like the religious schools in Israel and the schools
in Antwerp were getting good again—the very schools in the very
buildings that he had gone to before the war. Antwerp still seemed
to be his home. He never knew exactly why he didn't leave.
"Maybe I lost the guts," he sometimes speculated.

Many Jews did leave Antwerp in 1950. Europe was once again
looking dangerous. The old wartime alliance had broken up, and
the world was dividing into the Soviet and Western sides. In 1947,
General George Marshall gave a commencement address at Harvard about a new policy directed "against hunger, poverty, despera-
tion, and chaos." The Marshall Plan promised to rebuild Holland
at a point when the Dutch were becoming desperate. Shortly
before Marshall's address, the Dutch government, faced with

continued shortages of food and basic materials, had been developing wild contingency plans for survival. One such plan called for people to sleep longer and spend more of the day in bed.

The Soviet bloc chose not to participate in the Marshall Plan, however, and from 1947 on there were two Europes. While people in the eastern bloc continued to struggle for basic materials, the western bloc after a few years began to experience spectacular growth under the Marshall Plan. Soon, used tires were no longer in demand in Amsterdam, and Mauritz Auerhaan, the Bucharest piano player turned Amsterdam tire salesman, switched to importing used West German televisions. The new West Germany was developing so quickly that it was far ahead of the old European Allies in new industries such as televisions.

The creation of the State of Israel was one of the last things the old Allies did together. It was with the enthusiastic backing of the Soviet Union along with France and the United States that the close UN vote was carried. With the Soviets' backing, Czechoslovakia trained pilots and devoted an entire airfield to sending weapons to the new Israeli Army, playing a critical role in Israel's survival in 1948. But that same year, the joint occupation of Germany began to break down. In 1949, with tensions mounting and Soviet and Western foreign ministers no longer even meeting, the West created a separate Federal Republic with a capital in Bonn. The Soviets responded by establishing the German Democratic Republic with its capital in Berlin.

The following year, the first East-West shooting war broke out in Korea. This drove the West to do what had been up to then unthinkable: It rearmed the Germans. West Germany, which had been banned from military activity, was now once again to have an army, though only to operate on German soil. The Soviets responded by doing the same with East Germany. Meanwhile, the Korean War was causing such economic instability in Europe—inflation and shortages—that it threatened to undo all the progress of the Marshall Plan.

Many Jews thought a new war was coming, once again brought on by economic chaos and a rearmed Germany. It was all happening again. Thousands of Jews, many of Eastern European origin, decided to leave Antwerp, for the United States and Canada. They sold off their property and abandoned the diamond trade, which, as the world grew less secure, was rallying. In Paris there was a great deal of talk in the Pletzl about the new war and about moving again to safety. Most of the Jews there were still alive because they had left when the last war started. Icchok Finkelsztajn was convinced that World War III was about to erupt and seriously thought of moving as far away from Europe as possible. He kept talking about Madagascar, a place so far away—"the end of the earth"— that a Jew could survive the next war. Ironically, before the Third Reich decided on the Final Solution, Adolf Eichmann had contemplated deporting Jews to Madagascar.

Victor Waterman, whose family had been Amsterdamers for more than three centuries, remembered how long he had waited last time, how he almost hadn't made it out, how his brothers and sister and mother had stayed and died. He was worried about the Russians and about the soon-to-be-rearmed Germans and about what the Dutch, who had acted so badly before, would do this time. He concluded that he couldn't trust anyone in Europe anymore. He was still in the chicken business and still had contacts in the United States. In 1951 he and his wife and children moved to Union City, New Jersey, where he began working again in the kosher chicken industry. When people asked him why he had moved, he would say, "When you've experienced the Germans, you trust nobody."

10

In the
New Berlin

WHILE THOUSANDS OF SURVIVORS WERE WAITING IN Germany to arrange for a ship to take them away out of Europe so they could be far from Germany, a small number of German Jews went to English ports looking for ships to get back to Germany. Most of them had barely managed to get out only a few years before.

From the time Mia Lehmann left Antwerp for Berlin until she finally escaped to England in the late 1930s, moving to Germany had been for her a nearly fatal choice. Mia was a small woman — it seemed almost by design. She could lean close to people, ask them about their troubles, and then turn her head to listen so that her ear would be exactly at the level of the other person's mouth. Her strong and determined jawline contrasted with her soft and sympathetic eyes. An activist by nature, she did not think that Nazis coming to power and ruling the streets with brown-shirted bullies was any reason for her to be quiet. To her, it was all the more reason to speak out. She spent two years, from 1934 to 1936, in a Nazi prison in Silesia, accused of plotting to overthrow the government. She always laughed about the charge, because she thought it gave her undue credit; all she had really been doing was getting aid to families of political prisoners. She was one of six Jewish women in her cell block, all of whom served their sentences for political crimes and were released. The Nazis had not yet decided to murder every Jew. Maybe they would just send them to Madagascar. After her release, Mia had to report to the police once every week. She had no grasp of the extent of what the Nazis were planning, but as she watched Jews near the Oranienburgerstrasse synagogue being rounded up in open trucks and taken away, she understood that she would not survive if she stayed in Germany.

To leave, another country had to agree to accept her as a refugee. She had to have a sponsor to get a permit. It all took money. The Jews who had money were leaving, and those who didn't were being rounded up in trucks. Between 1933, when Hitler came to power, and 1938, half of the 500,000 Jews in Germany got out. Finally in May 1939, Mia's international Communist connections landed her a permit to go to England and work cleaning houses. Three months later, the war started and it was impossible to escape.

WERNER HÄNDLER'S FAMILY were German Jews who suddenly found themselves living in Poland when the borders were redrawn after World War I. Shortly after Werner was born in 1920, the family moved to the mountains a little to the west so that they would be in Germany again and not Poland. Eighteen years later, in November 1938, Werner and his father were among the twenty thousand Jews arrested during *Kristallnacht*, the night Jews and Jewish buildings throughout Germany were simultaneously assaulted. The Händlers were taken to Sachsenhausen.

In those days Sachsenhausen had no gas chambers or crematoriums. Werner, 18 years old, could not really understand what this place was, this strange triangle of barracks in Oranienburg. He and his fellow inmates were marched and worked and abused, and it seemed like some sort of prisoner-of-war camp, but there was no war. It was still peacetime. The camp had been set up for six thousand political activists and criminals. But Händler and his father were among another six thousand men who had been brought in, all Jews rounded up on *Kristallnacht*. Werner did not understand what the Nazis were doing in this place, but with twelve thousand men it was now very crowded. Their clothes were not warm enough, and there were not enough blankets. The inmates found sleeping mates to keep each other warm on the straw where they slept. There were beatings, and disease, and overworking, and the one thing Werner did understand was that "anybody who lives in these camps can be dead in ten minutes." The political prisoners taught the Jews how to survive there, what to do and not to do.

After a few months Werner and his father were both released. Before they got out of the camp, a group of political prisoners told Werner, "When you get out, wherever you go, tell about people like us. Tell what is going on. Tell them in England that Germany is preparing for an enormous war." It was the time of the Munich pact, when Western Europe had appeared to convince itself that "peace in our time" was possible.

Werner arrived in London with ten marks. On the boat over he had asked a fellow passenger what the English word for *war* was, and even knowing few other words, he told everyone he talked to that there was going to be "war." The English patted him patronizingly on the shoulder. Clearly the boy had been through some upsetting experiences.

While Werner and his father had been in Sachsenhausen, his mother had tried to arrange passage to England for the family, but she had been able to get only one permit, for Werner. It was now up to him to arrange papers for the rest of the family. When he got to London, he went to his mother's distant cousin, a barrister named Bernard Gillis, and told him about the camps, the storm troopers on the streets, and how his parents were being robbed of their money and property. He tried to make Gillis understand what it was like in Germany, and he said that he doubted his parents could survive there much longer.

The barrister listened sympathetically and then explained that if they came, he would have to support them, since they would not be able to work in England. But he could not assume this responsibility since he was already supporting a rabbi who had come over and he just did not have the money to support anyone else.

Both Werner Händler's parents were killed in Auschwitz.

When the war broke out, the British government decided it was too risky to trust any Germans in their midst. Werner Händler was sent to an internment camp on the Isle of Man and then to Canada. He had never been particularly political, but once again he found that the political militants were the people to know. They were the ones who spoke out for better conditions. They were the ones who knew how to survive, and he wanted to be one of them. In 1942 the British started allowing German Jewish refugees to work in defense jobs and even to serve in the military, but the

British Army rejected Händler because it regarded him as a socialist troublemaker.

Back in England, he worked repairing bomb damage. Mia Lehmann could now work in a factory. German Jews had their own world in wartime England, with political organizations such as Free German Youth and cultural movements and leftist movements. By the end of the war, Mia Lehmann, Werner Händler, and many other German Jews had met and married fellow refugees.

After the war there was little enthusiasm among them for returning to Germany. But a few German Jews, especially those still in their twenties, decided that even if they did not really want to, they had an obligation to return. Some thought they owed it to all the people they loved who were now dead. They believed that "a new Germany" was going to be built, one that was democratic and socialist—a complete break from the past. If idealistic young people didn't go back to build it and make sure it was very different from the old Germany, who was going to do it?

Händler and his wife, Helle, were among those who went back to build this new anti-Nazi socialist Germany. Helle had come from an old Sephardic family in a town near the Dutch border. She had left Germany to try to get to South Africa, where her father's older brother ran a hotel. But she had not been able to get farther than England. After the war her South African uncle went to England to convince her and her new husband, Werner, to take over his hotel. But Werner and Helle wanted to fight racism, and they reasoned that in South Africa they would be in constant trouble. In the new Germany they had an opportunity to change things. Most of their fellow German Jews were not as enthusiastic as they were about the promise of the new Germany and regularly urged both of them not to go back. Of the more than eight thousand refugees in the Free German Youth movement in England, only a few hundred returned to Germany. They did not return as Jews, and they did not expect to lead a Jewish life. Werner Händler, one of the few German Jews of his generation to grow up in a kosher household, had concluded, "I am *broygez* with my God." *Broygez* is a Yiddish word for when you quarrel, become angry, and stop speaking to each other.

In 1946, Händler stopped off to say good-bye to Barrister Gillis. "I have always had a bad conscience about your parents," Gillis said. "But we couldn't know what was happening. Not the truth of what the Germans were doing."

Händler understood. Before he had gone to Sachsenhausen, he would never have believed what the Germans were doing either. In fact, for most of the war he had hoped his parents would survive. Then in 1944, Russian troops had liberated Maidanek. When Händler read an account by a Russian writer of this death factory that operated day and night, he scoffed, "Why is he telling us this? Does he think we don't hate the Nazis enough already?" For an entire week he dismissed the story. Then he started thinking about what he had seen in Sachsenhausen and how afterward people in England had patted him on the back very kindly and said, "It's all right, my boy." He realized that the account was probably true and that he would never see his parents again. "Since then," he said, "I have known that the unimaginable can be true."

THE LEHMANNS WENT to Berlin in 1946. The mountains of rubble had been mostly cleared from the thoroughfares, but there were still entire neighborhoods without a single building or even a wall—blocks of brick and stone heaps, with claws of twisted pipe reaching up. Mia's husband was a Berlin Jew from Charlottenburg, a suburb to the West. The first commuter train in Berlin had run between the center of Berlin and Charlottenburg. Now Berlin was not a center with suburbs, but four zones. The old center was the Russian zone, and Charlottenburg was the British zone. The Lehmanns believed that with the help of the Soviets a new democratic Communist Germany would be built, and that this bold new experiment would in time so outshine anything else that it would be adopted as the model for all of Germany.

They moved to the Soviet sector, to Prenzlauer Berg, an area of three-story tile-roofed, vine-covered buildings in the stylishly severe Berlin design. It had no windows left, no heat and no hot water, but it still had its geometric bas relief friezes—little touches of detail on the gray, early-twentieth-century facades. Compared to most of Berlin, Prenzlauer Berg was in good condition. From Alexanderplatz, which had been the center, they could see little but rubble in all directions. Many people were still living in the basements of collapsed buildings.

They used rolls of plastic to cover the empty window frames, and they had a little coal-burning stove for the winter. In 1948, Mia, who was almost 40, became pregnant with her first child. The sector authorities had glass put in the window of one room for their baby girl. In the spring the trees that lined the streets of Prenzlauer Berg at methodically spaced intervals turned green again and birds nested in them. The Lehmanns felt as if they were part of an exciting experiment, working together with their old comrades who had fought and suffered and escaped and now were back to rebuild and this time make it work. They were not looking for Jewish life. Jewish life had ended for Mia Lehmann on that Yom Kippur morning in the Romanian Bucovina, when she found her mother sitting on the ground. They had other things in their life now. Mia had a whole city of people with troubled stories to listen to. Except that she knew that too many of those people had been Nazis.

The couple who lived below them had been Nazis—not major figures, but what came to be known as "little Nazis." They had been Nazi party snitches on the block. Mia avoided them, but one day she was walking with her baby girl, and the woman came up and peeked into the baby carriage. Her face rumpled into a goofy smile. "What a nice baby! What a lovely baby!" she cooed, while Mia stood in silence thinking that only three years earlier this same woman would not have allowed this baby to live.

After that Mia and the woman talked almost every day, although they never discussed anything of substance. The other woman didn't seem to mind Mia's reserve. How was she to know that Mia was normally a very different kind of person? The woman loved the Lehmann baby. When Mia had to go out, especially when the weather was bad and she didn't want to take her outside, she would leave the baby with her new neighbor. The neighbor would always visit on their daughter's birthday and bring chocolate, which was hard to get in the Soviet zone after 1949. She had contacts in the West.

WHEN WERNER AND HELLE HÄNDLER returned to Germany to begin their great task, they had nowhere to go. The Polish German border had been redrawn again, and the town Werner's family had adopted because it was in Germany, was now also in Poland. His only living relatives had escaped to South America. Helle's family, whose books traced their lineage back to the Spanish expulsion of 1492, was also gone. Her mother had last been seen in Minsk, and her father, she now learned, had been taken out in front of the inmates of Buchenwald and beaten to death. But that Germany was defeated and in ruins. They would help build the new one, a Germany that completely broke with its past.

They arrived in Hamburg, and Werner's only skill was as a woodworker. Surely, they reasoned, Germany would welcome dedicated young people who were ready to build the new Germany. Händler wrote to the Northwest German Radio station that he had returned to Germany to do something useful and that he had heard they were offering training in radio. I am back with no qualifications; will you train me? That was all he had to say. They took him immediately. There was a great demand for Germans who had never been Nazis.

With his tough, direct manner, Händler felt the ice of the cold war early. He was not a political sophisticate like Mia Lehmann, who had been active in the Communist party for more than fifteen years, or her husband, who had been thrown out of school in 1934 for forming a Marxist cell among his classmates. Händler was not even a member of the Communist party. He was simply an angry Hamburg radio journalist with a sense of mission, preaching the new socialist democratic anti-Nazi Germany when and wherever he had a chance. In late 1947 he was one of a number of journalists who were fired in what seemed to be a general housecleaning in western-sector media.

Shortly after that he was offered a job with Berliner Rundfunk, or Berlin Radio, the Soviet-controlled German radio station for Berlin, Hamburg, and Cologne. The Händlers moved to an apartment in the British sector of Berlin, where the radio station was located. To them there was nothing political about the sectors—it was all occupied Germany. But in 1948, after their first daughter was born at the Jewish Hospital, separate currencies were established for East and West. The money Werner earned no longer had value in the sector where he lived, so they moved to the East, where their second daughter was born.

When separate currencies were established for East and West, the Lehmanns understood what was about to happen and they were worried about it. The scenario was supposed to be a slow evolution toward a democratic socialist state. But if East and West split, the East would instantly be declared the new socialist democratic Germany. Both of the Lehmanns agreed that the Germans were not ready for this. Just a few years earlier, many of them had been Nazis. Now they would be socialists, and for the same reason—it was what the existing power told them to be. But how many of them understood socialism and were really prepared in their minds to embrace a totally new kind of society?

There had never been an East and West Germany. Linguistically and culturally, the division had always been between north and south. But although both sides were Germany, both peoples were German, and the division of East and West was artificial, a mentality of "us" and "them" very quickly took hold on both sides. Contributing to this frame of mind was an 858-mile border that followed no regional lines, no cultural patterns, and lacked all historical logic. Rather, it was defined by guards, barbed wire, and minefields. Still, the small group of Jews who had returned to build the new Germany felt that their German Democratic Republic had a new vision, while the Federal Republic in the West was simply a deplorable continuation of the old Germany—the part that refused to go along with progress.

One East German Jew, expressing a widespread point of view, said, "In West Germany the judges, the police, the civil service, the criminal police, and, once they started rebuilding it, the officers of the Army, were all people who had big jobs in the Nazi party, in the civil service, in the government." The only inaccurate part of that observation was the word "all." As the old alliance broke up and the West increasingly came to see the Soviet Union as its principle enemy, it treated Germany's Nazi past with an ever-increasing leniency. The first Bundestag election revealed a significant presence of extreme right-wing voters and political organizations. The American policy of "denazification" had been dropped in preparation for the creation of the West German state. Once created, that state in 1950 declared an amnesty for low-level Nazis. The Soviets had fired 85 percent of the almost 2,500 judges, prosecutors, and lawyers in their sector, and most of them went to the West, where they usually qualified for the 1950 amnesty. Of 11,500 West German judges, an estimated 5,000 had been involved in courts under the Third Reich. In the East, Nazis were also purged from the schools, the railroad, and the post office, and many of these ousted personnel found homes and jobs in the West as well. This fact was given enormous publicity in the East. Then there was the Globke case.

Hans Globke was West German Chancellor Konrad Adenauer's state secretary of the Chancellery. He had been known as an efficient, loyal administrator both in the Weimar government and in the Third Reich. At the 1935 Nuremberg rally Hitler had announced a new series of laws that gradually stripped Jews of their German citizenship, their right to own shops, their right to attend schools, and their right to mix with non-Jews. It was an important step in the dehumanizing of Jews that would lead to their being hauled off in cattle cars. To give legitimacy to these new laws, legal opinions had to be written, as they would for any other German law. These legal commentaries had been Hans Globke's contribution. Later, still serving in Hitler's government, Globke had proposed forcing all German Jews to take the middle name of *Israel* or *Sarah*. The East Germans denounced the Adenauer government for the presence of this Third Reich figure, but when Globke offered his resignation, Adenauer refused it. The East Germans demanded that Globke stand trial and eventually tried him in absentia and sentenced him to life imprisonment. In the ten years he served Adenauer, Globke offered his resignation five times, but Adenauer insisted that his aide had done nothing wrong in simply writing "an objective interpretation of the racial laws."

Werner Händler had become the Bonn correspondent for Berliner Rundfunk, and he covered the Globke affair. He also covered the organized extreme right, which reached a level in 1950s West Germany that it would not reach again until the reunification of Germany decades later. In 1954 there were almost fifty extreme right-wing organizations in the new West Germany, with an estimated 78,000 members. Expelled Nazis from the East, former targets of denazification in the western zones, and some who had been quiet for a time were now regrouping. Händler thought the West Germans were at best soft on Nazis. While he was in East Berlin in 1948, someone painted a swastika on the Berliner Rundfunk building, and when Händler and others protested, the station director called a meeting and said, "There is one thing you should know. We don't have discussions with Nazis. If we catch one, we beat it out of him. We don't discuss it."

THE FIRST TIME Irene Runge saw Europe, in 1949, she was a seven-year-old New Yorker, her ship had just pulled into Gdańsk, and she wanted to jump and swim back all the way to Washington Heights. Her father was a German Jew who might have been destined for the family's business in Mannheim. But when Hitler came to power, he went to Paris with his non-Jewish girlfriend and lived the leftist intellectual life of the days of the Popular Front, changing his name from Alexander Kupermann to Georges Alexan, which he deemed a fashionable *nom de plume*. He wrote articles and pondered larger works that he was never to write, but he did manage to use his base in Paris to get his entire family out of Germany.

When the Germans invaded France, he fled to Palestine, where he convinced his girlfriend to convert to Judaism before they married. Then they moved to the United States, settling in the Washington Heights area of upper Manhattan, west of the Broadway trolley. It was a Jewish neighborhood with a concentration of Austrian and German refugees. He opened a shop in the vast, dark labyrinth of the Times Square subway station, where he sold books and art. The shop became a hangout for German refugees, who drifted in and out all day, were served coffee, and passed hours arguing and debating in German.

Their only child, Irene, was born in 1942. After the war, the family did not go back to Germany. Irene's father still enjoyed his shop and his German intellectual life in Manhattan, and her mother liked living in the boom town that was postwar New York. But then came the cold war, and some of their friends—the crowd that passed through his shop—were called for questioning by the U.S. Congress on their leftist activities. In 1949, with the same quick instincts that had saved him from Nazi Germany, Irene's father told his wife and daughter to pack because they were moving to the newly formed German Democratic Republic. Over the protests of his wife and the whining of his daughter, they were soon living in Pankow, an East Berlin neighborhood just north of Prenzlauer Berg. Pankow had not been bombed, and so many of the East German ruling elite lived there that Westerners often sneeringly referred to the East German government as "the Pankow government."

Back in Washington Heights, little Irene's only notion of a place called Germany had been that she would see her parents and neighbors putting together packages, and she was always told it was to help the poor people in Germany. They would joke about putting her in the box and shipping her off. And now here they were, off to that miserable place where the poor people waited for packages. But she was told that her friend Johnny, with whom she played in Washington Heights, would be there too. He was. In fact, she grew up in Pankow around the same kind of people, and in some cases the same people, as she had in Washington Heights.

She grew up with the idea that East Germany was a place where Jewish intellectuals speaking a variety of languages had little houses with housekeepers. That was Pankow. Most of the people had fought the Nazis one way or another. There were no Nazis here. She never met one. She only met anti-Nazis. The Nazis must have been in the West, she thought.

As the cold war progressed, Irene learned to speak more and more German, because Americans and their language were not well liked. An American was an "Ami," and the look she saw in other children's eyes when they said to her "Ami go home" was enough to convince her to speak German. But she never did quite fit in. She learned to speak flawless colloquial Berliner, but she never thought of the language, the culture, or the idea of Germanness as being who she was. She was a Pankow Jew. Religion did not exist in Pankow and Irene did not exactly know what a Jew was—to her, a Jew was a Communist. But then, she did not have a clear idea of what a Communist was, either. To her, a Communist was a Jew. In her world all the Communists she met were Jewish, and all the Jews she met were Communists. Irene and her friends in their Pankow Jewish immigrant community had chewing gum and wore blue jeans. Some people said these things were symbols of imperialist culture, an idea she could not quite grasp. But her parents understood, and in time they stopped dressing her that way. Her mother never seemed to fit in, either. This life had been her father's grand scheme, and he lived happily in this neighborhood full of important builders of the new Germany and he talked with them and he thought and he wrote. But for her mother, it was an isolated life. There was nothing in Pankow for her. She was not building a new Germany and had been happy to be away from the old one.

Irene's childhood dream was to be a guerrilla fighter—a Soviet guerrilla fighter, popping out of the forest and attacking the Nazis. Her childhood literature contained many stories about the good Russians fighting the evil Nazis. Her father had very definite ideas about what children could read. He encouraged them to read the great German literature, but he strictly forbade German children's fables and folk tales. The old Germans had been raised on those dark myths. Mickey Mouse, on the other hand, was allowed.

Irene knew that the families in the Pankow colony were not the same as Germans. One of the ways they were different was that they were not supposed to eat pork. Also, if meat and dairy were served on the same dish, several minutes of *fleishig-milchig* jokes, most of which she didn't get, would follow.

When Irene's parents had dinner guests, which was very often, the meat was a great topic of conversation. In Germany most meat turns out to be pork. Irene's mother had a special recipe where the pork was cut in thin strips and then marinated, breaded, and fried. The guests would take a bite and murmur that it was chicken, that it tasted like chicken, what good chicken it was. Then someone would whisper, "Yeah, but it's really pork, you know." There would be a lot of whispering around the table, and finally someone would ask Irene's mother how she got the pork to look and taste like chicken. Her mother would explain the recipe, the cutting, the marinating, and the seasoning. It was called "koshering the pork."

Another peculiarity of Irene's secular childhood was her father's hat. Her father spent his days reading and studying, and as he did so, he wore a strange brimless hat. It was not a yarmulke. It was his own idea of a hat. But when people came over who were not in his regular circle, he would quickly remove it. He always said that he wore it because of a draft.

One of the Jewish writers from New York who visited the family told Irene that she was Jewish, which she thought was a great idea. The writer gave her a children's book teaching the Hebrew alphabet. To her father's chagrin, Irene loved this notion of being Jewish, because if you were Jewish, you got a completely different alphabet, like a secret language. She could be a *Jewish* Soviet guerrilla fighter with a special language that nobody understood.

When Irene started telling her schoolmates that she was Jewish, they paid little attention, except for once, when they came to her with a question. Since she was a Jew, they thought she might know the answer: Why did the Jews kill Jesus?

Irene had no answer. She went home that day with two questions for her father. "Why did the Jews kill Jesus?" and "Who was Jesus?"

One December day in 1951—by coincidence, Stalin's seventy-second birthday—Irene's mother was not home when Irene came back from school. Nor was she home the next day, or the next. Irene was sent to various people's houses to stay. At first, she was mostly aware that she didn't have to go to school. Gradually she came to understand that her mother had died, but she did not learn very much more because her father would not talk about it.

In time, she came to understand that her mother had killed herself. Only years later, talking to cousins, did Irene realize how much her mother had disliked being in Germany and how unhappy she had been in Pankow.

IN THE EARLY 1950s, West Germany launched a policy by the name *Wiedergutmachung*, which means "making it good again," or setting things right. Israelis always preferred the Hebrew word *shilumim*, meaning "reparation payments." *Wiedergutmachung* was the expansion of a program that had been started under U.S. direction in the American-occupied zone. East Germany refused to participate in this or any other such schemes, insisting that West Germany was the continuation of the Third Reich and thus should pay for its crimes, whereas the German Democratic Republic was a new society that had no predecessor. When the Federal Republic was created in the West, it agreed to pay an individual four marks, which was then worth about one dollar, for every day spent in a Nazi prison or concentration camp. It also made a payment for the loss of career and for loss of life. The payments amounted to billions of dollars. Much of it went abroad. In the Netherlands these payments financed the rebuilding of the Jewish community and remained the economic base of that community's activities.

Israel, facing a desperate economic situation and unable to obtain financing from anywhere else, saw *Wiedergutmachung* as a last hope. Many Jews in and out of Israel were appalled by the idea that Israel would enter into any kind of relationship with Germany. This was a time when extremists were demanding that Jews who chose to live in Germany should be expelled from Judaism in some way. But the 1952 treaty, signed in the Luxembourg city hall, earned Israel some $700 million in goods, services, and capital annually for the next fourteen years, at a time when tens of thousands of Holocaust victims were living in Israeli tents. For that price, the West German Federal Republic could claim to the world—in spite of what the East Germans were saying—that the Bundesrepublik was a new Germany trying to make up for its past, making it good again.

The reparations created an entirely new German bureaucracy, as millions of claims for individual payments poured into Germany. That was how the Zuckers, who had left Germany for good, ended up back where they started in Berlin. Ron Zuriel was born Werner Zucker in Berlin in 1916 to a family that had immigrated from Poland. The Zuckers, like the Wakses, derived their Jewish identity less from religious practice than from a passionate involvement in Zionism. When Ron joined the Zionist movement at 15, he was firmly committed to the idea of a Jewish state someday in Palestine, but he had no real plans to leave Germany personally. Two years later, Hitler came to power. After two more years the first of the Nuremberg laws were announced. The Zuckers heard Jews discussing whether to leave or stay, whether things would get better or worse. But the Nuremberg laws were all it took for Ron and his father to decide. They were not going to live in a country where Ron's father had to give up his textile business because he was a Jew. Ron was not going to live in a country where the law forbade him to date a non-Jew. Now Zionism gained a new meaning for the Zuckers. The following year, Ron and his father (his mother had died years earlier) emigrated to Palestine. Soon Ron went to England to study law, but two wars interrupted his education. First he went back to Palestine to serve in World War II. Then, soon after resuming his education in England, he went back to Palestine to fight in the 1948 Arab-Israeli war. During this war he changed his name from Werner Zucker to Ron Zuriel. In 1950 he was at last ready to open a law practice in Israel.

After three years as a lawyer in Israel, Ron returned to Berlin for a visit, at his father's request. Ron's father did not seem able to stay away from Germany. At first he had gone back on visits to see old friends. Being an Israeli, he was very aware of the *Wiedergutmachung* program, and since all his friends were survivors, he urged them to file claims. He would help them do it. Soon he was helping his friends' friends. Gradually his visits grew longer until, in reality, he was once again living in Berlin, with an office stacked with files for *Wiedergutmachung* claims and only vague ideas about how to pursue all these cases. His son was now a lawyer, and he needed his help. Ron agreed to come for a visit and try to help him, but neither he nor his Czech Jewish wife wanted to live in Germany. It was a grim and eerie experience just to be there at all.

A photography enthusiast, Ron took pictures of the ruin that used to be their house in the Schöneberg section. The entire neighborhood had been bombed and was now mostly cleared, but he could make out the ruins of his house and the nearby synagogue, which had survived *Kristallnacht*. No one wanted to touch the synagogue. If it fell down or had to be torn down, it would surely be said that Germans had once again destroyed a synagogue.

But there were no Jews around to use it. It just stood in a lot with some rubble and an empty space where the neighborhood had been. It was as though his upbringing were a badly fixed photo that was slowly fading. The next time he went to that spot even the synagogue was gone. Then construction began, and soon Schöneberg was a modern neighborhood of new apartment buildings, shopping malls, and wide highways—a place as removed from his childhood as if it were in another country.

Berlin was no longer home to Ron Zuriel, and he returned to Israel. But his father kept gathering more and more cases with which he could not cope, and he continued to ask his son to join him. They could work together, he said—make it a business. In 1956, Ron's father talked him into coming for "three or four years." Ron was reluctant. His wife was even more reluctant. But Ron's father argued that it would be just for three or four years. They thought perhaps they could stand Berlin for that long. They would live in their own world, Ron would have his work, and it wouldn't really be like living in Germany.

It was a strained existence. They formed a small circle of friends from a community of a few thousand Jews, and Ron worked from early morning until late at night. They avoided contact with non-Jews, but that was unnatural, and after a time they started talking to Germans. The Zuriels could speak with Germans as long as the Germans weren't of their own generation. If a German was Ron's age, he could only think about what this person might have been doing during those years. And just thinking about it, he didn't want to talk. It was actually easy to avoid those people. All Ron really had to do was to make it clear that he was a Jew, since Germans found it difficult to talk to Jews. It was too . . . awkward. They knew what Jews were thinking about them. Sometimes a conversation would start, and then it would drift to the war years, and then it would inevitably end up with the non-Jew declaring, "I didn't know. I had no idea." Ron didn't believe them. He kept waiting for just one German of his generation to say, "I knew. It was terrible, and I could do nothing." He would have accepted that. But he never heard it, and the rage pulsated through his body as he stood in silence, his face expressionless, his eyes cast toward the floor, and listened to these people politely explaining that they didn't know, as though they just happened to have been out shopping during the twelve years when his world was being annihilated.

11

In Czechoslovakia

JURAJ STERN'S EARLIEST MEMORIES WERE FROM underground. When he was four years old he was crowded into a small dark bunker with his parents, his grandmother, and his brother. The opening to their underground hiding place was concealed by a woodpile and a potato bin. He remembered the thwack of bullets being shot into the bunker from above while they huddled below, motionless, and braced themselves not to cry out or move if hit. But no one was ever hit. There were only those sickening dull noises.

Juraj also remembered a time when he was hidden alone, and a Slovak man would come several times a day and bring him food. The man would put an index finger against his lips and say, "Not a word. You have to be very quiet." After two days Juraj's father came and took him to another hiding place.

Juraj's fondest memory was of a Romanian division that came through the town on horseback. A Romanian soldier lifted little Juraj onto his horse and galloped him around a Slovak village. He wasn't hiding anymore. Juraj Stern's childhood had begun.

Jews and Jewish life had vanished from their village during the war. The Sterns went to Bratislava, where Juraj's father resumed his prewar work as an accountant in a factory. The small groups of Jews who remained moved to centers that still had communities.

Only a few Orthodox Jewish communities remained in Slovak villages. Most of the surviving Jews went to Bratislava, Brno, or Prague, where there were still Jewish communities.

Less than fifteen miles from the Sterns' village was Nitra, whose Jewish community, though greatly reduced, had survived. Only about one hundred Jews were left in this town of forty thousand people, yet there was a synagogue, a kosher butcher, and a traditional religious slaughterer. The Jewish community in Nitra dated back to the eleventh century, in a part of town called "Jewish hill." In 1947, Zuzana Šimko was born into a Nitra family whose background was seldom discussed. At the time of her birth her father was 44 and her mother 41. They were widow and widower. Her mother had had another family before the war, from which only a daughter survived. In 1946 the daughter, then 18, married and emigrated to Israel. Zuzana would be an adult before she would meet her half-sister and learn what had happened to her mother's other family during the war. Her father had also had another family, all of whom had been sent to Auschwitz. For Zuzana's parents, she was their new life.

Zuzana grew up in a building with six other Jewish families. Their household was kosher, like those of most of their neighbors. Her father remained an Orthodox Jew, clean shaven, but always wearing a hat. He had his own locksmith shop, which he would open up each morning after wrapping *tefillin* and saying morning prayers in the nearby synagogue. After closing the shop at the end of the day, before the last light was gone, he would go back to the synagogue to say his afternoon prayers. He would return again after dinner for his evening prayers. From Friday sundown to Saturday sundown he permitted no work, electricity, or sparks of any kind. Except for the smaller size of the community, Zuzana was being raised in a world very similar to the one her parents had lived in before the war.

The Slovak region, as always, was poorer and more anti-Semitic than the Czech lands. Aware of this, the government in Prague advised Slovak Jews not to push too hard for restitution of their property. In a number of violent incidents Slovaks resisted the return of Jewish property. But in general, Czechoslovakia was again a favorable place for Jews.

Moravia, a rolling pine-green farm region, once celebrated for its Jewish culture, now had a community only in its capital, Brno. This small town of wide streets, netted with streetcar wiring and sober nineteenth-century architecture, had a thousand surviving Jews. The main street running up to a triangular plaza in the center had been renamed by the Nazis, but it was now once again called Masaryk, after the first president of Czechoslovakia, an outspoken critic of anti-Semitism.

One synagogue in Brno was reopened, a simple concrete structure that gave no hint of Jewishness from the outside. It had been built this way not so that Judaism could be practiced secretly but because of a movement of the 1930s called "functionalist architecture." After the war, however, the remaining Jews thought this was a very sensible and discreet way to house a synagogue.

Postwar Prague, with its ten thousand Jews and two reopened synagogues, was again becoming a prosperous capital. Alice Kraus, who had survived Theresienstadt and forced labor camps, was back in Prague trying to live a normal life with her journalist husband František—trying to build a future as though their past had been normal. She never talked about what had happened to her. That unspoken chapter of her life was a mystery to her son Tomás, who was born in 1954. But the subject somehow remained present in his childhood by her weighty and conspicuous silence. Perhaps that was because Alice's behavior contrasted so starkly with that of František, who could not stop talking about his experiences, writing about them, and lecturing on them. There are, it is said, two kinds of survivors, and Tomás Kraus was raised by one of each—the one who could not speak, and the one who could not stop speaking.

Most Czechs remember the first few years after the war as the best time Czechoslovakia ever had. As in that other happy moment, before the Nazis came, the country had a well-functioning democracy and an industry-based economy that produced a satisfactory standard of living. František was now a well-known journalist, and both Czechoslovakian radio and the Czech news agency offered him jobs. He started a foreign broadcasting section for the radio station.

Since František had not been able to have the new tenants evicted from his former apartment on Kozi Street, the Krauses moved into a large and comfortable new home. While again becoming very active in community affairs, like most Jews, they observed their religion selectively. Some went to synagogue once a week. Few observed dietary laws. Some Jews kept no connection at all with the Jewish community in Prague. The unanswerable question—"How could God have allowed the Holocaust?"—kept being asked by people who appeared once or twice at a synagogue or community function and then never showed up again.

Only two synagogues reopened in Prague after the war— Europe's oldest, the Old-New Synagogue, and the Jubilee. The Jubilee was a giant, neo-Moorish art nouveau building from the turn of the century, when the Community had been replacing the synagogues lost in the slum clearance program. The Old-New Synagogue was in the former Jewish ghetto where František had once lived, but in spite of its presence there, the ghetto was not really Jewish anymore. The ten thousand Jews left in Prague were now spread throughout the city. Although there were far fewer Jews in Prague than before the war, traditional practice actually increased because of the arrival of Slovak Jews from the villages. More Jews had survived in the Slovak region—where they had been able to take to the mountains and fight with partisans—than in the Czech lands. The urban Jews in Prague and Brno, who had not lived the traditional life of villages like Nitra, were being brought practices that had not been seen in the cities in generations.

The Slovak village Jews came not only in search of surviving communities, but in some cases to be able to stay in Czechoslovakia. With the new map drawn by the Allies, many of the eastern Slovak villages from the regions of Carpathia and Ruthenia now lay within Soviet borders. Viktor Feuerlicht, a small Ruthenia Jew who had fought his way into Prague with the Czech Army, did not want to live in the Soviet Union. His home town, Khoust, was now part of the Ukraine. After the war Feuerlicht decided to stay in Prague. He went to a technical school and tried to hold a factory job, but one of his arms had been badly mangled during the war, and a constant series of operations made it impossible for him to keep the job. Feuerlicht had no interest in Prague-style Judaism. Any Saturday, you could see this little man with only one good arm clutching a torah that seemed almost as big as he was, determined to go on practicing the village religion of his father, even in Prague. He became one of a small nucleus of Slovak Orthodox Jews that formed around the Old-New Synagogue.

TO MANY in Czechoslovakia, the Soviets were still the heroes who had saved them and made possible the return of Czech democracy. In 1946 there were more than one million registered Czechoslovakian Communists. It was the one country in Central

Europe where the Soviets could truthfully claim that Communism was popular. In 1946 the Communist party got 37.9 percent of the vote, more than any other party, and it entered into a coalition government in which it controlled key ministries. It is also true that the Communist Ministry of Information once released a peculiar statement complaining about the presence in important places of "bearded Solomons." But in general Jews and non-Jews felt comfortable with the Czech Communist party. In the next two years the party's membership doubled to two million. One out of every five adults in the country was a registered Communist. Czechoslovakia seemed close to becoming a Communist democracy.

But the Communists had a ruling majority only in a coalition with the Social Democrats, and their hold on the coalition was not solid. Perhaps they feared losing their edge in the next election. Perhaps they—or more likely, the Soviets—just grew impatient with the power vagaries of a parliamentary system. In 1948, with the help of what appeared to be threats from Czech-based Soviet troops, the Communists simply ousted their partners and took over the government. There was little resistance, even though the foreign minister, Jan Masaryk, son of the national hero, was found dead outside his office building.

The Western Allies had not forgotten their own failure to act the last time Czechoslovakia had been taken over. This time they would respond. Their response was to greatly accelerate what was becoming the cold war by taking a harder line with the Soviets in Germany. But many Czechs took the news calmly.

For Jews, something much more important happened only three months later—the creation of the State of Israel. The new Communist regime in Czechoslovakia, like the democratic leftist coalition before it, was an enthusiastic backer of Israel. It trained pilots, shipped badly needed weapons, and sent volunteers. In addition, Czech and Slovak Jews—including many who had military experience fighting with Slovak partisans during the war—went to fight with the Haganah. One of Viktor Feuerlicht's brothers joined the Haganah and went to Israel. Feuerlicht's other brother, his only other surviving relative, had already emigrated to Israel. But Viktor, with his mangled arm, could not fight, and so he remained in Prague. Brno, where Masaryk Street had now been renamed Victory Street because Masaryk was considered too nationalistic, lost about one hundred of its Jews, which was one in ten. That was a smaller percentage than most communities lost. Whether related to the Communist takeover or not, Jews left by the thousands for Israel.

Those who stayed found themselves living in a very different system. Zuzana Šimko's father was told to close his little locksmith shop. Instead, he was placed in a workshop for a state-owned factory. He still could go to synagogue before work and take Saturdays and Jewish holidays off.

For some, it got rougher. About sixty miles from Bratislava was a town of twenty thousand people called Nové Mésto nad Váhom. It had been about one-quarter Jewish before the war, and a small community remained. A Jewish typesetter named Kraus (no relation to the Prague Kraus family) let it be known that he did not want to see his print shop nationalized. Mysteriously, the shop burned down. The town saw in this a Jewish conspiracy. He was arrested for arson and sat in jail for six weeks while the local press ran articles calling for Kraus to be hanged: "Kill the Jewish capitalist," one article said. But after six weeks an actual arsonist was discovered, and Kraus was released without explanation or apology.

At the time of the Communist takeover, Karol Wassermann, the pharmacist who had been liberated from the hospital at Sachsenhausen, was married to a Protestant woman, and they were both working in a little pharmacy outside Prague. He had kept his oath to never again live in his native Slovak region. Living outside Prague, he was still close enough to have contact with other religious Slovaks at the Old-New Synagogue. When the new regime closed the pharmacy, Karol's wife went to medical school and became an eye surgeon. The Communists were opening up opportunities. But Karol, although he was not a political man, suspected that he would not do well in the new system. For one thing, it seemed humorless to him. In 1950 he had been sitting in a movie theater watching a Soviet movie about Stalin, and he could not stop laughing. He was told to leave the theater. He tried to explain, sputtered out something about Joe Stalin, and then his body heaved and he was convulsing in laughter once again. This ridiculous heavy-handed artless propaganda seemed so funny—no doubt it was fine for the Russians, but here it seemed so . . . well, so silly. He broke into more wheezy laughter. Wassermann did not have a jovial laugh; it was angry, and it pulled tight the features in his face, so that he didn't even appear to be really smiling. He was shown to the exit.

Wassermann's wife found him a job in the largest state-run phar-

macy in Prague, where he was one of thirty-six pharmacists. Then
he had a revelation: He hated pharmacies. He had never wanted to
be a pharmacist. It had all been his mother's idea. What he really
wanted to do was—he wanted to be an art historian.

NEITHER THE COUP nor the nationalization shook the Jews of
Czechoslovakia the way the events of 1952 did. Until then, there
had been no association between anti-Semitism and Communism.
On the contrary, the Communists had been the great adversaries of
fascism and had taken in hundreds of thousands of Jewish refugees
fleeing the Nazis in Poland and Germany, at a time when the
United States, France, and Great Britain were not letting them in.
Communists had championed the cause of Israel, campaigned for
passage of the UN resolution, and armed and trained the Israelis at
a desperate moment when the United States and Great Britain
were refusing them weapons. But there were other things going on
in the Soviet Union that Czech Jews had not been watching. Stalin had always shown anti-Semitic tendencies—it was an undercur-
rent in his hatred of Trotsky. But after World War II, according to
many in the Kremlin, including Nikita Khrushchev, anti-Semitism
became a growing obsession, a hatred that consumed him. Stalin,
who had probably been mentally disturbed from the beginning,
was going mad. Those few psychiatrists who were so foolish as to
venture a diagnosis—paranoia—were killed on Stalin's own orders.
    Czechoslovakia got its first taste of Stalin's lunacy at the end
of 1951, when he ordered the head of the Czech government,
Klement Gottwald, to arrest the number-two man in his government, Czech Communist party chief Rudolph Slansky. He was
accused of being an agent of Israel and Zionists. This was not even
plausible, because Slansky had always opposed the Soviet policy of
supporting Israel. Indeed, the nascent Israeli government regarded
him as their only high-ranking adversary in the Czech government.
    Nevertheless, for one week in November 1952, Slansky and thir-
teen other upper-level Czech Communists were tried for plotting
with Zionists, Israelis, and American Jewish organizations to overthrow the Czech government. It was at once the oldest and the
newest accusation in anti-Semitism. Throughout the history of
Europe, Jews had been accused of plotting against the state—that
was the accusation that had been made against Dreyfus. Another
charge was that Jews are internationalists and have no loyalty. The

phrase that had gained currency under Stalin was "rootless cosmopolitans."

Of the fourteen accused, eleven were Jews, and their "Jewish origin" was clearly stated in their indictments. During the trial the Czech prosecution made regular references to the Jewishness of the defendants. Like many Jewish Communists, most of these defendants were not very Jewish. Bedřich Geminder, who had directed the party's foreign affairs department, never mentioned his Jewish background and for a long time even tried to conceal it.

But the accused fourteen, forced to play their parts, burlesqued confession and grotesquely contradicted the record of their entire careers. On the first day, Slansky somberly confessed—as though it made sense—that he had plotted with, among others, the Rothschilds, David Ben-Gurion, Bernard Baruch, and the American Joint Distribution Committee to destroy Czechoslovakia and turn Israel into an American military base. Two weeks after the trial began, three of the defendants, including one Jew, Deputy Foreign Minister Arthur London, began to serve their life sentences, while the other eleven, including Slansky, were hanged and cremated, their ashes tossed out the window of a speeding car in the suburbs. Then a second trial started of another three prominent Jews, including Slansky's brother. At the same time thousands of lesser-known Jews were arrested and charged with playing minor roles in the conspiracy.

At first, Czech Jews who were not serious political observers paid little attention. To Karol Wassermann, it was just another internecine conflict between Communists. He was not even aware that the defendants were Jews. But as the trial progressed, he started noticing troubling things in the newspapers. Words like *Zionists* and *cosmopolitan* were being used in that same vague way that a paranoiac uses the word *they*—the unnamed enemy. The official press adopted language reminiscent of Nazi propaganda. The defendants had "Judas faces" and "beady eyes." Graffiti that denounced capitalist Jews or that said "Jews out!" appeared on Prague walls. Anti-Semitism had become official policy.

Its repercussions were felt even after Stalin died. František Kraus was removed from the radio station and from the Czech news agency, and the Krauses were forced to give up their apartment. They had to squeeze into a small one and live on a meager pension that František was receiving for his ruined health at the hands of the Nazis. He died from those health problems in 1967 without ever again getting a job.

In Bratislava, at a time when unemployment did not exist, Jews who worked in large factories and offices of big companies were being told that their services were no longer needed. Juraj Stern's father lost his job as accountant. A thoroughly apolitical man, he was the only one dismissed in his factory. He too never again worked.

Even people who didn't know they were Jewish were losing their jobs for their supposed Zionist ties. The first time Bedřich Nosek had ever thought about his link to Jewishness had been when the Nazis examined his family tree and told him he had to leave the civil service and work in a factory. The second time was when the Slansky trial cost him his job. In fact, he wasn't Jewish. He had come of age in the 1920s and 1930s, and typical for that generation, he thought of himself simply as an enlightened modern man, an engineer with a role to play in the modern age. He was a secularist who liked science and progress and was not interested in religion. His parents were Catholic, but Bedřich was not interested in Catholicism. His mother's mother was very Jewish-looking and had in fact been born Jewish. But this was also of no interest to him—nor evidently to her, since she had converted to Catholicism and practiced devoutly. If Bedřich wasn't interested in his Catholic origins, he was even less interested in the fact that one of his grandmothers had been born Jewish.

At the time of the Slansky trial Bedřich Nosek was an engineer in charge of a section of a factory that built engines for the Soviet Union. One day Soviet agents came to his home and took him away. For four days his wife and son did not know what had happened to him. After being questioned about his loyalty and being told that since he had "Jewish blood," there was some doubt about his willingness to produce for the Soviet Union, he was released. After that he was no longer an engineer but a construction worker. Years later, when the climate softened, he was able to get a job as an instructor in a technical school.

12

From Moscow
to Warsaw

NINEL KAMERAZ LEARNED ABOUT STALIN AND JEWS AT an early age. Her name, fashionable among her parents' generation of Communists, is *Lenin* spelled backward. Ninel always called her name "a hunchback I've carried through life." She was born in Moscow in 1937, and that same day, after her parents gave her this name, her father was arrested. The next time she saw him, she was 11. Ninel calculated that between her father's eleven-year term, his sister's eighteen, and the terms of various others, her immediate family had spent sixty-four years in Stalinist labor camps.

The Kamerazes were rebels, or perhaps even true revolutionaries. Ninel's grandfather was an illiterate wagon driver from a Lithuanian shtetl who became involved in the anticzarist underground. An army deserter, he bought the family name along with Lithuanian papers from a man named Kamerazov. Her grandmother came from a rabbinical family that disowned her because she went to a university. When she first left to attend her classes, they announced, "You are no longer our daughter."

Under the czarist system the child of a small-town wagon driver had no opportunities except to also become a wagon driver in the same Lithuanian village. But once the Communists came to power, Ninel's father was able to study and after seven years to become a philosophy professor. His brother became the conductor of Moscow radio in the 1930s. Ninel's mother was in the music conservatory.

Thinking back on her parents decades later, Ninel said, "They had no chances in life. The Communists gave them a chance to be normal people. They could do whatever they wanted. They could do this, they could do that. They were talented people. They believed in this. They wanted to be normal people. They didn't only want to be Jews. They wanted to be people. This was the new religion. They threw everything aside, and they believed in this. And they paid the highest price for it. I understand them. I really do understand them. It was such a chance to take. To live. To be. But the price was—they didn't know. It seemed so pure, so right. It was—diabolical evil."

In 1948 her father was released but was told that he could spend no more than twenty-four hours in the European section of the Soviet Union. He moved with his family to a Jewish neighborhood of Warsaw, in the 20 percent of the city that was still standing. They found a prewar Jewish apartment building—an odd combination of baroque ornamentation and the streamlined curves of early art deco that had been built in 1914 by a leading architect of the day. Next to the building was a synagogue, and behind the synagogue was a *mikveh*, a ritual bath. Next door was a Jewish school.

Jews in Warsaw at the time were trying to live near other Jews for safety. When the Kameraz family moved to Warsaw other Jews warned them, "A Jew alone is a dead Jew." Though her father had never been a practicing Jew, he was so Jewish-looking that everyone in the building urged him to stay in the neighborhood at all times. The trams were not safe for people who looked Jewish. Bullies would throw them off. Trains, especially on the run between Warsaw and Łódź, were even more dangerous.

The Kamerazes felt safe in their Jewish building, even though from time to time, during periods when anti-Semitism was particularly active, someone would rub excrement on their door. Ninel's parents didn't know how to live a Jewish life—it was the Poles cursing "*Żyd*" on the street and shoving people out of trams that forced them into the safety of Jewish company. Ninel's mother and many of the other people in the building spoke Yiddish, but Ninel concentrated on learning Polish. Yiddish was only used to talk of terrible things, of camps and who was saved and how, and who wasn't and why. Ninel did not want to hear all this. It frightened her.

There was something temporary about life in their cozy apartment of little rooms and hallways, and stacks of dusty books, and the table they sat around with the electric samovar always heating water for tea. All around them Jews were leaving. Ninel's family didn't leave but only said good-bye to friends. Other Jews from Moscow would arrive. But then they wouldn't stay. So the Kamerazes made their life between things—between hellos and good-byes, between Russia and the West, between the Judaism they had abandoned and the Communism that had abandoned them.

In Warsaw, as in other Polish cities, new Jewish institutions started up after the war—schools, cooperatives, theaters, newspapers in both Polish and Yiddish, the Union of Jewish Writers, and even a publishing house. As long as there was still a sizable survivor population in Poland, foreign funds were available for such things. But with each pogrom and train murder the Jewish population shrank and the remaining Jewish community began turning its institutions over to the state because it could no longer operate them. The Jewish school that Ninel attended in the neighborhood became a state school, even though it still had a largely Jewish student body.

As in Czechoslovakia and everywhere else where Stalin's influence was felt, the Polish regime hardened in tone and substance after 1948. Władysław Gomułka, with his Polish-nationalist brand of Communism, was removed from power, even imprisoned, and a government that followed every hand-gesture in the Kremlin was installed. But once again as things worsened for Poles, Jews saw an improvement in their lives. As the police state cracked down on the population, fascist and anti-Semitic activities were no longer tolerated. A Pole caught throwing Jews off trains or scribbling anti-Semitic graffiti—or, for that matter, any kind of graffiti—was quickly arrested. Also, Jews profited from the anti-Semitic stereotype of the *żydokomuna* (Jewish Communist). Polish anti-Semites became afraid of Jews because their own hate propaganda had convinced them that all Jews had connections to top-ranking state security people.

In 1949, when Marian Turski moved to Warsaw, the reconstruction process was only beginning. The old center of town was being rebuilt, stone by stone, reproducing the pastel historic buildings. The heaps of refuse where the ghetto had been were starting to be cleared away and replaced with modern apartment buildings with huge gates and massive entranceways, as well as a relatively restrained touch of the neoclassic ornamentation that seemed to obsess architects in the last years of Stalin. Soon the area that had previously been a downtown district, then a Jewish death camp, then an ash heap, had become a desirable new housing project. Turski moved into one of these new buildings in 1951, in an apartment with a view of the new Old Town, and began his career as a journalist.

Most of the young men in Turski's circle of friends were pursuing the same young woman. He too thought her extremely beautiful, and he was amazed that she seemed to prefer him, then finally chose him. Turski, a small, dark-haired, awkward man with a slight speech defect, often pondered why she had chosen him. Even months after they started living together, he still shook his head in astonishment. One day after they had been living together for six months, he was talking to her about his Jewish background, and she told him that she too was Jewish. Her family had hidden in Warsaw and been caught and were all killed, but the Nazis had never caught her. She had lived openly as a Polish Catholic. After the war she continued living that way.

Her choice of him now made sense to Turski. Now he understood that she had chosen him because she wanted to find a Jew. After they had lived together for thirty-five years and raised a daughter together, Turski was still convinced of this. When it was suggested to him that perhaps she simply fell in love with him, he persisted, "Well, I hope so. But there were so many handsome young men surrounding her, and she chose me! I understood that this was because she wanted to have a Jewish boy."

IN THE EARLY 1950s both Jakub Gutenbaum and Barbara Góra were studying in Moscow on Soviet scholarships. Foreign students were given much higher living allowances than the Soviet students, and their lives were relatively comfortable. They could buy the food in the shops that Soviets could not afford, and attend museums, the opera, and the ballet. Student life in Moscow was pleasant, except for occasional signs that all was not well in the Soviet Union. A Soviet student was taken away from Gutenbaum's class and never again seen.

Gutenbaum and Góra knew each other because he was dating one of her roommates. But they had very different experiences. Gutenbaum never changed his name. He had already learned that a face like his would identify him faster than a piece of paper. So he filled out his papers correctly, writing "Polish citizen, Jewish nationality."

But Barbara Góra, the former Irene Hochberg, had learned to pass as a Pole. If things turned, no one even knew she was Jewish. Why should anyone think Barbara Góra was Jewish? It was rumored that some in her group were clandestine Jews. Barbara even knew of one, a friend from the Ukraine. Once Barbara was even asked how she had survived the war, so she knew that some of her fellow students suspected her. But she had been playing this game well for a decade, and she was confident.

On November 7, 1952, like thousands of Muscovites, she walked to Red Square and saw Stalin on the reviewing stand. Teams of experts around the world examined photos of that event, not only to see who was standing close and who was kept far away, but to search Stalin's face for signs of rumored illness, both physical and mental. But Barbara Góra simply went and saw Stalin. It was the last time he was seen in public.

On January 13, 1953, it was announced that nine top doctors from the elite Kremlin staff had misused their professional skills to murder two of Stalin's top aides. Although it was not mentioned that six of the nine doctors were Jewish, it was pointed out that these six had connections with that great bourgeois Jewish conspiracy, the American Joint Distribution Committee. The doctors, it was discovered, were part of a Zionist spy network that was plotting against the Soviet state. The Soviet press ran regular articles warning the citizenry against Zionist connivers and especially Jewish doctors. The people were advised to be on the lookout for these doctor-poisoners, who were allegedly committing ever more fantastic crimes, including changing children into animals. There was nothing more dangerous than contact with a Jew. Gentiles with Jewish spouses were encouraged to get divorces. Some did; others simply staged divorces for appearances.

Suddenly, Jakub Gutenbaum felt as though the air around him had lost its oxygen. No one wanted to come near him, talk to him, or be seen in his company. In addition to the distrust of Jews, there was a general distrust of anyone who had been in contact with Germans during the war or with any other foreigners. If you had had contact with foreigners, that meant you might have been recruited by foreign agents. One of Jakub's friends had lived in Rostov, north of Moscow, for three days while it was under German occupation. She had never mentioned it, knowing it would disqualify her from a university education, but now the authorities discovered the truth and she was thrown out of the university. And then there was Gutenbaum—not only a Jew, but a Jew who had spent the entire war under Germans. Those terrible years of survival in the Warsaw ghetto and the camps were now classified as "contact with the West."

One hundred students were gathered together and handed a sixteen-page questionnaire, on which they had to answer questions about their birthdate, parents, grandparents, military record, and parents' occupation. Do you know any foreigners? the questionnaire asked, and: Have you ever exchanged letters with a foreigner? Gutenbaum and a girl from Bulgaria were the only two foreign students in this particular group summoned for the questionnaire. There was one official present to answer the students' own questions, and Jakub and the Bulgarian girl very quietly asked what they should do about the question of knowing foreigners. "Since we are foreigners and grew up somewhere else, we have always known foreigners, but not in the same sense." The room grew quiet and tense. Everyone knew that the two students could not have it on their papers that they knew foreigners, no matter what the reason. And it would also probably be remembered that the other ninety-eight students in the group had been with the two who were caught knowing foreigners. The official left the room and did not come back for fifteen minutes. When he did return, he gave the ruling: "Since everybody knows it, it is not necessary to write it." Everyone in the room seemed to exhale as one, like a single organ. Reprieve.

Then, with the country's leading doctors in prison, being tortured and waiting to die, thousands of others awaiting a similar fate, and Soviet Jewry bracing for what might be a second Holocaust, the problem was solved in the manner of a badly written nineteenth-century melodrama: The villain, possessed with his own mad hatred, rolled his eyes up in his head and fell over dead. There are a number of different accounts of Stalin's death—even the date varies. All that is certain is that he had a stroke and that no first-rate specialists were available to treat him. One distinguished doctor later said that he had been consulted from his prison cell.

Once Stalin had died, things changed almost instantly. People were released from prison without explanation. The press discontinued its anti-Semitic campaign. Jakub Gutenbaum no longer felt isolated. People were friendly to him again. "The Russians are friendly people," he said.

13

In Budapest

In 1948 the Communist party, which had been in a coalition government, simply took over the Hungarian government the same way that the party had done in Czechoslovakia, except that in Hungary the Communist party had been only a small minority faction. The takeover was not popular with the general population. But many Jews at the time had been more concerned about the resurgence of extreme right-wing nationalist movements. To them, the Communist party was the alternative to fascism.

The new government was led by Matyas Rakosi, who had a Jewish mother and a number of close Jewish associates, including the head of internal police, Gabor Peters. But these ties did not mean that their ascension to power was good for Hungarian Jews. Zionist organizations were banned. Jewish publications were closed down. The only Jewish organizations permitted were those directly controlled by the state under the auspices of the official Jewish Community. The curriculum in Jewish schools was made to conform to the state curriculum, and the schools were eventually taken over by the state. One Jewish high school was allowed, the Anne Frank School, but it was maintained as a kind of second-class high school, since its graduates would find it difficult to be accepted by universities. As in Czechoslovakia, any Jewish religious activities or affiliations would greatly damage the chances for advancement not only of an individual but sometimes of the family.

The policy of nationalizing the economy also came as a hard blow to many Jews, because they happened to be of the merchant class. To Ilona and Géza Seifert, now married, the antireligious policies meant a dismantling of three years of hard work by the community in building Jewish institutions. In addition, Ilona's father lost his soda factory. Gyula Lippner tried to keep his family china shop—since he was a party member who had enthusiastically supported the regime, he hoped one little china shop in Újpest would be permitted. Originally, it was said that the nationalization was only for substantial businesses and that little shops would not be bothered. But in 1949 a few Jews were arrested on charges of Zionism, and Lippner decided that this was no time for a Jew to test the limits of the new system. He voluntarily turned over the china shop and accepted a job with a large state-owned paper company.

The Lippners were not practicing Jews, but they told their two sons that the family was Jewish and they repeatedly explained that they should be careful with this information because "it is a very dangerous thing to be a Jew in Hungary." In general they tried to be good Communists and raise their sons to be good Communists and join the young Communists, and they did all the other things good Communist families did to get ahead.

Even the Konráds' hardware store in Berettyó was nationalized. Many of the surviving Jewish men had started new families with Jewish women from elsewhere or non-Jewish women from town, and they had opened small shops in their traditional trades. In 1949, once they realized that even these little shops were to be taken, signs appeared on the doors of little ateliers all over Berettyó saying that the owner was away and would be back shortly. The shop owners and their families loaded themselves into trucks and drove to Czechoslovakia, from where they could still travel easily to "the new Soviet ally," Israel. They settled in a small town on the Mediterranean coast, where they reopened their shops, and continued to speak Hungarian. For two decades Berettyó Jewish life was preserved in this Israeli village.

In Berettyó itself, Jewish life had ended. The more affluent and better-educated families did not get on the trucks to Israel but instead drifted, a few at a time, to Budapest. György Konrád, now 16, went to Budapest in search of something to do after the family hardware business was nationalized. Having struggled to learn Russian ever since those first curious troops had appeared in Berettyó in 1945, he had now learned it well enough to work translating articles from *Pravda* and other party organs into Hungarian. These were wordy, tedious thousand-word items that tortured language to assure political conformity. Each of György's translations was carefully filed in an archive, where in all probability it was never again seen.

THE GAZDAG FAMILY lived in Ferencváros, in southern Pest, where a small tributary forks off the Danube, only to rejoin it south of the capital. Both parents were party members who enjoyed the opportunities of the new system: Ervin was a chemical engineer, and Zsuzsa, no longer a nurse, was a film editor. A successful Communist family, they believed in the future of this new egalitarian society. Their son Gyula, born in 1947, was six years old walking home from first grade with several other children. Suddenly his friends started pushing one boy because he was fat. Gyula decided to defend the fat boy—he was being raised with this kind of idealism. For the rest of the walk home, the boys shouted, pushed, and scuffled until, one by one, they broke away at their homes. When they got to the street where the Gazdags lived, only Gyula, the fat boy, and one of the other boys were left. They were neighbors. Each boy went to the gate of his building, but they continued to shout at each other. The fat boy shouted at the other boy, "You dirty Jew!" That seemed to put the other boy in his place, so Gyula also started shouting "Dirty Jew!" He went right over to the gateway and shouted it in the boy's face. At that moment an elderly woman who lived in Gyula's building was trying to get through the gate. She glared at Gyula and said, "You silly little boy. You are Jew too," and pushed past him to the street.

Gyula could not understand why this nice old lady had cursed at him. He had done nothing wrong. He had just been keeping some bullies from picking on a fat boy. He told his mother what had happened and asked why the woman had cursed at him.

Zsuzsa explained what a Jew was. Then she explained that her family had gone to Vienna and come back to Budapest to flee the Nazis, and that the Nazis had put his grandmother in the ghetto, and that the Arrow Cross had been about to shoot her by the Danube when she hid her in the hospital. And she told Gyula about his grandfather, and how he had been taken to Auschwitz and killed. Then she had to explain what Auschwitz was and how he was killed. Then she told him that his father was a Jew also, and that he had escaped to France, and she told him about his fighting with the Resistance.

Hours later, six-year-old Gyula was changed. He took to saying openly in school that he was a Jew. And he angrily denounced children who used the word *Jew* as a curse. He could not stop thinking about the things he had learned, about the deportations and Auschwitz. When he was eight years old, he resolved that he would be a filmmaker and make movies about the Holocaust.

THE GADÓS LIVED in Újpest. To them, the essential fact remained that the Red Army had saved them. Both Béla and his wife joined the Communist party. As a lawyer with Red Army experience and a party member, Béla soon became a judge in the Hungarian Army. But at the time of the Slansky trial, Hungarian Jews were being removed from prominent places, and he was among the Jewish officers who were thrown out of the military. Nobody told him that it was because he was a Jew. Like many other Jewish officers, he was dismissed with no explanation at all. Eventually, the most prominent Jew, Matyas Rakosi, was removed as head of government and replaced by Imre Nagy, who was charged with cleaning up the party. *Cleaning up* meant expelling Jews, even some of his own close friends.

Béla Gadó's son, György, who had been rescued in his hiding place by his father and the Red Army, had also become a party member. But he was growing angry about what was happening to the party and the country, and increasingly he said so to other party members, which was a risky thing for a civil servant to do. Soon there came a restructuring in government that left no job for him. After nine months out of work, he realized his civil service days were over, and he became a schoolteacher.

Many Hungarians were getting angry not only about the abuses of power but about the economy, which was lowering Hungary's living standard. Under these pressures, Nagy turned out not to be Moscow's man. He made the economic policy less rigid, allowed a small degree of private initiative, and released political prisoners, including those accused of Zionism. In doing so, he pleased some Hungarians but not the Soviets, who removed him from power in

February 1955, just as a few years earlier they had removed the populist Władysław Gomułka in Poland. Matyas Rakosi was returned, and Hungarians grew angrier. Encouraged by a Polish movement that came so close to open revolt in October 1956 that Moscow had to bring Gomułka back, a popular movement in Hungary started openly demanding not only the return of Nagy but free elections. Hoping there was a choice between the two demands, Moscow rehabilitated Nagy.

The concession was a tactical error, one that the Soviets were to make again. Spurred on by their small victory, the Hungarians pressed for more, demanding the removal of Soviet troops, democracy, and free speech. Nagy himself pressed further demands on Moscow, such as release from the Warsaw Pact, and neutral East-West status. Austria, Hungary's historical partner, had successfully negotiated such an arrangement the year before.

Once all demonstrations were banned, a huge spontaneous rally filled the streets of Pest. The police opened fire on the demonstrators, which turned a protest into an uprising. The well-organized working class joined the rebellion. "Revolutionary committees" were set up to take control throughout the country, and as the uprising increasingly became an open rebellion, Hungarian soldiers were called out. But the troops only chatted and commiserated with the rebels. The Soviets called out their own troops, but there were not enough of them in Hungary to contain what was now a nationwide armed rebellion.

In October 1956, György Konrád was editing a new literary magazine, which by chance had been scheduled for publication on October 27, the day of the outlawed demonstration. He had finished his studies that summer, and he and his classmates had been inducted into the military. Their training included not only instructions on the use of weapons but lectures by officers on abstract notions such as "the nature of the enemy." Konrád would listen to these lectures with his mouth slightly twisted in his ironic smile, but the "nature of the enemy" lecture proved to be too much for him and he exploded in great heaves of laughter. Soon he was declared an "anarchist" and thrown out of the army. This was the same army from whom his university colleagues obtained weapons a few months later, in October 1956. Konrád, not wishing to take part in a shooting war, stayed home for a few days after the illegal demonstration. But since it did not wind down and was too interesting to miss, he decided to wander over to the campus and around town.

At the university, rebels had stacks of boxes. There were boxes of apricot jelly from the far right-wing Otto von Hapsburg, and boxes of light weapons from the police. Somebody had sent cans of corned beef. When György arrived at the campus, it was all being distributed to the young revolutionaries. "Who wants a submachine gun?" someone shouted. Konrád raised his hand and was handed the weapon.

It was amusing to walk around Budapest wearing an armband and holding a submachine gun at your side. "I carried it like an umbrella," he said. He did not want to shoot anyone, but he did have some things he wanted to do. He visited the various publishing houses, this tall young man with a mop of curly brown hair leaning on a submachine gun, and asked to see the director. He was always ushered into the director's office immediately, and the director always readily agreed that writers should have far greater artistic freedom. A submachine gun, it seemed, was a useful tool for a writer.

But it also had some disadvantages. A small elderly woman pulled on his arm and said, "Young man, please come here." Without waiting for him to answer, she dragged him down the street, over to where a group of women were standing and pointing up at a building.

"There on the third floor is an AVH man," one woman said. The AVH was the despised internal police. Then all the women started shouting at once.

"What do you want?" Konrád finally shouted over their voices.

The small elderly woman looked at him as though he were an astonishing simpleton. Then she shouted, "Shoot him!"

"No, no. I'm not going to shoot him."

"Of course. He's AVH. We have him cornered," she said, trying for a conspiratorial tone.

"No, no."

"Why not? You have the gun!"

Konrád tried to explain that although it was true that he was carrying a weapon, he did not shoot people. He tried to calm the women. But one of them shouted, "If you won't shoot him, I will go find someone else to shoot him."

"All right," said Konrád. "Take me to him." The woman led him into the building and up to the third floor, where they found an unarmed man crouching in terror. Konrád pointed the submachine gun at him. "All right," he said. "Get up and start walking."

While the women cheered, he marched his prisoner out of the building and down a quiet street to shoot him. The man explained that he was from the AVH, but he kept insisting that he only played in a band. This brought the same mischievous smile to Konrád's face that had caused the army to declare him an anarchist.

"What instrument do you play?"

"Tuba," was the shaky-voiced reply. And Konrád laughed as he marched his prisoner safely away from the angry women.

"I think you'd better find a safer place to hide," Konrád said, shaking his head as the man ran off. He wasn't going to shoot a tuba player.

Konrád went home and decided he should get rid of the submachine gun. But the next morning, November 4, when he went to return it to the university, there were Soviet tanks on the street— entire armored columns that had been brought in from somewhere. People kept pulling him into doorways and warning him not to get near any major streets with that submachine gun. He could find himself standing in front of a Soviet armored division with nothing but a submachine gun. He returned home and dropped off the weapon, and then went back to the university, unarmed, only to find the campus wedged in with large steel clanking Soviet tanks. The university rebels were sitting around with their weapons. They certainly weren't going to start shooting at this many tanks. By the end of the day, the Soviets told them to give up, or the university would be leveled. They gave up.

IN SOUTHERN PEST, in Ferencváros, the shooting started on October 24. A tank rumbled into firing position in front of the Gazdags' building, firing with an enormous *boom* down their little street. At the end of the street were rebel-held barracks, which answered with the steady *pop-pop-pop* of machine guns. The tank responded with *booms* so large, they shook the windows, which had to be opened to keep from shattering. For six days the fighting prevented anyone from leaving the Gazdags' building, and they had been caught with nothing to eat but potatoes. There was not even anything to put on the potato. Gyula's grandmother baked them by the rackful for three meals each day. On October 30 the shooting stopped, and Gyula's grandmother went out and bought food and spent the quiet day cooking and preparing for when the fighting would start again.

Sunday morning, Gyula was sleeping in his bed. At six o'clock he was awakened and given some new books that had been wrapped for Christmas. These Jewish atheists celebrated Christmas. Then he was led to the bomb shelter that had been set up in the basement of the building in preparation for World War III. Gyula had spent his childhood dreading World War III, the inevitable showdown with the Americans that could happen at any time. All buildings had to have bomb shelters where the residents could sit out the nuclear holocaust.

The fighting grew heavier—more than just one tank and a few machine guns. There was a war up there, not with the Americans but with the Soviets. But for nine-year-old Gyula, this was the best time of his whole childhood. The children of the building spent the entire day in the basement playing. Each family set up beds in the cubicle used for their belongings. The whole family was there. No one went to school. No one went to work. And making it even more exciting, they sat around all day by candlelight. And when the parents got dull and started debating, the children could just roam from cubicle to cubicle and find other children with whom to play. To Gyula, this seemed some sort of model lifestyle.

His parents sat on the bed and talked about leaving Hungary. But Zsuzsa was adamant that she was not going to spend any more of her life moving. She had started in Budapest, fled to Vienna, then back to Budapest—it was enough. She was staying here, come what may.

GEORGE LIPPNER was also nine years old, and he also was hiding with his family in the basement of their home in Újpest. But he wasn't enjoying it. The family spent a night in the basement when the shooting was particularly violent, and when they came up in the morning, they found that two crosses had been painted on their door. Looking outside, they found similar markings on all the homes of neighbors of Jewish origin. These neighbors, like the Lippners, did not practice Judaism or talk about it. Nevertheless, somebody had known which doors to paint. George had no idea what Jewish practices were, or the difference between one kind of Jew and another. But now he understood what his parents had been telling him: It was dangerous to be a Jew in Hungary, and he was scared.

But another nine-year-old boy, Andras Kovacs, did think it was fun. *Kovacs*, like *Konrád*, was changed from a Kohen name in the last century. Andras's father, Imre, was a Sachsenhausen survivor with many relatives who didn't survive. Living in the sixth district in central Pest, not far from the traditional Jewish area, they had many Jewish neighbors. This was also a convenient location for the uprising. Only a few yards from the Kovacses' building was a barricade, and neighborhood people would go home and shower or eat or rest and then go back to the barricades. One young man in their building went to the barricade faithfully every morning at eight o'clock. Andras remembers it as "a sort of comfortable revolution." His parents seemed confident that soon United Nations troops would arrive and Hungary would be declared neutral—the Austrian solution. But one day, as Andras was walking in the street with his mother, two rebels raised their arms in fascist salutes and greeted each other, *"Sieg heil,"* and then his mother started to be frightened.

György Gadó, a schoolteacher at the time, enthusiastically participated in the demonstrations. In fact, he was one of the party dissidents who had been attending meetings for a year leading up to this rebellion. But when the shooting started, he backed away. He saw that there were really two factions in the rebellion. One wanted to reform Communism and make it live up to democratic egalitarian ideals. The other wanted to resurrect Horthy's fascist Hungarian state. Gadó feared the latter would triumph if the Soviets backed down. Although in later years he would modify this view, at the time he concluded that the Soviets were the only safeguard Hungary had against fascism.

Even György Konrád, while involved in the rebellion, had noticed that it had some worrisome elements. When it first erupted and Konrád was trying to put to bed his new literary magazine, he had to work over constant shouting both on the street and in the building. At one point someone in the building from an office near his shouted, "Jewish murderers!" Konrád later heard similar comments on the street. Konrád's wife sat on a committee of schoolteachers that began talking of purging the teaching staffs of Jews. Konrád believed that the rebelling Communists would in the long term lose out to a conservative element. But he thought that the moderate wing of the conservative movement would gain control.

The subject will always be debated, because Soviet tanks preempted any political process at all. A working-class Hungarian Communist, János Kádár, was placed at the head of a government that ruled by martial law. Once again, when the Red Army came to Újpest, the Lippners and some of the other Jewish families were relieved to see them. Gadó, having been frightened by his glimpse of counterrevolutionaries, rejoined the Communist party. Zsuzsa Gazdag, on the other hand, quit the party.

Gyula Lippner used his connections at the big state company to get a good supply of glass and, being an experienced window man, he was kept busy replacing missing panes all over Újpest. Since the Kádár government had a more liberal attitude about economic activities, he was able to turn this into a small shop that did windows and picture framing.

An estimated 180,000 Hungarians emigrated. At least 20,000 of them were Jewish. The Seiferts stayed, though most of Géza's family left. A relative of Ilona's who had survived Auschwitz left with his wife and child, leaving behind the unnerving warning, "It's starting again." But Geza and Ilona had been more frightened about "it starting again" during the uprising. At first they thought it was a grand thing. They had not liked the way the institutions they had built had been shut down and replaced by an official Jewish Community. They had thought there were many things wrong with the way the Soviets had been doing things, and they liked the way the Hungarians were standing up to them. Then, for the first time since the Red Army had entered in 1945, they started hearing the phrase "true Hungarians." In Geza's legal circles a distinction was being made about "true Hungarian" lawyers being the only ones who should be allowed to practice once the Soviets had been driven out. Anyone who had lived through the Horthy era knew that this was code for the exclusion of Jews from the practice of law. Now that the uprising was crushed and the Soviets were back in control, the Seiferts were ready to take their chances. "I am sure," said Ilona Seifert, "that lots of people were killed who did nothing. And they are also martyrs. But it was not the same, '56 and the Holocaust. . . . I have to say that there were a lot of martyrs from that time, but not one child, not a ninety-nine-year-old man or woman. I am sure they did terrible things and people suffered, for example, people who were in the prisons in '56 . . . but it was not the same."

To the Seiferts, Budapest was home. The Communists, even the Soviets, were people they could work with. They allowed an official Jewish Community, and by being active in the official community you could negotiate things, accomplish things, maintain a Jewish life. It was a question of negotiating skills.

But many Jews did not agree. So many families from the Jewish neighborhoods left that Andras Kovacs's school went from four classes to only two. On November 11, György Konrád's cousin and one of his best friends came to him and told him people were being arrested. It would be years before Hungarians learned how many people had been arrested and eliminated. Even Imre Nagy was quietly executed without an announcement. But Konrád's friends understood what was happening because some of their circle, including the brother of György's closest friend, had been among those rounded up. György's friend and his cousin had decided to leave the country. They wanted Konrád to come too. "Don't stay here and be arrested," they argued.

But there were forces holding György Konrád to Hungary. His wife and her three-year-old daughter could come with him, but could he leave his parents alone? In truth, he was more afraid of leaving than staying. He was determined to be a writer. If he was arrested, he could write about that. "I believe prison would be a good school. As long as I survive, nothing that happens to me here can be bad for me as a writer." But if he left, he would cut himself off from the Hungarian language, his language. He wasn't sure he could ever write in anything but Hungarian, and Hungarian is a language that has no cousins. Only in Hungary can you be a Hungarian writer.

14

From Moscow to Berlin

MEDICINE HAD BEEN ONE OF THE GREAT SUCCESS FIELDS of Soviet Jewry. At the time Stalin exposed the "doctors' plot," Moritz Mebel was among the more than 15 percent of doctors in the Soviet Union who were Jewish. He could not understand what had gone wrong. After his family fled Nazi Germany, he had never experienced anti-Semitism while he was growing up in Moscow. To him, anti-Semitism was a German sickness that he had escaped by moving to the Soviet Union, a nation that had welcomed him and his family. Then he went off to war, and after fighting in the Ukraine, Hungary, Czechoslovakia, and Germany, he was even shipped east to fight the Japanese. But when he returned to Moscow, the Soviet Union seemed different. He didn't feel welcome anymore.

After the years of frontline combat, he was now hearing that Jews were cowards and couldn't fight, that they all hid far from the front lines. Two hundred thousand Jews had died fighting in the Red Army, an army that—though certainly nobody wanted to mention this while Stalin was in power—was founded by a Jew, Trotsky. Yet it was a popular insult to ask a Jew with a combat medal where he bought it.

As Mebel the veteran was finishing his education, he started feeling that opportunities for advancement were closed to him. He certainly would have no future in the foreign service. But medicine

147

was a field where many Jews had advanced and even made it to the exclusive Kremlin staff, as the entire world soon learned. Even though he had known many Jewish doctors during his studies, even though the urologist under whom he interned was a Jew, he was still certain that he would not be allowed to hold a good position in Moscow or Leningrad. He went to Estonia, and there he was quickly elevated to medical director of his hospital. Once the "doctors' plot" was announced, he was advised that it was only a matter of time until he was removed from his position in the hospital. Then Stalin died, and his problem, along with those of many other people, was solved.

Mebel was in love with a German Jewish microbiologist, Sonja, whose family had also fled Germany when Hitler came to power. She was eight years old at the time, and unlike Moritz, she did not remember Nazi Germany. Sonja worked in the Microbiology Institute in Moscow. Of the five hundred qualified microbiologists, doctors, and chemists there, she had the lowest position, and she was convinced that this was due to the combination of being a Jew and a German.

Sonja reached a conclusion that many Jews before her had also reached: Even if she could not advance, she could learn. She was in an excellent department headed by a distinguished professional, a Spaniard who had been chief medical officer for the Republican Army. She worked for a renowned expert in her field. "The most important thing for me is knowledge, because nobody can take it away from me," she said.

Unlike the Mebels, Sonja's family had always intended to return to Germany. Since the day they fled it had been their dream that someday the Nazis would be defeated and they would go back. But when the Nazis were defeated, Sonja's mother was seriously ill, and the family stayed in Moscow until she died at the age of 46 in 1948. By then, Stalin had closed the borders and they could not leave.

In 1957, Sonja moved to Berlin with her family, although the following year she returned to Moscow to marry Moritz Mebel. Then the two of them moved to Berlin. Moritz had never thought he would go back to Germany. He had been a Soviet citizen for more than twenty years. But he felt that the new GDR wanted him and the Soviet Union no longer did. He, too, felt certain that he was not going back to the old Germany but to a new Germany to which he could make a contribution. The

Soviet Union seemed to have no role for him anymore. In an odd way he felt as though he were coming home. But he was not sure he liked the feeling.

He worked at the Charité Hospital in East Berlin, in Mitte, the old historic center of the city where the government had been, and the university and the opera, and famous cabarets. It did not look very different from the last time he had seen it while serving in the Red Army at the end of the war. The Reichstag was still burned black and peppered with bullet holes and shrapnel gashes. The great museums and government buildings of the wide Unter den Linden were also still war-scarred. The tight bullet patterns on the fronts of dark buildings reminded him of those days of house-to-house fighting when you would realize that someone was shooting from above somewhere, and you would just raise your weapon in a cold sweat and unload everything at the building overhead, hoping to stop whoever was up there.

Mitte was left standing, but with hardly a flat, untouched surface in the neighborhood. A few missing blocks had been cleared. Some buildings still weren't inhabitable. But none of this was upsetting to Mebel. Restoring buildings was not a priority for the new East Germany. Education, social service, and health care were. The Charité was a good hospital. But it was there that he found something he had not expected in this new society: He found the old Germany. The rest of the staff was acutely aware that he had been an officer in the Red Army. He certainly would never hide that fact. On the contrary, as a Jew in the Soviet Union he had become accustomed to defensively asserting his war record. He had served in what was supposed to be the good army. The problem was that many of the people with whom he was now working had been in the bad army. The hospital's director had been the surgeon general for the Sixth German Army, of which all but a few thousand had died at the hands of the Soviets when trapped in a subzero showdown at Stalingrad. He and the other former army officers did not talk to Mebel. Mebel had fought against Germans.

Although he was an experienced urologist and former hospital director, Mebel was allowed only to do anesthesia. After a time he changed hospitals, but the situation was not much better. Finding that if he worked hard and alone he would at least not be obstructed, he did research in the evenings in an empty laboratory that he was not allowed to use during the days.

Sonja did microbiological research. The head of her section was rumored to have been an important Nazi. That was not supposed to be possible in the GDR, but there he was. Another one of the scientists with whom she worked was a known former Nazi party member. But most of her colleagues were younger than she was, too young to have been Nazis. Soon, it seemed, all the Nazis would be gone. Germany had only to raise a new generation and be patient.

Like the rest of the Soviet bloc, the GDR had flirted with official anti-Semitism at the time of the Slansky trial. It was a relatively brief episode in the GDR. This was Germany, and if it was not a "new" Germany, it was nothing. But at the time, some Jews lost official positions. There were a few trials. A friend of Mia Lehmann, a loyal party militant, was tried for a mythical crime. The Lehmanns were deeply disturbed. Many Jews were more than disturbed. About eight thousand of them migrated to West Germany.

Jews weren't the only ones leaving. Discontent was closely related to economic failure. On June 16, 1953, East Berlin workers protested a ten percent increase in production norms. By the following day it had become an open revolt put down by Soviet troops. About 1,500 people received prison sentences and 109 were killed, including 41 Soviet soldiers executed for refusing to fire on German workers. That year, 300,000 East Germans left. In the subsequent calm, 150,000 was an average yearly figure for emigration. By the late 1950s, the West German economy had grown dramatically and lifted its people from the misery of 1945. East Germans were still digging out, and the economy would not show dramatic improvement until the 1960s.

A guarded border divided the two Germanies, but Berlin was an open city. From East Berlin, West Germany was only a few stops on the S-bahn. The neighborhoods adjacent to Mitte on the western side were in West Berlin, where tall cranes were erecting new buildings; old historic buildings, of which there were far fewer than in Mitte, were being refurbished, and the consumer product deluge of the 1950s, cranked out by the U.S. economy and the Marshall Plan, was beginning to become part of the new lifestyle.

Germans crossed back and forth every day for work and shopping. But many were not coming back. In East Berlin the endemic labor shortage was growing into a serious problem because of people migrating West. In a culture that creates a word for everything, the new word for leaving the East was *Republikflucht*, which in 1957 became a crime. After that, anyone who wanted to leave had to do so without warning anyone. Children would go to school and find their teacher gone. At Moritz Mebel's clinic it became difficult to schedule surgical procedures, because you never knew who was going to show up the next day.

Mia Lehmann's Nazi neighbor who had grown so fond of her daughter suddenly announced that she would have that operation she had been needing. Although she had always flaunted her contacts in the West, she went to an East Berlin hospital. Back from the hospital, she could not say enough about the East German medical service, how nice they were, and free! and so efficient— and free! When she was well enough, she and her husband vanished to the West.

The two-tier economy was becoming unbearable for East Berliners. Prices were much cheaper in the East, especially with West German marks worth far more than East German marks. In fact, East German marks weren't worth anything outside of East Germany. East Germans like Mia Lehmann who had no interest in going to the West would go to their neighborhood store or hairdresser and be told that their money was no longer accepted. With West German marks being offered, no one wanted the low-value eastern currency.

ALL OF THESE TENSIONS were hardening the regime, instilling the "us or them" brand of official paranoia, making the state increasingly insistent on conformism and increasingly distrustful of rebellious individualists. Georges Alexan's teenage daughter Irene was not fitting in.

Her father had remarried, to an outsider in their circle of outsiders. She was a German, not Jewish, not from abroad. Irene, resenting her, had divided the world into her father's world, which she loved—Jewish and American—and her stepmother's world, which she hated—gentile and German. She continued to insist that she was Jewish, and her father continued to be ambiguous. The day before Christmas, he would hand Irene some money and tell her to buy a tree. She would run out to the street, buy one, and bring it back. But neither of them knew what to do with the tree. Her father went back to reading, back to his customary posture, bent over a book with his hat on.

Irene's rebellion grew. She dropped out of school and later took a lover, ironically a non-Jewish lover, and became pregnant at 18. Her father didn't want them to marry, because they seemed an obvious mismatch. A classic parental mistake, his opposition fueled their determination.

She had a job in the East German news agency, where her skill in English was valued, though she mostly distributed English-language copy to the right desks. As she went through the office reading copy, she made comments with that New York brand of irreverence that had become her style. These were not times for irreverent pregnant teenagers in the GDR. She was informed that she was a "bourgeois leftist revisionist" and that she needed to be reeducated. This was to be accomplished by sending her to work in a factory assembly line.

Factory work? She had never done anything like that. She had grown up among the privileged Communist elite. She didn't even know people who worked in factories. Wandering East Berlin, 18 and pregnant, she contemplated the fact that for the first time in her life she was not going to be in a privileged position. She was not going to be in the vanguard, not a Soviet freedom fighter—she was going to be a faceless German in a factory.

And then someone came to her and said he was from the government and that he understood she was scheduled to go to a factory because she was a bourgeois leftist revisionist. She said that was true, but she didn't want to go, that she was a good Communist and she didn't know what had happened. The man's face glowed with a hospitable smile. "If that is true, if you are right, if you are a correct person, then maybe we could work together." He explained that he would appreciate having conversations with her, not very often, just from time to time. Maybe once or twice a year. She could just talk about what she thought was going on, her views on people and events in the office, and these would be secret conversations that no one else in the office would know about.

Now she would not have to go to a factory. She would do undercover work! She liked that idea. It seemed like the guerrilla fighter of her childhood fantasies exposing the Nazis.

That summer of 1961, Irene gave birth to a boy, Stefan. Alone, she took her new baby home to her small apartment on a quiet war-scarred street of Mitte. Her street was quieter than usual that night, and she was feeling very alone with her baby, whom she was not exactly sure how to care for. Soldiers had erected a makeshift gate at the entrance to her block, and she had to prove that she lived there before she could pass through. To Irene, that meant that she would be alone with the baby. Visitors would not be let into the block—unless they came from the other direction. But when she looked down the block, it appeared to be completely closed off on the other end with swirls and tunnels and spirals of barbed wire suspended between new concrete posts. It looked like some kind of military construction project winding through the center of the city. The border was closing.

PART THREE

'68

"Living just to survive—that would never end well."
JIŘÍ WEIL, Mendelssohn Is on the Roof

15

---

*From
North Africa*

T HE MAJORITY OF FRENCH, BOTH JEWS AND NON-JEWS, had a deep-seated desire to pretend that World War II never happened. Most French Jews went back to being Frenchmen. Just as before the war, they were a diverse group, not well organized, and usually attached to the French Republican ideal of fitting into France. They spoke out from time to time, as happened during the Finaly affair, but they were not a political force. Nor did most of them want to be. Among French Jews it was widely believed that when Jews hold political power, it always leads to trouble. In 1954 the French government was headed by Pierre Mendès-France, an assimilated Jew who once proudly asserted, "I do not remember ever making a decision in my political life—and even less so in government—inspired by the interests of the Jewish community." Yet when he resigned as head of government after a controversial seven months and seventeen days, during which he had withdrawn France from Indochina, started the autonomy process for Tunisia and Morocco, and won French ratification for the rearmament of West Germany, his final speech to the National Assembly was shouted down by deputies screaming *"Sale Juif!,"* dirty Jew. The Jewish community had little reaction. Emmanuel Ewenczyk fatalistically explained, "When a Jew is in a highly responsible position in France, there is always some anti-Semitism heard."

Emmanuel and Fania Ewenczyk had two daughters, one born in

1945, and one two years later. Emmanuel had kept the business in the Jewish garment area in the center of Paris. But as it prospered, he and his family moved to western Paris, to the sixteenth arrondissement, where they had the kind of ornate Paris home that is surrounded by swirls — in oriental carpets, in gilded molding on the furniture, in bas-relief on the walls and ceilings, in chandeliers, and even etched in the crystal. In one generation they had been able to rise from poor eastern immigrants in the garment district to the assimilated grand bourgeois life like that of the Altmanns.

The Altmanns were raising three children in a nearby western Paris neighborhood, an area of manicured streets and grand turn-of-the-century buildings with sculpted detail. The steel trading business had to be carefully managed in a fast-growing but unstable world marketplace, and their lives as affluent Parisians, not much different from non-Jews of their economic class, had resumed. Once a week, a rabbi would come to the children's school and teach them Hebrew for one hour. Such things were important, but they were not the center of life.

The Ewenczyks sent their children to an afternoon Jewish school, a Talmud-Torah, for a few hours a week. But their passion was Zionism, not religion. Atypical of French Jewry, the Zionists were organized and rented huge Parisian halls for mass rallies, which Fania and Emmanuel always attended. Emmanuel was consumed with his fast-growing business, but Fania missed the activism of their Resistance days. Most of their old Resistance group from Grenoble was now in Israel. In fact, most of the real activists in French Jewry, the ones who wanted to remember and did not think life could be put back the way it had been, had gone to Israel.

Less than ten years after the war, the Jewish population of France was approaching the 340,000 prewar population. France had opened its borders to Jewish refugees, and 55,000 DPs moved there. The immigrants gravitated toward the Pletzl or the Rue Bleue area, but French Jews lived throughout Paris, often not in Jewish neighborhoods, sometimes almost clandestinely. Wartime experiences had convinced many Jews to change their names to French ones. Many times more Jews changed their names between 1945 and 1957 than in the century and a half between 1803 and Nazi occupation. In towns and villages where a mere name change could not hide a family's origins, there was an unusually large number of conversions to Catholicism.

THE PLETZL, after losing so many people to deportation, never regained its original size. It was now only Rue des Rosiers and the few streets running off it. But new people were moving in. One of the first new groups, after the 1948 Middle East war, was the Egyptian Sephardim—strange Jews for the Pletzl, who spoke perfect French but no Yiddish and didn't eat the heavy potted food of central Europe.

The neighborhood always smelled of food. Inexpensive restaurants, like the ones before the war, opened in the narrow storefronts, the steam from dense Polish Jewish cooking drifting out doorways. In the 1950s these restaurants often closed after only a few months because of a lack of customers. In time, people learned that the Pletzl was now a smaller place and could no longer support a restaurant in every third door.

Horse-drawn ice wagons struggled down the narrow streets past black marketeers who bought silverware and gold and sold U.S. dollars. Next to Finkelsztajn's bakery was a shop not much wider than a doorway that sold live carp from a tank. Across the street from Finkelsztajn's, on Rue des Hospitalières-Saint-Gervais, a block-long street off of Rue des Rosiers, an Ashkenazic family, Klapisch, opened a second carp store. A delivery truck would get to the corner and scoop out the scaly amber fish in big nets, dumping them into the tanks of the two stores. Young Henri Finkelsztajn would wait for the truck to leave and then run to the gutters, where he would find small carps that had slipped through the nets, smacking themselves uselessly against the curbstones. He would gather them up and bring them to his parents.

One block east of Finkelsztajn's, on the corner of Rue des Ecouffes, was the Korcarz bakery, with the same blue tile mosaic front, still owned by Icchok's Aunt Leah and her husband. In the 1950s, Korcarz's brother, a camp survivor, arrived and opened another bakery on the western end of the street next to the Blums', whose *charcuterie* was the last of the original Alsatian Jewish shops. Korcarz's brother was still a traditional religious Jew, and his bakery was one of the few strictly kosher shops in the Pletzl.

Most of the buildings remained dilapidated, the blackened facades broken by fissures and wandering cracks, some of the buildings buttressed by huge wooden beams. The Finkelsztajns' apartment above the bakery seemed spacious in comparison to most of their neighbors'. Large families stuffed themselves each evening into little studios. The other side of the Finkelsztajns' building, the side with the carp store, was particularly deteriorated and dirty. Soon the carp store gave way to a small café owned by a Polish non-Jew. It catered to a poor alcoholic Polish clientele who got very drunk and often violent. Because the café lacked space, the fights usually took place in the street. From time to time the dead body of a Pole would be found in the hallway of the building. The police would come and remove it without asking many questions. A dead Pole on Rue des Rosiers didn't even make an item for the newspapers.

In the 1950s the café was taken over by a Belgian Jew who ran a small restaurant and whose son became one of Henri Finkelsztajn's neighborhood friends. Henri had a happy childhood in the Pletzl, and the bad years were behind him, perhaps only recalled in a nervous stutter that held him back in school.

Small Orthodox storefront prayer rooms, *shtibls*, began reopening, but they rarely had the two dozen men that would make them seem full. Henri and his neighborhood friends were not religious but attended weekly instruction in a small Talmud-Torah on Rue des Ecouffes. They, like the Ewenczyk children, were among the fewer than three thousand Jews in all of Paris's sizable Jewish population who received this modest form of Jewish education. Henri and his friends also belonged to a Zionist youth organization, which to them was more of a social club than anything political. Growing up in a crowded neighborhood with narrow streets, they needed a meeting place.

AT THE TIME when Mendès-France decided to cut loose the French protectorate of Tunisia, Roger Journo, like his father before him, was a successful cloth merchant in southern Tunisia. The Journos were Jews in a country where Muslims and Jews did not mix socially but worked together and seldom had conflicts. The Tunisian nationalist leader, Habib Bourguiba, valued the hundred thousand Jews in the protectorate and tried to keep Jewish leaders informed on negotiations with France for Tunisian independence. Bourguiba told Tunisian Jews personally that the independent Tunisian state would guarantee the equality and citizenship of Jewish Tunisians. Some Jews believed him and even worked for the independence movement. But Journo feared that if things turned out badly after independence, it might be difficult to get out. In 1951 he gave up his good life in the sunny Mediterranean port town of

Sousse, where one in five people were Jewish, and moved his wife, two daughters, and two sons to one of the smudged little damp and badly heated apartments on the bad end of the Finkelsztajns' Rue des Rosiers building. Only on rare days would they get sunlight through their three small garret windows on the top floor. They bought a small storefront across the street from the apartment and sold Jewish food. But with the exception of three or four other North African families, none of the Jews on Rue des Rosiers had ever before seen such Jewish food—olives, hummus, tahini, couscous, and halvah. Not a gefilte fish or a herring in sight, and not a word of Yiddish. The neighbors on Rue des Rosiers found these too to be very strange Jews.

More of them were coming. French North Africa had a population of a half-million Jews. Morocco alone had some 285,000, mostly impoverished or struggling peddlers and craftsmen. After Israeli statehood in 1948, a wave of poorer Jews emigrated to the new Jewish state from both Tunisia and Algeria. In Oujda, Morocco, a mob attacked the Jewish quarter during the 1948 Middle East war, killing more than a dozen people and wounding many more. More than a third of Morocco's Jewish population, mostly the poorest, emigrated to Israel. These emigrants sent reports back to Tunisia and Morocco of a hard and sometimes dangerous life, and few Jews were interested in following this first wave. After independence the new Moroccan government kept its promise to treat Jews fairly and even appointed Jews to ranking government posts. But the new country had virtually no economy, and with Moroccans sending back troubling reports from Israel, the remaining Jews began an orderly three-decade-long retreat to France.

Algerian Jews never called themselves Algerian. Algerians were Arabs. These Jews, though they had been in Algeria since the Spanish expulsion, considered themselves French, which was legally correct since 1870, when the *décret Crémieux* had granted French citizenship to Algerian Jews. Adolphe Crémieux was a passionate nineteenth-century advocate of French revolutionary idealism who had championed the abolition of slavery. He successfully argued that extending citizenship to Jews in Algeria was the overdue fulfillment of the rights granted other French Jews by the French Revolution. They were simply thought of as French Jews. In fact, Algeria was thought of as part of France. Mendès-France, after getting France out of its bitter colonial war in Vietnam and dropping Tunisia and Morocco, balked at Algeria. "Algeria," he said, "is France and not a foreign country." There was enough anger about his "giving away" Tunisia and Morocco that he never could have discussed doing the same with Algeria; it would have been seen, as he himself said, as an attack on "the unity and [territorial] integrity of the Republic." Instead, France had to fight one of its most divisive and brutal wars before finally letting Algeria go.

Algeria had three almost completely separate populations—the Muslims, the French, and the Jews. The war for Algerian independence was a war between Muslims and French in which Jews were caught in the middle. The National Liberation Front, the FLN, hoped that Jews could serve as mediators in its bid for independence. Some Jews among the intellectual class were militant members of the FLN. Others served in the French Army. To most Jews, it was time to take their French citizenship and move to France. But for all their talk of being Frenchmen, many were reluctant to leave Algeria and move to a strange, inhospitable, and cold northern country.

Lazare Bouaziz, son and brother of rabbis, was born in 1933 in Oran, Algeria's second city and a major center of North African Jewry. Up until the independence war, the only anti-Semitism he had ever experienced was during the wartime Vichy regime, when the *décret Crémieux* was withdrawn and Jews were expelled from the schools. In 1954, like many Algerian Jews, he went to Paris because the educational opportunities were too limited in Algeria. He studied dentistry and planned to establish a practice in Oran. But when he went back, it was as an officer in the French Army at war with Algeria. He, like thousands of other Frenchmen, had been drafted and was sent to Algeria from 1960 to 1963, where he served as a dental surgeon in the medical corps. The radicals of the FLN would plant bombs and ambush. The extreme right wing in the French military would torture and murder. The violence became increasingly gruesome, and Lazare, in a French uniform in his native Algeria, could only watch. But he still hoped that this would all pass and he could remain in Algeria when his military service ended. His family, like many of the Jews of Oran, was divided on whether to stay or leave. His parents wanted to leave. He and two of his sisters wanted to stay. Algeria had been good for Jews. It had been bad during the Dreyfus case and Vichy, but the bad times had always been caused by a problem in France. This too was a French problem that could pass, and life could go on for the Jews and the Algerians.

On June 1, 1962, Algeria became independent. One week later, an Arab mob went into a berserk killing frenzy in the Jewish section of Oran. "It went on all day," said Lazare Bouaziz. "They killed and killed and killed." That ended the debate in the Jewish community. The Jews left, and their synagogues were turned into mosques. Six months later, Bouaziz was discharged from the army and moved to France.

To Bouaziz, Paris was a familiar city, but for many Jews from Algeria it was a strange place with inhospitable people and unfriendly ways. As the European Jews received a small measure of success and moved from the Pletzl to better neighborhoods, North African Jews took their places. They also moved into the garment district as well as the garment trade. The area around Rue Bleue became a Sephardic ghetto, as did some of the new suburbs north of the city.

In retrospect, hardly any Ashkenazim recall any problem with the Sephardim. But the Sephardim remember it differently. "The Sephardim complain to an extent that I find unfair," said Henri Finkelsztajn. His neighbor Roger Journo's son André said that at first, "the Ashkenazim took us for Indians. They called us *shvartze*." In Yiddish, a shvartze is a black. They were Africans. The Sephardim—who were so proud of their Frenchness, their perfect mastery of the language—were perplexed by the fact that these people with heavy foreign accents looked on them as the foreigners. Even when they came from such noted centers of Jewish scholarship as Bône, they were regarded in Paris as ignorant third-worlders from a primitive backwater.

On Rue des Rosiers, the Sephardim went to Sephardic stores and the Ashkenazim to the Ashkenazic stores. There were people who ate couscous and people who ate knishes. The café that a Belgian family had taken over from a Pole was now taken over by an Algerian Muslim and became a hangout for Sephardic youth. To the Finkelsztajns and most of the other Ashkenazim in the building, these teenagers were "*voyou*," juvenile delinquents. It was an unwelcome element. Several times the police raided the café for drugs. Suddenly, the Ashkenazim were concerned that in this dilapidated space where, not long before, drunken Poles had been leaving knifed corpses, something unwholesome was now going on.

16

In Paris

I{F SUCH THINGS CAN BE PREORDAINED, THE F}INKELSZTAJNS seemed fated to be bakers. Even if he didn't have to work in a basement anymore, Icchok Finkelsztajn still had not wanted to be in a bakery. Now his son, Henri, was working there with him. Although talkative and sociable, Henri's stutter had made school difficult, and he stopped his education at age 15. Icchok wanted his son to do something better and sent him to apprentice in the garment district. Looking for a way out of the bakery himself, Icchok bought a small hotel on Rue de Rivoli, the wide boulevard nearby. But it did not make a profit, and Henri gave up the garment trade to rescue the hotel.

More by instinct than design, the hotel was run like a casual family boardinghouse with a small group of regulars who were charged low rates. One of the regulars was an American soldier whose life's dream was to own a store, even though he seemed incapable of navigating through simple arithmetic. The soldier bought anything with francs that he could sell for dollars. It seemed to Henri that almost everyone cheated the American on the exchange rate, but the rate was so good that the soldier made money anyway. Eventually, to his great excitement, the soldier opened his first store in Fontainebleau, near U.S. Army headquarters, and he invited Henri to look. It was an American supermarket—something unknown in France at that time. Henri was amazed by all the space, the aisles, all the different products and the little metal wagons for wheeling purchases around the store. Henri, who had always thought this American incapable of doing anything, could not help but be impressed by this huge orderly market. It also made an impression on the U.S. Army, which called the soldier in for a talk about his sideline and then sent him back to the United States.

The Finkelsztajn hotel did not fare much better, and it soon closed. Henri went to work for his father in the bakery once again. He hated the work as much as Icchok, but he enjoyed being with his father, whose rippling muscles and good spirits betrayed a love for physical labor that Henri had not inherited. In 1958, Henri married Honorine Paul-Jean, who was from Madagascar, the end of the earth his father had talked about running off to only seven years earlier. Neither Honorine nor Henri claimed to be religious. Nevertheless, because Honorine had only one Jewish grandparent, they worried about their children being legally Jewish. Honorine submitted to the long, arduous process of religious conversion. They named their son Sacha, after the little brother of Henri's mother, the boy shot in the road near Kielce by the Nazis.

THE SONS OF RAHMIN NAOURI, a famous rabbi from the Algerian city of Bône, started working at the Klapisch carp store on Rue des Hospitalières-Saint-Gervais. They did not think the carp business was very interesting and, instead, they decided to sell smoked salmon. Although this is a traditional Ashkenazic food, lox, it was not known on Rue des Rosiers because the people there were too poor to afford it. Non-Jewish French people knew nothing about smoked salmon, either, except for a handful of the elite, who paid dazzling prices. Buying a German machine that sliced and wrapped, lowering the price just a little, the Naouri brothers believed that *saumon fumé* could become one of those French luxury products like lobster and foie gras for holidays and birthdays. They got the trade unions to buy enormous quantities for union galas, especially New Year's Eve. Soon every blue-collar union worker in Paris associated *saumon fumé* with holiday extravagance.

Today there is rarely a *charcuterie* in France that doesn't sell smoked salmon, but in the early 1960s, Parisians who wanted it went to Rue des Rosiers. Although a little out of the way, the street had tremendous potential because it was not far from the central market, Les Halles, which had everything but smoked salmon. To get smoked salmon, people walked over from Les Halles to Rue des Rosiers, turned up the little side street, spent hundreds of francs at Klapisch, then walked forty yards back to Rue des Rosiers, noticed a little bakery with challah and bagels and other exotic breads in the window, and spent a few francs at Finkelsztajn's.

Henri always watched what was going on in the neighborhood, and he was becoming irritated by this trade. He wanted to see a little more of the money spent at his shop and began offering herring and other traditional family foods, as well as a few Sephardic dishes and even Madagascar specialties from his wife. Soon others started doing the same. The Ashkenazim started noticing that hummus and vine leaves sold well. The Sephardim started catching on to poppyseed strudel and cheesecake. Soon it was hard to tell a Sephardic store from an Ashkenazic one.

But although they looked the same, the people were still different. They were not as different as a Pole and an Algerian (they did, after all, share common religious, moral, and intellectual traditions), but one was a Mediterranean and the other a Central or Northern European. Significantly, the North African Jews who settled in Marseilles and other points along the French Mediterranean found it far easier to adjust to living in France than did those in Paris or Strasbourg. But the jobs and opportunities were not in the south.

It was not only the climate but the history of the two peoples since 1492 that had shaped different mentalities. While North African Jews had experienced occasional persecution and even violence, especially in Morocco, they had not had a Holocaust; nor had their society been shaped by centuries of Cossack raids and regular pogroms. While the Ashkenazim had learned to either keep a low profile or assimilate in a world controlled by Christians, the Sephardim had learned to be a separate but assertive subculture in a society composed of separate groups.

There are slight differences in practice between Ashkenazim and Sephardim. Religious Sephardim wear the four fringes, the *tzitzit*, tucked in rather than showing on the outside of their pants, which is a sign of piousness among Ashkenazim. Even the most religious Sephardic boys do not wear *peots*, curled side locks. Ashkenazim consider rice not to be kosher for Passover but Sephardim find eating rice on Passover completely acceptable.

Traditions also vary among Sephardic groups. In the Sabbath

service at the Esnoga, the Dutch royal family is blessed in old Portuguese. Algerian Sephardim have a lamb feast the night before Passover. Yiddish, essentially German dialect written in Hebrew, is uniquely Ashkenazic. But North Africans speak Judeo-Arab, which is Arab dialect written in Hebrew. The Dutch, Turkish, and Greek Sephardim speak Ladino, a Jewish dialect based on fifteenth-century Spanish.

One of the richest differences among Jewish subcultures is in music. The biblical readings of both the Ashkenazic and Sephardic service are chanted on a five-tone medieval scale. The music is not noted on a score but simply alluded to by marks above the Hebrew lettering indicating the direction of pitch. This leaves considerable latitude in the actual melody of the music, and a wide range of religious music has been created, much of which is passed down by unwritten tradition. The Sephardim are particularly noted for the beauty of their chants; a number of celebrated operatic singers have recorded Sephardic airs.

While the music can be very different and unfamiliar, any Jew should be able to go to a synagogue anywhere in the world and follow the service.

What the North African Jews were not prepared for in Paris was the degree of Christianization that had taken place in the French spirit of Republicanism. This would not have been surprising to someone who had seen the German Enlightenment or the American Reform movement, but there had been nothing like this in North Africa. The synagogues of Paris, instead of chanting, played organ music. The capital had three kosher butchers for 120,000 Jews, and only two or three kosher restaurants. And the strictness of the kosher was, to North Africans, highly dubious. Few Paris Jews were kosher at all. In a typical North African assessment, Lazare Bouaziz said, "Paris Jews were very discreet. They were Jews who did not want to say they were Jewish."

The North Africans also found French Jewish education to be inadequate, and since most of their distinguished rabbis, scholars, and educators had moved to France, they began to make their own arrangements. Rabbi Naouri was now in Paris, along with the younger rabbis who had gathered around him in Bône. One of these younger Bône rabbis was René-Samuel Sirat. Sirat had first come to France in 1946 as a sixteen-year-old student, and then went on to study at the École Rabbinique de France. At the time he was studying in Paris, there were few Sephardic Jews. On Saturday

mornings he would walk across Paris to Rue Popincourt, on the
eastern edge of the city, where the Salonikan community had a
synagogue. These were Sephardic Jews from the Greek port of
Thessaloniki. Before the war 20 percent of Thessaloniki had been
Jewish, and it had been one of the most important and culturally
rich Sephardic communities in Europe. The Nazis had deported
45,000 of the Thessalonikan Jews to concentration camps. The
Gestapo officer in Greece, an Eichmann favorite named Aloïs
Brünner, was later transferred to Paris, where he was able to deport
more Salonikan Jews from this neighborhood, and after the war the
few remnants of Salonikan Jewry were vanishing. (Brünner, who
was then only in his twenties, also vanished, but he was sighted in
Syria in 1986.) The synagogue on Rue Popincourt and another on
Rue St.-Lazare, near Rue Bleue, were among the few places where
the fifteenth-century rites and passionate music of Salonikan Jewry
could still be heard. Sirat, who would not take a bus on the Sabbath, walked for more than an hour on Saturday mornings to hear
this service. Today, the Rue St.-Lazare synagogue is Algerian, and
the Rue Popincourt synagogue no longer functions. Another
nearby Salonikan synagogue is now Moroccan.

Sirat was saddened by the general level of Jewish education in
France. Few Jews went to synagogue, and on the rare occasions
when they did go, they could not really carry it off because they
could not read Hebrew. Jews would say a kaddish for their deceased parents by reading a text transcribed into Latin. A Holocaust
survivor had written a book that was in wide usage on preparing
young people for bar mitzvah. Instead of the customary intensive
Torah study, it simply offered a few passages. To Sirat, the Talmud-
Torah classes such as Finkelsztajn had attended were "really
nothing at all." There were only three full-time schools for Jewish
studies in the entire country, all three of them in Paris.

Sirat saw it as his mission to stay in France and build the Jewish
education system. With few truly Orthodox Ashkenazim, the
Salonikans dwindling and only a handful of North Africans, it was
a lonely struggle. Then suddenly, he was joined by another
350,000 North African Jews. North African Jewish communities,
especially in Algeria, had been tightly organized and extremely
activist. Even the departure was well organized and carefully
funded to help the poorer Jews. Now France itself needed to be
organized. Naouri directed the French rabbinical board, the Beth
Din. Created in 1905 to regulate religious law, the Beth Din was

chiefly in charge of certifying marriages and supervising kosher practices. Naouri began to enforce strict laws on the slaughter of animals and the regulation of kosher shops.

In 1964, with Paris suddenly experiencing a renaissance of strict observance, it seemed natural that a new rabbi, tall, thin, with a fine brushed beard, boundless energy, and the fixed features of a man who does not compromise—Antwerp's Chaim Rottenberg—should arrive in town.

In 1911, the same year Chaim Rottenberg's father decided to move from Poland to be a rabbi in Antwerp, a small Ashkenazic community was established in the Pletzl. They had raised enough money from small contributions to build a new synagogue, and full of optimism for their growing community, they commissioned the leading Parisian architect of the day, Hector Guimard, to design it. Guimard was changing the look of Paris, bringing the long graceful curves of art nouveau to everything from *métro* entrances to apartment buildings. The building site was on a rundown street off of Rue des Rosiers, Rue Pavée.

The synagogue that was built, in a simple and stylish way, may be the most beautiful in Paris. Rising in a narrow space between two old Pletzl buildings, it was designed with long elegant vertical lines to exaggerate its height, and with a three-quarter balcony and a simple, tall leaded-glass window at the back. Typical of the period, the long lines are softened by graceful curves. From the posts supporting the balcony to the tulip-style light fixtures to the pattern in the leaded-glass window, the design recalls the graceful bowing of long-stemmed flowers.

In the fall of 1964 the rabbi for the Rue Pavée synagogue died, and Chaim Rottenberg was invited to replace him. In the Antwerp community it is said that, "It was in Paris that Chaim really found his work." In Antwerp a community with numerous ultra-Orthodox rabbis, Rottenberg was constantly clashing with the other rabbis. But in Paris he was a phenomenon.

The building where the Rottenbergs were to live, next to the Guimard synagogue, was a cramped, damp Pletzl tenement. They had to clean it and build closets and virtually make an apartment out of the space. Chaim earned a modest salary, and Rifka had a small reparations payment from West Germany. Chaim had refused his own German payment, calling it "blood money."

Chaim, with his long stride and peering eyes, was seen every-where in the neighborhood, inspecting, and most of the few kosher shops were, by Rottenberg standards, all too lax. Sometimes in these early days Rifka was even seen buying a challah from Henri Finkelsztajn, something that in later years would be unimaginable. The Finkelsztajns had never claimed to be kosher and always did a good trade on Saturdays. In fact, once the other shops became more observant, Saturday turned into the Finkelsztajns' best day.

Rottenberg found that the milk was not kosher. Milk that was not under rabbinical supervision could come from anywhere and could have had contact with meat. Rottenberg insisted on a supply of rabbinically supervised kosher milk for the entire year, and not just for Passover. He was troubled by the lack of *mikvehs*, or ritual baths. There was only one, very old-fashioned ritual bathing place in Paris. *Mikvehs* are used for purification. Converts immerse themselves there, as do married women after menstruation before they resume sex. Single women presumably have no need for a *mikveh*. Men bathe there to reach a purified state before a particu-larly holy moment, especially Yom Kippur. The fact that there was only one *mikveh* for all this activity had not greatly troubled the community up until then, because in reality few modern Jews ever use one. Most French Jews—in fact, most Jews—have never seen one.

But Rottenberg wanted not only a new *mikveh*, but an ultramod-ern one. Anyone who knew Chaim Rottenberg knew what the next step would be. He would start insisting that people use the *mikveh*. His plans required an enormous sum of money, much of which he raised by going one by one to people in the Pletzl and suggesting they pay what they could. If they were poor, he would take coins. If they were rich, he wanted to see ample checks. Sometimes he would smile at people, and sometimes he would shout at them. Once the *mikveh* got under construction, his regular visits to the builders and architect insured that everything would be strictly according to rabbinical law, even at the cost of the workers' sanity. He was relentless. But people liked him. He was from an old rabbinical tradition in which a community is held together by the singular force of a rabbi's personality—the kind of rabbi that was called a Rav, a great one. Their lives would take on the daily rhythm of religious practice because his did, and his presence would bring people into the community.

He would also grab them, scouring the Pletzl on a Saturday

morning for a few loose Jewish men to fill up the minyan, or quorum. Soon he had no problem with minyans, but he would still grab people. "Come stay with me," he would say. Some people avoided the Pletzl because of Rav Rottenberg. Others became daily members of the Rue Pavée community. He would grab them, house them, teach them, arrange their marriages, then teach their children. His fanaticism was blended with love and a tireless enthusiasm. He could instill fear and then surprise people with his tolerance.

He ran around, stuck his head in everywhere, and knew everything that was going on. One man whom he had pulled in studied in his group every night for two years, then finally got the courage to confess that his wife was not Jewish. This was a terrible confession to a man like Rottenberg. It meant their children would not be Jewish, and for all the man's studying, his Jewish line would end. But Rottenberg only nodded and said, "I know that." Henri Finkelsztajn, who did not go to synagogues and was never going to be grabbed, still loved the sight of Rottenberg. He thought this tall, elegant, dark-coated rabbi with the long beard darting through the narrow streets was a welcome addition to the old Pletzl.

Rottenberg, of course, still liked to be "a troublemaker." When Henri Schilli, a Grand Rabbi of France, died, a funeral procession was arranged with a Rothschild baron in the lead. In France, Rothschilds always lead anything run by the Consistoire Israélite, the central Jewish authority in France. It is with good reason that the Consistoire's synagogue is commonly referred to as "the Rothschild synagogue." But Chaim Rottenberg did not think a rabbi's funeral should be led by a man who was not a rabbi or even a religious Jew by Rottenberg's standard. He walked in front of the baron so that he himself was then leading the procession—in his words, "out of respect for the torah."

LAZARE BOUAZIZ was now a Parisian dentist, and he maintained the religious practices of his father's rabbinical household in Oran. He was active in an organization that arranged vacations with kosher food and Sabbath observation. The hope was that Jews would meet on these trips and marry. Intermarriage has long been a great threat to the continuance of French Jewry. In 1965, Bouaziz led a group tour in Greece and met Suzy Ewenczyk, daughter of Fania and Emmanuel. Two years later, they decided to get married, which was to be exactly what Lazare's organization wanted to happen. The problem was that many Jews saw this match as a mixed marriage between a Sephardi and an Ashkenazi.

To the Ashkenazim, a Sephardi was still a strange and very different kind of Jew. But Bouaziz had been around Ashkenazim for many years and had no problems about marrying one. His parents were not particularly happy about the marriage, but he had a brother who had already married an Ashkenazi, so they were coming to accept the idea. Emmanuel Ewenczyk does not recall the marriage presenting any great problem, but Suzy and Lazare remember it very differently.

"It was a big, big problem," Suzy said. "My parents were not at all happy." They did not discuss their unhappiness with her but instead sent friends and Fania's mother, all of whom carried the message, "It's not the same thing when you marry a Sephardi. They are good people and well-educated, but it is just not the same."

In 1958, De Gaulle's Fifth Republic came to power with a new constitution. The minister of culture, André Malraux, a war hero and respected intellectual, began doing what Icchok Finkelsztajn had dreamed of for more than twenty-five years—cleaning the buildings of Paris. Slowly, building by building, Paris brightened into limestone shades of cream and beige. At first it was not even noticeable to Finkelsztajn and the other old guard on Rue des Rosiers, but the new cleaning policy had another side to it that was to profoundly affect the Jews of the Pletzl. Not only were buildings to be cleaned, but the slummy areas in the central eastern part of the city, especially the fourth arrondissement, were to be restored and improved. What Finkelsztajn thought of as the Pletzl, the government called the Marais, the swamp. The area had, in earlier centuries, been a swamp or at least a marshy area along the Seine, providing swans and other wild birds for the feast tables of the aristocrats. But by the sixteenth century the aristocrats had ruined their own game preserve, draining it and building large private homes. The section deteriorated after the revolution, when the aristocracy lost its standing. The rose-garden street became the heart of a crowded immigrant slum.

Now the government wanted to restore the area, buying properties as they became available and renovating them. When a property goes up for sale in Paris, the city has the option of buying at a fair market price. The market price in that part of Paris was very little for a dilapidated sixteenth-century building, and few but the government had the capital to restore such large, ancient properties. Slowly, the city began buying up the Marais. If anybody was thinking about it, they would have known that a Jewish immigrant-based social phenomenon like the Pletzl was not going to be part of the government's urban planning.

The Paris face-lift was a small part of De Gaulle's larger scheme to restore "the glory of France." This was to be accomplished partly by rewriting history, a Gaullist project that began in 1944, when he persuaded the Allies to let him enter Paris and pretend that the French Army had liberated France from the Germans. De Gaulle had argued that France needed to believe this to restore its pride and confidence and achieve stability. Myth-building also required forgetting not only about the Vichy collaboration but about the role of the Resistance in the war. The war between the Resistance and the collaborators had been a civil war between Frenchmen, and the lynching and even the legal trials of collaborators were, in his view, threatening France with a continuing civil war.

According to the De Gaulle version, World War II was much like World War I, and the French in unison had fought and defeated the Germans for the greater glory of all France. He always emphasized the 1918 armistice celebration and played down anniversaries of World War II victories, in which France had played only a minor role. The betrayals of French Jews by their fellow Frenchmen, the history of deportations, the fact that there were French concentration camp survivors—all that was inconvenient for the Gaullist myth.

Nevertheless, De Gaulle did not have particularly bad relations with French Jews. He was remembered as a leader who had worked closely with many Jews in the fight against Pétain. Politicians did not think about "the Jewish vote," which to this day is thought to be an American concept. Even on policy toward Israel, the sentiments of French Jews were not a key factor one way or the other. Mendès-France felt that he had to prove that he did not favor Jews because he was Jewish. De Gaulle had nothing to prove, and Jewish interests were not an issue for him.

As it happened, his relations with Israel greatly pleased French voters, Jews and non-Jews alike. There was probably no foreign leader with whom De Gaulle had a better relationship than David Ben-Gurion. France had hated the British Mandate because it was

British, and from the beginning it had been a strong backer of the State of Israel. De Gaulle continued this policy. In 1961, France provided Israel with sixty-two state-of-the-art jet fighters, the Mirage III, and five years later it provided fifty more. First-class French tanks and helicopters were also furnished. If Israel had a military force that could stand up to the Arab League, it was in part thanks to France. No doubt in De Gaulle's mind, it was entirely thanks to France. The policy made French Jews feel good about their country, but it had the same effect on French non-Jews. France was proud of what it was doing for Israel at a time when France needed to feel proud.

Since De Gaulle's treatment of his own countrymen was marked by almost unbearable paternalism, it is not surprising that he treated poorer, weaker nations the same way. It seemed that since France had supplied the arms, it should be able to tell Israel how to use them. When on May 22, 1967, the Egyptians decided to block the Gulf of Aqaba, De Gaulle and his military advisers determined that this was not a serious threat to Israel. The Israelis, however, saw it as the first step in a joint Arab war against Israel. Rather than wait for what they were certain would be a coordinated military attack, they decided on a preemptive air strike. While Arab leaders were once again talking about the destruction of Israel and the massacre of Israelis, the President of France forbade Israel to go to war and announced an arms embargo to the Middle East. On June 5, when the Israeli air force began to obliterate the Egyptian air force, De Gaulle was furious.

From the perspective of French Jews, a war of extermination against Israel had begun, and France was not only refusing to help, it was embargoing. A fundraising committee quickly formed under the Baron Guy de Rothschild, so quickly that no one stopped to think that French Jews had never launched such an emergency fund drive before. Tightly organized demonstrations were immediately planned. To the Ewenczyks, there was nothing new about demonstrating for Israel, only this time they were really worried. If Israel did not get help quickly, the entire population, they feared, would be massacred. Their daughter Suzy marched with Lazare. Men in the Pletzl got shots and medical certificates and prepared to go fight in Israel. Henri Finkelsztajn marched with his father, Icchok, and with most of the people in the neighborhood. Chaim Rottenberg, the anti-Zionist troublemaker from Antwerp, organized his own Orthodox contingent and marched them to the mass show of support that was building in front of the Israeli embassy. Daniel Altmann, a wealthy seventeen-year-old student with no religious feelings at all, demonstrated and helped with the fundraising drive.

Each group had leaders with portable walkie-talkies to coordinate movements. An estimated 100,000 people brought Paris traffic to a standstill for hours in front of the Israeli embassy. Standing there 100,000 strong, Jews suddenly realized that French Jewry had changed. The North Africans had more than doubled the Jewish population of France to 650,000, almost twice as many Jews as before the war. It had become, after the United States, the Soviet Union, and Israel, the fourth largest Jewish population in the world. And now it was a population that was speaking out.

The Jews may have been surprised by their own numbers and the effectiveness of their organization, but De Gaulle was astounded. Even when Israel triumphed in only six days and most French cheered the Israeli victory, he turned French foreign policy away from Israel. In a November press conference called to explain the new policy, the French president reflected, "Some people even feared that the Jews, hitherto dispersed but remaining what they have always been—an elite people, self-assured and domineering—might, once reassembled on the site of their former grandeur, transform into ardent and conquering ambition the very moving wishes that they had been formulating for nineteen centuries: 'Next year in Jerusalem.'"

Jews reacted with shock and fury to the statement, and that surprised the general too. When Grand Rabbi Jacob Kaplan told him that his statement had been anti-Semitic, De Gaulle seemed baffled, insisting that it was a compliment. Possibly it was. The whole thing resembled a kleptomaniac revealing his suspicions of thieves. De Gaulle himself was elite, self-assured, and domineering. Put in Ben-Gurion's position, he might very well have succumbed to all kinds of ambitions. The notion of a people returning to "former grandeur" was pure Gaullism, a phrase he frequently applied to France. But at that moment a new generation of French Jews changed their mind about their parent's World War II hero, Charles De Gaulle.

Nothing was going to ever be the same again. The Jewish community noticed that they were now sizable and could organize and be heard. The Sephardim had brought a new militancy along with a new population. If nothing else, never again would a deputy be able to stand up in the National Assembly and shout *"Sale Juif"* without hearing a huge outcry in response.

FRANCE'S " '68" had begun. It began in most places in '67 or even a little earlier. It is difficult to understand exactly why, but 1968, like 1848, was a year of spontaneous combustion. The year 1848 had seen similar rebellions for similar reasons in similar countries, but it is more difficult to find a pattern to 1968. In the United States the reason for the rebellion was opposition to the Vietnam War. In Paris and Berlin the Vietnam issue was thrown in as an extra course. French students were tired of the essential myths of Gaullism, a system that had dished out half-truths in the shape of platitudes as their future grew ever more bleak. More than half a million Frenchmen could not find jobs in 1968. Under De Gaulle, these students had seen the economic boom of their childhood slowly evaporate. The Paris movement was loosely related to similar student protests in Berlin and Rome. The Italians started with university issues and ended by protesting the venality of society. In Spain students demonstrated against Franco. The Basques became militant, revived their language, and founded the armed group ETA. In Berlin students started by protesting the way the university was controlled and then moved to protesting the capitalist press monopoly, but ultimately they protested a corrupt German society that could not grasp democracy because it was founded on lies. Young people started asking what their parents had done and what they had not been told in school.

At the same time, Czechs, not just students but government officials, were turning away from the Soviet model, much as the Hungarians had tried to do, and they were realigning Communism with the ideals that had made it attractive in the first place. Polish students, carefully watching Prague, wanted the same.

But all these uprisings had a spontaneous quality, starting with smaller issues and growing to increasingly broad intellectual concepts. Perhaps the one thing they all had in common was that the generation had been raised on a glossy version of the horrors their parents saw. The first nuclear generation, who had spent their childhoods from Budapest to California learning to go into the shelter and cover their heads when the bombs that would destroy the earth were dropped, were coming of age, and they felt that their parents had swallowed too many lies. For young European

Jews, there was another issue: Why had their parents not resisted
the Nazis more? Why had Jewish communities cooperated in deportations? Why, in 1961 at his trial in Jerusalem, was Eichmann,
who negotiated with Jewish leaders for the orderly deportation to
death of their people, able to assert when asked about his conscience that he had never encountered any opposition to what he
was doing?

In Paris many of those who had demonstrated for Israel in 1967
also demonstrated in May 1968. Not coincidentally, many of the
same organizational techniques, such as walkie-talkie communications, were used. Daniel Altmann, after demonstrating for Israel,
had his curiosity piqued enough to spend time on an Israeli kibbutz. But he returned to demonstrate in May. Henri Finkelsztajn,
a thirty-year-old high school dropout, also demonstrated. What had
begun as a demand for coeducational dormitories was now a general protest backed by the major labor unions.

One of the leaders of the student movement was Daniel Cohn-
Bendit, a German Jew whose parents had returned to Frankfurt in
1949. He was called Dany the Red both for his politics and for his
very unsemitic-looking red hair. A kind of folk hero in France, for
years afterward French journalists would look him up in Frankfurt
and ask him how he became a student radical. "What was the
turning point in your life?" asked André Harris and Alain de
Sédouy, the team who had written the celebrated 1970 Max
Ophuls film on French collaboration, *The Sorrow and the Pity*.

"It was the war," said Cohn-Bendit.

"World War II?"

"No, no . . . "

"The Algerian war?"

Finally he had to tell them. It was the Middle East Six-Day War.
The Palestinian cry, "Drive them to the sea" had rallied him too. It
had stuck in his mind. Another thing that stuck in his mind was
something said to him when he was arrested in the police crack-
down in Paris. Taken to one of the infamous French police com-
missariats, a policeman said to him, "You're going to be sorry that
your parents weren't roasted at Auschwitz."

17

West Germany
and the
Promised Land

O NE THING THAT RUWEN WAKS CAME TO UNDERSTAND
growing up in DP camps was that beyond the camp was
Germany, and the people who lived there were Nazis. This was the
general impression of the entire Waks family, and when they
settled in Düsseldorf, their world was to be the 400 to 600 other
Jewish people who had also settled there. They had learned
German, but the first language of the family remained Yiddish. It
was the kind of Jewish life more typical of Jews in their native
Poland than of German Jews.

In the beginning Lea was afraid. She did not want to walk on the
street. They were all Nazis out there. Aaron felt that he knew how
to deal with these Germans. If there was a disagreement—over a
price, over the right of way while turning a corner, anything at
all—he would angrily glare at the German and shout, "You Nazi!"
One day, he had an encounter with a policeman and he called
him a Nazi and angrily walked away. The policeman was stunned.
He had been a small child during the war. Why did this man, who
seemed to be a Jew, a survivor of some kind, think he was a Nazi?
Because the Jews, especially the foreign Jews, were few and stayed
together in Düsseldorf, the policeman was able to find out who
Aaron was and locate his apartment. Once he found Aaron, he
asked him, "Why did you think I was a Nazi?" For the policeman
to live his life as a German of his age, it was essential to understand

why this survivor was accusing him of this terrible thing. They talked, and in time the policeman became a close friend of the Waks family. Then they understood that there was at least one German who was not a Nazi.

Aaron and Lea continued to work with Zionist organizations, and their sons started working with the Zionist Youth Movement. Ruwen and Moishe were sent to school to learn Hebrew in preparation for their move to Israel. As for Łódź or the war or what happened in Poland or what happened to relatives, this remained a mystery to the children. The Waks family shouted about Nazis, but they did not discuss the Holocaust.

Lea's parents continued their nomadic life, now returning to Düsseldorf and then going back to Israel. Then they settled near Düsseldorf, in Dortmund. Then back to Israel. When they were in Israel, they said that life was too hard. When they were in Germany—Germany was German. They moved almost once a year for the remainder of their lives. Lea's mother died in Israel. Her father died in Germany.

The five-year age difference between Ruwen and Moishe reflected the change in West German society. When Ruwen was in school, the East German accusation that West German schools were full of Nazi teachers had been true. Ruwen's history teacher had been a Nazi, but he had been a little Nazi. If he was careful about what he said in class, he could keep his job. And so in the busy year-long curriculum, there simply was never any time to discuss the years 1933 to 1945. When Moishe went to the same school, to his fascination, they studied the Holocaust in detail. He would come home with a torrent of questions. But his parents would not talk about it.

In nearby Cologne, on the day before Christmas in 1959, a monument to the victims of Nazism and a synagogue were marked up with Nazi graffiti, the handiwork of two youthful members of Deutsche Reichspartei, or DRP, a postwar extreme right-wing group. Neither was old enough to have had a real wartime Nazi past, although one had joined a Nazi youth group, Deutsche Jungvolk, just before the end of the war. The two had been school-boy friends and had joined the DRP together the year before the synagogue attack. They later gave as reasons for joining that it was the only party that truly addressed the Jewish question and stood for the ideals of National Socialism. It was Germany's first glimpse of a new generation of Nazis, the neo-Nazis.

The Federal Republic shuddered at the realization that the poison had spread to a new generation. There was even a drop-off in membership in extreme right-wing groups. The DRP was accused of being a resurrection of the old Nazi party. It had to publicly declare itself to be "antifascist," and even that only gave it a temporary reprieve. Eventually it disappeared, only to be re-formed as the Nationaldemokratische Partei Deutschland, the NPD. This game with names was to become part of the standard procedure of neo-Nazi organizations.

All of West Germany was talking about the rebirth of Nazism. It led to a Nazi graffiti crime wave. In the half-year after the first two youths were arrested, 685 cases of anti-Semitic acts were recorded by law enforcement. In school, a fellow student walked up to Ruwen and simply said with no real fervor, "Heil Hitler." Ruwen went home and told his father. Aaron immediately went to the school director. The boy's parents, in a refrain that would become commonplace in the 1990s, said that they could not understand why he had said such a thing. They certainly were not Nazis.

A sullen misfit in Moishe's class also adopted Nazi rhetoric. He became conspicuously anti-Semitic and even turned his exam questions into diatribes against the Jews. But for this he got very poor grades, and while Moishe was well-liked by his classmates, this unhappy colleague was an outcast. He was a curious figure for Moishe because for all he had heard about Germans, this friendless boy was the first openly anti-Semitic German he had ever encountered.

The Jewish community in Düsseldorf grew slowly. Romanian and Hungarian Jews, escaping the problems of their own countries, arrived in small numbers. In Budapest, György Gadó was divorced, and his wife and daughter moved to Düsseldorf. The official Jewish Community was eagerly receiving these new Jews, struggling to build itself up. But the Waks family was actively trying to get Jews to leave. Ruwen and Moishe worked hard for the Zionist Youth Movement. Youth were Israel's future. Too many older people like their grandparents had found Israel to be too difficult a life, but young people could build Israel. Nowhere did Zionists apply more pressure than in Germany, because the idea of Jews staying in Germany was particularly distasteful to them. Yet they were never very successful in Germany. In a good year one or two Jews would move to Israel, but often they would not stay.

Nevertheless, Ruwen and Moishe were trying, and the Community was not happy about their efforts. The Jewish leadership was in
a difficult position, because they did not want to say they were
opposed to Zionism. They simply didn't want people to leave.
Wanting a Jewish community in Düsseldorf does not make you an
anti-Zionist, but it does make you unhappy to see Zionists recruiting people in Düsseldorf.

Throughout West Germany the same tension emerged between
the Zionists and the Community leaders. In Düsseldorf there was
usually no room available at the Jewish Community Center for
Zionist meetings. Ruwen and Moishe would sometimes hold their
meetings in a stairwell. And they had to find their own financing. The Jewish Community had no funding available for Zionist
activities.

Then suddenly in 1967 came a big boost to the Zionist cause —
the Six-Day War. It was more a boost in sympathy than in actual
numbers. Of twenty thousand Jews in West Germany, four hundred were members of the Zionist Youth movement. Only twenty
actually went to Israel at the time of the war, and most of those did
not stay. Yet it was a record year for German Zionism. Ruwen
volunteered and stayed permanently in Israel. His parents had to
sign papers to give him permission. Moishe was too young to go.
Aaron could not even attempt to conceal his pride in his son who
had volunteered for Israel. Lea jutted her jaw and wore a stiff face
of approval as she sent her son off to a faraway war. She wasn't
supposed to think of it that way. She had raised her sons to speak
Hebrew and be Israeli. She had no choice but to approve of what
Ruwen was doing.

The war turned out to last only a matter of days, but Ruwen was
sent to work on a kibbutz run by the German Zionist movement
near the Lebanese border. After two months he returned to Düsseldorf, a hero in the Jewish Community, no longer confined to stair-
wells, giving talks about his experiences in the city's major halls
and meeting places to Jews and non-Jews. After several months, he
returned to Israel, and soon he was running into many of his
friends from Germany who had also decided to emigrate. But time
passes swiftly in Israel, and to Israelis the war was already long over
by then. The Germans lost their sense of purpose and, a few at a
time, went back to Germany. Only Ruwen stayed to make his life
as an Israeli. He married Carmela, an Iraqi Jew who had lived in
Israel since she was a small child.

Aaron and Lea may have had their hearts in Israel, but their pants store was in Düsseldorf. Every year, while they preached Zionism, their lives became more deeply entrenched in West Germany and the German economic miracle. The store was prospering, and they had a large apartment on a wide rebuilt boulevard near the center of the city, not far from the birthplace of Heinrich Heine, the Jewish poet who a century earlier had written passionate verses of his love for Germany.

And others, like Lea's parents, were returning from Israel. One German Jewish family that had lived in Israel since Hitler came to power moved to Düsseldorf over the sad protests of their two Israeli-born children. In Tel Aviv this family of four had lived in one room of a four-room, four-family house with a common kitchen and bathroom. Educated people, the father worked small teaching jobs and his wife was a maid. In 1953 they were evicted from the house and were about to move to a distant housing project in a slum. Instead, to their children's great chagrin, they moved to Düsseldorf, where he worked as an editor on the Jewish newspaper and lived in an apartment in the center of town. He had a love of the language and culture, and in truth it was the country where he was most at home. Still, no one in this family loved Germany the way Heine had. They loved German literature and no doubt knew Heine's famous verse, *"O Deutschland, meine ferne Liebe,"* but to them, for the past twenty years in exile, Germany had been not a far-off love but a horror they had escaped. Now it was simply a place where they could have a good job and a decent apartment. Israel had not offered that.

DÜSSELDORF, like all West German cities, was being rebuilt with a modern opulence it had never before seen. Within walking distance from the Wakses' was the Königsallee, where trees were planted and rococo bridges built over a little dark canal. Both sides were lined with cafés and shops, where enormous quantities of money could be spent on anything with a label on it. Nothing creative or original was being offered, only status name brands, so that West Germans could spend their money and display their wealth.

West Germans embraced materialism with the same set-jawed determination with which they had done everything else. The people who, when blockaded from munitions in World War I, had made their own by learning how to extract nitrogen from the air, were now focusing their ingenuity on becoming rich. Economic growth became the all-important measure between the two Germanies. West Germany had it, and East Germany didn't. West German growth was so rapid that in the early 1960s there was a labor shortage—a need for foreign laborers, guest workers to live in Germany without citizenship and do the work that Germany needed done. These growth figures were a point of national pride for the West. Every sign of prosperity was an important benchmark. Germany had been mired for too long in ideologies. The East Germans were still stuck in one. But West Germany would be the successful new Germany, a land of material wealth. As the ruined cities were rebuilt, each one had a boulevard like the Königsallee, the most important being the Ku'damm, because it was in West Berlin, the ultimate display case of the Federal Republic deep inside the GDR.

Protz is a German word for showiness, too many gold rings, flaunted wealth. The Israeli-born daughter of the man who took the newspaper job in Düsseldorf concluded after years of reflection that it was this flirtation with gaudiness, the *Protz,* that seduced. It was a dramatic contrast to the harsh life in Israel. It kept bringing German Jews back, and it held them there. Aaron and Lea Waks would go to Israel someday, but for now they had the trouser business, just as for Ron Zuriel his law practice was keeping him in Berlin.

But the Wakses and the Zuriels had distanced themselves from the fact that they were in Germany by not associating with non-Jews, by preserving their stern and critical distance from "the Germans." When student demonstrations began erupting in Berlin in 1968, Ron Zuriel found it an encouraging sign. Here was a truly new generation of Germans rejecting their parents' world. "They actually revolted against the attitude of their parents . . . they were rejecting everything institutional," he said. This was a German movement of which he could approve. They were saying the same things about Germany that he had been saying. He even began to hope that new Germans were being made who could construct a new Germany.

But if the 1968 demonstrations reassured Ron Zuriel because a new generation was rejecting their parents, they also showed that all was not well in the new German shopping paradise. In June 1967 demonstrators had greeted Willy Brandt and the Shah of Iran in

Berlin, and while they were in the opera house listening to Mozart, police attacked the student demonstrators outside, killing one. In April 1968 two Frankfurt department stores were burned, and a week later a leader of the student movement was shot by a psychopath, who hanged himself. The incident led to a week of rioting in Berlin and around West Germany in which two were killed and four hundred wounded. The new, nonideological consumer society was turning out to be an angry and violent place after all.

MOISHE WAKS, five years younger than his brother, had to wait six years before he too could move to Israel. When he finally did, he found himself feeling a bit alone in a strange land. He had Ruwen and Carmela, and a friend of Carmela's family whom Moishe had met in Germany became his only friend. He played soccer well, and that gave him an activity. It was a beginning.

Ruwen seemed very nervous during the holidays that year. As Yom Kippur approached, he warned Moishe not to go anywhere by car, saying, "They will kill you." Moishe did not know what to think about that—the presumably Arab "they" was not explained. That evening, from his apartment near the university, he could see an almost infinite line of buses speeding by. But he had no telephone and lived alone, and he had no way of finding out what the buses might mean. The next day, Yom Kippur, he was tired of being alone and decided to visit some friends from Germany who were staying at a nearby hotel.

Moishe drove to the hotel without incident. Surely his brother was overreacting, he thought, and had been needlessly worried. Nobody seemed to be out killing anyone. He spent the day with his friends, and only when his brother, who had been frantically looking for him, finally found him, did Moishe understand that a war, the Yom Kippur War, had begun. There was no soccer, nothing for him to do, and he went to a kibbutz to replace someone who was fighting. His only friend was killed in the war. Moishe began to understand what his grandparents had always told him: Life was very hard in Israel.

18

===

Passing
in Warsaw

T HE LATE 1960S WOULD HAVE BEEN A GOOD TIME FOR
Jews in Poland to have had amnesia. But as perverse fate
had it, it was at this time that memory started returning. In 1965,
Marian Turski accidentally discovered his loss of memory at the
twentieth anniversary of the liberation of Theresienstadt, where he
was talking with a well-known Polish Jewish figure with whom he
had been in the camps. The man started reminiscing about the
time Turski had saved his life.

"I saved your life?" asked a perplexed Turski.

"On the death march! Remember?"

Turski tried to look into his own memory, but he had no idea
what this man was referring to. "Tell me about it," he said, and he
questioned the man for more and more details. Then he realized
that he remembered almost nothing of his experiences in Auschwitz, Buchenwald, Theresienstadt, and the murderous marches to
them. He began reading books about the Holocaust. Until then,
accidentally scanning the cover of such a book in his peripheral
vision had been a disturbing experience. Now he was soaking them
up with a hunger that was like the end of hibernation. He also read
books about Judaism. He spent his time thinking about his experiences and the collective Jewish experience. The following year, he
visited Auschwitz, officially "the place of martyrdom of Polish
nations and other nations." He rummaged through barracks and

visited the subcamp where he had been held. Facing the horror of it was a price he could pay to get back his memory. It was the beginning of what Turski was to call his "comeback."

This was a time when Poles were also thinking more about Jews, which is generally not a good thing in Poland. For all its impact on Western European Jews, the Six-Day War affected Jewish lives in the Soviet bloc even more profoundly. The Soviet Union had reversed its Middle East policy twelve years earlier, when the British had tried to forcibly prevent Egypt's Gamal Abdul Nasser from nationalizing the Suez Canal. By the time of the Six-Day War, the Soviet bloc was firmly on the Arab side, supplying and training Arab armies. To the Poles, the spectacle of Soviet-trained armies being routed in less than a week by a bunch of Jews brought glee and pleasure to an increasingly anti-Soviet people. *"Jojne poszedł na wojnę,"* the Poles snickered—"Jojne went to war," the phrase being cute in Polish because the first and last words rhyme.

Jojne is Polish slang, the anti-Semitic stereotype of the cowardly Jew who can't and won't fight. But finally the *Jojne* had fought, and they won in six days, defeating all those armies so carefully trained and equipped by the Soviets. It was a wonderful joke. Some Poles, even though they never called a Jew a Pole, started taking pride in the Polishness of Israelis. After all, a large part of the Israeli population had been born in Poland. And many of the most warlike Israelis—the organizers of the Haganah, for example—came out of Jewish defense movements in Poland. Was the Six-Day War not in some way a victory of Poles over Soviets? Marian Turski, who was traveling around Poland for his newspaper, constantly encountered such contorted observations.

But party boss Gomułka was not amused. Though he was a Polish nationalist who had fought many political battles with Moscow, the intensity of anti-Soviet feelings in Poland troubled him. He worried about what would happen if war broke out with the West. And, of course, Moscow was even less amused than Gomułka. According to Turski's sources from the period, Gomułka attended a secret meeting in Moscow in which it was decided that something had to be done about the Polish attitude.

WHILE IT WAS TRUE that there were many Polish-born Israelis, Jews were getting to be rare in Poland. After the upheaval of 1956, about half of the remaining Jews had left. Available figures are imprecise, but at most there were between 25,000 and 35,000 Jews left. Everyone had their own count because divining who was or was not a Jew had become an arcane Polish hobby.

No one would have counted the Gruberskis, for example, who lived in Sochaczew, a town near Warsaw. They were Polish Communist atheists, although on occasion they sent their fourteen-year-old daughter Barbara to mass. She wasn't baptized; nor was she encouraged to believe. Barbara was stubborn and different and a little difficult, and other children didn't like her. They would call her that standard Polish curse, "Żyd," Jew. Sometimes they would call her Dreyfus or Beilis, after Mendel Beilis, who had been accused of ritual murder in Kiev early in the century. They would deliberately stretch out and distort vowels to make these names sound especially heinous.

Barbara didn't know who Beilis or Dreyfus had been, and she didn't really know what a Jew was. When she asked her parents why the other children called her Jew, they explained that it was because she was adopted. Many people her age were adopted, including a girl in the next house. But nobody called that girl "Żyd." Her mother explained that it was her dark thick hair. Her mother also had dark thick hair, but she was not called a Jew, perhaps because she had light blue Polish eyes. Barbara had dark eyes.

Finally, in 1958, when Barbara was 16, her mother decided to tell her the truth. Barbara had been born in the Warsaw ghetto. Her real parents may have been from the nearby town of Lovice, but that was not certain. Her mother may have been the daughter of a doctor. In any case, they were Jews and had some money, and they had been trapped in the ghetto and desperate. A contract was drawn up in which they paid Polish people to take care of their baby daughter, Barbara. In addition to the monthly payments, a substantial settlement would be made after the war if the parents survived and took back the child. Three months were paid in advance, but after the three months there were no more payments, and the Polish foster parents had lost interest in caring for the child. When the Gruberskis first saw her at the foster parents' home, she was starving. They offered the seven-month-old baby a piece of bread, and she hungrily ate it. Childless, the Gruberskis happily adopted her and had a new birth certificate drawn up.

Even more shocking for Barbara was the news that the original foster parents were people she knew—the Kwiatkowskis, who rented an apartment from the Gruberskis in the neighborhood. Kazimiera Kwiatkowska was a first cousin of Barbara's adopted mother. They often visited and had four children with whom Barbara would play.

At first, Barbara was not certain how she felt about all this. She kept thinking about the fact that the Kwiatkowskis, who she still saw regularly, probably still had the contract, something from her real mother. It would probably have her mother's signature on it. She decided to confront them, a reckoning, a showdown. Once faced with the embarrassing news that Barbara knew the truth, the Kwiatkowskis were willing to talk to her about it. But they did not want to give her the contract. "It was written by my mother, and I want to have it," Barbara argued. She had a way of setting her jaw and turning her eyes into cold shining dark stones. Realizing that she would never relent, they gave it to her.

According to the document, Barbara had been turned over for 700 złotys per month, with three months to be paid in advance. In 1942 this had been a substantial payment, far more than care for a baby would cost. But, of course, the foster parents were taking a risk, for which they had to be paid. If they were caught hiding a Jewish baby, the entire family would be shot. The baby was young enough that there was no reason to suspect it wasn't theirs. As the Kwiatkowskis told Barbara, nobody in the neighborhood would have turned them in, because they were all involved in black market meat for sausages—the Kwiatkowskis stored the meat. One raid on their home, and the whole neighborhood would have been in trouble. For years afterward, Barbara liked to tell people, "If I am alive today, it's only because of all the kielbasa the Poles eat."

Barbara took the contract home with her, but could not leave it in a drawer. Whenever she was home, she had to take it out and look at it. The paper was signed *Karolina Leboida*. That signature was the only trace of her real mother—just the signature, not the name itself. It was a Polish name, because her parents had tried to survive outside the ghetto by taking other names, just as Barbara (Irene Hochberg) Góra had done. But the name *Leboida* hadn't worked like *Góra*, and they were rounded up and put in the ghetto.

Who were they? What was her mother's real name? What was she like? Barbara Gruberska asked herself these things. Then she started asking, "And who am I? What is my real name?" She went back to the Kwiatkowskis for more information, but they had no more to tell. She took the signature to a handwriting analyst who compared the signature *Karolina Leboida* and with Barbara's own. The handwriting expert told her that Karolina Leboida was extremely intelligent, fearless, and well organized. Analyzing Barbara's signature, he concluded that these two people would not get along well.

Barbara decided that she would be best off, after all, as Barbara Gruberska, Polish Catholic Communist. She tried to be even more Catholic than her upbringing. But even with regular church attendance, she was not completely safe. At a youth camp in Bulgaria a Russian boy said to her, "You have Jewish hair." she became furious and repeatedly denied that her hair was Jewish. She went to Moscow, and a man on a subway platform asked her where she was from. When she told him she was from Poland, he said, "Ah, a Jew from Poland." And once in Wrocław, on a tram, a man made his way toward her. She looked at him and knew he was Jewish. "So when are you moving to Israel?" the man said. Once again, Barbara became furious. "What are you talking about? Going to Israel! Me go to Israel? As a matter of fact, I am on my way to mass right now!"

EVEN BARBARA GÓRA, with years of practice, could not always pass. When she finished studying agriculture, she moved to a small Silesian village, Stare Olesno, where she worked on a state-run experiment developing a new breed of potato. That was the system: Take a bright young Pole and invest years in training her to be an agronomist—only to bring more potatoes to Poland.

Even though she was a party member, she did not have the usual tensions with the peasants, and she also got along well with the other scientists. She found that the Silesians, for all their German language and culture, were not anti-Semitic. But like other Poles, they had a knack for spotting a Jew when they saw one. Although nobody ever said that she was Jewish, things were often said that made her realize that everyone simply assumed that she was. One of the workers confessed that he had worked with the German Army and then asked, "How did you survive?" The name Góra didn't seem to be fooling Poles anymore. She would look in the mirror at her same light hair and reasonably broad features and wonder if somehow as you get older, the face changes and becomes more Semitic.

In 1965, Barbara Góra went to Israel. She had relatives to see and the opportunity to travel. To get the travel permission she had to say that she wanted to go to Israel to visit family, which was a great deal more than she customarily said about her background. And she was saying it on official documents. Traveling by Polish freighter, she first arrived at the port of Tel Aviv. As the freighter glided into this modern harbor, a Polish crewman explained to her the harbor's layout, how well organized and modern and efficient it was.

Funny. Just an odd feeling. On reflection, Barbara Góra realized that for the first time in her life, for just a moment, she had felt proud to be Jewish. Here was this Pole. He was not telling her about the dirty Jew. The Jew who produces nothing. He was admiring the efficient work of these Jews.

Her father's sister, whom Barbara's father had also saved, was among the Jews who had left Poland in 1956 with her entire family, and Barbara went to visit them in a small town near Tel Aviv, where she stayed for seven weeks. She also visited her mother's sister, who had emigrated to Palestine before the war and had eight children. Then she returned to Poland as she had left, Barbara Góra, Polish agronomist.

WHEN JAKUB GUTENBAUM RETURNED from Moscow in 1955 — after the "doctors' plot" and the death of Stalin, he had completed his scholarship — he could find almost nothing that looked familiar. The city of rubble had been replaced by a city of massive blocks, unidentifiable rooftop statues eerily watching, and towers with neoclassical details that looked as if they had been stuck on later with glue.

It was a good time for Gutenbaum. Nobody seemed to particularly care that he was Jewish. He got a doctorate and a second doctorate and worked on research at the Polish Academy of Sciences. He lived in an elite Polish world. He married a Pole in 1960, and he worked with Polish scientists. No one ever made an issue of his Jewishness.

In the meantime an entire new postwar generation was growing up, learning of their Jewish background only on a need-to-know basis. The previous generation had tried to save their children this way. The less the child knew, the less danger for everybody. After the war it was as the Lippners had told their sons about Hungary; being Jewish could be dangerous. Since the families were not practicing Judaism, there was no need to discuss the subject unless the child was taunted and needed to know why. Some children were told because they were picking up Polish anti-Semitism. When children who spent their childhood going to church came home repeating anti-Semitic words they heard in school, they were told, "You are a Jew, I am, your father is, our whole family is." Then the child had to be told what a Jew was.

Some children were told by dying parents who felt obligated at the last moment to let the children know. But other parents never told their children. In truth, even today it is impossible to say how many people of Jewish origin live in Poland.

The postwar generation was too young to remember the violence of the late 1940s. They had grown up in the 1950s, when people were arrested for anti-Semitic outbursts. It was a Poland in which the entire subject of Jews was taboo. The Jews didn't want to talk about it, and the anti-Semites did not dare. When Gomułka returned to power, there was a widespread belief that Jewish issues would be laid to rest. He was not considered an anti-Semite. He was even married to a Jew, although Jews later quipped that it was his horrible wife that had turned him anti-Semitic.

A power struggle bubbled up in the slow-simmering way that happens in countries that do not replace their leaders through elections. General Miczlyslaw Moczar was trying to position himself to overtake Gomułka. In Poland, Jew-hating is always an available card that can be played. In 1966, Moczar established a "Jewish department" to look into the suspicious past of Jews. Moczar thought anti-Semitism would play well with another longstanding Polish sentiment, anti-Germanism. After the Six-Day War, Gomułka came under intense pressure to go along with Moczar. A new version of Polish history was floated in which the Poles had tried to help the Jews during the Holocaust, but the Jews had destroyed themselves by their own cooperation with the Germans. The Jews were foreign sympathizers.

Moczar began a purge of Jews in the echelons of the party and the army. In June 1967, Gomułka gave a speech about "fifth columnists" to a trade union congress, which was seen as a signal of approval for Moczar's purge. Most of this maneuvering was barely perceptible to the general population until the student movement of 1968. A production of Adam Mickiewicz's popular nineteenth-century drama, *Dziady*, or *Forefather's Eve*, was forced to close by the government. This in itself was a strange move, since the play, though nationalist in theme, was an established classic of Polish literature. But the Polish regime was nervously watching a reform movement led by Alexander Dubček in Czechoslovakia that they did not want to see spread to Poland. There was a student slogan in 1968: "All of Poland is waiting for Dubček." In March 1968, Warsaw students demonstrated against the closing of the play. Two student leaders were arrested, and students started demonstrating against the arrests as well as for freedom from censorship.

Joanna Wiszniewicz was a Warsaw student at the time. She knew that the government would have to react to the demonstration. She didn't know what they would do, but she felt that she had to demonstrate. She couldn't act afraid. What could they do? "I felt safe in this country with its socialist ideals." The first shock came when she found herself with hundreds of others fleeing from policemen who were mowing through the demonstrators with clubs. A bigger shock came two days later, when she bought a newspaper and read that the entire protest had been carried out by Jews.

This was astounding. She didn't recall anything ever being said about Jews. She was Jewish, though she only learned that when she was ten years old, and she had never even been to a synagogue. Suddenly, Zionists were supposedly everywhere, and the newspapers were full of warnings. Comic slogans were being used with deadly seriousness. She read phrases such as "Moishe, go to Israel!" and "Zionists, go to Dayan!" Now Jews were being expelled not only from the party but from their jobs and even schools. Well-established careers ended abruptly, with a quick message that their services were no longer needed.

Konstanty Gebert was 15 when he was expelled from his school as a "political security risk." His father was an old-time Communist labor organizer in Detroit who had been one of the founders of the Communist Party of America and had returned to Poland after the war. Konstanty had grown up in elite circles and lived much of his childhood abroad while his father served in diplomatic posts. His mother was Jewish. By escaping to the Soviet Union, she became one of four people in her family to survive the war. His parents had met through their common Communist ideology, and that was the family religion. Then suddenly, at the age of 15, Konstanty's long, sixties-style hair was clipped off in front of the school with the pronouncement, "This is not a Jewish school. We don't wear long hair." A yellow star of David was painted on his desk. It was all so silly, he thought, the way grown-ups acted. He couldn't believe this was all happening.

Even grown-ups could see this purge was not without its comic aspects. An insignificant factory engineer with a Jewish name was dismissed as a Zionist. He went to the government with his World War II Latvian certificate, which had established to Nazi satisfaction that he was of good "Aryan" stock. The government apologized and reinstated him.

It was both a thrilling and confusing time for a fifteen-year-old boy. Once Konstanty was thrown out of school, he was free to demonstrate. Coming home from his first demonstration, although he arrived home three hours late, he felt triumphant. This was a Communist household, and he had been on the streets fighting the cops for freedom and equality. Breathlessly, he told his father, the veteran Detroit organizer, about his day. Now he, too, had a story like his father's stories, and his father would be proud. But instead, his father was angry and made him stay in the house for three days. The old veteran was also a father and did not want his son to be beaten up on the street.

Then something even more confusing happened. Konstanty was walking in his neighborhood, not far from the Polonia Hotel, in an area where enough had survived and been rebuilt to vaguely suggest old Warsaw and conceal the steel and glass giants only a block or two away. Two men grabbed him and slapped him in the face while calling him "dirty kike." Afterward, he rubbed his sore face and wondered who he was to be so abused, to be called a dirty kike and be hit.

The older generation was frightened by the Polish regime's purge of the alleged Zionist German conspiracy. Barbara Góra read the newspapers and felt as if she were back in the Nazi occupation. She started finding out who among her friends were Jewish: They were the ones who were suddenly losing their jobs. The state scientific publishing house where she now worked on an agricultural newsletter dismissed all of its Jewish employees. They were Zionists and could not be trusted. For the moment she was still untouched, but all of the party members where she worked—and she was a party member—were asked to sign a resolution against Zionism. The publisher was told to draw up the resolution. Scared and uncertain of what to do, he wrote a simple statement, "Down with Zionism." The statement was passed around at a special meeting, awaiting the signatures of all who hoped to keep their jobs. But Barbara Góra's supervisor handed the paper back to the publisher and said, "This is not necessary. It's completely irrelevant, because we don't have any Zionists here." A few days later, the same supervisor ran across an editor he knew who had been fired from the state publishing house. The supervisor hired him for his publication.

There were many such acts of defiance. They were sometimes less a reflection of sympathy for Jews than of opposition to the government. It was the beginning of an antigovernment coalition that would bring together many diverse groups, including Jews and the Catholic Church. The legal press was state-controlled and dutifully ran the anti-Semitic diatribes handed out by the government. But two weeklies refused to cooperate and instead tried to report on what was really happening. One was a small Catholic weekly called *Tygodnik Powszechny*, and the other was *Polityka*, where Marian Turski had made his career.

Turski was to look back on 1968 as one of the best years of his life. It was a sad year in which many of his friends' lives were uprooted, but the atmosphere at *Polityka* inspired him. No one there cared who was Jewish. It was simply a newspaper working against the lies of the state. It was a Communist newspaper practicing adversarial journalism. The other newspapers ran daily attacks on *Polityka*, calling it the voice of the new money class. But those who worked at *Polityka* were party members, Jews and non-Jews, comrades taking a stand together. It felt like Communism was supposed to be. The paper was run by Mieczysław Rakowski, who years later would move on to the dubious perch of being the last head of the ruling Polish Communist party. Every day, the *Polityka* staff would go to work wondering what was going to happen to them. But they always felt good about what they were doing. Marian came home at night and with great excitement told his wife, "Tomorrow or maybe the day after tomorrow, we will all be dismissed. I think I will drive a taxi. I have a car and there are not that many cars in Warsaw, so I think I will be able to do all right as a taxi driver."

Jews were being offered one way out: They could forfeit their homes and whatever property they might have and emigrate to Israel. Only Jews were allowed to emigrate, and Israel was the only acceptable destination. Most of the Turskis' closest friends left. Marian had an offer at the University of Denver. He and his wife had visited and loved the Rocky Mountains. They reasoned that his wife, as a well-established engineer, could find work, and between their two careers it seemed they would live well. To exit for Israel and then change destinations once they were in Vienna was a common tactic. But there was a problem: Turski was working with non-Jews who were risking everything to stand up to this smear campaign. They could have gone along with it, like the other newspapers, and Jews like Turski would have been dismissed, but nothing would have happened to them. Now they had risked everything, and yet if *Polityka* were closed down, the Jews could leave but the non-Jews would have no escape. They had been loyal to him, and now he would be loyal to them. Once again Turski decided he would stay in Poland.

Jakub Gutenbaum didn't emigrate either. While he was never a party member, he did believe that Communism stood for some ideals, and this anti-Zionist campaign was a complete contradiction of those ideals. But he could not imagine what he would do in Israel. "'I would be a foreigner there," he thought. And his wife and child were not Jewish.

In 1968 the Kameraz family was through with Poland. Their Jewish building was no longer Jewish. The synagogue in the courtyard had been torn down and was now a playground. The *mikveh* next to it was no longer used, and the Jewish school was now a movie theater. Ninel's sister and her husband were both dismissed from their jobs, and they left Poland with their three children, as did most of their friends and neighbors. Their mother had died, and their father was ill and depressed. He wanted to emigrate but was too weak and soon he too died. It seemed to Ninel that everyone was leaving. Even her Jewish assistant at work was dismissed and left. In the mysterious ways of Polish Communism, no one ever bothered Ninel. She kept her job as an electrical engineer. But she too wanted to leave.

Ninel had been married since 1956 to a non-Jew. Since their marriage he had become fascinated with Jewish culture. Abandoning his physics career, he now taught Yiddish and the Kabbalah to Poles. When Ninel approached him about emigrating, he would say, "I'm a Pole!" He would talk about their good life and the literature and film projects with which he was involved.

From Ninel's senior class in high school, which had been three-quarters Jewish, only two Jews remained in Poland—Ninel, and a very disturbed schizophrenic who was under treatment.

HAVING ALREADY BEEN to Israel, Barbara Góra was certain that she did not want to live there, even though one of her closest friends emigrated there and two others moved to the United States. Although she decided to stay in Warsaw, her attitude about the city and Poland generally had changed. After seeing the Holocaust and the subsequent waves of survivors driven out every ten years, she finally reached the conclusion that somebody should stay in Poland and say, I am a Jew and I am still here. "If they don't want me, they have to have me," she declared. "If they don't want Jews, then I should be here."

This idea came to her on a spring afternoon as she sat in her living room with three non-Jewish friends reading in the newspaper about how the student demonstrations had been organized by the Zionists. One of her friends, a longtime Communist party member, said that they had managed to arrest a number of students and had singled out the Jews among them. The newspapers did not give their names, but she had contacts and she knew who was arrested. Many, like Barbara Góra, had Polish names. And yet, her friend had said, they knew. They knew who the Jews were. How did they know?

And Barbara Góra, without a moment's reflection, said, "Well, I'll tell you something. I am a Jew."

Her friends reacted as though she had just said her hair color wasn't natural. It was of no great importance. But Barbara suddenly realized what she had done. She had just said publicly, "I am a Jew"—and nothing had happened. And she didn't think anything was about to happen. For the first time in twenty-six years, ever since she had presented a piece of paper bearing her new name to a German guard and walked out of the Warsaw ghetto, Barbara had volunteered to non-Jewish people, "I am a Jew."

She stayed in Poland. She did not change her name. She did not take up the Jewish religion, but every now and then she would tell someone, "I am a Jew." Next time Poland had one of its bouts of Jew-hating, she resolved, she would still be there, and she would still say it. "Where they beat Jews, you have to be a little Jewish," she decided. In Paris, students were demonstrating with signs saying, "We are all German Jews." Why shouldn't she say "I am a Polish Jew"? It was time to say that in Poland. Except that nobody ever says "Polish Jew" in Poland. You are either a Pole or a Jew.

Even Barbara Góra's mother, who had spent her life so afraid of her Jewishness, finally got angry in 1968. When she went to a newsstand to read the latest anti-Semitic slurs, the woman in the stand looked at her and, just as she had always feared, pointed to her and said, "You are a Jew!"

Góra's mother glared back and said, "Yes, and you are a Nazi!" and walked away.

The Jews of the university in Warsaw, the '68 generation, left. Joanna Wiszniewicz was one of the few who remained, lonely without her friends from the momentous university days. But they could never come back to Poland for a visit. She arranged to meet friends who had gone to Israel in places in Hungary and Romania in the next few years, but she had in fact lost her friends. Many Jews discovered that their friends were Jewish only when they saw them all leave.

Joanna stayed, because her field of study was Polish culture and she would have nothing to do if she left Poland. "It's not patriotism," she said. "It's a lack of imagination."

BARBARA GRUBERSKA became a doctor of internal medicine, just as she had learned her mother's father had been. Though she married a non-Jew, she decided to stop hiding her true identity. Her husband, an electrical engineer, was a third-generation Communist who hated the Catholic Church and had many Jewish friends. Unfortunately, the year she decided to become openly Jewish and even become involved in community affairs in Warsaw was 1968. In that year Jewish life virtually shut down. There were no longer even religious services available, or places to learn about Jewish practices. She decided that she would do what every Jew she knew was doing: she went to the ministry to apply for permission to emigrate to Israel. The government demanded proof of her Jewishness. She had none—neither parents nor ties to the Jewish community. Her application was denied.

Two years later, Kazimiera Kwiatkowska, who had taken 700 złotys a month to care for her, was dying and asked to see Barbara, who came to her bedside. Barbara pleaded with her, "There must be something more you know about my mother."

Kazimiera Kwiatkowska, lying in her deathbed, admitted that she had met her mother once. She had come to sign the contract with a bribed German policewoman and another woman whose business was brokering such contracts. She had come holding

Barbara on a pillow, saying she had to leave the country and wanted someone to take the baby for a time.

"What did she look like?" Barbara Gruberska wanted to know.

Kazimiera said she was very thin, dirty, and dressed in rags. "She was more like an animal than a human being." The woman had stayed the night in Kazimiera's home, just sitting on a chair, crying until morning light.

19

Czechoslovakian Summer

THE EVENTS OF 1968, FOR A FEW EXCITING MONTHS, caused the name of Victory Street in Brno to be changed once again back to Masaryk Street.

The Czechoslovakian economy, which was supposed to be the best in the Soviet bloc, had been failing. Economic reform was halfhearted and unsuccessful, and in search of change the conservative leadership was removed and the party put in the hands of Slovak party chief Alexander Dubček. In a quip borrowed from Bertolt Brecht after the 1953 GDR uprising, the new party leader said, "We couldn't change the people, so we changed the leaders." Dubček was a courageous man whose destiny it was not to be thanked by history. He was a Communist who tried to save Communism in a country where the ideology had once been broadly popular. Taking a slogan from Hungary in 1956, he called for "Communism with a human face." The mistakes of the Hungarian movement were not repeated. There was no demand for an independent foreign policy, but instead, Dubček gave repeated assurances that Czechoslovakia was a loyal member of the Soviet bloc and a firm participant in the Warsaw Pact. Dubček even made clear that he wanted to continue one-party Communist rule. In the end, the results were no different than in Hungary. Communism may have been capable of a human face, but Soviet power wasn't.

Dubček offered a Communism that might have taken hold with

Czechs and perhaps East Germans and Hungarians and possibly even with Poles. That was what the Soviets feared. Dubček seriously pursued things that in the past had only been proclaimed in speeches, such as economic reform based on decentralization, destalinization to remove the infamous monsters from the power structure, and liberalization, which included free speech, a critical and uncensored press, and freedom to travel abroad.

For the few thousand Jews who were left in Czechoslovakia, Dubček was a reprieve. The exact number of Jews is uncertain, because after the Slansky trial in 1952 the majority of Jews who stayed did not openly show their Jewishness. The fifteen thousand Prague Jews who were registered with the official Jewish Community were thought to constitute only a third of the Jews in Prague. "Anti-Zionist" persecution had considerably eased since the years immediately after the Slansky trial, but after the Six-Day War, the press once again felt moved to run a steady diet of anti-Zionist opinion. "Spontaneous" anti-Zionist demonstrations were organized. Jewish Community plans for a celebration of one thousand years of Prague Jewry were canceled.

The politically astute saw that the anti-Zionist campaign was simply a desperate attempt by the ruling conservatives to outmaneuver Dubček and his emerging reformers. Most Jews were not aware of this. They only knew that words like *cosmopolitans* and *Zionists* were showing up in the newspapers. But once Dubček gained control, everything changed. Foreign travel, religious activities, and open criticism of government policies were suddenly commonplace. People who had never been political in their lives were drawn in by the excitement. Karol Wassermann, who had limited most of his conversations to antiques and art history, was talking about political reform in the pharmacy where he still worked. He had completed his studies in art history at the university up to the doctorate level. Just as he was starting to write his doctoral dissertation, he was informed that "the proletariat will not finance two degrees." He was already a pharmacist, and he would not be given an art history doctorate.

So art history remained his hobby. Among his other new interests was theater. He regularly attended rehearsals of new plays. Although he had always avoided politics before, he now became fascinated by the young absurdist movement in theater, which was clearly political. He was particularly enamored of the young playwright Václav Havel. Wassermann also studied at the state-operated

Jewish Museum. When the Nazis had occupied Prague, they developed a ghoulish obsession with the Jewish Museum. They selected a team of Jewish experts to carefully catalogue all the antique Judaica that was found in the homes of Jews who were deported to the camps. Reinhard Heydrich, the Nazi who established the first ghetto and was the first concentration camp administrator, wanted to create in Prague a definitive collection of relics from what he hoped would soon be an extinguished culture. The Jews who were made to work on this project painstakingly catalogued each article, because they thought the Jews would come back and their property could be returned. Most never came back, and the collection ended up in the hands of the Communist state.

Bedřich Nosek's son, also named Bedřich, became a historian for the museum. As an undergraduate at Prague's Charles University, he studied Czech history. Then he discovered, to his amazement, that a Hebrew course was offered in the state-run modern language school. Even more surprising, the course had been taught for years by an Israeli woman who was married to a Czech. She had been dismissed from the university at the time of the Slansky trial, but when the anti-Zionist campaign cooled off, she was able to start a course at the modern language school. An even greater stroke of luck was the fact that the Jewish Museum needed a new historian, and just as Nosek had completed his undergraduate work in Czech history, the university opened up its graduate program in Jewish studies—an opportunity that was offered about once a decade—to a candidate with a history degree. There were three students and four professors. None of them were Jewish. One of the professors had studied at the museum in the late 1940s under the last surviving Jewish expert on Judaica.

In Prague, Brno, and Bratislava, the Dubček era was a time when the postwar generation of Jews started to openly express their Jewishness. Synagogue attendance increased, and social meetings and community functions became regular events. The head Czech rabbi, Richard Feter, who lived in Brno, had been quietly giving instruction to Jews on request. But now he could run a full-scale Jewish Community, even if it was only for a few hundred. He gave open lectures on Judaism and supervised community celebrations of Jewish holidays. For the first time in their lives, a new generation of Jews experienced Judaism as a living culture, and they participated excitedly, forming a range of youth groups with meetings, discussions, and social events. In 1968 Prague, suddenly the

eighteenth-century Jewish town hall, the rococo building on Maislova Street next to the Old-New Synagogue, was a lively place with
young people rushing up and down the dark wood stairways. Bratislava had its own rabbi and a Jewish youth group that more than
fifty people attended every week. Being Jewish was now something
more than becoming worried when you read the newspaper.

ZUZANA SKÁLOVÁ was seven years old, and her sister Eva was
nine. Although Skálová is the feminine ending for the family
name, Skala, originally their father had been named Spitz. But
once he returned from Denmark where he had been saved during
the war, he thought it would be safer to have a typical Czech
name. He married a Jewish woman whose name had been Gerty
Kirchner, although her parents had always cautioned her that it
was safer to just use her middle name, René. She survived Theresienstadt and was looked after by an uncle named Schonhauser,
who by coincidence had also changed his name to Skala because it
would be safer. And so one fake Skala married another.

When Eva was born, the Skalas gave her the Jewish name Eva
Ruth, and for a fee they had it officially registered at the Jewish
Community in Prague. By the time Zuzana was born, they thought
better of this and told her that her name was Shoshana, but they
didn't register it. For Passover the girls would go to a seder at the
Jewish town hall with about two hundred other children. Their
parents were members of the Community, but they only went to
synagogue for major holidays. One day when Zuzana was in the
second grade, one of her schoolmates ran around the classroom
saying, "Don't talk to Zuzana, she's Jewish." Zuzana knew she was
Jewish and didn't take this accusation very seriously—until she
realized that it worked. No one in the class would talk to her for
the rest of the day.

In 1968 things were different. The girls started going to Hebrew
lessons, and there were meetings for children every Saturday afternoon. While the Skalas never observed the Sabbath, now they
often met their daughters after their lessons and took them next
door to the Old-New Synagogue for the Havdalah service marking
the end of the Sabbath. It was a popular service for children, and
the youngest child would get to hold the candle that is extinguished.

The newspapers also were different. Far from threatening Jews in coded language, they were now denouncing anti-Semitism as a political tool. The millennium of Prague Jewry was rescheduled as a major international event, to take place in June 1969.

For seven and a half months Czechoslovakia was an exciting place. Not the least of the new possibilities was the chance to travel. On August 20, when a strange scream was heard in the skies—the sound of Soviet MiGs flying over an incoming armored invasion—many Jews were out of the country and watched the fragmented reports on television. Seven Soviet and one East German division headed to Prague and Pilsen from the GDR, one Polish and two Soviet divisions came in from Poland, three Soviet divisions came into Slovakia from the Ukraine, and smaller Soviet, Hungarian, and Bulgarian forces rolled into Slovakia from the Hungarian border. It was as though they were coming to fight a rebelling army. The Warsaw Pact, as the Soviet ambassador explained to U.S. President Lyndon Johnson, was moving against forces "hostile to socialism" and rescuing Czechoslovakia.

But what they encountered was angry, unarmed young people. Some at first tried to block tanks by sitting in front of them, but they quickly realized that they would simply be run over, as were walls, cars, and anything else that stood in the way of these clanking steel giants. In Bratislava girls seductively pulled up their miniskirts, and while Soviet tank and truck drivers stopped to ogle young Slovak thighs, young men ran up and smashed headlights with rocks and managed to set some oil drums on fire. A tank column from Hungary noisily squeaked and rumbled across the Danube bridge into Bratislava as university students cursed and threw bricks. A Soviet soldier dropped to firing position on the back of a tank and shot and killed a fifteen-year-old nursing student. The crowd that had gathered became furious, but the Soviets fired a few more rounds, killing another four unarmed people. The Soviets moved 175,000 troops against young Czechs and Slovaks throwing stones and bricks, which rang like off-key bells against the armor plating of unstoppable tanks.

By daybreak, August 21, every town of any size in the country was under the control of armored divisions. The foreign press reported spectacular acts of futile defiance. In Prague a legless World War II veteran dared tanks to roll over him. A girl ducked past the bayonets of a tank crew to mark a swastika on their tank. The Soviets were attacked with burning rags and Molotov cocktails. A few tanks burst into flames, and one ammunition truck exploded.

Young men wrapped themselves in Czech flags and charged tanks armed only with empty cans to stuff down the barrels. Flaming rags were dropped on tanks, and more of them caught fire. Scraps of furniture, car parts, and trees were tossed across streets for barricades. The tanks rolled effortlessly over them. On Thursday and Friday one-hour nationwide work stoppages were announced by the honking of horns. In one small village a tank column was turned back from a bridge by villagers who would not move. In Bratislava brown paper was stuck over tank periscopes to momentarily blind crews, and some tanks were set on fire.

For the first time in almost two decades, Czechoslovakians had been allowed to spend their summer vacation abroad. This was the news from home they were picking up on radio, television, and newspapers. František Kraus had recently died from his wartime ailments. Alice and their son Tomás were visiting friends in West Berlin. Reading the news, they were in no hurry to return.

The Skala family, on vacation in Denmark, started picking out the words *Czechoslovakia* and *Prague* in Danish conversations. Then they turned on the television and saw their hometown. The airport, the national museum, and the television center were shot up. At least twenty people had been killed in Prague alone. Russian troops had torn up the Czech Writers Union with crowbars.

In the new freedom of 1968 a youth trip to Israel had been organized by the Joint. Milana Mandl, born, like Israel, in 1948, was one of a number of Jews her age from Brno on the trip. Because of the presence of Rabbi Feter in Brno, her generation had grown up with an isolated but fairly active Jewish life. But the summer of 1968 on a kibbutz was their first opportunity to be around other Jews. Her younger brother Martin was in a Jewish youth camp in Yugoslavia. Their parents were on vacation in the mountains of Austria. When the news broke, they gathered up Martin and went to Karlsruhe in West Germany until they could decide what to do.

A difficult decision had presented itself. It was apparent that some kind of deal had been made with Moscow. The Soviets, who had five hundred tanks positioned in Prague alone, would gradually withdraw as conditions "normalized." Normalizing meant going back to the old ways. At the moment the borders were still open for travel, but it was likely that they would not stay that way. Those who remained outside would never be allowed back in, and those inside might not have another opportunity to leave. It also seemed likely that the "normalization," although unpleasant for everyone, would be particularly unpleasant for Jews. Already an anti-Zionist campaign was in full swing in the Soviet bloc.

A popular Czech singer, Karol Cernoch, came out with a new song that captured the mood in Czechoslovakia: "I hope this is just a bad dream." Thousands of Jews left the country permanently, along with tens of thousands of other Czechoslovakians.

The Skalas went back to Prague and the "normalization." Zuzana's parents explained to her what had happened along the way, so that she would not find it too shocking when they got home to five hundred Soviet tanks. One tank, she found, was stationed in front of her grade school. There was a Russian in a padded helmet who stuck out from the top looking very lonely, she thought. Sometimes the older children would throw stones at him, but most of the time he was alone with nothing to do but stare out.

Her parents' closest friends, three couples with whom they did everything, all moved to Bad Nauheim, a town near Frankfurt in West Germany. The Skala parents visited Bad Nauheim to see what it would be like. Their friends wanted them to move there immediately. Other friends in Prague could arrange for Eva and Zuzana to be flown to Frankfurt. They would not even need to go back. Their friends would arrange everything. These people were living very well, because the man was a distinguished doctor. Skala, on the other hand, was a clerk, and his wife had no particular skill. Under Socialism, they had lived comfortably. But they could see that the West was different. Their friends would live very well, and they would struggle along like the poor side of the family. They returned to Prague.

There was no longer much life at the Old-New Synagogue and the Jewish town hall. Security agents were positioned in the building across Maislova Street to report on who went there. The official Jewish Community could function only because it cooperated with the regime. The Jewish officials could not be trusted, and so people stopped attending the few Community activities. It was no longer fun to celebrate holidays under watchful eyes on Maislova Street. At a Hanukkah or Purim dance, the community leaders would tell the young participants not to play music or dance because it might disturb people in the neighborhood. Soon there were no activities for Jewish youth. Old people with their old ways would be tolerated, but there was no reason to encourage young people. Zuzana Skalova kept going on occasion until she was a teenager. Then, by chance, when she came across a document from the official Community leadership stating that Jewish life in Prague was free, open, and lively, she decided that she was participating in a sham staged by the Community leadership for the government. She stopped going.

Rabbi Feter was still in Brno, and Prague had Rabbi Gustave Zicher, but they were both aging, and the two younger rabbis who were to be the next generation of rabbinate emigrated. A good Sabbath turnout at the Old-New Synagogue was twelve or fifteen older men. Only the pensioners were not worried about their careers. The second synagogue, the Jubilee on Jeruzalémská, also managed to stay open, though the neo-Moorish synagogue was too eerie and lonely for the handful of aging men hoping for a minyan, and services were moved to a small dusty upstairs room.

Viktor Feuerlicht now led the services in the Old-New Synagogue. But he, too, had been contemplating leaving. He only wore a yarmulke indoors and did not make an outward display of his Orthodoxy. Still, he was the cantor and was seen regularly at the synagogue. No new apartment or opportunity was ever available for him. He still lived in a shabby postwar apartment with his wife and two sons who could not expect to have many career possibilities. With the "normalization" they would probably have even fewer choices. One of his sons had gone to England to study mathematics, and after the occupation he decided not to come back. But Viktor still had trouble with his arm, injured during the war; and Czechoslovakia had a good, free health-care system that looked after him.

Under "normalization," even apolitical people were worried about what they told their children. If children heard something different at home than at school, they might say the wrong thing at school. The Skalas did not talk very much about Jewish affairs and said even less about political affairs in front of their daughters.

Czechoslovakia's only teacher of modern Hebrew had to leave the country because of articles written by her journalist husband. As they left for Vienna, she asked Bedřich Nosek to take over the course. Nosek called it "a miracle" that all during the long hard "normalization" years, he was able to teach modern Hebrew to regular classes of up to eighty students. Of course, some of his students were called in to official offices and politely interrogated about why they were studying Hebrew. Nosek was also periodically questioned about his materials. The regime had to make certain he was not using Zionist books. But since his books were in Hebrew, they could only guess at their contents. Nosek would always assure them that they were normal language books. This response worked until an influential man from the Soviet Union, a director of adult language programs, arrived in 1982. Meeting with the heads of the school board, he simply asked, "How can you be teaching modern Hebrew? Isn't it Zionist propaganda?" After he left Czechoslovakia, Nosek's course was quietly canceled.

In the early years of "normalization," many people were being questioned. The Krauses had hesitated too long in West Berlin before returning, and they had some explaining to do. Even Karol Wassermann was called in, the art-collecting apolitical pharmacist. That was the way Wassermann thought of himself, but another view was that he was a nonparty member, seen regularly not only at the Old-New Synagogue but at rehearsals for theater pieces that were now banned. He decided not to tell his wife when he was called in. She was a Protestant and had not been through the experiences he had. To him, it seemed nothing that terrible could happen now. If it went very badly, he could lose his job. He hated his job.

After more than an hour of questioning—normally such sessions lasted fifteen minutes—Wassermann started to get that taut, ironic look to his face that was always a prelude to losing his temper. He told the three men questioning him what he really thought of the Russians and the occupation. After two hours he was sent home. Later, he was informed to his complete astonishment that while he had been very critical, he had criticized with "a Marxist vocabulary." He was removed from his job but was sent to direct another pharmacy, one that he was convinced was the smallest pharmacy in Prague.

ZUZANA ŠIMKO had been to Israel three years earlier and had met her half-sister, who had told her the stories their mother never spoke about: how Slovaks had hidden them during the war and an informer had turned them in. Zuzana's half-sister was hidden in corn husks, the father was beaten to death, and their mother escaped. After two months in Israel, Zuzana went back to Slovakia to her parents and her home in Nitra in the building full of Jewish families where they kept kosher and observed the Sabbath and every holiday. In Zuzana's mind, Jewish life was a normal and permanent thing in Czechoslovakia. She did not have to go to Israel to find it. On a rare occasion she would hear something vaguely anti-Semitic, but in general she had no problem with non-Jews. Friends gave her Hanukkah presents, and she gave them Christmas presents. Nitra was her home.

But in 1968 she saw most of the other Jewish families in her building and community pack and leave. Although she was only 20, her parents were already in their sixties and she could not bear to leave them. Her father, with whom she was especially close, candidly stated that he did not think he would live much longer if she left. Then, too, Zuzana believed in the diaspora. For her, it had become Jewish life: "I think Jews need to have communities in other places in the world."

Within six months following the Soviet invasion, her Jewish world had vanished from Nitra. In what had been a building of six Jewish families, only the Šimkos remained. Most of the Jewish people who had been clustered in the apartments near the synagogue left. The few Jews who stayed were mostly party members, though many of them were soon ousted from the party. Almost no one of Zuzana's age was left. Nitra's nine centuries of traditional Judaism, which had even survived the Nazis and Stalin, this time had finally been extinguished.

At the time of the invasion Fero Alexander had been performing folk music in Budapest. In between performances he heard on the radio that there was shooting in Bratislava and Prague. The Alexanders were a musical family, and Fero played violin in a Slovak folk group, while his brother Juraj, born in Theresienstadt, was a concert cellist. Born in 1948, Fero was one of the few boys of his generation to be bar mitzvahed in Bratislava. But with the changes of the Dubček era, he had been able to participate in a lively new youth group for Jews of his age in Bratislava.

Fero and his folk music group went back to Bratislava while there were still tanks on the street. But he was to soon find that all his friends had left. Out of the fifty or sixty Jews his age who had taken part in the Jewish youth movement, not one stayed. The only remaining rabbi in Bratislava also left. But the Alexander family stayed. Fero's brother Juraj did not want to leave because he had been hired to play in the cello section of the Slovak Chamber Orchestra. Juraj and Fero reasoned that their parents were aging and felt too old to start a new life. Fero pictured them sad and

alone, the way some of the other people of their generation soon
would be.

The rabbi was gone and all his friends had also left. The Jewish
community consisted largely of lonely older people whose children
had emigrated. This was the fate from which he had saved his
parents. But soon these deserted older people were smiling, showing everybody photographs of their families in foreign lands. They
seemed so proud when showing the pictures. The photos were
usually in color—the first color snapshots most of them had seen.
Fero imagined his family proudly showing snapshots of him in his
new home somewhere and silently wondered if he had not made a
mistake.

Urban renewal hit Bratislava like a bombing. A wide modern
bridge was built across the Danube, connected by a new highway
that cut a gash a hundred yards wide through the frilly historic old
center. The bridge landed in Bratislava exactly where the old Jewish section of town had been before the war. To government plan-
ners, it had just been an abandoned neighborhood. The synagogue
was no longer used and could also be torn down to make way for
the new thoroughfare. Bratislava no longer had a Jewish quarter,
nor did it have enough Jews to fill one.

IN KARLSRUHE a debate had gone on between Martin Mandl's
parents. Like many Jews from the prewar Czech lands, Martin's
father had grown up with a German education. Since he had been
raised as an ethnic German and since West German policy in any
case was to be open to Jews, they would have few difficulties ac-
quiring the normally elusive German citizenship. Martin's father
wanted to do it, but his mother did not want to be a German.
While the arguments volleyed back and forth, a letter arrived from
their daughter Milana, still on the kibbutz. She missed her home
and wanted to see Brno once more. She loved being in Israel, but
once she understood the situation—that the Czechoslovakian borders would soon be closed and she would never be able to go
back—she realized that she was not prepared to never again see
Moravia.

The Mandl family flew back to Prague and from there to Brno,
where they met their daughter at the small Brno airport. It was now
1969, and travel restrictions would soon be reimposed. When

Milana saw her family, her first words to them were, "I only came back to tell you that I am moving to Israel."

She did not understand that she had already made her choice. It would be another twenty-two years before she had the chance to return to Israel. In Brno the Jewish life she had known was gone. There were no more meetings for young people or Hebrew lessons. In 1970, Rabbi Feter died, and there was no one to take his place. Martin did not have an opportunity to be a Jewish teenager, as his sister had had only a few years earlier. In 1974 their father was able to visit his brother in West Germany. While he was away, Milana was called in for questioning. Many young people were questioned during the "normalization." Seated in a room with three very polite interrogators, she was presented with a long list of places she had gone, people with whom she had talked, words that had been spoken. Then the questions began. Milana was supposed to realize that people all around her were informants, and so she might as well be one too. But instead she laughed. All their information and all their questions seemed so inconsequential. Apparently it was decided that she did not make a very good informant. She was never called back.

In Brno, Masaryk Street was renamed Victory once more. But the victory of 1945 was fading. Now when Czechoslovakians thought of the Red Army, they thought of the 1968 invasion.

PART FOUR

THE
RITE
OF
PASSAGE

"As a Jew I have been persecuted, as a Jew. Waiki, my beloved, my husband, had been murdered. I couldn't put being Jewish aside, like a dress that had become old-fashioned.

Being Jewish is a fact, but I'm not successful in giving it any content. Not possible without belief in God."

GRETE WEIL, The Bride Price

20

East German
Autumn

ASIDE FROM A VERY SMALL NUCLEUS THAT KEPT ONE synagogue on Rykestrasse alive, Jewish practice in East Berlin by the 1970s had become largely a death cult. The biggest event of the year at the synagogue was the annual memorial on November 9 to *Kristallnacht*. One Berlin Jew who attended every year with his two sons was asked if he did anything else to practice Judaism. "I take my sons to the cemetery," he said. "They know they are Jewish."

The only functioning synagogue in East Berlin is a large, tasteful, moderately neo-Moorish building on Rykestrasse in Prenzlauer Berg, discreetly tucked behind a courtyard. Most surviving German synagogues are somewhat tucked away. Irene Runge had first walked into a synagogue when she was in her twenties. "It was a Friday night, and I was really in the mood, and it was my step forward." At that time a handful of young American Jews who were opposed to the Vietnam war had gone to the GDR, and Irene, with her New York English and her hunger for anything American, met most of them. One of them, an American Jew for whom a trip to the synagogue was a banal event, took her to the Rykestrasse synagogue for this major step.

"It was horrible. It was like Germany. No one would say hello or nobody would be friendly, and I thought Jews were like the people I knew and I thought, 'This can't be Jewish.' And I was never going to go there again." It was, in fact, very German. One hundred people was a huge turnout for a major holiday. Twenty was more typical. The people would file in quietly and take their places in their pews as in a church. There was none of the wandering the floor, debating, match-making, or gossiping that went on in the Rue Pavée synagogue or even the one favored by Jews of *Ostjuden* background on Joachimstalerstrasse in West Berlin which was even more hidden from the street. On Rykestrasse the East Berlin Jews would take their places silently, sit through the service in silence because few could read Hebrew, and then silently walk out, much like any other kind of German public meeting.

Several years after Irene's first synagogue visit, her Jewish friends—and that was most of her friends—were talking increasingly about their Jewish identity. Their parents had always said they were Jewish, and yet they knew nothing about being Jewish. Now, in their thirties, they were beginning to ask themselves exactly who they were. If they had a Jewish identity at all, it was a negative one. They were Jews because they were not Germans. They couldn't be Germans because of what Germans had done to the Jews. But they wanted to be something more than just not German. A group of them, all officials in the university youth organization, started going together to lectures and cultural events at the East Berlin Jewish Community. Irene found this only slightly more impressive than going to synagogue. "Also very German," she reported. "You know, they had all the chairs, and then there was the lecture, and then 'I thank you in the name of blah, blah, blah and thank you for coming.' and that was it!"

Nevertheless, in 1975 she became a registered member of the East Berlin Jewish Community. The following year she took her son, Stefan, who, a year past bar mitzvah age, had never been to a synagogue, to a Rosh Hashanah service on Rykestrasse. Stefan said, "For me it was interesting to sit in a synagogue with all the people and to get a hat."

Stefan had been raised by his non-Jewish father's parents in a village near Berlin. When his father remarried, they moved back to Berlin, a five-minute walk from the Rykestrasse synagogue. Now he was having more contact with his mother, who informed him for the first time, shortly before taking him to the synagogue, that he was a Jew. After Irene had taken him the first time, he would often drop in on a Friday evening. He knew no Hebrew and could not follow the service, but in time he memorized certain passages. Eventually he decided to be circumcised and bar mitzvahed. The circumcision was easy to arrange, since the head of the East Berlin Community, Peter Kirchner, was a doctor and a *mohel*, someone who performed ritual circumcisions. Stefan remembers almost no one coming to his bar mitzvah. Irene remembers it as a big community success. But Irene was the only family member present. Her father not only would not go, but for years after he refused to speak to his grandson. Stefan's father and stepmother, both non-Jews, were very upset by what they saw as a bizarre extremist activity.

But Stefan was not religious. He simply did it to have a Jewish identity. "In Germany the people don't know Judaism as a religion. They know it as a population," he explained. "I thought it was a bit of solidarity, and I loved being a member of this population." He had spent his childhood being moved from one home to another and one identity to another, and as he approached adulthood he was looking for solid things to hold onto. He was drawing closer to his mother at a time when she too was in search of an identity. Mother and son became Jews together. "My mother is Jewish, so I am a Jew," he said.

But Irene rarely went to services, and when she did, not knowing Hebrew, they made very little sense to her. The first time she ever understood a service was when a rabbi came from Toronto and gave a Yom Kippur service in German. The other thing that stood out about that service was an argument that broke out on the women's side about whether the service was a legitimate excuse to skip the Monday local Communist party meeting. Gradually, Irene got increasingly involved. She began attending the annual Hanukkah party and a few other social events. In the early 1980s she was invited to join the board of the Jewish Community. Once she was a member, she wanted to weed out the non-Jews who had always been welcome at Community events. Most Community meetings had a majority of non-Jews. "Because they love going to Jewish places and listening to those boring lectures," said Irene. "Whereas the Jews, you know—they just come for the Hanukkah party." To Germans going to Jewish events was an attempt to come to terms with history, and it was always a way to assert that you were "one of the good Germans." Irene, raised in the Communist elite, always held the notion of members and nonmembers. If you were not a Jew, you were not part of the club and you did not belong at the meeting. Why should Jews have to help the Germans work out their problems?

Irene started having informal meetings to which non-Jews were not invited. She called her group Uns für Unsere, We for Ourselves. For four years they had monthly meetings, a small group of Jews who discovered that they all had the same background. They had been born in the United States, France, England, or Australia, wherever their parents had found shelter from Hitler. They had all been brought back to Germany when young and had never felt completely German but had never given much thought to being Jewish either, because they were all from good Communist households. They became like archeologists brushing off the rocks of their lives, looking for clues to a bygone civilization. Irene arranged lectures on Jewish law, on holidays, on Israel. She started arranging for Lubavitch rabbis from the West to come for holidays.

Most of the East Berlin Jews had other things on their mind. Their religion was the new socialist Germany, but it was getting harder to stay a believer. When Brezhnev decided to invade Czechoslovakia in 1968, he meant to send a message to people throughout the Soviet bloc. The event marked the beginning of a slow decline in which idealism turned to disillusionment. It made loyal Communists wonder about the entire system. If East Germany went its own way and reformed its errors, which was what many loyal Communists were hoping would happen, would not the Soviets treat them the way they had the Czechoslovakians? The Warsaw Pact was for mutual defense, and a central concept was that the USSR was not supposed to intervene in the internal affairs of its members. But obviously the Soviets would intervene.

When the Soviets invaded Czechoslovakia, in East Germany it was mainly the intelligentsia who were upset. But as the economy failed to perform year after year, discontent spread. East Germans grew a little angrier every year, and as the Stasi accurately reported on growing discontent, the regime grew more repressive and distrustful. "There was not physical repression but mental," said an East German journalist of Jewish background, "I mean people were never afraid to voice their opinions, especially in factories. They voiced their opinions very openly, but of course the state authorities didn't like it and the people were deprived of fundamental freedoms like travel, to read what they want. I mean, they could see television, they could listen to the radio, but if you wanted to read *The New York Times* or *Le Figaro*, you couldn't, unless you were a privileged person like I was, who was working as a journalist. Of course we had everything, but that was only a privileged smaller group—writers and journalists."

Mia Lehmann and her husband often talked about how things were not going well. They had understood the need for the Berlin Wall as a temporary measure, but not as a permanent policy. By the time of her husband's death in 1963, he had become extremely critical of the GDR system. Mia knew that the dream—the new egalitarian Germany—was drifting far off course. As a trade union official, she earned her living doing what she did best. She spent her days in factories asking people why they were unhappy. "I had to deal with people in the factory. I knew what the economic side was. And it went down and down."

While the average East German was worried about the economy, the Communist elite, like Mia Lehmann, was troubled by incidents such as the Wolf Biermann affair in 1976. Biermann was the West German son of an Auschwitz victim who moved to the GDR and became a popular poet and ballad writer. He had the kind of impeccable "antifascist" credentials that made friendly criticism permissible. But by the mid-1960s, he was being almost entirely censored, and in 1975, after being granted permission for a visit to the West, he was not allowed back into East Germany. This was a shock to many East German Jews who, like Biermann, had suffered under the Nazis and gone to the GDR for idealistic reasons. What had gone wrong that the new socialist Germany would treat in this way one of their own who had come back to rebuild?

21

In Budapest

HUNGARY HAD A LONG-DISTANCE RUNNER OF EXTRAORDI-
nary endurance who had never won any Olympic medals.
Rather than compete in sports, he ran to publicize political events.
For the centennial of Lenin's birth he ran from Budapest to Moscow. He had carved out a strange career for himself—a runner who
never competed. To Gyula Gazdag, it was what everyone had to
do—shape and fit a career to the needs of the state, let yourself be
used; rather than compete in the real world, offer yourself to the
state in a symbolic gesture. This was the subject of his first documentary film.

The state, not surprisingly, did not like being portrayed in
documentary films in this ironic light. Under János Kádár, Budapest had begun at last to lose the dark, bombed-out look from
the war. The last of the great historic bridges that connected
Buda and Pest across the Danube was rebuilt in the 1960s. By
1970, the last of the bombed-out lots had been cleared and
rebuilt. Limited private initiative was tolerated. But films satiriz-
ing the system were not.

Most of Gyula's subsequent films were not appreciated by the
state either, and six of them were banned. After Gyula made a film,
he would be called into a political office, and the ideological problems of the work would be explained to him. Sometimes he would
be told that if he did such a film again, he would no longer be

allowed to make films. He was frequently spied on. "I didn't know Gyula was applying to military school," a neighbor once said to his parents.

"What!?"

"They came by. Said he had applied to military school and needed to ask us certain security questions about him."

Gyula had been one of only eleven accepted out of some 900 applicants to the film institute. But while being a film director was a privileged position, it earned a very low state salary. Because Hungarian Communism believed in incentives, the bulk of a film-maker's income was paid on delivery of projects. When a film was banned, not only would the filmmaker not get his money, but neither would anyone else who worked on the film. When Gyula's film was banned, he was letting down his friends and colleagues. That was how the system worked under the soft Hungarian dicta-torship of János Kádár, the man known as Father Joe. "It seems that people here, even when grown up, need a father to tell them what to do," György Konrád wrote.

Konrád also tested the limits of the system's vaunted tolerance. Two-thirds of the essays he wrote following the 1956 uprising were not published. He would play with the system. With a certain editor, certain things would get by for a time. Then editors would change. Classics would work. Politics would not. Things had to be hidden or carefully woven. Thinking there must be something more worthwhile to do than write essays that no one was allowed to read, he became a social worker, and from 1959 to 1965 he worked with troubled children.

"I believed it was better to have jobs that were independent from the ideological literary scene because there I was more dependent. Here, I do something that corresponds to my own values, because to do something for children is okay. And to edit the classics is also okay, so I can earn my livelihood and support my family in two solid activities, and I'm not depending on the censors."

In 1969, Konrád's first work of fiction was published, a novel based on his work experience, called *The Case Worker*. This was a surprisingly liberal period in Hungary, considering the repression taking place in neighboring Czechoslovakia. The Hungarian upris-ing was now more than a decade in the past. During the Six-Day War the government attempted an "anti-Zionist campaign." The government official who led it was of Jewish birth. But Jews re-sponded with surprising assertiveness. Even the official Jewish

Community, which was often resented for legitimizing government policy, dared what was to be remembered as its bravest moment. Community leader Geza Seifert, without the customary gerrymandering of phrases, declared the support of Hungarian Jews for Israel in its struggle.

Unexpectedly, the Six-Day War had stirred up forgotten sentiments in Konrád. He had gone to a newsstand, bought a newspaper, and started reading. Suddenly he felt faint, the sickening flutter of anxiety in his stomach. The war had broken out. Jews were once again being singled out for a slaughter. Could this be happening again? He began to think increasingly about the fact that he was a Jew and to read Jewish history. But when the anti-Zionist campaign started attacking Jewish government officials, attacking some of the very people who were censoring writers, Konrád had little sympathy for the Jewish officials. "I am not interested in the fact that they are Jews," he would say. "Only that they are censors."

György Gadó was so angered by the government's only slightly modified Soviet anti-Zionist line that he turned in his party membership. In the government statistical bureau where he worked, he was demoted to a low-level clerk.

As in Poland, support for Israel during the Six-Day War was seen as an expression of anti-Russian sentiments. Jews found themselves with the most unlikely of allies. Andras Kovacs took an excursion on the Danube and visited a small village inhabited by ethnic Germans who had been living in Hungary for many generations without losing their German identity. Kovacs was sitting on a park bench enjoying the setting when the village guide came over to him and started talking in German. Kovacs answered in German, and as they talked, he realized that the guide was extremely drunk. The guide at about the same time realized that Kovacs was Jewish.

"Aha," said the guide, scrutinizing Kovacs through drooping eyelids. "Are you Jewish?"

"Yes," said Kovacs, preparing himself.

The guide, leaning forward, stared into Kovacs' eyes. "I am German," he said. "We are eternal enemies. I fought in the SS in the Second World War, and I was put in a prison for twelve years."

Then he clamped a thick hand on Kovacs's shoulder and lowered his voice. "Now times have changed. Now we are on the same side. I fought the same Russians that you fought in Israel."

In the early 1970s, Konrád helped to smuggle a friend's manuscript out of Hungary. The friend had been expelled from the university and given a laborer job and had written about his experience. For his part in the smuggling, Konrád lost his job, but he was able to get another as an urban sociologist for a planning institute. This experience led to his second novel, *The City Builder*. He was informed that the novel was "too dark," lacking in optimism, and it was refused Hungarian publication. The book was published in the United States.

Since Hungarians do not learn other languages and others do not learn theirs, translations are always in demand. When György Gadó's low-level clerical job was finally taken from him, for the next twenty years he could not get a job and he survived by doing translations from Russian and German. Andras Kovacs was also forced into the free-lance translation trade. He had been an editor in a publishing house as well as a teacher of philosophy at the university. But like Konrád, he was writing for the underground press, and he decided as a deliberate provocation to run an article that, rather than being anonymous, would bear his byline. He was removed from both the publishing house and the university. In 1980 a West German university offered him a one-year teaching position. After descending into a labyrinth of bureaucracy, Kovacs finally got a Hungarian passport so that he could travel. But it came with only one exit visa. He could leave but he could not come back. It was a virtual invitation to emigrate. Konrád received a similar passport.

Kovacs left and taught in Bonn for a year, then moved on to Paris and New York. But Konrád stubbornly held to his Hungarian-speaking country.

Zoltán Gardos was born two years after the Hungarian uprising. He had always been aware that his parents had a painful secret. They would be watching television, and if something about World War II came on, Zoltán would look over at his father, staring silently into the blue light of the television, and he would see tears running down his cheeks. Nothing was said.

When Zoltán was 13, he met a girl in school who, although not a practicing Jew, talked very openly about being Jewish, and in his conversations with her Zoltán began to suspect that he might also be Jewish. At 15 they were in love, and he wanted to know more about Judaism.

Slowly he got the truth from his Communist atheist parents. He learned that his father, who was an accountant, had wanted to be a lawyer but had been barred from higher education before the war because he was Jewish. While his father was in a Russian forced labor camp, his family had been deported to Auschwitz—his mother, wife, and son—and were all killed. After the war, he re-married to Zoltán's mother, also a Jew, who had survived in hiding. Zoltán never did learn more than these vague details, which were so fraught with emotion that he too started to find the subject difficult to talk about.

He would not think about it for the present. Someday, after his parents died, he thought, he might try to explore this secret more. But his girlfriend wanted to talk about it. Soon he began to realize that some of his friends also had the same secret. Then he realized that most of his friends had this secret. Why was it, he wondered, that unknowingly he had been drawn to so many Jewish people?

At 19, Zoltán nervously made his way through the dark old Jewish section of central Pest, to the ornate cathedrallike Dohány synagogue, said to be the largest synagogue in Europe. He observed strange things going on in this imposing building, in a strange language with strange music. Zoltán may have been drawn to other Jews, but he did not feel that his place was in the Dohány.

When he was 21 he met Kati Kelemen. As a small child, Kati had come home from school mouthing anti-Semitic slurs, meaningless curses she had learned from other children. Her parents, Communists who believed in working toward the egalitarian society, told her then that they were Jewish, but they never told her much more about it.

Zoltán and Kati married and continued to ambiguously pursue Judaism. Budapest was the capital of officially sanctioned Judaism in Central Europe. It had the largest community and the only rabbinical seminary. Everything Jewish was either officially sanctioned or unofficial and banned. There were official social functions. The seminary offered a *Kiddush*, a social gathering centered around a wine blessing to sanctify the Sabbath, and the turnout for this was generally large. Zoltán and Kati sought out other Jewish gatherings, and they began to stumble across the unofficial ones, including one in the home of a couple who had secretly invited people there for a Passover seder. The same couple would also invite five or six young people over for Friday nights. The couple were regularly warned by the police against these activities, but they continued to invite people to their home. The police would call them in for questioning and would warn them that they would lose their jobs and have their passports revoked.

Zoltán and Kati also met a young dissident rabbi, Tomas Raj, a graduate of the Budapest seminary in a class of four. Raj had already aroused the displeasure of the authorities for attempting a Saturday afternoon study group in the town of Szeged, where he had been rabbi. When he produced a play about Moses at the synagogue, the Jewish Community leaders had removed him and sent him to work at a home for the elderly in western Hungary. He continued his activities, and in 1970 he was expelled from the rabbinate.

The officials of the seminary and the Budapest Jewish Community leadership, MIOK (the Hungarian acronym for National Representation of Hungarian Israelites)—which was directed by Géza Seifert and, after his death in 1976, by his wife Ilona—worried about maintaining their own positions and about keeping what they had operating and on good terms with the state. Because of this, the state could often rely on the central board to stop unapproved activities. This was the system for state management of Judaism throughout Central Europe. An older generation remembered that it had also been Eichmann's system. To a younger generation, including Zoltán and Kati, it meant that they could expect no help in learning about Judaism from the official Jewish Community. There were no courses or books or any guidance for Jews wanting to learn the basics. Their only chance was to meet other Jews, and for this reason they started going regularly to the synagogue.

"You couldn't catch a word," said Zoltán. "I can't catch a word because I don't know Hebrew, and even if you know Hebrew you can't possibly understand what is going on if you are not told where you are."

They joined a group of young professionals who studied with Rabbi Raj. Studying rendered them ever more confused: What did it mean to be Jewish? Was it a nationality, like being Hungarian? Or a religion that they did not know how to practice? If it was a nationality, then did they belong in Israel? In 1983, through an Israeli contact in Budapest, Zoltán and Kati were able to arrange an illegal trip to Israel. They told the government they wanted to visit neighboring Austria and were given passports and visas. In Vienna they were met by a Jewish organization with visas and plane tickets to Israel. In Israel they were taken around the country to meet Hungarian Jews who had immigrated. Everyone told them of the good Jewish life in Israel and showed them only the best and most beautiful sights.

But they could not make the decision to move there. Their lives, all their friends and relatives, everything they knew was in Hungary, and they hadn't even had a chance to say good-bye. They hadn't dared to tell anyone what they were really doing. After four weeks they returned to Hungary even more confused, and for years afterward they would periodically think about Israel.

22

In Warsaw
and Cracow

GOMUŁKA WAS FINALLY DESTROYED, NOT OVER ANY OF the student issues, not over democracy or free speech or anti-Semitism, but rather because of the price of meat. A 36 percent hike during Christmas 1970 led to strikes, and he was replaced by Edward Gierek. The change was welcome news for Marian Turski and the staff of the besieged *Polityka*. The independent Communist newspaper had been advocating a shift toward Western financing, opening opportunities for a private sector, and making infrastructural improvements such as a highway system.

This was exactly Gierek's approach. Gomułka had wanted nothing to do with the West. "In a way, there was something in common between him and De Gaulle," Turski later said of Gomułka, " . . . a very selfish man with a very large, unlimited ego." Gierek was a pragmatist who had been educated in the West. Promising economic growth, he obtained Western loans and started a Polish automobile industry and built roads, including the main highway from Katowice in the south to Warsaw. Poland showed impressive growth rates and was soon ranked the tenth strongest industrial nation in the world, only slightly behind East Germany. At the time these were probably the two most overrated economies in the world. By 1976, supposedly thriving Poland was forced to reveal that it was literally bankrupt and could not even service its debts.

Just as Gomułka could not be forgiven his sins once his great virtue
of holding down prices was proved hollow, Gierek without economic growth did not have much appeal.

It was a period of change when the old faiths weren't working,
a time when Poles were asking many questions. Ever since a
thug had called him a Jew and punctuated it with a smack in
the face, Konstanty Gebert had been asking himself, "What was
I supposed to do about things? How come I'm a Jew? What does
it mean?" He was not going to start going to a synagogue. Synagogues and churches were "relics of the past," not something for
an enlightened modern Communist. Gebert was not even sure
where to find a synagogue. He suspected that some of his friends
were also Jewish. But you could not go to your friend and say,
"Are you Jewish?" He compared it to saying to someone, "Are
you an ape?" In Poland to ask someone if he or she is a Jew is to
make an accusation.

The alternative was reading. He tried reading the Bible, but it
did not speak to him. So he turned to the great nineteenth-century
Yiddish literature. Writers such as Russian-born Sholem Aleichem
and Polish-born Isaac Leib Peretz had been recognized by the regime as part of official culture and therefore were translated into
Polish and made available to the public very inexpensively. Culture for the masses was a Communist ideal, and these writers had
been included. What amazed Gebert when he read these stories of
Jewish life in Poland and Russia—the world that had been exterminated shortly before he was born—was that it did not seem alien.
Though he had never seen a shtetl or met religious Jews, they
seemed very familiar and understandable, as though somehow certain values and ways of thinking had been passed on to him without the hat, beard, language, or rituals. Was Jewishness, then, a
way of thinking?

In 1971, Gebert decided to visit the United States and look up
some of his father's old Jewish Communist friends. He discovered a
great-uncle in Sacramento, California, whose family included a
grandson his age. They were not deeply religious, but they did
observe the Sabbath, and Gebert, for the first time, went to a synagogue and to a family Sabbath meal. Although he was intrigued,
he could not imagine living like that. In 1976 he met the family
again in London. He even tried hosting his own Sabbath meal with
Warsaw friends. But it didn't really work.

By then, Gebert, a psychologist by training, was reading more intellectual Jewish writers such as Martin Buber. When Carl Rogers, the American humanist psychologist, came to Poland to meet with Polish psychologists, Gebert and most of his friends went to see him. After a general talk, Rogers suggested that they break up into groups of special interest. There could be a group on divorce, one on parents of small children —

"How about a Jewish group?" someone said. Everyone laughed. Jews were always a good joke. But the person who had said it wasn't joking. He ignored the laughter and stubbornly added, "Well, anybody who is interested, meet me in my room at eight o'clock."

Gebert went, pressed his way into the packed room, looked around, and discovered that most of his friends were Jewish. After that, he started talking to his friends about being Jewish. He found that most of them had in some way been abused in 1968 and that for them, too, the experience had led to reflection, but they hadn't known what to do. Gomułka's 1968 campaign had driven most Jews out of Poland but it had rekindled a Jewish consciousness in the few who remained. An unofficial Jewish group formed to meet twice a month in the hope that their common questions would lead to some common answers.

THE GIEREK YEARS —from 1970 to 1980—were a good time for this kind of activity. Under Gierek, Western fashions and culture started to appear, and there was a minor boom in the publication of what were perceived as "Western-type" books, which included a wide variety of titles on Jewish subjects including Holocaust history, World War II memoirs, studies of Jewish art, and reprints of prewar Jewish books.

The history of Eastern European Communism has been colored by the irony that opposition most flourished during periods of relative freedom. Gierek couldn't go after Western loans while he was busting up meetings and arresting intellectuals. When he eased the repression, it gave an opportunity for groups to organize. An accidental by-product of the anti-Semitic campaign of 1968 was that for a rare moment in Polish history, Jews and the Catholic Church were thrown into the same camp. Then the Catholics and the Jews began working with trade unions. By 1980, a wide range of opposition groups had formed an unlikely but solid coalition called Solidarity. The coalition between Catholics and Jews lasted throughout the early 1980s. Gebert, as a Jewish dissident, was sometimes invited to speak at Catholic churches, which, like synagogues, he had never expected to enter. The congregations always seemed very excited and a little embarrassed to have a Jew among them. One priest introduced him as "Mr. Gebert of the Mosaic persuasion." Just as the influence of the Catholic Church was increasing in Poland, Karol Wojtyła from Katowice became Pope in 1978, giving the Polish church even more confidence.

This prosperous time for Konstanty Gebert, Marian Turski, and many other people in Poland ended harshly in 1981. The meat price went up again, and Lech Wałesa, the Solidarity leader with his base as an electrician in the Gdańsk shipyards, organized nationwide strikes. The Gierek regime suddenly realized something astounding: Most Polish workers were now Solidarity members. Ten million Poles belonged to Solidarity. To settle the strike, Gierek agreed to sweeping reforms and then resigned. Most of the reforms were not carried out, but the Communist party was now in such disarray that Poland by default became the freest society in the Soviet bloc. But on December 13, 1981, General Wojciech Jaruzelski led a coup d'état and established martial law. The small measure of Polish freedom was over.

The little Polish Jewish revival also ended with the coup. Gebert's group was discontinued, because any gathering of more than eight people had to register with the police. Since almost all of the sixty group members were active in the underground political opposition, they could not afford to do this. But the group still unofficially met on Jewish holidays and observed its own annual commemoration of the Warsaw ghetto uprising, shunning the official one. Fifty Jews would quietly walk through the few monuments in the 1950s housing project where the ghetto had been. The police didn't object until 1983, when Solidarity decided to join in and invited the people of Warsaw to participate. Not coincidentally, this was the year when the government, trying to improve its badly degenerated international image, invited Jewish leaders from abroad to come to an official commemoration of the fortieth anniversary. Marek Edelman, the last surviving veteran of the ghetto uprising, was now involved in the underground opposition; he urged world Jewish leaders not to come because they were being used to give the regime the appearance of international approval.

Gebert's little group could barely be found among the thousands of Solidarity supporters and sympathizers who joined in the unofficial ceremony. They were surrounded by police with clubs and machine guns as they made their way through the trim, straight streets to the Umschlagplatz. The plan was that survivors and relatives of survivors would lay wreaths in front of the plaque that marked the site where the ghetto Jews had been herded for deportation. But as these elderly mourners approached, the armed police blocked them from coming near the plaque. The crowd grew as angry Poles from the neighborhood joined the mourners. It was not that Poles were supporting Jews but that they were all opposing the regime together.

World Jewry ignored Marek Edelman's plea, and the government was able to bring more rabbis to Warsaw than had been seen there since the war. The fact that none of these visiting Jews would participate in the unofficial ceremony to which they were also all invited left Gebert with a lingering bitterness. It was the logic of the time. When you are visiting a Communist dictatorship, you do not publicly participate in dissident activities—not if you ever want to come back. The result was that instead of having a rabbi to say the prayer for the dead, Gebert's group had to use a Catholic priest.

The day after the Umschlagplatz ceremony, Gebert and some of his group participated in a small private memorial over a ghetto hero's grave in the Warsaw Jewish cemetery. This was not a large Solidarity show but was planned for a few local people. As the group was arriving at the cemetery, the official Jewish Community, which was sponsored and controlled by the regime, had the solid steel gates to the cemetery closed. Unable even to see past the rusting metal, they laid their wreaths on the gate. There were not even ten Jewish men, a minion, to say Kaddish for the dead. Some of the foreign Jews came to the cemetery in tour cars driven by Orbis, the state travel agency, and shot photos without getting out of their cars. Gebert tried to see their faces through the closed windows of the air-conditioned cars, and for the first time he did not feel proud to be a Jew.

NINEL KAMERAZ AND HER HUSBAND were part of a small group of Solidarity supporters who produced pamphlets and books on taboo subjects, often contradicting official versions of history. Printed on a hand press, each sheet of four pages had to be placed in the press, printed, and then lifted off. It was a common process in the Solidarity movement. Gebert's overfed black and white cat was named Offset after the piece of equipment they could only dream of getting.

The pages had to be collated and stapled and then clandestinely handed out by the thousands. To Ninel, it was a fight against the system that had broken her family. "Jews would come and say to me, why are you involved in all this? Why do you have to fight this? There are no Jews. Why is this your business? This was my business because Communism destroyed so many Jews. It was terrible in my own family. It was my business, and I'm glad I did it."

In 1983, Jaruzelski allowed Warsaw's one remaining synagogue—the spacious, decorative turn-of-the-century Nozyk Synagogue, which had survived the war by serving as a stable for German horses—to be reopened. Ninel started going to services for major Jewish holidays. A hard core of a half-dozen elderly Yiddish speakers formed the beginning of a minyan. One of them, Moishe Shapiro, approached Ninel and asked if she wanted her two sons to learn Hebrew.

Ninel had already come to the conclusion that she would never be able to adapt to a Jewish way of life. It was too alien after two generations of Communism. The one thing she could do was pass Judaism on to her sons. "But there was nothing Jewish around. It was up to me. This was my responsibility," she said. "For me, the most important thing is that my children know that they are Jews. What they do with it, that is their business. But they have to know, and then they will have to choose."

Lukasz was already 13 and Mateusz was 11—Luke and Matthew. Mateusz immediately loved the idea, but Lukasz was not interested in religion. His mother decided he had no choice: They both had to study Hebrew for one year. "How can you say you don't want it when you don't know anything about it?" she argued. After a year of study Lukasz was still certain that he didn't want it. But Mateusz continued. He had spent his childhood delivering his parents' underground literature through the Warsaw streets— "between the tanks," he liked to say. He had grown up with the idea that Poland was his country and that it was his responsibility to make it a country that still had Jews.

Mateusz asked Ninel if he could have a bar mitzvah. It was what she had wanted, but having never in her life done anything religious, she had felt she could not talk about it. "I didn't feel I could dare to tell him to do it. But if he came to me and said I want a bar mitzvah—it gave me such happiness."

A bar mitzvah marks the moment, on the thirteenth birthday,

when a male takes responsibility in the religious practices of a community. He now wraps *tefillin* on weekday mornings, is counted in a minyan, and can be called up on Saturday morning for Torah reading. In traditional Jewish life, as it was practiced in Poland before the war and as it still is in Antwerp and on Rue Pavée, all of these functions are a normal part of daily life. The bar mitzvah is the first time in which he is called up to read Torah— presumably the first of many times. But in assimilated communities since the war, the bar mitzvah, rather than being a beginning, is the singular moment, often the only time in his life that the bar mitzvah boy will go up and read in a synagogue. For this reason, assimilated Westerners have approached bar mitzvahs with ever greater fanfare. Central European communities, many of which had not seen a bar mitzvah in decades, saw bar mitzvahs as nothing less than a reaffirmation of the existence of Judaism.

Ninel was secretly afraid the entire thing would be an embarrassment. Did Mateusz really know how to read Hebrew? It was difficult for her to imagine Mateusz standing on a *bimah* reading in Hebrew. No one she had ever known in her family had ever done anything like that. But in fact Mateusz had learned Hebrew and gave a well-studied delivery to a synagogue filled with the people he had invited. Praying in a full synagogue stirred many memories for the few elderly survivors, and they wept. Mateusz's bar mitzvah—the first Poland had seen since the 1950s—received international press coverage. For months afterward, Ninel and Mateusz were interviewed on foreign television. A few years later, when she visited Israel, people recognized her on the streets from television interviews about her son's bar mitzvah. But her best memory from Israel was learning that Ninel is not only *Lenin* spelled backward but that in Hebrew *Nin El* means "great-granddaughter of God."

"Finally," she said, "the hunchback fell away."

AMONG THE MANY foreign rabbis who arrived in Poland to help the struggling Polish Jews, none came as a greater shock than Emily Korzenik. She was a feminist-turned-rabbi in Stamford, Connecticut, where she particularly delighted in weddings and bar mitzvahs because they symbolized the continuation of Judaism. "A bar mitzvah," she said, "is a celebration of the continuity of the Jewish people."

Several members of her congregation were part of a tour of

Poland and Israel. Such tours were a growing phenomenon. A group would be taken to Poland, where they would visit cemeteries and concentration camps, and then go on to Israel to see "Jewish life." In Cracow they visited a Jewish canteen where the elderly remnant of a once-major community gathered for lunch. The canteen was run by a woman in her late seventies, the youngest person there. The group asked her if there was anything she needed from America, and she replied, "Bring us life." She told the story of her nephew who had been taken away and killed by the Nazis while preparing for his bar mitzvah.

When Emily Korzenik heard this story, she decided that she would bring these people a bar mitzvah. Not that she would train a Cracow boy. Rather, she would choose among the boys in Connecticut whom she was preparing. She picked a handsome blond of Polish Jewish origin. Korzenik thought it would be a wonderful thing for the people of Cracow to have his bar mitzvah in their synagogue.

Two Cracow synagogues had been reopened after the war, and until 1968 they both offered daily services. The more famous was the Remuh, named after a sixteenth-century Talmudic scholar whose work is still regarded by the ultra-Orthodox as defining precepts for their way of life. Every year on the anniversary of his death, the Orthodox had made a pilgrimage to his nearby grave. When the regime would let them, ultra-Orthodox from New York took up the practice again. With the help of such visitors, the Remuh Synagogue was able to get a minyan.

The other Cracow synagogue was the Templum, which had been liberal. Before the war, there had been a reform movement in Polish Judaism, but the few surviving Jews in Cracow had no memory of this. Although they could not keep kosher or maintain most Orthodox practices, they felt attached to orthodoxy, thinking of it as the genuine thing. "It's a paradox," said Henryk Halkowski, a Cracow Jew. "We have only Orthodox synagogues now, but almost no Orthodox Jews."

Too large to fill, the Templum was used only on rare occasions. None of the locals objected when the New York Orthodox built a mikveh next to it, even though liberal synagogues do not use mikvehs. There were no liberals left. No one in Cracow had used a mikveh since before the war. The New York Jews would bathe in the mikveh to purify themselves before making a pilgrimage to the cemetery at the Remuh. Word spread among Poles that these Jews could not refuse a panhandler once they had been to the *mikveh*. They were in a purified state, and if they rejected a beggar they would have to go back to the *mikveh* and bathe again before going to the cemetery. Believing this, the Poles would line up to greet the Orthodox as they left the *mikveh*.

Emily Korzenik arrived in Cracow without speaking a word of Polish or Yiddish. But she had an entourage of translators. Also with her was an NBC television crew, a documentary film crew, and a photographer from *People* magazine. The elderly woman who had said "Bring us life" had not said anything about bringing press coverage, and she gazed uncertainly at these Americans. Not knowing what else to do, she invited them to lunch. Korzenik looked at the well-kept little Remuh and at the larger Templum, where the walls were rotting and old papers were stacked along the walls, and decided that she liked the Orthodox synagogue better. "It seemed like the most cleaned up," she said.

Czeslaw Jakubowicz, a white-haired man with a sturdy broad-featured face, was the president of the handful of people that was the Cracow Jewish Community. He was the old-timer who hadn't left. He had not stayed out of principle, however. In 1956, when large numbers of Cracow Jews were leaving, he decided that he would emigrate to Antwerp with the remainder of his family. They already had relatives there. But Jakubowicz's family did not understand the rules of this game, and so instead of lying and saying they were going to Israel, they applied to emigrate to Belgium. Permission was denied. During the 1968 purge he again missed the open door because his uncle, the president of the Community, was arrested, and by the time he was released five months later, the government had stopped offering the visas.

Jakubowicz stayed on to become the president of the few dozen remaining people. At most there were 250 people in Cracow who would call themselves Jewish, and the majority of them were not active. At his lonely post Jakubowicz received word that Americans wanted to do a bar mitzvah in the Remuh with a woman rabbi. He could barely remember the last Cracow bar mitzvah—in the early 1950s, in the Templum. But who was this woman who said she was a rabbi? "There was never such a thing in Poland. It was not Polish tradition. Can you imagine a woman priest?" he said. Women pray in a separate space, they are not allowed to do the Torah reading, and they do not wear prayer shawls. How can a woman be a rabbi? Troubled by this, he contacted a Bobover Hasidic rabbi who was visiting Poland and told him that an American woman rabbi wanted to bar mitzvah an American boy in the Remuh. The Bobover rabbi called New York, the home of an Orthodox rabbi named Nacham Elbaum. Elbaum was eating a bowl of soup when he received the news of a woman rabbi in the Remuh. He put down his spoon and ran for a taxi to Newark Airport for a flight to Warsaw.

The ceremony was moved to the Templum, and Elbaum led the prayer with a cantor he had recruited while changing planes in Vienna. Emily Korzenik found herself in the balcony with the rest of the women. Nor was the media very happy. Rabbi Elbaum would not allow them to use cameras, since this would be contrary to Orthodox custom. One photographer who happened to be Jewish was called up to read a passage from the Torah and hid a compact Leica under his prayer shawl, shooting between the lines of Hebrew with this almost soundless, exquisitely crafted German shutter.

For two and a half hours Elbaum and the cantor chanted, periodically walking over to the press to tell them to put down their cameras. Then the blond American bar mitzvah boy was brought up and read his passage. He then signaled for Emily Korzenik to come down from the balcony. Korzenik could stand it no longer in any case, and she pushed her way downstairs through the media to the *bimah*, the reading area. Elbaum physically stopped her from putting on a prayer shawl. A woman wearing a prayer shawl was too much for him. But he had to retreat when the bar mitzvah boy threatened not to recite anymore. Korzenik shouted from Isaiah, while Elbaum shouted "Ladies cannot speak in the synagogue!" which made Korzenik shout Isaiah even louder. As the service ended, "Violence shall be heard no more in thy land" was the passage she was screaming over Elbaum's insistent voice. The few Cracow Jews watched in dismay.

PART FIVE

THE
SILENCE

April 14, 1987, Miami Beach, conversation between the author and Isaac Bashevis Singer:

MK: Do you think that the Holocaust was an anomaly of history?

SINGER: No. It's a part of human history. The whole of human history is a holocaust.

MK: If that is true and there is a God, what is God doing?

SINGER: (*shouts with real anger in his voice*): He did it! HE did it! I didn't do it! He created a world in which animals and man and God knows what else fight like hell all of the time. Fight! They fight for sex. They fight for territory. They fight for all kinds of cultures. They fight about religion.

MK: What is it like to be 83? What does the world look like?

SINGER: The same like 23 because I am the same man. I have the same troubles. I have the same passions. I have even somehow, although I don't have as much, hope as I had at 20, but more or less the same. Maybe I'll write another good story.

MK: But you mean all of the questions you have been asking all of your life, none of them have been answered?

SINGER: No. No question can be. Of course if I ask what time it is and someone gives me the time, a question has been answered, but when it comes to the so-called eternal questions, none of them were answered.

MK: So you keep asking them?

SINGER: I was always compelled to. We always say what did God do. And God is silent as ever. We have to make peace with it or else.

23

===

Belgium,
On a Bank
of the Yser

IN THE 1970S, WHILE JEWISH LIFE WAS PROSPERING IN Antwerp's diamond district, something very different was happening sixty miles away by a bank of the Yser River along a flat, muddy stretch to the North Sea. In the Flemish language it was called the *IJzerbedevaart*, the pilgrimage to the Yser. An annual event that began in 1920, the IJzerbedevaart was the kind of internecine Belgian affair that had rarely interested Belgian Jews. It had to do with the animosity between the Flemish, who are essentially Catholic ethnic Dutch, and the French-speaking Belgians. It was a dispute between Catholics.

The pilgrimage was supposed to be a demonstration for peace, a ceremonial march to a dank and stark monument, a 150-foot-high tower with a bulky Celtic cross on the top. The words "no more war" are written on the tower in four languages. But it has never been a very peaceful pilgrimage. In the beginning, the Flemish made the pilgrimage to commemorate their staggering losses in the World War I trenches under the leadership of French-speaking officers. Why had the frontline troops been 80 percent Flemish without any Flemish-speaking officers? The IJzerbedevaart quickly turned into an expression of Flemish nationalism—the desire of the Flemish to have a separate country. Flemish nationalism is not popular with Belgian Jews because Antwerp is in the Flemish region and because, while Antwerp Jews claim to have a generally good relationship with their Flemish neighbors, those who lived through the German occupation remember that the extreme nationalists had many Nazi sympathizers in their ranks.

By the 1970s, the Flemish, once the minority, made up more than half of the Belgian population, and within that population was a strong Flemish nationalist movement. At the same time a new crop of Europeans was emerging, and the IJzerbedevaart drew them with a magnetic force. Europe's second generation of Nazis, neo-Nazis, were coming into their own, and the Flemish pilgrimage gave them a place to meet—a place for British Nazis to meet Spanish Nazis, and more important, a place for the older ideological Nazis to connect with brutal young men who were looking for a reason to hit someone. A half-century after it started, Jews began to notice the IJzerbedevaart and the one-story village of Diksmuide where it took place.

Among some 30,000 Flemish nationalists, only a few hundred foreign fascists attended the weekend. The organizers claimed that the foreign extremists were unwelcome but did nothing to keep them out. They virtually took over the town for the weekend. The few main streets of this village, the cozy Belgian cafés and dark bars, were filled with men of varying ages in gray and black uniforms and jungle fatigues, sporting swastikas, SS insignia, and other fascist emblems, passing out books and brochures—many of them printed in the United States in a variety of languages—praising the Third Reich and berating immigrants, Jews, and Zionists.

While the pilgrimage was sponsored by groups with strongly antimilitary sentiment, uniformed young paramilitaries marched, legs high, through the little main street of Diksmuide. In Belgium, as in much of Europe, there are laws against "the open display of Nazi nostalgia," which includes wearing Nazi insignia and uniforms and goose-stepping through town. But while the gendarmerie stayed vigilant and occasionally confiscated a club or knife, it did little to enforce the anti-Nazi laws. The city authorities were concerned only that the Flemings to whom they had given permission to march appeared to have had their ranks thoroughly infiltrated by West Germans.

Diksmuide is in the heart of militant Flanders, and the great majority of the Nazi nostalgists were Flemish nationalists. The town's mayor, Hendrik Laridon, was a member of the Flemish Christian Democratic party, a moderate center-right party that often dominated Belgian governments. He stood passively on the main street as hundreds goose-stepped by and, in a familiar refrain, asserted that the wise policy was to let the young people "blow off steam."

After they marched, they blew off more steam in the taverns at one end of town, where they traded contraband Nazi memorabilia concealed in the innermost compartments of wallets, drank a great deal of beer, and expounded on their visions of Europe. The British, some in uniform, preached against Pakistanis. The Dutch denounced the Surinamese, the French lashed out at North Africans, and the Germans raged against the Turks. They also denounced each other. The northerners hated the Mediterraneans, although Spanish and Italian fascists were present. Scuffles with clubs and knives periodically erupted. As one neo-Nazi explained, they were, after all, nationalists. The one harmonious note in these beer-soggy interchanges was that they could all agree on their hatred of Jews. Most of them seemed to greatly enjoy explaining their own particular racist theories. These were young men with an inner anger because no one had ever wanted to listen to them. Neo-Nazis were usually instantly seduced by the proposition that someone thought they were significant. The appeal of being a neo-Nazi was that people paid attention to Nazis. Nazis had a history, and they frightened and worried people.

Not all of the neo-Nazis were young. The older ones did not seem to want attention and shied away from uniforms and fascist salutes, instead quietly talking to the younger ones. Toward the end of the 1970s an even newer crop of Nazis began to appear at Diksmuide—the skinheads.

The skinheads were different. They, of course, looked different. Their heads were shaved and often tattooed and their laced boots were often the largest thing about them. The fashion had recently started in the working-class districts of British cities, where the boots were used for "Paki bashing"—attacking Pakistani immigrants. But the idea had already spread to Germany, and the German skinheads were the scariest-looking people in Diksmuide. For one thing, they tended to be larger than the other Nazis. Maybe it was just the boots. Or maybe it was just that they were German and spoke German and thus resembled the real Nazis.

The skinheads did not mix with the neo-Nazis. They mainly kept to themselves and drank. Later, when there was less debating and more fighting, the skinheads came into their own. Nazis and neo-Nazis could hammer out the arguments. Skinheads just wanted the action.

By late Saturday night, there was enough action to keep the skinheads happy. The northerners had to show the Mediterraneans their place, and the Flemish had to show all the foreigners their place. It is not easy to have an international gathering of violent xenophobes. A dark bar called the Flemish House was the center of the beer-drinking and Sieg-heiling. Everyone liked to Heil Hitler. But the Flemish House was also the neighborhood pub, and townspeople were still there too—housewives, families with children, and cuddling young couples—none of whom showed any sign of seeing anything disturbing this night. The Flemish sporadically gave straight-armed fascist salutes and shouted "Sieg Heil!" They were particularly happy when they could get a chorus going—sixty or more Flemish nationalists rhythmically jutting their arms out and shouting "Sieg Heil" over and over. These volleys greatly excited the foreign visitors. German skinheads stood up and stuck out their muscular tatoos and joined the chant. A small contingent of Italians from the neofascist party MSI (Italian Socialist Movement) got excited and started countering with shouts of "Il Duce!" This angered the German skinheads, which in turn reminded the Flemish nationals that the Germans were shouting in German, not in Flemish. "We can say it, but the Germans have no right to say it in Flanders," said one Belgian Army sergeant stationed near Dortmund who had come in for the weekend festivities. The Flemish looked for opportunities to jump the German skinheads, but this was difficult to do because the Germans stuck together in a large group.

The British—an assortment of brown-shirted National Front members, Scottish nationalists, members of a fascist movement called League of Saint George, and skinheads—were easier to isolate and run out of the bar. Some of them were severely clubbed.

The British were upset by the quantity of pro-German literature. Most of it celebrated the exploits of Flemish volunteers who fought for the Third Reich against the British and Americans. A British National Front member said in a wounded tone of voice, "I feel sort of unwelcome here with my Union Jack." This was particularly problematic since his Union Jack was tattooed on the top of his shaved head.

Only their hatred of Jews tied these groups together. They could always turn to this subject when they got bored with Dutchmen railing against Surinamers and Germans ranting about Turks. The Diksmuide meeting was, in fact, what monitors of anti-Semitism most feared—a meeting place for extremists from very separate segments of European society, people who did not often have occasion to encounter one another. With neo-Nazi groups growing in the 1970s, a new set of political opportunists was also emerging. As European unemployment figures steadily rose, they could exploit irrational anti-immigrant sentiments. In France the National Front was flourishing under Jean-Marie Le Pen, a veteran of the anti-Semitic Poujadeist movement that had briefly gotten into the National Assembly in the 1950s. The Dutch Centrum party won a legislative seat in the early 1980s on an anti-immigrant platform. In 1983 a former SS officer, Franz Schönhuber, founded the Republican party in Germany. These new parties avoided overt association with anything Nazi. They were sophisticated politicians looking for voters. They kept their language coded so that it would appeal to racists without scaring those who feared Nazis. They denounced immigrants and said they should be sent back where they came from, but they always argued that the immigrants would be better off there. Anti-Semitism was to be avoided as sounding too Nazi-like, although there were occasionally slips, such as Le Pen calling the gas chambers a minor point in World War II history.

In Diksmuide, activists from these political movements could make contacts with disreputable neo-Nazis and even skinheads, as well as the new crop of intellectuals that had emerged to say that the Holocaust was a lie that the Jews had foisted on history. In 1978 a group called the Institute for Historical Review was founded in California, offering $50,000 to anyone who could prove that at least one Jew had been gassed in Auschwitz, $25,000 for evidence that Anne Frank's diary wasn't a fake, and $25,000 for a bar of soap made from Jews. They later backed down, saying that this was just a publicity stunt. They also advertised the European Revisionist Tour, which was to visit Dachau, Bergen-Belsen, and Auschwitz, then wind up in Diksmuide for the IJzerbedevaart.

The IJzerbedevaart was a place where the men of thought could recruit the men of action.

24

In Antwerp

IF ASSIMILATION REMAINED A DIFFICULT ISSUE AMONG JEWS in Paris, in Antwerp it was simply a dirty word. But of course, in Antwerp there were always other things to argue about. The official Community had split into two organizations. One described itself as Orthodox. The other insisted it was more Orthodox. The Hasidim did not join either but remained about a dozen small cults centered around their own rabbis and their own small synagogues, often just a room in a building. All of these groups enjoyed good relations with each other. They would occasionally pray at each other's synagogues. They would go to each other's celebrations. Only an expert in Jewish affairs would have been capable of discerning the difference between the two principal "communities." But whenever a communique from Antwerp Jewry was needed, they would be certain to disagree on the wording.

Wandering through the Jewish neighborhood at sundown, the mutter of *minchah*, short prayers of the afternoon service, could be heard from buildings and houses on most blocks. Each synagogue had its own atmosphere, often determined by the personality of the religious leader. The Van Den Nestlei, rebuilt in 1954 to replace the ruins, served as the center for one community. It was large and modern, with its white pillars supporting a balcony, modernist stained glass, and a renowned silken-voiced cantor. The other community had restored its old synagogue, farther down along the turreted stoneworks of the train tracks. Past that was a block of ordinary Flemish stone buildings where no prayer was heard, but in one of these houses, down a long, dark tenement corridor, was a room on the right with a high enough ceiling for a small balcony. There a small group of Jews of German origin quietly prayed. This was the Eisenmann Shul, the one the Nazis had never found. The explanation always given was that the Nazis had missed it because these Jews were so quiet when they prayed. While every other synagogue was filled with gossip and chatting, at the Eisenmann Shul there was still a strictly kept rule of silence. It was the kind of German Jewish thing that Irene Runge so disliked.

A Jew looking for a Friday-night service in another European city might go to a Jewish neighborhood, sight a man with a hat or yarmulke, and follow him. It would be more complicated in Antwerp because the streets were full of hatted men, and they headed in twenty different directions, clutching their hats and darting through the train line's dark underpasses of ornate ironwork and tattered posters. Christians stroll to church. Jews always seem to be rushing to synagogue, as though late for an appointment.

In its Jewish neighborhood of about thirty blocks Antwerp gives the impression on a Friday night that it is the most Jewish city in Europe. In truth, this provincial center of a half-million people is in some ways Belgium's most Flemish city, with its northern Renaissance old center chilled by harsh gusts of wind from the mouth of the Scheldt, its trim and serious nineteenth-century housing, and its wide modern boulevards. The architecture offers an assortment of symmetrically ornate old Dutch brick, elegantly swirled art nouveau, and stark modern—all set against a chronically gray sky. The Flemish do not go out at night, unless to go to their neighborhood pubs, or if they do leave their neighborhood, they drive. There are no traffic jams in Antwerp. Virtually the only pedestrian crowds, aside from tourists in the old town, are the Orthodox Jews who cannot drive on the Sabbath. By the late 1970s, their neighborhood seemed so prosperous, so concentrated, that it was easy to forget that some twenty thousand Antwerp Jews was less than half the prewar population, which had lived in a far larger area of the city.

Flanders as a safe harbor for the late flourishing of Orthodox Judaism is not without its logic. The Flemish, while achieving an affluent modern standard of living, have remained Europe's most steadfast traditionalists. They have kept their folk customs and the local rituals of each town. They still cling to the Catholic Church, and like the Jews they usually send their children to their own religious schools. Like Orthodox Jews, the Flemish believe in large families (though in recent years the Flemish birthrate has not been keeping up with the Hasidim). Like their Yiddish-speaking neighbors, they refuse to part with or dilute their dialect. Flemish, which varies from town to town, has remained a purer form of Dutch than in Holland, where Amsterdamers like to adopt foreign words. Flemish eat their own cuisine—stews, husepots, and waterzoois—which are not flashy enough to interest foreigners but help fight the chill of a North Sea wind. Were it not for the fading memories of World War II recalled by the extreme Flemish nationalist movement—which grew more boisterous in the 1970s and by the end of the decade openly violent—Antwerp Jews could have felt totally at home in this Flemish heartland. There is even a marked preference for beards among Flemish men.

Not all Antwerp Jews were religious, and it was sometimes whispered that the nonreligious might count for more than 50 percent. But the nonreligious also sent their children to Jewish schools. More than 90 percent of Antwerp's Jewish children attend Jewish schools, the highest attendance record of any Jewish community in the world. And even the nonreligious will often keep kosher homes so that they can invite their friends and business associates.

But the many Jewish schools do not include a university. The community is not a particularly well-educated one because it is centered around diamonds, a trade where a good income can be earned without an education. Jewish education in Antwerp emphasizes fluency in Yiddish and Hebrew and religious study. Yiddish is the most commonly heard language in the Jewish quarter, and it is the working language of the diamond trade.

Dress is one of the ways that Antwerp Jews stand out. It is intentional. The clothing of the ultra-Orthodox serves to make a statement about commitment to a special life, a uniquely Jewish life. The belief is that a distinct exterior guards against assimilation and separates a Jew for a particularly pious life. Before the war, in places where Jews lived separate and pious lives, married women wore wigs, men wore curled side locks, long beards, black wool clothing, and broad-brimmed hats over their yarmulkes. The war generation, remembering their yellow stars, felt ambiguous about this idea of being visually set apart. Orthodox men simply wore a hat. They usually did not even grow beards. But their children, raised on tales of the Holocaust, grew up defiant. They thought their parents' generation had paid for being too meek, for trying too hard to get along. They wanted to dare to make the statement, "I am a Jew and I am here." The more outrageous, the better, according to the thinking of this new generation of observant Jews. Hats became even bigger. The *shtreimel*, a wide sable fur hat from pre-twentieth century Poland, became popular for young men to wear on the Sabbath in Antwerp. Beards and *peots*—curled side locks—became longer and were brushed, shampooed, and curled for greater elegance.

Dwora and Hershl Silberman were of that more modest wartime generation. Although he was strictly religious, Hershl Silberman shaved every morning and dressed like any other Belgian man. But his son Mechilim, named after Dwora's father, started wearing Hasidic clothes as a child in the late 1950s, even before it became fashionable. Mechilim did not approve of the way his father appeared to hide his Jewishness. If a gentile even knocked on the door, he noticed his father would quickly remove his hat. That was not the kind of Jew he wanted to be. Where had that attitude gotten his parents' generation? Mechilim wore black and *peots* and hats, and when he could, he would grow a beard for everyone to see. At first, he was thought a little odd, but by the time he was an adult, this was the normal look for Antwerp Jews.

THE MEN IN ANTWERP started their weekdays at seven-thirty in the various synagogues, where they wrapped *tefillin* so tightly that their arms turned red, and they said their morning prayers. Then they had breakfast together—coffee, herring, eggs. A few deals were made. A broken watch could be shown to the jeweler, some silver might be discussed with the silver dealer. And there were family matters—matches to be made, marriages to be arranged. By nine o'clock, they were all off to work. It was all in Yiddish, and some older immigrants, finding that Yiddish was all that they needed, never learned Flemish.

They intermarried with the world's other traditional communities. Antwerp, New York, Jerusalem, and London were places where traditional Jews searched for marriage partners. Young people were constantly marrying in and out of Antwerp. The families had four and five children, and with some leaving and others marrying in, the population remained fairly stable at a little more than twenty thousand.

246 | A   C H O S E N   F E W

A typical new arrival was Levy Kohane. His family were Bobover Hasidim who had fled Poland in the 1930s and settled in Antwerp. At the beginning of the occupation, all but the father had been shot during a Nazi roundup of Jews. After the war the father had settled in Paris where, though he said he had lost his beliefs, he raised his four children according to Hasidic tradition. Levy was allowed no contact with girls until he was 20. Then a marriage was arranged with an Antwerp girl. A contract was signed, and the two were brought together. Levy's first impression: "What could I think? It was one of my first meetings with a girl. Her first with a boy." They settled in Antwerp and started having children.

SLOWLY DURING THE 1970s the diamond industry changed. Before the war most of the world's diamonds had been made in Antwerp. It was the only center that handled large quantities. But now, as in all manual labor industries, there was competition from impoverished countries. Sawing, cleaving, and polishing could all be done cheaper in India. In Antwerp, when cleaving was done at all, it no longer involved much labor since it was generally executed with amazing speed with the use of laser beams. Antwerp's diamond district gradually began moving away from the manufacturing of diamonds, but it remained prosperous as the world's great diamond trading center. Brokers peddling rough stones to manufacturers and dealers trading in finished diamonds remained. About three-fourths of the rough diamonds in the world still passed through Antwerp. But fewer of them were being cut there.

Sam Perl closed his sawing factory. After the war there had been about 250 sawers in Antwerp, but by 1980 only some twenty-five remained. Perl used his knowledge from a lifetime in diamonds to become a successful dealer.

Pinchas Kornfeld started as a cleaver like his father, Israel. He did not pass the time listening to people's troubles while cleaving, as his father had. He had heard enough of that as a child and wanted to avoid Holocaust stories. Instead, he carefully recorded major passages of the Talmud and other commentaries on a reel-to-reel tape recorder, so that he could study while cleaving at home. By the 1970s, he too could see that manufacturing was moving away from Antwerp. In 1979 he became a broker. Then he was a businessman and not a craftsman, and for that, he said, the only thing that was needed was "*mazel,*" luck. Behind the Pelikaanstraat near the train station, is a little S-hook of four streets lined with modern glass buildings high enough to block the sun on the rare sunny day. This is the diamond district, concentrated mainly in three buildings, the Bourse, the Club, and the Kring (ring). Diamonds are traded there, often around a table in a small office with a small, accurate scale. The Diamond Kring, where brokers such as Pinchas Kornfeld traded, specializes in the rough stones.

Kornfeld was active in Jewish institutions such as Agudat Israel, a worldwide Orthodox organization. Because Pinchas was soft-spoken and diplomatic, he seemed a good choice for handling anxious parents whose children would be attending an Agudat Israel summer camp in the Ardennes. Someone had to talk to the parents, assure them that their children would be well looked after, that the vegetarian wouldn't get meat, and that the boy who had to leave early would get back.

In the summer of 1980, on the day the children were leaving, Kornfeld went to the Agudat Israel office where the bus would be parked and the parents would gather with their children, waiting for him to reassure them. It would take patience, but it had to be done. Trying to make the day more enjoyable, he brought his own six-year-old son and his little daughter, who were both still too little for the camp. They could play around the bus where the older children were gathering.

Levy Kohane was there with his father, seeing off his younger brother David. David was very quiet and studious. He had been very attached to his mother and had seemed depressed since her death a year before. At 15, he was the baby of the family, and everyone fussed over him and worried about him. The summer camp would probably be good for him. His brother and father said their good-byes and walked away. As Levy crossed the street, he noticed a young man at the corner throwing rocks. This kind of thing was happening sometimes now—some troubled kid would decide to throw a few rocks at the Jews.

But then he realized that the man on the corner was not throwing rocks, he was throwing hand grenades. He threw two, and then sprinted down the street. Kornfeld heard the explosion and ran outside. Children were standing wide-eyed in the street. People were scurrying in different directions, not knowing where to run, while younger children stood paralyzed with terror. Kornfeld caught a glimpse of his own children, but he did not have time to comfort them because there was so much blood on people, on the street. He called the police and ambulances arrived in two minutes, which was still too late for David Kohane. With a piece of shrapnel through his chest, he writhed in agony for a few seconds, and when his father leaned over him, he whispered, "It hurts." Then he died, the only fatality. But 20 of the 55 people present were wounded.

Minutes later, the police caught the killer. The attack had been on a narrow treeless street of solid, high-ceilinged big-windowed houses in the heart of the residential section of the Jewish neighborhood. The killer had apparently planned to escape to the Belgielei, the wide-open boulevard that led to the train tracks by the Van Den Nestlei synagogue. From there, it would have been easy to follow the tracks up Pelikaanstraat to the train station. To run almost the entire length of the Jewish ghetto through the main thoroughfares on a lazy, uncrowded summer day does not seem like much of an escape plan. But the attacker didn't even do that. He got confused on the Belgielei, where there is a traffic circle that always confuses out-of-towners, and he turned the wrong way, heading back toward the scene of the crime and into the hands of the police.

The man was a twenty-five-year-old Palestinian, Nasser Al-Saied. A resident of Saudi Arabia, he claimed to be working for a dissident movement of El Fatah, acting under the orders of someone named Wahid who was never found. His attorney pleaded that he was "a Palestinian soldier" and pointed out that he had been raised "in a particularly abject brutality." The attorney described the plight of homeless Palestinians and how his parents, farmers near Jaffa, had been forced off their land in the 1948 war. Nasser was said to be a good soldier who unquestioningly followed instructions and was not a criminal. Proof of this, according to his attorney, was the fact that although armed, he did not resist arrest.

The jury pondered these issues for one hour before returning with a verdict of guilty. He was sentenced to death, a symbolic gesture since there was no capital punishment in Belgium. A death penalty is automatically reduced to twenty years with the possibility of release after ten years.

In his own defense, Nasser Al-Saied had stated that he had acted "out of conviction." He denied being anti-Jewish. His only quarrel was with Zionism. Nasser, the anti-Zionist, had attacked a program of Agudat Israel, itself a somewhat anti-Zionist organization that had accepted the founding of the Jewish state with considerable ambivalence. As for his victim David Kohane, who was buried in the Jewish cemetery in Putte, across the Dutch border, he and his family were Bobover Hasidim. They spoke Yiddish as a first language but rejected modern Hebrew. Ancient Hebrew was reserved for prayer. David's brother Levy explained, "Yiddish is the language of Jews. [Modern] Hebrew is the language of Israelis." To him, Israel was in a sense "anti-Jewish," because it led Jews away from traditional Jewish life, the kind of life that he followed in Antwerp. This was the kind of Zionist that was killed at the age of 15 by this Palestinian soldier.

The attack was in July 1980. In 1990, Nasser Al-Saied was set free. The Belgian government denied it had made a deal, but prior to Nasser Al-Saied's release, a Belgian family, the Houtekins, were taken hostage by Arabs. The Antwerp Jews immediately saw what was coming and wrote the government, saying they knew a trade would be proposed and asking the government to reject it. The foreign minister wrote back that such a swap would never be made. But elections were coming, and this typical wholesome Belgian family, the Houtekins, were in the newspapers every day until one day, miraculously, they were released. Soon after, Nasser Al-Saied, the Palestinian soldier, was himself released for good behavior.

25

In Paris

ISRAEL WAS STILL A GREAT PLACE TO BE YOUNG, AND WHEN
the Six-Day War was over, the demonstrations and fundraising
finished, Daniel Altmann went back to his northern kibbutz. Palestinian children would occasionally throw a rock, but you could still
have fun. A group of friends from the kibbutz volunteered for an
archaeological dig in the Greek Orthodox sector of Jerusalem. Digging in the bottom of a pit, they found oil lamps, not all of which
they turned over to the archaeologist. In addition to these souvenirs
they would save small shards of pottery that were of no archaeological value and sell them by the kilo to Arab merchants, who ground
them up and made "oil lamps from the time of Herod" to sell to
tourists.

But the Altmanns did not raise their children just to have fun,
and so Daniel returned to Paris, where he attended the prestigious
Paris Institute for Political Science Studies, "Sciences-Po." In this
leading university he met many of the Jewish intellectuals who a
decade later would emerge as key figures in the Socialist government of Sciences-Po graduate François Mitterrand. Daniel then
attended an elite officers' school and afterward, served as an officer
in Berlin. For major holidays he would go to a West Berlin synagogue that was packed with American soldiers. After a two-year
tour as a French officer, he joined the family steel business in
northern France, where he had no contact at all with Judaism.

He had never lived much of a Jewish life, but in Valenciennes, a town near the Belgian border—where, for the first time, he was completely cut off from other Jews—a question came to him: "Am I a Jew or not?" It seemed to him, at 26, that he had to make a choice. He had behind him the whole history of the Blums, the Lévys, and the Altmanns. He thought about his great-grandfather, who had believed he was an established businessman until the Dreyfus case forced him to flee; about his grandfather, who lived the good life in Paris until the Nazis came and he had to sell his business; about his uncle, who was deported despite his changed name; and about the way his parents had raised him and his two sisters to be affluent Parisians who only occasionally entertained the idea of Jewishness. You can't be a little bit Jewish, can you? Aren't you either Jewish or not Jewish? Isn't that what we had all discovered by accident?

Daniel became active in Jewish fundraising activities, and soon he was president of a group called New Leadership, an organization of people like him—young Jews from wealthy families working to raise money for Israel. Daniel organized visits to Israel, going back himself several times. More than fun and funny pottery, this work had become a way for him to feel Jewish, feel involved with Jewish life. But did giving money, raising funds, mean being involved in Judaism? He was still troubled, and one day at a Jewish wedding he began talking about this to a man he met. The man said, "Listen, if you want to search a bit, call me."

Altmann began spending one night a week studying the Mishnah, the first part of the Talmud. After a year his teacher said he needed a more advanced teacher and sent him to Rue Pavée, to the dank and moldy building next to the Rue Pavée synagogue where Chaim Rottenberg and his wife Rifka lived. On the top floor, in a large threadbare room with worn floorboards, Rav Rottenberg taught a small group of men on Thursday nights. They were the people he had somehow grabbed to join his fast-growing community.

In 1978, the year that Altmann met him, Rottenberg was still a man of boundless energy, a rigorous, uncompromising enforcer. Before Passover that year, he had gone to Strasbourg to inspect the matzoh makers, storming into the factory in his black coat, asking questions, looking around, making sure the matzoh was baked in no more than eighteen minutes because, it is thought, leavening could take place if it were baked any longer. The matzoh dough was being mixed in a huge vat, and Rottenberg had to climb up a ladder to peer in and make sure everything looked kosher and chametz free. Preoccupied by the inspection, he lost his balance and fell off the ladder.

To Rifka, this was the fatal fall, the fall from the matzoh vat, somehow God's will. In truth, the doctors examining him after the accident discovered he was suffering from Parkinson's disease. Thereafter he slowly weakened.

It took four years of study to turn Daniel Altmann, the wealthy assimilated Parisian, into a devout Orthodox Jew. He decided to marry and start a traditional family. Not exactly like Levy Kohane, who had never been in the company of a girl, thirty-year-old Altmann went to the synagogue, to the study group, the cheder, and asked for a suitable woman to marry. The community found him Lynda Abitan, a woman from a deeply religious Marrakesh family. Lynda's father had died when she was very young, and her mother had raised six children by herself, working in a factory, making sure they were all religious and well married. Lynda was the outspoken, independent, and still-unmarried one. Her mother was beginning to worry about her. She was religious, but she just didn't seem to be conforming to the Orthodox mold.

Thirteen years had passed since Lazare Bouaziz married Suzy Ewenczyk. More than half the Sephardic marriages were now with Ashkenazim, and it was no longer an issue that was given great importance. French Jewry had a Sephardic majority that had strongly colored the community and was thoroughly blending with it. The two groups were no longer distinct. In January 1981, the same year that Altmann married Lynda Abitan, René Sirat became the first North African Grand Rabbi of France. Much was made in the general press of the fact that this ruling Ashkenazic bastion was now falling to the Sephardim, as though the struggle for control of the community had been won by the North Africans. But Sirat's first official act the day he became Grand Rabbi was to go to the Soviet embassy and request a visa to visit Soviet Jews. The application was denied, but Sirat continued to apply pressure on the Soviets and to make sure that French Jewry did not forget about the struggle of Jews in the Soviet Union. Given the numbers and activism of Sephardic rabbis, it may be a long time before there is another Ashkenazic Grand Rabbi, but the ascent of Sirat may also have been the last time anyone would ever give it a thought. Even separate congregations were becoming increasingly rare.

The Altmanns were not concerned that Daniel was marrying a Sephardi, and in fact they greatly admired Lynda's mother as a tough, hard-working, industrious woman. One of Daniel's sisters had also married a Moroccan, and no one had seen that match as an issue. But after ten years, when that marriage failed, even happily married Daniel suspected that differences between Ashkenazim and Sephardim were to blame. "Matching an Ashkenazic woman with a Sephardic man is a big problem," he observed.

In 1981 the issue between the Altmanns and the Abitans was not Sephardim versus Ashkenazim. It was assimilation. Lynda was already a little wild, and it was worrisome to her deeply religious mother to see her marrying into this bourgeois French family. Even though Daniel had studied hard and had turned traditional, they worried about it lasting. Lynda's mother loved the Rue Pavée synagogue, because she claimed it was the only one in Paris that had never committed the outrage of having organ music. The other Altmanns rarely went to any synagogue at all. When they did, it was to the "liberal" synagogue on Rue Copernic, over in their expensive sixteenth arrondissement. At Copernic it was not just the music that was untraditional; there was not even separate seating for men and women.

The Altmanns had been eager for their son to get married. He had been "fooling around" for long enough. But his marriage to Lynda Abitan exposed them to a strange world that they did not like. They had tried not to say too much when their son grew a beard and started studying. But it was not until Daniel's wedding that they saw what his new world was really like. At the wedding not only did men and women sit apart, they did not even touch. They did not even dance together. Instead, Daniel would dance with the other bearded men while the women were off in another corner. What century was this all from? Modern successful Jews did not act like this. Who had influenced him? Who had changed him? Was he really going to live like strange oppressed people from some faraway backward country?

To LIVE A TRADITIONAL JEWISH LIFE means to live in a community centered around a rabbi and a synagogue that has to be within walking distance. But to live within walking distance of Rue Pavée was increasingly difficult. The Marais was getting refurbished. New museums were opening to draw tourists. Bit by bit, the old buildings that used to be propped up with thick timbers running into the narrow streets were getting reconstructed, resurfaced, carefully divided into apartments and sold for prices previously unknown in eastern Paris. The city had timed the Marais renovation well, and the buildings were becoming ready just as real estate prices were starting to rapidly inflate. It had closed the central market, Les Halles, and the entire historical center was being reworked. The Marais was no longer a working-class, commercial area. There was no longer a lively market to drift toward late at night. The working-class residents were being moved to the suburbs, while the buildings that had been working-class tenements for centuries were being turned into luxury apartments. The official claim was that the original tenants would be given opportunities to move back to their old neighborhood. But working-class people did not want to move into a deluxe neighborhood that offered high prices and few jobs.

The Altmanns—Daniel and Lynda—were not working-class people, and they could afford to live in the Marais, buying a large, two-floor apartment with a terrace a few minutes away from the synagogue. There was enough space to comfortably raise a large family. But most of the fifty families that belonged to Rottenberg's community were not wealthy international businessmen and had to find apartments ever farther away. Many had to walk forty minutes or an hour to attend Sabbath services on Rue Pavée.

The Pletzl, too, was being shaved away. It was now no more than Rue des Rosiers, Rue des Ecouffes, and Rue Pavée. It was becoming a curiosity for tourists, mentioned in guidebooks. You could buy a little pastry at Finkelsztajn's or some Sephardic treats from the Journos'. Or you could have lunch at Jo Goldenberg's, which had been one of the last surviving steamy one-room eateries in the Pletzl but was now expanded and cleaned up for foreign visitors.

Like many of the old Pletzl generation, Icchok Finkelsztajn had left for a better neighborhood before the renovation had gotten under way. It was this migration of the old working class that had opened up much of the property to renovation. In 1971, Icchok retired, and he and Dwojra moved to the north of the city behind Montmartre, where for a reasonable price they could rent a more spacious apartment in a nineteenth-century building that was not collapsing. In 1974, Leah Korcarz died, and the blue-tiled bakery on the corner of Rue des Ecouffes was sold out of the Finkelsztajn family. Henri, who had taken over his father's bakery, was the only family member still in the Pletzl, although he and his wife also now lived away from the crowded center. The apartment above the bakery could be used as an additional work space, making it possible to expand the offerings of foods to keep pace with the Journos across the street.

DURING THE 1970s, France experienced a fashion called "forties revival." Once De Gaulle and his official version of World War II faded from power, there was a great burst of interest in what had taken place in France during the war. Books were being written and movies produced. Film director Marcel Ophuls made *The Sorrow and the Pity*, a television documentary on daily life during the war in the provincial town of Clermont-Ferrand. The soon-to-be president of France, Valéry Giscard d'Estaing, happened to be from that region, and his family happened to be among many that the film showed in various degrees of collaboration and acquiescence. While the film was a sensation in New York, it never made it on to French television, which was state-controlled, until a decade later, when Giscard was defeated by François Mitterrand.

The more French people looked into the 1940s, the more toxic the atmosphere became. In 1978 a journalist for *L'Express* went to Spain to interview Louis Darquier de Pellepoix, the one-time head of Vichy's Office for Jewish Affairs. Darquier told *L'Express* that "only lice were gassed at Auschwitz." He then proceeded to deny that there had been a Holocaust. This was the same year that, while the Institute for Historical Review was coming into being in California, a crackpot professor in Lyons named Robert Faurisson started attracting attention by making outrageous statements. He was to become one of the most publicized of the Holocaust revisionists.

There were more serious problems than this in daily life. Attacks against both immigrants and Jews were becoming increasingly common. In 1975 there was an explosion in a synagogue near Rue Bleue. The following year, several organizations that monitored anti-Semitism were attacked. In 1977 anti-Semitic graffiti on Jewish sites noticeably increased, and several leaders were attacked. The rhythm of these attacks seemed to accelerate. In 1979 a Molotov cocktail was thrown at a synagogue, and a Jewish leftist, Pierre Goldman, was openly assassinated. In March a bomb went off in a Paris student's kosher restaurant at lunchtime, wounding dozens.

The next month a Molotov cocktail was thrown at the door of a Jewish hostel. In September one of the Paris stores of Daniel Hechter, a Jewish clothing designer, was bombed. In November firebombs were thrown at a Strasbourg synagogue.

Nineteen eighty was even worse. A synagogue in the Marne was attacked in April. In May an organization for deportees and Resistance fighters was hit. In September a Jewish business was set on fire. A few days later, automatic weapons were fired on the central synagogue, a Jewish day care center, the Memorial to the Unknown Jewish Martyr, and a school.

On Friday, October 3, at 7:30, when the evening Sabbath service should have been ending, a bomb exploded in front of the Rue Copernic synagogue. Because the service had run a little late, there were fewer fatalities than planned. Still, more than twenty people were injured, including some inside the synagogue. Four people who had happened down the short street at the time were killed. One of them, by coincidence, was an Israeli tourist. The others were non-Jews. French Prime Minister Raymond Barre was quick to denounce "this odious attack which was intended for Jews on their way to the synagogue and which struck innocent Frenchmen crossing the street."

Was not this statement a symptom of one of the problems? A government which distinguished between Jews and innocent Frenchmen? The Jewish community had had enough. A huge demonstration was quickly organized with the labor unions and opposition political parties. Some 300,000 people marched against racism and anti-Semitism. Some estimates of the crowd were as high as 500,000. The wide, long boulevard that extends from Republique to Bastille was filled.

An hour after the explosion, a telephone call claimed authorship of the attack for a small neo-Nazi group called Fédération d'Action Nationaliste Européenne, commonly known as FANE. The organization was officially banned one month later, which in practical terms only meant that it had to change its name. In Belgium and West Germany there were similar laws, and neo-Nazis had become skilled at running a variety of organizations and quickly turning one that was banned into another. The Flemish Military Organization, after being banned in 1983, became the Flemish Bloc. In Germany the Aktionsfront Nationaler Sozialisten was banned and became the Nationale Sammlung, which was banned and became the Deutsche Alternative. Year after year, the same people showed up at Diksmuide with different names for their organizations. The year after the French government banned FANE, the FANE activists were at Diksmuide under the name FNE. A mere inconvenience for the neo-Nazis, the name changes created total confusion for law enforcement.

The police investigation could not show who had planted the bomb at the Rue Copernic synagogue. Accusations landed all over the political spectrum. Extreme right leader Jean-Marie Le Pen accused the KGB. Arabs and Basques came under suspicion. Increasingly, so did the French police, recalling that Pierre Goldman's unsolved murder was claimed by a group called "Honor of the Police." A police union official, Jose Deltorn, asserted that he knew of thirty police officers who were active in extreme right-wing organizations, including FANE. But when the government challenged him, he was discredited because he could prove that only nineteen of these policemen were neo-Nazis.

Jean-Marie Le Pen's National Front was becoming better organized. There was also something called the New Right, which was supposed to be highly intellectual. A popular newspaper magazine, *Le Figaro*, published articles in their Sunday magazine about biological determinism and the inherent inferiority and superiority of certain peoples. *Le Figaro* is published by France's leading press baron, Robert Hersant, who had gotten his start contributing to the collaborationist press of Vichy France.

Middle East politics was also a factor in Europe's increasingly dangerous atmosphere. In 1977 the Labour party lost the Israeli elections, and power passed to Menachem Begin, a man who had previously been labeled a disreputable terrorist because of his war against the British Mandate and his extremist view on Palestinians. Begin's rise divided Jewish opinion. Aaron Waks in Düsseldorf cheered Begin's victory, but his two sons in Israel were appalled. The idea of a disreputable right-wing extremist as Israeli prime minister made the European leftist press even more sympathetic to the Palestinians, but an overall impression that the world was turning against Israel had already contributed to the rise of Israeli hardliners. In 1975 the UN General Assembly passed a resolution giving official sanction to a favorite European line of anti-Semitism. The resolution, in language that was very familiar in Central Europe, declared that Zionism was a form of racism. Yasser Arafat, leader of the Palestinian Liberation Organization, after committing numerous acts of terrorism, denounced the future use of terrorism and was accorded head-of-government status by the United Nations.

UNDER GISCARD D'ESTAING, French foreign policy became overtly pro-Arab. The PLO was permitted to open an office in Paris. Between 1973 and 1980 the price of oil went from $3 a barrel to more than $38, and undeveloped Arab nations were awash in cash that they were ready to spend on arms and other projects. Among the lucrative contracts France grabbed was one for a nuclear reactor for Iraq. The radical Arab nations also had money to finance small Palestinian breakaway groups that rejected Arafat's newly moderate position. It had been one such group that had sent Nasser Al-Saied to Antwerp.

But the Jews of France were worried about Nazis, not Arabs. That was who history had conditioned them to fear. Even if the Copernic investigation was pointing toward the Middle East, it was clear that fascists were becoming increasingly active in France, and now at last, French people were united as never before against them. At last pressure was being put on a government that was so indifferent to right-wing extremism that President Giscard d'Estaing had not even interrupted his hunting weekend when news of the fatal synagogue bombing broke.

The only group that ever claimed responsibility for the attack was FANE, in a telephone call made by a bodyguard named Jean-Yves Pellay. Pellay was a giant with close-cropped gray hair, a scar on his forehead, and a menacing grin with one tooth missing. He had a nervous twitch that caused him to blink both eyes tightly closed so that he always looked as if he were trying to make sure he was awake. At the time he was only 28 years old.

Curiously, Pellay had been arrested in January 1980 for illegal possession of a firearm. He had been held for three months, during which time he was regularly questioned about which policemen were involved with FANE. This was nine months before the bombing and Jose Deltorn's accusation against the police.

Warily looking around a café one year after the bombing, Pellay whispered a strange story of a Jewish mother and time he had spent in Israel and then in service with the French Foreign Legion. In Paris he had been approached by a small radical Jewish group that wanted him to infiltrate FANE. While he was providing the neo-Nazis with paramilitary training, he was passing on information to the Jewish group. He said that he made the telephone call claiming the synagogue bombing for FANE not at the request of FANE but at the request of his Jewish contacts. This was confirmed by the contacts. A few more established Jewish figures also confirmed that they were involved in the recruiting and use of Pellay as a double agent. Involved in monitoring and reporting on the extreme right, they wanted the government to move against FANE. They were not concerned about obstructing the police's search for the real perpetrators, because they reasoned that the police investigation would lead nowhere. The French police never solved these cases. In time the Israeli secret service would solve it, and in the meantime they would have forced law enforcement to mobilize against the extreme right.

As predicted, the French never solved the case, but in 1984 the Israeli secret service identified the Rue Copernic bombers as a dissident faction of George Habash's Popular Front for the Liberation of Palestine.

AUGUST IS Paris's quietest month. It is the month favored by Parisians for their month-long vacation. The only shops and restaurants that remain open are the ones trying to catch August tourists. In the old days this didn't have much to do with the Pletzl, since the poor immigrants who lived there had nowhere to go. But by the 1980s, even Rue des Rosiers closed down in August, except for Goldenberg's, whose business had become largely with tourists visiting the newly discovered Marais. At the height of the lunchtime rush on August 9, 1982, two men walked into Goldenberg's with Polish-made automatic pistols, and as staff and customers dove under tables and crawled behind counters, they sprayed bullets, systematically working from the cashier's counter along the bar to the tables, and even into the kitchen, where they shot a cook. Then, with the confidence of professionals, they backed out, still firing, and worked their way down Rue des Rosiers, walking calmly behind a white getaway car being driven by an accomplice while they watched doorways and windows and fired at anyone who appeared.

Finkelsztajn's was closed for the month of August, but Henri was in the shop, seated behind the counter watching television. He heard small explosions, and since the shades were down on the storefront windows, he wondered what was going on in the street. He got up and went to the door and then realized it was probably just kids with firecrackers left over from Bastille Day. And so he went back to his seat behind the counter instead of walking outside into the automatic pistols of the two men, who were now in front of his store deciding whether to continue on Rue des Rosiers or turn up Rue des Hospitalières-Saint-Gervais. They took the smaller street past the Journos and fired on a café before vanishing from the neighborhood.

A few minutes later, a bulletin appeared on television that there had been an attack on Rue des Rosiers. When Henri Finkelsztajn opened his door, people were running down the street. He walked down to where a crowd had gathered in front of Goldenberg's. There was blood on the ground, and people were wailing and shouting. Six people were dead and twenty-one wounded. Eighty spent bullets were found in the restaurant. A young Arab whose father, a longtime Goldenberg employee, had been killed was sobbing uncontrollably. The Algerian who now ran the café in the space next to Finkelsztajn was there. André Journo, who had taken to smoking large Cuban cigars, turned up and was making strong angry statements to journalists. Pletzl people stayed in the street all afternoon and argued about the Nazis and the PLO, which still had a Paris office, and the government and the police.

When Finkelsztajn went home, he turned on the television news, which reported that young Jews had come to Rue des Rosiers and shouted anti-Arab slogans in a demonstration. Finkelsztajn had not seen Jews shouting anti-Arab slogans. There was no logic to it, since some of the victims were Arab and the neighborhood was increasingly mixed. He angrily telephoned the television station, France-3, told them who he was, and said that he had been there all day and there had been no such demonstration. It was explained to him that nevertheless the story was true, because a reporter had been there. Finkelsztajn was furious. There was no Arab-Jewish problem in the Pletzl—the press was inventing one.

Mitterrand, the newly elected president, demonstrating the difference between himself and his predecessor, spoke at a memorial service at the Rue Pavée synagogue. But once again the French police could not find the attackers. Goldenberg stayed open the rest of the summer, but only a few friends or an occasional reporter came. No one wanted to eat lunch there. One Jewish woman went there to eat lunch at the counter out of defiance. "It's disgraceful. Disgraceful," she said. "People have to come here to show them. Otherwise they have won."

Goldenberg sat in one of the red-upholstered booths looking defeated. He had been born on Rue des Rosiers in 1923. Three years later, his father, who came from Odessa by way of Turkey, had opened the little restaurant. In 1943, Jo Goldenberg came home late one day just in time to see the police take away both his parents and two younger sisters. They were all killed in Auschwitz. Now Goldenberg thought about how he seemed to always miraculously escape, always arrive a moment later. He had missed this attack, too, coming in fifteen minutes later. He preserved the window with the bullet holes just where it was and erected a plaque to the six victims. It was decided that the anniversary, August 9, should become a Pletzl event. "We must commemorate August 9 every year," André Journo would say solemnly whenever a journalist showed up.

Angry young Jewish men, some armed, some only claiming to be, began to patrol the Pletzl, stopping people, demanding identification, asking questions. They were often rude and abrasive, a belligerent amateur burlesque of tough cops. They were not going to leave the safety of Jews in the hands of the French police any longer, and their deliberately exaggerated demeanor was to advertise the point that the Jews here on this street, where the police had quietly gathered up a previous generation forty years earlier, were no longer going to be the way they used to be.

A YEAR BEFORE the Goldenberg attack, two people had been killed and seventeen wounded when a grenade and automatic pistols were turned on a Vienna synagogue. The same type of W Z-63 Polish automatic pistol had been used and traced to a Palestinian dissident group led by Abou Nidal. Although this group and that of Arafat were bitter enemies, the Vienna Jewish Community angrily blamed the Bruno Kreisky government for its friendly relations with the PLO. They believed that Kreisky, who happened himself to be Jewish, inadvertently encouraged terrorism.

Three months after the Goldenberg attack, a bomb exploded in front of a synagogue in the Antwerp diamond district. Once again, the attackers had completely misread their target. They imagined that a synagogue in the heart of the diamond district, the only

nonmodern building in that little hook of streets behind the
Pelikaanstraat, would be a direct hit on the Jewish establishment.
In fact, the synagogue has little to do with the diamond district and
serves the small Sephardic community. The bomb was placed
there on the morning of Simchat Torah, a holiday which celebrates
the conclusion of the annual cycle of Torah readings, when all of
the Torahs are removed from the arc and carried around the synagogue to the accompaniment of singing and dancing. Children
join in, carrying candles and little flags. The next morning, the
celebration is repeated. But because in Antwerp Jews tend to be
excessive about these events, the night before they had danced late
into the night. Realizing that they would have only a few hours to
sleep, they postponed the nine o'clock morning service to nine-
thirty. The bomb went off at nine-fifteen, blowing out the metal
and glass facades of the diamond district and killing three and
wounding 106 people, all of them non-Jews. The Jews who worked
in diamonds were all in synagogues outside of the diamond district.

The bloodshed continued around Europe. Another man armed
with an automatic pistol opened fire on the entrance to a Brussels
synagogue during Rosh Hashanah services in September 1982. A
few weeks later, as a crowd was leaving a Rome synagogue at the
end of Sabbath morning services, assailants tossed hand grenades
and opened fire with machine guns, killing a two-year-old boy and
wounding thirty others. The Chief Rabbi of Rome charged that
such attacks had been encouraged by the Italian government's wel-
coming Yasser Arafat on a recent visit.

But the Palestinians were not the only problem. Even if an attack
such as the one on Goldenberg's showed every sign of Palestinian
work, the assailants clearly had their European admirers. Mysteriously, mimeographed flyers appeared around Amsterdam saying in
Dutch, "In the heart of Paris freedom fighters have done a brave
act." The statement attributed the attack to French "Nationalists . . .
nauseated by the fact that there are Jews in the Red French government. Fiterman, a real French name isn't it?" Charles Fiterman, a
Jewish Communist, was the minister of transportation in the new
leftist French government that had come to power in 1981.

Two of the bloodiest incidents of the period—the 1980 bombings of the Bologna train station, killing eighty-five, and the Munich Oktoberfest, killing 13—were both attributed to the extreme
right. The Munich bombing was traced to a "martial sports group"
led by Karl-Heinz Hoffmann. Shortly before the bombing, former

Bavarian Prime Minister Franz-Josef Strauss had been quoted describing the group as people who were picked on for doing nothing more than spending their Sundays hiking. Many leaders of the German extreme right spent time in Hoffmann's sports camp. Hoffmann was released for lack of evidence in the Oktoberfest case, and after his sports group was banned, he became involved with the PLO and for a time centered his activities in Lebanon.

In France alone, between 1977 and 1981, 290 violent acts were attributed to the extreme right. A 1981 West German government report claimed there were 200,000 right-wing extremists in Germany, but that "only" 3,000 were armed and ready to commit violence. In March 1981 the Sinus Institute, a West German pollster commissioned by the chancellor's office, found that 13 percent of the West German electorate—some five and a half million West Germans—held extreme right-wing political views. These views included hatred of foreign minorities and hatred of democracy and a reverence for what in German is called *Volk*, Germans as a racial entity. Almost half of these extremists said they approved of the use of violence.

Throughout Western Europe, verbal and physical attacks on immigrants became increasingly common in the early 1980s. The Germans, as is the habit of their culture, invented a word for hostility to foreigners, *Ausländerfeindlichkeit*. The neo-Nazi groups that had emerged in Germany in 1960 declined in the 1970s, but by 1980, they were larger and more active than ever before. As in France, the West German police seldom arrested right-wing extremists. On the other hand, in June 1983, when ten thousand people turned out to protest a planned rally of two hundred neo-Nazis in the Kreuzberg section of West Berlin, the police moved in with clubs and tear gas, and a pitched battle ensued in which 203 anti-Nazis were arrested. *"Ausländer ins KZ"*—foreigners to the concentration camp—became a common graffiti slogan. "Foreigners out!" in various languages was becoming a common slogan throughout Western Europe. What was no longer common anywhere in Western Europe was an unguarded synagogue or Jewish institution. A Jew looking for a Sabbath service needed only look for the armed guards strolling in the street.

FOR THE FIRST YEAR anniversary of the Goldenberg attack, French television did a special documentary interviewing Jo Goldenberg and other people in the Pletzl. André Journo eagerly took his turn to explain his theory of how defeated President Valéry Giscard d'Estaing had been behind the attack. Henri Finkelsztajn, whose schoolboy stutter occasionally flared, was not eager to make such media appearances, but he was still angry. After the attack the people of the Pletzl—Arabs, Jews, Christians, even some gypsies— were scared and worried and had spent that afternoon together talking, but no one had chanted anti-Arab slogans. This had to be made clear to the public.

With the camera running and lights so bright that his little bakery looked twice its size, Finkelsztajn found himself face to face with the old lines. He was asked if he was a Frenchmen. If so, why did he call himself a Jew? There was no stutter. Finkelsztajn, the high school drop-out, had a smile of wisdom and eyes that seemed to be winking as he explained, "I say I am a Jew because we are in France. When I am abroad, I say I am a Frenchman."

The interviewer, not content with this, pointed out that he was a Polish Jew. Henri, with the patience of a man who has spent a lifetime answering the same needless question, explained that he had never been to Poland, had had no contact with the country nor the slightest feelings for the place. Then he smiled his pleasant, amused smile—the same smile you get after buying one of his challahs.

PART SIX

EUROPE, NEW AGAIN

Denk ich an Deutschland in der Nacht
Dann bin ich um den Schlaf gebracht
(When I think of Germany in the night, I'm robbed of
my sleep)

—HEINRICH HEINE

26

In Poland

IN SEPTEMBER 1989, HENRYK HALKOWSKI, THE DIRECTOR of the musty, nearly deserted Jewish social club in Cracow, was eager to show foreign visitors his town. For the first time since immediately after the war, Poland had a non-Communist prime minister. The Polish Communist dictatorship was over, and among the new freedoms was the possibility of showing your town to a Westerner without being watched by the secret police. Halkowski was an enthusiastic man in his late thirties with steel-rimmed glasses and a sardonic smile. On the day that Tadeusz Mazowiecki was installed as the first non-Communist prime minister, a New York University professor was in Cracow and Halkowski wanted to take him to the place where Tadeusz Kościuszko had first vowed to fight for Polish independence almost two centuries earlier. Halkowski liked the idea that at this historic moment of the new Polish state, he should take someone to this historic spot. He also knew that Kościuszko was the one Polish patriot whose name was known to New Yorkers—because of the bridge bearing his name on the Brooklyn Queens Expressway.

Halkowski led the visitor to the large, empty medieval market-place in the center of town that a few years later would be filled with tourist cafés. As he and his guest stopped at the very spot of the Kościuszko vow, six young people with shaved heads and laced boots whom he had never seen before pulled him from behind and knocked him down. As they beat him with their fists, they shouted in German, *"Jude, Jude, Jude,"* and then ran off. There was a police station nearby, but the militia that didn't allow youth to roam the streets attacking Jews, let alone curse them in German, had already been disbanded.

THE NEW POLISH STATE, which had for Halkowski so inauspiciously begun, was the fruit of two decades of political resistance. The crisis of the Communist state had become so extreme that the military had sought the help of the opposition but in the process gradually negotiated itself out of existence. The opposition had to be legalized, and then parliamentary elections had to be allowed. Power evaporated from Communist hands more rapidly than even Solidarity had been prepared for.

It fell to the former *Polityka* chief, Marian Turski's longtime editor Mieczysław Rakowski, to ease the transition, first as prime minister, then as Jaruzelski's replacement, becoming the last first secretary of a ruling Polish Communist party. In July, Rakowski appointed the last Communist-led government, but it lacked a following, and in August he had to replace the prime minister with a non-Communist.

The dream had failed. The Communist state for which people like Marian Turski had been working all their lives had collapsed, bankrupt in every sense. Turski and his associates had been fighting this failure for thirty years. Ever since the Soviets invaded Hungary in 1956 and they saw that the Communism they had dreamed of was betrayed, they had been trying to get it back to what it was supposed to be. Turski said of the final collapse, "It was not a certain must. There could have been a lot of change." The existing power was to Communist reformers like Turski a monster that used the label "Communism," although they themselves were never able to mount a successful reform movement. "For myself and many of the people close to me," Turski said, "the regime was not Communist. It was nothing but a nationalist, imperialist policy of Russia."

Barbara Góra, another longtime Communist, did not mourn the regime's passing, either. She had never married and had always been absorbed in her work. She had found a position compiling a weekly newsletter on foreign agriculture. The three-page publication was intended to be a serious journal for professionals who wanted to keep up with interesting ideas around the world. She tried to make it her contribution to improving Polish agronomy. But it was difficult to fit all the information into only three pages, and she worked under a man who desperately wanted to embellish his standing in the party by having his own articles published. His studies were usually arcane and irrelevant and sometimes ridiculous. She particularly remembered his pointless study of Swedish bears. When they were that silly, she would simply take the article home with her and never mention it. But she was often obliged to run his pieces. Dissatisfied, she left when the first opportunity to retire came up in 1987. "We all waited for the changes. We were so disappointed with our lives. This was not socialism. It was state capitalism. There was a privileged class, the owners of Poland."

But the new Polish state would also have its disappointments. Konstanty Gebert understood that in spite of its coalition of Jews, Catholics, unionists, and intellectuals, Solidarity had always had an anti-Semitic element, especially within the Warsaw chapter of the trade union. During the 1990 presidential campaign, a poll indicated that 30 percent of Poles believed "Jews have too much influence in Poland." Among those who said they intended to vote for Wałesa, 50 percent agreed with that statement.

In the local elections that year several small parties expressed anti-Semitism. A small conservative Catholic party with the backing of Polish Primate Józef Cardinal Glemp produced a poster that showed a happy worker tossing out a barrel-load of people bearing the sinister rapacious faces that have become the standard anti-Semitic stereotype for Jews. The caption said, "Enough of socialism, comrades."

In the 1990 presidential race, Mazowiecki, having been the first post-Communist leader, appeared to be mounting a major challenge to Wałesa's candidacy. Although Mazowiecki was a devout Catholic, his campaign was dogged by persistent rumors that he was secretly a Jew. No public figure ever uttered this, but it appears to have been widely believed. Konstanty Gebert, who by that time had become a well-known journalist, would question people on why they believed this. One person explained to him, "He is sad, and he prays too much," while another told him, "Well, he did get to be prime minister, didn't he?"

While Wałesa had always been outspoken in condemning anti-Semitism, he did nothing to deflate the anti-Semitic tone of the campaign, no doubt since it had turned against his principal opponent. He started playing with Polish anti-Semitism, vaguely alluding to hidden Jewish activities and asserting that he was "a hundred percent Pole" and that he had documents going back "for generations untold" proving his Polishness.

In a speech to a Solidarity group Wałesa referred to rumors that "a new clique is at the trough again." He went on to say that he had heard they were Jews. A group angrily walked out of that meeting and established its own party, the Civic Movement for Democratic Action. Wałesa complained that he could not attack the new movement without being accused of anti-Semitism. When Gebert asked him at a press conference if he considered the Movement to be "a Jewish party," he said no but then added, "Why do they conceal their origins?" As he went on the campaign trail, he was regularly confronted with questions about when he would throw the Jews out of government. Some would shout, "Gas the Jews."

Wałesa did not confront these comments at his rallies and when he later talked about such incidents, latent Polish anti-Semitism kept slipping into his rhetoric. In the meantime anti-Semitic graffiti, which had appeared occasionally even in Communist times, was becoming increasingly common, especially "Gas the Jews" written in Polish and *"Juden Raus,"* Jews Out, written in German. Anti-Semitic literature was once again being sold openly on the streets. In Kielce the performance of a Jewish folk group was interrupted by firecrackers and the shouting of anti-Semitic epithets. A month before the election, a group of reportedly more than a dozen youths stormed the Jewish Historical Institute in central Warsaw, smashing windows but failing to break down the door. They tried again one week later. Although the Institute is located near police headquarters, the siege continued for more than an hour without the police ever intervening.

Wałesa won the presidency by a landslide. Mazowiecki did not even come in second, trailing behind an unknown return émigré from Canada who promised to improve the life of Poles within one month. Gebert described Wałesa as "a consummate opportunist. He used anti-Semitism because it was expedient." The longer Wałesa stayed in office, the more Poles would see this electrician who spoke rough and uneducated Polish as a self-serving egotist focused on power politics with few programs. In 1993 even the Solidarity trade union broke with him. The old opposition had been certain to break up once it came to power, but one of the first rifts in the victorious anti-Communist coalition was when Jewish intellectuals split with Wałesa over the 1990 campaign. Shortly before the election, Adam Michnik, who first came to prominence in the 1968 student protests, wrote to Wałesa in his paper, *Gazeta Wyborcza*, "I have never accused you of anti-Semitism, but I do want to say that what you had said—that people of Jewish origin should reveal themselves—and I am a Pole of Jewish origin—was for me as if I had been spat in the face. I will not forgive you this."

At the same time, the short-lived amity between Jews and the Catholic Church ended over the existence of a Carmelite Convent at Auschwitz. It was foreign Jews and not those in Poland who strongly objected to this Catholic shrine, which had stood just outside Auschwitz since the 1970s. In 1987 the Catholic Church came to an agreement with Western European Jewish leaders to close the convent by February 1989. But no steps were taken to close it down, and as the deadline approached, Cardinal Glemp began vaguely denouncing the accord. Avi Weiss, a Riverdale, New York, rabbi, went to Poland with his group to protest. Barred from the convent, they climbed over the walls to stage a sit-in. Workmen attacked them with urine, water, and paint and had started to beat them when the Polish police reluctantly intervened. Glemp delivered a homily in traditional anti-Semitic language, accusing the Jews of thinking themselves "a nation above all others" and asking them not to use their "power in the mass media."

The upsurge in anti-Semitic attacks around Poland at the time of this homily was probably not coincidental. Glemp had never been popular because he had been seen as too soft on the old Communist regime (even in his anti-Semitism, he would slip into official rhetoric, such as referring to Jews as Trotskyites). But after this homily he suddenly gained a following. The international controversy over the convent went on for several more years, and in the end the Jews were the great losers. Instead of the convent the Catholics built a far larger visitor complex two hundred yards outside the camp. As the relationship between the Church and the Jews regained its more traditional tensions, the era of Solidarity ended.

As Wałesa was losing his mass following, a sign of the confused state of post-Communist Polish anti-Semitism was a graffiti message on a Cracow wall which said "Send Wałesa to Madagascar."

NINEL KAMERAZ had simply wanted to overthrow Communism. She was not disappointed nor did she continue her political activities.

Though her building was no longer Jewish, her apartment was unmistakably the home of a Jew, even if the mezuzah was on the inside rather than outside of the doorway. It was a warm dark place in earthen colors, with antique books and a sense of organized chaos. She had taken up painting, and the walls were covered with her slightly macabre tempera paintings. She had an old Victrola with a horn through which she played prewar recordings of Yiddish songs. The one small room—almost filled by a large wooden table with an electric samovar whose on-off switch was built into the table—was her conversation room. She would flip on the hot water for tea and reflect on the changes in her adopted country. "The Poles see themselves altogether differently from what they are. They see themselves as having always struggled for the freedom of all nations, that they waited for centuries, that all around them are animals—the Germans, the Czechs, the Russian, the Lithuanians—who are always stupid or evil or mean, all kinds of things, and about the Jews we know already. But they, the Poles, are pure and wonderful and good. When this was a closed state under Communism, they couldn't go anywhere. They looked in on themselves, they had to analyze themselves. And when the borders opened and they began to travel again, it turned out that people didn't say such nice things about Poles after all. They said they were thieves, that they didn't know how to work. And the Poles said, 'What? How can that be? We fought for liberty and freedom of all nations. How can you say such terrible things about us?' It's good that these lessons were learned. They were hard lessons, but they were necessary. And now they are finding out that they are normal people. They are good. They are bad. All kinds."

How many Jews are in Poland remains unknown. It is often said that there are five thousand, and some think there are perhaps seven thousand. There is one operating synagogue in Warsaw, a small Jewish community in Wrocław, another in Łódź, and two synagogues in Cracow, though only one is used at a time. Łódź and Wrocław on occasion get ten men. In Warsaw the half-dozen aging Yiddish speakers scour the area near the synagogue three times a day looking for the two or three more Jews they need for minyans, and the Cracow synagogues make their minyans on tourists. It would be difficult to show that there are one hundred Jews in Poland who practice the Jewish religion with regularity. But there are many hundreds more in search of some relationship with Judaism.

After the fall of Communism the three most likely places to find foreign visitors in Warsaw were the old town, the hotel strip by the central train station, and Grzybowski Square. The historic old town, so carefully restored after the war before anything else was, became one of Poland's first experiments in capitalism, with cafés, restaurants, and bookstores all of limited appeal to foreigners, even though they were a new phenomenon for Poland. The hotels by the train station were also an experiment in capitalism. Even before the fall of Communism, they had become a center for prostitution. Most of the hotels were new glass high-rises catering to the few bold foreign businessmen looking for investments in Poland. The Polonia Hotel, that once-elegant survivor where Barbara Góra had followed diplomats up stairways, was no longer draped in flags, but it was still international. Women in the Polonia who were dressed in peculiar and revealing outfits could say, "Let's have a drink," in Russian, Polish, German, English, or French.

The third tourism center in Warsaw, Grzybowski Square, was the closest there was to a Jewish tourism area. Since a large portion of the world's Jews had roots in Poland, Jewish tourism ironically became the greatest part of the new Polish tourist industry. So many tourists were Jewish that the Poles had to change their little souvenir Hasid dolls. These wooden carvings that were sold in Poland's main tourism centers — such as Warsaw's old town and the center of Cracow — portrayed Hasidim much as in Goebbels's hate films, with sunken avaricious eyes and jagged menacing noses. It was an authentic Polish souvenir but in time the Poles noticed that the tourists, being mostly Jewish, didn't seem to like these dolls, and so they softened their appearance.

With the growth of Jewish tourism, Grzybowski Square, the green triangle on the opposite side of the Culture Palace from the Polonia, became an attraction. The Culture Palace itself — a tower ornamented in the basic medieval/Moorish/art deco/neoclassical architecture that had become a symbol of Stalinism — though hard to ignore, was not an attraction. But a guidebook for Jewish tourists could describe the Grzybowski Square area as offering a synagogue, a Yiddish theater, and a kosher restaurant.

The kosher restaurant, decorated in white and blue, was one of the more expensive restaurants in Warsaw and struggled to survive with a small, mostly foreign clientele. The synagogue also often needed a tourist or two to have a minyan. The Yiddish Theater was of some distinction until 1968, when its director, Ida Kaminska, and most of its actors emigrated. Now it was run by a dramatic white-haired man, Shimon Szurmiej, who was one of the least-liked figures in the Warsaw Jewish community. During Communist times, as head of the Social and Cultural Association, Szurmiej was a token "Jewish leader" and was ready to give credibility to any position that the regime took, from rejecting criticism from world Jewry to establishing martial law.

The Yiddish Theater would not be much of a draw for Polish Jews in any event, since only Moishe Shapiro and a handful of others understood the language. Next to the synagogue was a free lunch program—a very basic lunch weighted with a lot of potatoes—where these few could socialize with each other and speak Yiddish. These people had very little money and went neither to the kosher restaurant nor to the Yiddish Theater. The rarely-more-than-half-filled theater was made up of a few Poles curious about Yiddish theater and schoolchildren who had no choice. Headphones were provided with a monotonous, droning translation into Polish, but many of the schoolchildren did not even put the headphones on. Aside from Szurmiej, his wife, and his son, most of the actors were not Jewish. They had been coached in Yiddish but were not conversant. And since they knew nothing of Hasidim or shtetl life, their attempts to imitate it ended up as buffoonish anti-Semitic stereotypes. It was the performance equivalent of the carved wooden dolls.

Pinhas Menachem Yoskowitz, a Gerer Hasid from Łódź who had survived the ghetto, Auschwitz and Bergen-Belsen, was brought from Israel to Warsaw by American Hasidim to be the rabbi for the Nozyk Synagogue. He came from an important Hasidic family, and a marriage had been arranged between one of his seven children and Chaim Rottenberg's son, Mordechai, who took over from his father on Rue Pavée. Yoskowitz, in his sixties, was a tall, thin, meticulously dressed figure in the long dark garb of Gerer Hasidim with an expensive-looking black broad-brimmed fur hat. His eyes seemed to sparkle with a sense of mischief, and his long white beard caught the breeze and rippled across his chest.

Yoskowitz was given to making outrageous statements to the press, at one point talking about the evacuation from Poland of the Jewish community because of growing anti-Semitism. Many of

Poland's Jews, especially the young ones who were just discovering their Jewish identity, found Yoskowitz a difficult man with whom to talk. He appeared to have a short attention span and little patience for lengthy conversations, which was an odd trait for a rabbi. In fact, although he had been ordained a rabbi in Germany after being liberated from Bergen-Belsen, he had spent most of the subsequent years in Israel as a businessman.

When he arrived in Warsaw as the rabbi for the Nozyk Synagogue, he took the title Chief Rabbi of Poland. A second Chief Rabbi of Poland showed up from New York during a service, and their dispute ended up with the two rabbis in a physical tussle. The other Chief Rabbi was Wawa Moreino also from Łódź. Moreino had been the Chief Rabbi of Poland, traditionally a lifetime position, but he had been removed by the regime in 1955 and forced into exile.

Three times a day, Moishe Shapiro and about six other elderly men waited at the Nozyk for a minyan. Simon Heustein, the kosher slaughterer for the restaurant, would walk over to be the eighth. When Yoskowitz was in town, he made the ninth, and they only needed one tourist, any Jewish man. They looked out toward the square and waited to pounce. Tourists did show up full of questions—how many Jews are here, how did you survive the war, what happened to your parents—all very sympathetically posed. "Later," they would say to the tourist. "Come to the shul. We need a minyan."

The kosher restaurant was funded by the Ronald S. Lauder Foundation. Lauder, the heir to the Estée Lauder fortune and a Reagan-appointed ambassador to Austria, had an idea that with his considerable financial resources, he could make a difference in the future of Central European Jewry. He made his greatest effort in Poland. But to many of the Jews here, he simply created the illusion of Jewish life. Yes, there was a kosher restaurant, an education program, a summer youth camp, a Jewish youth newspaper, and an organization to help the so-called "hidden children" who were just discovering their Jewish origins after a half-century, but all of this was done by an American financier and without him it would collapse. The idea was to create a foundation on which Jews in Poland could build, but Jews in Poland were skeptical. "Lauder is trying to resuscitate things," said Ninel Kameraz, "but it won't work. If you want to live a Jewish life, you have to leave Poland."

Simon Heustein, the *shochet*, or kosher slaughterer, was born in Przemyśl in 1929, and survived the war in Siberia. When he returned, he had found Cracow to be a relatively thriving Jewish community in need of a kosher slaughterer. There he learned the *shochet* trade and then in the 1950s emigrated to Israel, along with most of his customers. In 1991, Yoskowitz persuaded him to come to Warsaw. "I wanted to do something for the Jews," Heustein said. He kosherized the Polish restaurant with $6,000 worth of new plates and new pots and pans, and he trained the non-Jewish staff in the dietary laws. Its clientele was a combination of Orthodox Jewish tourists who complained about the prices, and Polish non-Jews who believed that the high quality of kosher food justified the price. It was always a Polish belief that kosher things were better because the Jews knew secrets and took special care and got only the best. On a Friday afternoon in any store, workers in overalls lined up to buy bottles of vodka. While waiting in line, they argued with each other over which kosher vodka to buy. They were not interested in the quality Polish vodkas that are prized in gourmet circles in Paris and New York. They wanted the kosher stuff because the Jews really know how to make it. It's cleaner. It's stronger. It's healthier. It gets you a better drunk. These were all commonly offered reasons for drinking kosher, and they consumed the vodka with frightening speed.

Kosher vodka was also one of the issues in the fight between Yoskowitz and Moreino: which of them had the right to put the seal of the Chief Rabbi of Poland on a profitable line of kosher vodka? Yoskowitz, who was, after all, a businessman, wanted to expand his line to more than just vodka, and he even offered a kosher mineral water with the brand name Chaim.

Still, Poland's only kosher restaurant barely survived. The shuffle of Simon Heustein, the small disheveled *shochet*, in his limp gray suit and hat, with his scruffy beard and dust-clouded eyeglass lenses, making the minyan and going back to the restaurant three times daily, became one of the Jewish sights of the Grzybowski Square area.

"Hello, Mr. Heustein. How are you?"

"Oiy," he said. "It's slow, this kosher business."

"That's because you charge too much. The Poles can't afford it."

"No. The Poles come. If it wasn't for the Poles, we would have been out of business two years ago. But the Jews—"

THE MARKET FOR KOSHER PRODUCTS was only one of the signs that Jewishness, along with anti-Semitism, had become fashionable in post-Communist Poland. Jewish studies became one of the fastest growing fields in Polish universities, and Jewish books grew in popularity. Every sidewalk bookstand offered Polish translations of Isaac Bashevis Singer's novels. Poles with only one possibly Jewish grandfather were saying they were really Jewish. But most Jews suspected that this philo-Semitism, or Jew-loving, was simply the newest trend in anti-Semitism. It was also something that was left over from the old Solidarity days. The anti-Zionist campaign of 1968 had fixed in people's minds the idea that sympathy for Jews was an anti-Communist act. A young man from Cracow who had never before met a Jew—in itself something that would have been unimaginable in Poland even one generation earlier—took the opportunity to apologize on behalf of Poland to the first one he met for the anti-Semitic campaign of 1968, which he termed "Poland's greatest disgrace." He apparently knew of no earlier disgraces for which Poland should apologize to Jews. It was the Communists who had destroyed Polish Jewry, he believed.

At the same time, to walk around Poland in Hasidic garb is an act of physical courage. Yoskowitz was assaulted more than once by skinheads punching him in the face, shouting "Żyd." The few religious Jews left in Poland do not even go outside with a yarmulke on—that is only for the house or synagogue. Mezuzahs are placed inside, not outside doorways. A New York rabbi, not understanding this world, walked into a small-town store in southern Poland in search of a soft drink. The local peasants, who were already visibly drunk though it was still morning, spied his small knit yarmulke. One of them said, "You're a Jew, aren't you?"

"Yes," the rabbi replied.

"Give me your money."

"I'm not going to give you my money."

"You owe me your money."

In the back a few were angrily chanting, "Żyd, Żyd, Żyd." But the rabbi was able to leave with no more than a little shoving.

Yoskowitz, however, was not only assaulted, he was also frequently assailed by young Poles who wanted him to convert them to Judaism. He refused. He did not want Christians. He wanted to find the hidden Jews, people like Barbara Gruberska who had been placed in non-Jewish homes by Jewish parents who did not survive.

Nobody could be certain how many now-middle-aged people like her there were, who had not yet discovered the truth.

A YEAR AFTER Mateusz's bar mitzvah, Moishe Shapiro prepared a second bar mitzvah for Barbara Gruberska's son, Andrzei. Barbara had wanted very much to give her son and daughter the Jewish identity out of which she had been cheated. Her husband, a non-Jew whose family had been socialists since the nineteenth century, despised the Catholic Church but had no ill will toward Judaism.

Andrzei would have been perfectly suited to continue the cover-up in which Barbara had been raised. Tall and blond, with pale blue eyes, his appearance could be described as that of "a typical Pole," which is what he was until his mother took him to Moishe Shapiro. Andrzei approached this Jewishness with considerable ambivalence. He had never needed any identity other than being Polish. What initially made a difference for him was the charm of this small elderly man with his permanent hat and his Yiddish-accented Polish. Andrzei, always a good student, had never had a teacher he enjoyed so much. The bar mitzvah was a great moment in his family's life. His non-Jewish father started talking about the family moving to Israel. But Barbara knew that as a doctor, she would have to work much harder in Israel than she did in Poland, if she could get work at all. It was even more doubtful that there would be any job for her husband, an electrical engineer.

Andrzei was pleased with his bar mitzvah, and though he started calling himself Avram, he still felt ambivalent, especially about the news that his foreskin should be removed. Assurances that it would not hurt did not completely convince him. A Bobover rabbi was impressed with the former Andrzei and wanted to take him to New York to join his Hasidic community, but Barbara adamantly refused to let him go, a refusal that came as a tremendous relief to Andrzei.

For the next two years Andrzei drifted back into his Polish life in the small town near Warsaw. But then he was offered a scholarship to a Jewish high school in Paramus, New Jersey, by the principal who happened to be passing through Warsaw and who recognized in Andrzei an unusually likable, curious, and intelligent boy. Andrzei accepted. His second day in America, he was circumcised in a Brooklyn hospital—a simple surgical procedure with a medically qualified *mohel*. It didn't hurt. In New Jersey, living with a religious American family, Andrzei for the first time learned what traditional Jewish life was, observing the Sabbath, praying three times a day, eating only kosher food, and keeping his head covered even on the street. He was living in a world where Jewishness wasn't hidden. After a snowstorm he built a larger-than-life snowman on the front law of the house where he was living in Teaneck. The snowman was in the shape of a long-bearded Hasid and for a hat he had a huge *shtreimel*. It wasn't a provocation—just fun. This wasn't Poland.

What most affected Andrzei in America was a new version of history. To him, World War II had been a struggle of Poles against Germans. No one had told him that not only Germans but Poles had been involved in the murder of Jews. He began studying about Polish Jewry, and one day he ran across a photograph of Jews in the 1930s purging themselves in a river for Rosh Hashanah. In the picture he could see thousands of Jews on the riverbank. He recognized the spot. It was in his town. "I started thinking about all those people, the Jews that are no longer here. There are no empty houses. No burnt-out houses. Every place in town is full. And yet all those thousands that were in the picture are missing."

After high school Andrzei went to Yeshiva University in New York. By that time, he spoke almost flawless American English. He sometimes worried about his ability to fit in and thought that he was sometimes too easily influenced by the people around him. He was faced with a difficult decision: Did he want to be an American or a Pole? The choice was not easy for him, because he had always felt very comfortable in Poland. No one had seemed to whisper about his Jewishness there. He could play sports and drink with friends. "I love Poland. This is my country. I can walk down any street and act like a Pole," he said. But could he walk down that street and act like a Jew, with his head covered and tassels hanging off his hip? Could he find kosher food? Could he openly act Jewish and still fit in, or did he fit in only because he didn't look or act Jewish? He reached the sad conclusion that if he wanted to be Jewish, he could not live in Poland anymore. "You can be Jewish and American, but you can't be Jewish and Polish," he concluded. It was still the way it always had been. You were a Pole or you were a Jew. The phrase "Polish Jew" was still only used in Western countries.

It was very different for his younger sister, Maigorzata, who started calling herself Malka. She was not a tall, blond athletic Pole. She was short and dark, with what in Poland is called "Jewish hair." Like her mother, she grew up with few friends. Her one friend was Catholic, and she never discussed being Jewish with her. But by then, the entire town knew her mother's history. Perhaps they had always known it. Children shouted "Żyd" at her before she ever knew what it meant. No one ever shouted "Żyd" at her brother.

"Boys are different," explained Andrzei. "If you can play sports, that's all they care about. I've never experienced anti-Semitism. American Jews see something written on the wall, and they call it anti-Semitism. But I've never experienced what a Jew in Poland calls anti-Semitism."

Malka also went to school in New Jersey. For her, one of the deciding factors had been the mounting power of the Catholic Church in Poland. It was able to get mandatory Catholic religious classes into the school system in 1990. Malka was allowed to skip the classes, but that fact was noted by her teachers and might be reflected in her grades. She also felt set apart. She, in fact, was put back into the same dilemma in which young Barbara Góra had found herself in the 1930s. There were other signs that the Catholic Church was again going to be controlling life in Poland. Priests were denouncing the concept of a separation of church and state as Communist. The Church succeeded in getting a law passed reversing the liberal abortion policies and making Poland one of the most difficult countries in Europe in which to obtain an abortion.

In America, Malka felt free to be Jewish without being set apart. But she missed her parents and came back after the first year. It only took a few weeks back in Poland to decide: "I know I don't want this," she said resolving to return to New Jersey.

Barbara Gruberska felt she had to square things away with her mother, who she couldn't even remember. When she saw her children become Jews, she felt she had done that. The price, however, was losing them, shipping them away to a distant country whose language she could not even speak. She could no more imagine living in America than in Israel. "I'm too old to go to America," she said, though she was only in her fifties. "Too old to move. . . . Well, maybe to raise my grandchildren."

WHEN THE WAKS FAMILY made their trip to Łódź, they went directly to the cemetery to find what was left of Jewish life in this city whose population had once been one-third Jewish—home to the Wakses, the Turskis, the Yoskowitzes and the Moreinos, the Finkelsztajns, the Silbermans. Jewish families from Łódź were part of every Western Jewish community. Where else to find Jews on a Saturday morning in Poland but at the cemetery? Lea chatted with what was left of the Łódź community, none of whom remembered any Wakses or Lessers. Then Lea and her family went to the area that had been the ghetto, in search of the houses in which she and Aaron had grown up. The closer they got to Lea's house, the more distraught she became. She had not wanted to take this trip. She found her old building and struck up a conversation with a woman in the back, where the housekeeper had lived. When the woman explained that she was the housekeeper's daughter, Lea introduced herself and recalled that they had played together as children. The woman did not seem to remember her.

The building, the entire neighborhood, was exactly the way Lea Waks remembered it, except for the deterioration from almost fifty years of neglect. The Jewish owner of the house had fled to Canada before the war. By coincidence, Ruwen Waks knew a relative of his in Tel Aviv. But the tenants only knew that the owner had left a long time ago, and they were still hoping that one day he would return and repair his property. The *sukkah*—the little hut for celebrating the Jewish harvest-time holiday, Sukkot—was still on the balcony where he had built it. It had not been used since 1940, and when Lea pointed it out to residents, none of them seemed to have any idea what it was for. Apparently, no one had ever asked why there was a hut on the balcony.

The people in Łódź did not see Jews very often anymore. In Communist times the few Łódź Jews had had a second-floor cockroach-infested canteen in the once-Jewish neighborhood that claimed to offer kosher meals. Their only noticeable dietary concession, however, was that they did not serve pork. The staff was non-Jewish and wanted Sundays off, so the canteen stayed open on the Sabbath. With the change of regimes, the canteen lost its state funding and got even dirtier and more infested. Finally, the Warsaw Jewish Community insisted that it be closed.

Łódź had one restored synagogue. The fact that it was concealed from street view in an alleyway behind a building was not significant. Many buildings in Łódź have a tunnellike entryway, with two iron gates leading to an alley full of shops. The real life of the city is in these alleys. The synagogue, a rose-colored building of distinctly Jewish architecture, was behind the buildings on Rewolocja Street, one of the last streets to retain its Communist name. Even on a Saturday morning the synagogue was usually locked up, because there was rarely a minion. A man working on his car in the same alley on a rainy Saturday morning said that the synagogue was sometimes open but certainly wouldn't be on this morning. He looked up between the buildings at the gray sky and said, "It's raining. Besides, it's Saturday. Maybe on Monday." Though there was not always a minion, there was a cantor. In the nineteenth century, the student of a famous Bobover rabbi had a son who assimilated and survived the war as a Pole in a small town. After the war the son's daughter also grew up as a Pole. She married a Polish engineer and had a round-faced blond son named Krzysztof. Krzysztof Skrovronski played the flute and had a lyric singing voice that in time matured into a rich baritone. When he was 16 years old, his grandfather—the man who had survived the war by concealing his Jewish identity—was dying. He looked up at Krzysztof from his bed and said, "Do you know who you are?"

"Who I am? What kind of question is that?"

"There is something you need to know. Me, your grandmother, your mother—we are all Jewish."

The news did not have the anticipated impact. It didn't change his life, his flute playing, his friends. But more than ten years later, in 1985, when the Communist regime was losing its grip on society, Krzysztof started studying Hebrew with the last knowledgeable Jew in Łódź—a ninety-year-old man. Krzysztof's parents warned him that it would not be good for him to be Jewish. But he continued his schooling and eventually went off to Israel to study and become a cantor and a religious Jew. When he returned to post-Communist Łódź, his parents began to feel proud of him. Being a cantor in a community with at most twenty practicing Jews did not seem like much, but people noticed his voice and soon he was riding the commercial crest of philo-Semitism. A Warsaw producer contracted him to record Jewish songs, which were becoming a big seller in the Polish record industry. He had television singing appearances. He became a celebrity. Jews had been as essential to Polish culture as Blacks are to American culture, and Poles missed Jewish culture. But still, Krzysztof would not wear a yarmulke on the streets of Łódź, because, he said, "I want to live."

He did not see any Jewish future for Łódź. His wife was Jewish, and they decided that when they started having children, they would move to Israel.

IN THE POLISH SUMMER the rolling hills of the south near the Slovak border are plowed in quilted patterns of yellow and chartreuse. Distant ridges appear blue on the horizon. Wild raspberries grow along the curving roads that lead to little villages of wooden houses with statues of saints carved into the gate posts. Bulbous church towers stick out from thick green foliage of fruit trees, and the fields are studded with flame-colored poppies and violet and yellow wildflowers. In this setting, in an abandoned hilltop estate, the Lauder Foundation set up a summer camp for Jewish teenagers to learn about Jewishness.

Most of the teenagers had only recently discovered they were Jewish and were trying to learn something about it. Most had been raised as socialists; a few even as Catholics. Even those not from Catholic homes knew much more about Catholicism than Judaism just by living in Poland, and the bells of summer masses echoing off the blue hills, and the shrines and churches that punctuated this rural countryside seemed far more normal to them than the exotic rituals and practices they were learning about at the camp. For most of them, Judaism was a new idea. One girl first heard of it when her mother told her their family was moving to Israel.

"But they won't let you unless you are Jewish," pointed out the daughter.

"We are Jewish," said the mother.

Some of the children had discovered photographs of a grandfather in a long black coat with a beard. Sometimes they did not even know what that odd clothing meant. A few of the teenagers were not Jewish but were simply curious. They, too, were welcomed, because it was hard to say who was Jewish. One non-Jewish girl who had come out of curiosity afterward told her mother how much she had enjoyed the camp. The mother only then confessed that she was Jewish.

A teenage boy who had only learned that his mother was Jewish when he was 12 said, "The funny thing is, the Poles knew first. They always know before the Jews. I don't know how they do it. Kids used to call me Jew, and I didn't know why. How do they always know?"

After a month the teenagers would go home. Some took up

praying. Some tried to keep kosher. But they found that out in Poland, they could not continue to live the life they had learned about at the camp. At least at the camp these young Poles had experienced what Jewish life would be like. The food was uncompromisingly kosher. The men wore yarmulkes even outdoors, though it wasn't required. They sat around with their yarmulkes on, talking about how they could never do this in their home town. Two boys from Warsaw estimated that in the Praga section, a notoriously tough part of Warsaw on the other side of the Vistula, "someone with a yarmulke on would live for about two minutes." Another boy told a story of a family he knew in Praga that drew blackout curtains every Friday night so they could light Sabbath candles.

These teenagers had had socialist educations in which equality of the sexes was a strong belief. As they learned about Judaism, they had hard questions. They wanted to know why women didn't wrap *tefillin*, why they were not called up to read the Torah, why they were separated from men. They would consider abandoning atheism but they would not give up equality of the sexes.

The camp forged amazingly good relations with the locals in the area. There was a farmer who let them milk his cow so that they could be assured it was kosher milk. Michael Schudrich, the American rabbi who ran the camp, talked a baker into setting aside a separate room with separate mixing bowls and pans, where he would bake for the camp, under rabbinical supervision, an excellent round, crusty Polish peasant bread. The camp ordered dozens of loaves, and the baker was pleased to have the business.

One day in the summer of 1992, two men from a nearby village rode their ten-speed racing bikes to the door of the main estate building at the Lauder camp. One had the broad, rough, beat-up hands of a farmer. The other, who looked a little more refined, started speaking in Polish to an American who asked the nearest bilingual teenager to translate—a good-natured fifteen-year-old with shaggy long blond hair and a borrowed Lauder yarmulke. The two bicyclists looked around admiringly at the wood-paneled manor house. They talked about how it used to be in a complete shambles. Then it had been rebuilt with glass and aluminum. Now it looked like the old manor. Very nice, they both agreed.

After a few minutes they said, "Well, thank you," and shook the long-haired boy's hand, got on their ten-speed bikes, and pedaled off to continue their trip.

"What strange men," said the boy.
Why?
"They don't hate Jews. He even shook my hand!"

NOT FAR AWAY from those flowered summer hills is Cracow, whose untouched medieval center makes it Poland's best bid for a tourist destination. Cracow also has location going for it. When tourists get off the train from Warsaw, they are greeted at the platform by eager taxi drivers offering, "Taxi? Hotel? Auschwitz?"

The splendidly preserved walls of this rare city are papered on seemingly every available eye-level space with posters that say "AUSCHWITZ" in large block letters. "Go to Birkenau and be back in Cracow at 4 P.M." one of them advertises.

A thirty-minute taxi ride away is the most famous death camp of all. It may also have become Poland's biggest tourist attraction, with some half-million visitors a year and growing. While Poles think fondly of their country's variety of cultural and historical attractions, in the West Poland is largely thought of as the killing ground. Foreigners come to see what is left of the ghetto, the Jewish cemeteries, and the death camps—Sobibór, Maidanek, Belzec, Treblinka, Chelmno, Stutthof, Auschwitz-Birkenau—Poland was the site of the Holocaust. In Warsaw there is a heroic monument to the resisters of the Warsaw ghetto. Tourists come by the busload, sometimes even posing for group pictures on the steps. Nearby, a man sells assorted souvenirs, mostly books. The vendor is ready with an ink-pad and stamp to mark the endpaper with his souvenir "Warsaw Ghetto" stamp.

Some of the Jewish tourists, the groups who go to see death in Poland and then life in Israel, were understandably irritating to the Jews in Poland who prefer not to think of their home as the absence of life. But for the other Poles in the new Poland trying to embrace capitalism, it was good business. When a Cracow taxi driver got an Auschwitz fare, he would merrily inform the others at the stand, "I'm off to Auschwitz. Bye!" It was far better money than going back and forth to Kazimierz, the Jewish section on the other side of town.

The landscape between Cracow and Oświęcim has probably not changed much since the camp was operating—rolling farmland, yellow strips of harvested hayfields, orchards with branches drooping from the weight of summer apples, towns with traditional log houses, and even some horse-drawn carts. Coming into Oświęcim a wide railyard is passed, a junction of so many tracks it appears to be set on the outskirts of a major city. That is why the Germans chose this spot for a death camp. For all those tracks only twelve thousand people had been living there. The majority had been Jewish. There was still one Jew left in Oświęcim, and he, not surprisingly, was a recluse.

Outside the death camp is a parking lot filled with tour buses. There is a bookshop and a snack bar and a pretty green area with rows of two-story brick barracks and a small gateway in the shade of a slinky willow with the words *"Arbeit Macht Frei"* in decorative ironwork overhead. In the summer, the wildflowers are in bloom, and the seedlings that the doomed prisoners were forced to plant are now rows of tall straight shady trees, thick with leaves. Different tour guides are available in different languages and with different agendas. Some talk about martyred priests, others about the heroic antifascists. There are also survivors walking as though in a trance, leading their families.

Auschwitz shows things that are beyond commentary—the human hair, the eyeglass frames, the piles of toothbrushes, and an unremarkable-looking oven, like a bread oven. And there are gallows where prisoners were hanged and walls where they were shot and laboratories where they were worked on.

Somehow people drifted through all this. A little French girl, perhaps eight, sat down outside one of the display barracks and refused to go in. "Come on," pleaded her parents, pointing to the sign identifying the display. "This is about the life of the prisoners."

"I don't want to see that," said the little girl, hunkering into the wooden stoop.

Many of the visitors were weeping, others looked stunned, some looked like bored tourists shuffling from exhibit to exhibit, taking snapshots to mark each spot.

Birkenau, the sister camp down the road, was far more devastating. There were no exhibits, little documentation. Just the barbed wire, sentry towers, and a few barracks, though most had been stripped for their wood so that only the chimneys remained. Through Birkenau ran more than a mile of train tracks, with platforms for selections and at the end the caved-in crematoriums that the Germans tried to blow up at the last minute. It was a factory, designed for efficient mass production.

But at Auschwitz, many of the intact barracks had been turned into national pavilions, each displaying the suffering of its country, some with cold documentary style, others almost artsy. Auschwitz had become a kind of world's fair of genocide. The new Catholic visitors' center outside the camp, the result of the fight over the Carmelite convent, was just one more attempt to claim the moral high ground here on the killing site. Who would be the voice in this place? That was to be a seemingly endless struggle, first with the Communist state, which called the site "A Monument to the Martyrdom of the Polish and Other Nations." Their information was mainly about antifascism, with little mention of Jews. The plaque was later changed. Exhibits were changed. Literature was rewritten. Then there was the fight over the Carmelites and the resulting visitors' center offering the Catholic Church's interpretation.

Every institution with any pretense of moral authority wants the last word on Auschwitz. The problem is that there is very little that a truly moral voice can say. It remains incomprehensible. But if there is nothing that can be said, then the moral voice falls to the greatest victims, which were the Jews. To cede the moral voice to the Jews was an intolerable notion to some Polish Catholics. As Konstanty Gebert said, "The world owes us the right to exist because we have suffered. However, on the pinnacle of suffering, there is room for just one."

The spectacle of Jews wrestling for the mantle of martyrdom could be seen, theologically, as a Catholic victory after all. Martyrdom is a Catholic thing. It is the Catholics who chose as their symbol of faith an implement of torture, the cross of martyrdom. Judaism, however, has always been a religion with relatively little to say about death, other than that it should be kept clearly separate from life. Synagogues and cemeteries are not to be on the same site. For the Jews of Łódź to go to the cemetery on Saturday morning instead of to the synagogue is very contrary to Jewish law. Kohenim are not supposed to go to cemeteries at all. Priests should not gaze on death.

But Jews are forced to contemplate Auschwitz, because otherwise someone else will speak for them to hundreds of thousands of visitors and to history. Auschwitz survivors like Marian Turski do their duty and sit on the International Auschwitz Committee and are thereby regularly forced not only to think about but to visit the site of their nightmares. The International Auschwitz Committee tried to reach a consensus on what to do about Auschwitz. Turski, who for twenty years would not even allow his mind to remember what he had seen there, became an active member. Now he had to go with some regularity for speeches, conferences, and meetings. In time he no longer found it difficult. "Of course, when I am there, there are two or three places which have special bonds to my memory. There is something there in myself, in my heart. I would say it's a sore spot. I go there. I sift through the archives," Turski said, and then added with self-amazement, "I am really an expert!"

The well-landscaped Warsaw neighborhood where he and his wife lived for three decades, in a comfortable but not palatial apartment, indicated the limited measure of privilege he had enjoyed as a party member, albeit a troublesome one. His study was decorated with his collection of antique wooden carvings of Catholic saints. But there was no escaping who he was and what he had seen. In 1993, Turski appeared on a British television panel with three neo-Nazis from France, Austria, and Germany. One of them would not even shake Turski's hand because he was a Jew. The oldest of them was 32 and the youngest 21, and they sat across from him and, quoting from Faurisson, claimed that the Holocaust that Turski had survived had never really happened. Turski's wife had pleaded with him not to do it, fearing he would get so upset that he would have a heart attack. But he believed that these people had to be faced. "I was so quiet, so absolutely fully organized," said Turski. "She was amazed."

EVEN THOUGH MORE PEOPLE in Poland declared themselves Jewish every day, the community remained small. In the fight to at last receive German reparations after the fall of the Soviet bloc, applications in Poland were only in the hundreds. There was a loneliness to Polish Jews living in a non-Jewish world with non-Jewish friends. Even if it was known that they were Jewish, their colleagues, being broad-minded, would include them in Christian holidays and give them flowers and cakes on the saint's day of their name, forcing them in misguided friendship to act out a charade that to the non-Jews was simply being Polish. Only among other Jews did the few Jews of Poland feel safe being candidly what they were. Many would admit their Jewishness only to other Jews. No matter how many non-Jewish friends you had, it was only with a Jew that you were always sure, no matter what happened, that you could still say, "I am a Jew." It was only with Jewish friends that you didn't have to pretend to care about your saint's day or Christmas, lest they be offended. Your Jewish friends were never going to slip and say one of those things that are just part of Polish culture. But the Jews saw their valuable Jewish friends vanish, emigrate, and die. Survivors clung to distant cousins as though they were siblings, because it was all they had. An impoverished elderly woman who ate at the lunch program by the synagogue would gather scraps of food and give them to a middle-class Jewish woman in her thirties because the young woman's father had given her food during the war, and this was the only connection she had left.

Konstanty Gebert married a non-Jew, which meant that according to Jewish law their four children were not Jewish. With the help of Lauder programs, he was bringing them up with Jewish instruction in the hope that they would convert. "I don't want to make their decisions for them. I do desperately hope that they will make the decision to formally convert," he said.

He recognized that even he was a kind of artificially constructed Jew. In the anti-Communist underground days when he was working with Marek Edelman, Edelman would question Gebert's Jewishness, saying, "You invented it, you made it up." The Gebert household observed the Sabbath and most of the holidays. Gebert was not kosher because it would be too arduous a discipline in Poland. But he did not eat meat, a practice that was not necessarily Jewish except that it precluded the risk of mixing meat with dairy. "Why can't we be free like Dad and not eat meat?" his children asked.

Gebert wore a yarmulke indoors. Sometimes he forgot to take it off when he left the house, but nothing happened. Still, he was uneasy about his role in Poland. "The problem is there are so damn few of us. I don't want to be turned into a professional representative." He recognized that there were limits to how Jewish he could be in Poland. He too had made his choice. "I would prefer to live in circumstances that would make more observance possible, but if that means leaving Poland, I'm not about to do it."

Jakub Gutenbaum, who lost faith in Communism in 1968 but did not want to be a foreigner in Israel, became a full professor in 1977. He had never been a party member and was not political. Science was his religion. But he said that after the fall of Communism, "I thought maybe I could do something about problems outside of my field." In 1991 the Lauder Foundation was trying to organize an association for Jews who had survived the war because

they had been hidden as children, and Gutenbaum became involved, eventually becoming the head of a group of 140 people.
There were twenty older ones, like himself and Barbara Góra, who
had survived the ghetto and concentration camps. The rest had
been hidden as babies. All but fifteen of the 140 members were
women. It had been too dangerous to hide a boy with the telltale
circumcision. The people in Gutenbaum's organization had experienced a broad range of childhood traumas. One woman spent
her infancy in the bed of a prostitute who serviced German soldiers. One child had been living with Christian peasants, and after
the war a Jewish committee came to claim him. At night he escaped through a window and ran back to the peasant family, crying, "No, I'm not Jewish!"

Most of these children grew up to be achievers. The majority of
people in Gutenbaum's group held advanced degrees. Many were
doctors. Four were medical professors. But very few had stable
family lives. Many were divorced. There was a high rate of schizo-
phrenia and other mental disorders.

For Gutenbaum, the work was therapeutic because it forced
him to talk about his own experiences. After a time he could
calmly talk about the fire overhead as he hid in the ghetto, about
being led through the charred ghetto at gunpoint, about the selection process at Maidanek. These were all things he had never
spoken about, not even to his wife or their son. There were other
things he still would not speak about—things he would never utter,
even though he had learned that the more he talked the better he
felt. His nightmares became less frequent. He was looking for activities to throw himself into because soon he would have to retire.
He feared the day when he was no longer absorbed in his scientific
work and his mind would be free to wander. This was why the
hidden children had been achievers.

Barbara Góra had her own reasons for joining the hidden children group. "I decided to join because, you know, I have a lot in
common with them. I am alone. I am alone not only because I
didn't marry. I want to have my own social group, and this society
is not typically Jewish because they are people brought up like me.
Some of them are even Catholic because they were brought up
like that. I have more in common with them than with typical
Jews. I never wanted to be a member of this Jewish cultural society.
I have nothing in common with them. I am a hidden child."

Barbara's sister, who was ten years older, had married a Greek
Communist immigrant. They visited Greece every year and raised

their daughter to be Greek. When the girl was nine, she read a book about the Warsaw ghetto and asked her aunt Barbara about it. But when Barbara told her that her mother was Jewish, her niece didn't believe her. A cousin of Barbara's father was spending three months in Paris, and while she was there she looked up relatives who lived in a Paris suburb. She discovered, to her amazement, that they were Jewish. She came back and told everyone in her family, "We are Jewish!" To Barbara she said, "Did you know that we are Jewish?"

"Yes," said Barbara. "I know."

"Then why don't I know?"

The story makes Barbara laugh. "Now everybody knows. Now it's all open. It was silly. It was stupid. It doesn't matter!" The fact so amazed her that she repeated it several times. "It doesn't matter. It doesn't matter!"

IN THE SUMMER OF 1992, Henryk Halkowski hosted the last meeting at the old Jewish club in Cracow. After forty-six years they were abandoning the musty rooms and auditorium for a small, one-room meeting space. "Smaller, but without the mold," said Halkowski. Four people showed up, and they made tea and drifted from room to room. They still had the red velour flag with gold embroidery, with the Polish Communist party marked on one side in Polish, their local chapter marked on the other in Yiddish. One of the four said he had heard that an Israeli had recently come to town and told Czeslaw Jakubowicz that they should all move to Israel. They snickered. They weren't going to move to Israel, just to a smaller space.

Although Halkowski's family was originally from Łódź, he became a local historian in Cracow and enjoyed studying the sixteenth and seventeenth centuries, when Jews from Germany and Bohemia had migrated to this city where they could live in peace. The Cracow Jews were so secure in their home that many believed the name *Poland* was of Hebrew origin. Their popular theory was that it came from the Hebrew words *po* and *lin*, which together mean "stay here."

27

In Budapest

In 1984 an advertisement from a Hungarian travel agency led documentary filmmaker Gyula Gazdag to realize at last his childhood dream of making a film about the Holocaust. The advertisement was for a package tour of Auschwitz. Thinking that this was a peculiar idea, Gazdag investigated and discovered that the package was being put together at the request of the official Hungarian Jewish Community for the fortieth anniversary of the liberation. All of the tourists who took the package were Auschwitz survivors. *Package Tour* is Gazdag's documentary about the trip. He finds watching it almost unbearable and could hardly stand looking at it long enough even to edit it. The film crew moves from barrack to barrack across the shady Auschwitz grounds as the survivors point to the spot where someone was shot, where they were forced to line up for Mengele's experiments. A cheerful, enthusiastic Polish guide insists on telling them at every turn information he has been trained to recite. The survivors get increasingly annoyed with this uncaring Pole and finally take him aside to inform him that the people he is talking to are survivors and don't need to hear all this. But then we find out that the Polish guide, one of the early political prisoners, was also an Auschwitz survivor. He had worked hard at being cheerful because that was his job.

Most Gyula Gazdag films were still being censored by the regime. Although Gazdag never became active in the democratic movement, he and other Hungarian filmmakers provided one of the few vehicles for the expression of discontent. In the 1980s the Democratic Charter movement that György Konrád had helped create and other opposition movements were emboldened by the seeming weakening will of the Communists. Groups were forming around underground publications. György Gadó's apartment was searched eight times by police looking for illegal publications, which they generally found.

As György Konrád got more deeply involved in the opposition movement, he became convinced that Central Europe—Poland, Czechoslovakia, and Hungary—would in time break from the Soviet Union. He even developed a pet theory that it would happen in 1992. This was not a deep political insight but instead was based on the observation that every twelve years something happened. There was 1944, then '56, then Prague in '68, and Warsaw in 1980, and so surely something big would happen in 1992. But he also saw the entire superpower structure of global politics as destined to break up, and he wrote about it in a prophetic book called *Antipolitics*.

In 1988, János Kádár was replaced as head of the government by Karoly Grosz, who tried to offer economic reform as a substitute for political reform. But as in Poland, events outran even the opposition. By late 1989, the Communist party had voted to dissolve into a different kind of socialist party and to give up its power monopoly. New political parties were formed to fill the vacuum. The two leading ones, the Democratic Forum and the Free Democrats, offered similar programs, although the Free Democrats wanted to move a little faster. The major difference was that the Democratic Forum appealed to nationalism and the Free Democrats avoided it. Nationalism was about to turn neighboring Yugoslavia into a brutal battleground. Hungarian nationalism could get pulled in. Yugoslavia had ethnic Hungarians, as did Romania and the Slovak side of Czechoslovakia. Even before the 1990 election a vocal right wing of the Democratic Forum talked about who was and was not a "true Hungarian." It was being implied that Hungarians of Romanian, gypsy, or Jewish origin were not "true Hungarians." This was a code that everyone in Central Europe understood. The same thing was happening in Romania, except there, it was Hungarians, gypsies, and Jews who were being singled out. Hungarian nationalists were saying that Hungarian Jews were not "true Hungarians," but they also claimed that Hungarian-speaking Slovaks were. But many Slovak Jews are Hungarian-speaking—would they be "true Hungarians"?

The Democratic Forum was saying that the Free Democrats were not "true Hungarians," which was their way of reminding voters that some of the Free Democrats, including parliamentary candidate György Gadó, were Jews.

This was free speech. No one had been allowed to talk like this for forty years. It all may have been predictable, but that did not stop it from being a shock. The activists of both parties had worked together against the Communist regime. An angry György Gadó said, "I hoped, like many other people in my field, that a liberal democratic change had come. We knew, of course, that there were other forces in the society that did not hope for such a liberal change but for a Christian change or a change that had another ideology. But for many months we thought that our first enemy was the former system, the former government, the Communist party, the Communist movement. In this historic change our first enemy is not the former regime. It is people with whom we previously sat together and participated in the so-called opposition round table."

The nationalist line of the Democratic Forum paid off, when shortly before the 1990 election ethnic Hungarians were attacked by Romanian nationalists in Romania, killing four Hungarians and further infusing the political atmosphere in Hungary with paranoid nationalism. After the Democratic Forum came to power, the tone worsened. The man of the moment became István Csurka, a popular comic playwright who had risen to be vice president of the ruling Democratic Forum. Csurka talked a lot about "legitimacy." In repeated statements he expressed the idea that only "true Hungarians" should have a voice in Hungarian affairs. To expound on this message, in September 1992 Csurka staged a rally that was attended by a reported seventy thousand people. Shortly thereafter, thugs murdered a gypsy in a rural town. Konrád and his Democratic Charter organized a counterdemonstration of equal size, filling the large square by the many-spired parliament building with candle-bearing protesters. He was not surprised that it was difficult at first to line up speakers. "I am accustomed to this fact that people generally are afraid in this country. I wouldn't say that this government is aggressive or violent, but there are aggressive forces. A teacher is now afraid of what he has to say in history lessons to the students. Journalists are afraid, and writers are afraid."

Hungarians, especially Hungarian Jews, had to deal with things that had not been seen in a generation. There was an extreme right-wing group called Jobboldali Blokk, and neo-Nazi literature was appearing on the streets. In September 1993 an elaborate ceremony marked the transfer of Hitler's ally Admiral Miklós Horthy's body from where he died in Portuguese exile to his hometown in Hungary. It was an unofficial ceremony sponsored by navy elements who called him "a great seaman"—dim praise in a country with no coastline and no fleet. The government said they had had nothing to do with the transfer, but several ministers attended the ceremony and a commemorative coin was issued. Prime Minister József Antall, who usually distanced himself from the more nationalist elements, referred to Horthy as "a great patriot" because he had gained back lost Hungarian territory. The fact that he had done this by allying Hungary with the Third Reich was not discussed. Nor were the deportations under his rule mentioned.

Jews were becoming uneasy but also angry. Konrád had a ninety-two-year-old uncle, a veteran of the Hungarian independence struggle, who was furious. "I fought with Kossuth, I survived Auschwitz. Why do I want to be told now I'm not Hungarian?" his uncle would shout. It had become a common scene in Jewish households in post-Communist Hungary. A Jewish businessman who had emigrated to Switzerland and then returned after the change was discussing events with his family over a Rosh Hashanah dinner. He still had his house in Geneva and his Swiss papers. "If things go badly, I can move the whole family there," he said. But his family had not gone abroad with him before, and they were not interested in moving now. They had survived a lot in Hungary, and they were determined to survive Csurka. A cousin, a meticulously dressed older woman across the table, began talking with a rage that grew like a swell at sea. "This Csurka, he talks about who is a Hungarian and who is not a Hungarian. The Romanians aren't Hungarians, the gypsies aren't Hungarians. The Jews. Nobody can tell me I'm not a Hungarian. I have paid to be here," she said, at which point she shoved up her sweater sleeve and showed the bluish Auschwitz numbers tattooed on the pale inside of her forearm.

AFTER THE WAR the Budapest Jewish Community leadership, the MIOK, had estimated that there were 240,000 Jews left in Hungary. About 150,000 fled following the 1956 uprising. For years the estimate of the Jewish population ran between 80,000 and 100,000.

But this had always been a guess. Only about 10,000 Jews were registered members of the Jewish Community. After the change in regimes, in spite of nationalists and neo-Nazis, the number of acknowledged Jews steadily increased. By 1993, the common figure was 120,000 Jews. Budapest had three Jewish schools, and the Community was growing more active and more diverse.

One of the first things to be done was to remove the old leadership. Ilona Seifert was asked to leave the MIOK. Some Jews, especially younger ones, were bitter about her stewardship of the Community, and this judgment angered her. In her mind she and her husband had done what had to be done to keep the Community operating. "It was written what we had to do, and we were allowed all the elements of Jewish life. It's not true that you couldn't do what you wanted. Unless it was Zionist. That was very strict, and sometimes they thought things were Zionist and they weren't. But that didn't come from Hungary, it was from Russia. Because they didn't know what a Zionist movement was. Young people would try to do something and they would think it was Zionist."

But what those young people remembered was that the Community had not stood up for them, had obstructed rather than helped them in their efforts.

THE LIPPNERS, even though they did not want to be party members after 1956, raised their two sons to do the things that would insure them a career. Being Jewish was dangerous. You could know you were Jewish, but you didn't talk about it. Like the overwhelming majority of Hungarian youth, the Lippner boys belonged to the Federation of Communist Youth. George excelled in mathematics, coming in fourth in the national competition, and went to a technical university and became a mathematician. It really didn't matter that he was Jewish, as long as he didn't do anything about it.

George married a Jew of a similar background. Her parents had drawn one conclusion from the Holocaust—either there was no God, or God was not watching. It was inconceivable that God had intended this fate for Jews. Either way, nobody was looking after Jews, and so it was better to be quiet about being Jewish. George and his wife had two children and raised them, like themselves, without Jewish education. After the regime changed in 1989, George took a job in a Florida community college.

He read newspapers, trying to keep up with the changes in their country, but still, when a new Jewish school in Budapest asked him to be principal, the job offer came as a surprise. Lippner didn't think there would be any interest in a Jewish school in Budapest. There had been one Jewish high school for years, the Anne Frank School, which was not even allowed to teach modern Hebrew because it was considered a Zionist language. No one who wanted to go to university and have a successful career went to the Anne Frank School.

The new school was supported by the Lauder Foundation, but Lippner found it hard to believe it would attract enough good students to survive. Nevertheless, he decided to take the job. It would be an interesting challenge, because the school was trying to be Jewish without being either religious or secular. It did not even keep records of how many of its students were Jews, although they were certainly the majority. In addition to aiming for high general academic standards, the school taught Hebrew, Jewish history, and the Old Testament. Each Jewish holiday was studied as it came up. Anyone between the ages of 3 and 18 who was open to the curriculum was welcome. They were averaging more than four hundred students.

One incentive for a Jewish school was the growing movement to offer some kind of religious program in the Hungarian school system, which inevitably would be Christian. Jews were to be given the right to excuse themselves, thereby stating to bigots that they were not "true Hungarians" and would not fully participate in the "Hungarian" curriculum.

Even a third Jewish school sprang up in Budapest. Sponsored by the Joint and a Canadian financier, it served the Orthodox community. László Herzog, general secretary of the Orthodox community, said, "If anybody told me ten years ago that I would see a Jewish school with five hundred students—" It was particularly surprising since membership in the Orthodox community, adults and children, had hovered for many years at about 1,000 people.

Herzog's father had been head of the Orthodox community in Újpest. His wife and two children were killed at Auschwitz. After the war the Orthodox rabbinate arranged marriages for those who had lost their families, and since his wife and two children had been killed at Auschwitz, he was matched with a woman who had also lost two children and a husband at Auschwitz.

Their son, László, was one of the few Hungarian Jews of the

postwar generation who stayed in Hungary and grew up in a traditional Jewish life. Orthodox children were given special permission
to observe the Sabbath. László went to a small Jewish school in one
of the old dark buildings in the Jewish section of Pest, the run-
down neighborhood where the ghetto had been. His family managed to eat kosher, although it meant an extremely limited diet
since not many kosher products were available. This Jewish life
came at a price. Children like László Herzog grew up knowing that
they simply had no future in Hungary. All of Herzog's forty classmates left the country in the 1960s. László also intended to leave,
but at the age of 17 his father died, leaving only him to look after
his ailing mother. He naively dreamed of becoming a doctor, but
coming out of a Jewish school, he was not admitted to a university.
Later, he was able to go to London and receive the medical training to become a *mohel*.

Whenever he was outside, Herzog's yarmulke was always discreetly covered by a hat. But although his dress was not Hasidic, he
looked clearly like an Orthodox Jew. He had short blond hair and
was clean-shaven and serious-looking, with his wire-rimmed
glasses. What no one knew about him, unless they were one of the
few who went to services in the small, soiled, shop-worn synagogue
on Dessewffy Street—a plain room whose only architectural detail
was a painted design on the peeling walls—was that he had a rich
lyric tenor voice.

After the Communists fell from power, Herzog, who had always
circumcised the few male babies born into the Orthodox community, was suddenly in demand for the circumcision of teenage boys.
They would decide to be bar mitzvahed and would learn that they
were supposed to be circumcised and the family would ask Herzog
to do it. But in the course of interviewing the family, it often
became clear that the boy was not really Jewish. In most of these
cases the father but not the mother was Jewish. Herzog turned
down an average of twenty circumcisions a year for boys who he
found were not Jews.

ASIDE FROM this little Orthodox group, Budapest Jewry belonged
to the Neologue movement, a Hungarian variation that, like the
American conservative movement, was fairly traditional with some
liberal tendencies. Neologue was all Zoltán Gardos and Kati Kelemen knew, and it felt too conservative for them. Then they met an

English couple at the rabbinical seminary. The English couple had
noticed that there were a number of young people at the Kiddush
who seemed uncomfortable and out of place. "And this," as Gardos
said, "is how we met other young Jews from the big world outside."
For the first time in his life he was now free to have contacts in
other countries. He and his wife went to England, and they made a
discovery that greatly surprised them—"Other young people consider themselves Jews, and they don't live in Israel and they are not
even Orthodox!" It was a new kind of Jew to him. Until the trip to
England he had thought he had three options: He could move to
Israel or he could stay in Hungary; if he stayed in Hungary, he
could attend a Neologue synagogue, which to his mind was Orthodox; or he could not be Jewish. In London, he and Kati discovered
liberal Judaism, where the synagogue had Western music rather
than traditional chanting and where women were called up to read
Torah. They were astonished to find a Judaism that corresponded
to the ideas of women's equality that had been a part of their
Communist upbringing. And they were not made to feel inadequate because of their ignorance of Hebrew and customs.

Kati and Zoltán decided to bring this new kind of Judaism to
Budapest. They would start an entirely new community of liberal
Judaism. As a woman, Kati would not be allowed to attend the
rabbinical seminary in Budapest but would have to go back to
England and study. She would either become a full rabbi or at
least study for a year to become a religious leader.

They began by holding Havdalah services, the pretty little ceremony that ends the Sabbath. After the short service they had study
sessions. But the official Community was not happy. The rabbinate
declared that nothing liberal would be accepted, and it barred the
liberals from establishing a formal Community of their own. In the
official Community's statement, it declared that liberal Judaism led
to assimilation. Hungary had experience with assimilation before
the war, and what happened to all those assimilated Jews? The
Holocaust had proven that assimilation does not work, the Community argued. They could never be "true Hungarians."

GYULA GAZDAG left Hungary in spring 1989 to teach film at
UCLA. There he got Hungarian newspapers and read about his
friends, marginalized rebels, many of whom were now deputies in
parliament. The film institute had thrown out the old bureaucracy

that had been censoring them. It wrote to Gyula and asked him to
come back and head the film department. In May 1991 he returned to what seemed like a different country. But in the new
Hungary Gyula found a different obstacle to his film work. The
state, in the process of denationalizing everything from manufacturing to pastry shops, also wanted to stop funding films. That
meant Hungarian filmmakers would have to get financing from
other sources, of which there were few in Hungary. Foreign financing was also difficult because Hungary was a small country with a
small local market and a language no one else understood. In the
future Hungarian films would have to have some kind of foreign
appeal to attract foreign investors, or they just wouldn't get made.

Though László Herzog saw a trend toward more religious education for Jews in Hungary, neither Gyula Gazdag nor George
Lippner gave religious training to their children, even though they
both had Jewish wives. "They are aware of the fact that they are
Jewish," said Gyula. "But it is not natural for me to deal with
religion."

George Lippner felt the same way. His two children did not
attend the Jewish school where he was principal. Still, he did not
give them the same upbringing that his parents gave him: He did
not want to teach them that it was dangerous to be Jewish and
something to keep to themselves. "I tell them that if you are a Jew,
you cannot avoid being a Jew. If somebody else wants to pick on
you or say something rude because you are a Jew, he will not ask
you whether you think you are a Jew or not. So you have to be
ready."

Gyula was ready. He listened to the speeches about "true Hungarians," read about the occasional murder of a gypsy, and found
himself for the first time thinking about emigrating with his family.
"It's very strange. I had many conflicts and many problems during
the former regime. But I never thought of leaving. I felt that I was a
part of this culture, that all my roots were here, and that I couldn't
live in another country. But when it becomes about life and death,
then you don't think in these terms, and somehow you have to
think about how deeply your roots go and how the whole society
moved away from all those things which kept me here."

GYÖRGY KONRÁD, now an international literary figure and the
first Central European to head the writers' advocacy group PEN,

liked to meet people at sunset on the top floor of the Budapest Hotel and stroll on the circular outdoor terrace of this drab cylindrical high-rise. He would watch the Pest spires turn to silhouettes, the lights come on along the Buda Mountains, and the Danube turn black, its rebuilt bridges once again looking permanent, with lights that sparkled in the mist rising from the river. "It's an ugly building but a beautiful view," he would say with his impish smile while gazing at the voluptuous epicenter of his Hungarian-speaking universe, hard fought for and—for the moment—won.

At 60, he was in a new marriage and starting a second family. He was again going to synagogues on some occasions. He liked the atmosphere there, the way men wandered wrapped in their prayer shawls chanting a little in Hebrew and gossiping a little in Hungarian. It reminded him of Berettyó and the vanished Jewish world where he had held strings at his hip to fool the rabbi into thinking he wore religious garments.

His two sons, five and six, were of late contemplating the possibility of death. They thought it was unfair that God never dies and yet expected them to. They were also bothered by the story of Adam and Eve. They wanted to know why God punished Adam for wanting knowledge of good and evil. If we have to distinguish between good and evil, we have to know about them. So why was God angry at Adam? The two boys were increasingly suspecting that God was not always fair.

28

In the
Czech Republic

I T WAS INDICATIVE OF THE BAROQUE QUALITY OF REPRES-
sion in Czechoslovakia that playing jazz was a way to oppose
the regime. Jazz was the Czechoslovakian equivalent to Hungarian
filmmaking, the dissident activity that went just far enough to make
opposition clear but not so clear that it was crushed. All the regime
had to do was ignore the jazz musicians and they would have been
reduced to being jazz musicians. But jazz was Western, from
America, imperialist, decadent. Power, unchecked for long enough,
will invent its own enemies to feed its addiction to crushing them.

František and Alice Kraus's son, Tomás, became a lawyer. But he
also played drums—rock and jazz and the jazz/rock fusion that was
popular at the time. His group not only played, it brought in
groups from the West, becoming a major link to imperialist culture. The government objected so vehemently that the group,
which began in the early 1970s as "unofficial culture," ended the
decade as a famous dissident organization.

Artists of all kinds were at the heart of a dissident movement
born out of the postinvasion repression. Writers had enjoyed the
freedom of the Dubček era, and as their works were banned they
formed into a tightly linked underground. Playwright Václav
Havel, novelist Ivan Klima, playwright Pavel Kohout—in all, about
fifty writers met regularly, planned underground work, smuggled
manuscripts to the West, and celebrated New York and Vienna

opening nights in their Prague apartments. Among these writers was Karol Sidon, a playwright and screenplay writer who had collaborated on films with a celebrated Slovak director, Juro Jakubisko. During the brief Dubček era, they had won first prize at a film festival in Pilsen.

At the time of the 1968 Soviet invasion Sidon worked for an underground newspaper that tried to inform people of the true events of that summer. The new hard-line regime still permitted him to write for film and television, even though it knew about his newspaper activities and that he contributed to a small underground theater group. Because of his youth the government thought he might still come around. But by 1970, party officials would visit Sidon and casually suggest that he change his writing or face having all his work banned. He ignored the warnings, and soon he could not work as a writer anymore and had to find manual labor. For a while he was a coal stoker in a steel mill. Havel and Klima were also working such jobs.

In 1977 a defiant declaration of human rights, Charter 77, was circulated. Twelve hundred people—a wide range of academics, disgruntled Communists, and religious activists—had signed this dissident declaration between the late 1970s and late 1980s. But the authors, Havel and Kohout, and all of the original signers, including Sidon, came under intense harassment. They would regularly be arrested for a day or a few days and then be released. It was impossible to hold down any job. Sidon could not even be a coal stoker anymore. Each time he was arrested, government agents, strangers in dull suits, would arrive at his apartment and search it, shuffling through his and his family's possessions, upsetting his wife and terrifying his three children.

Sidon had been thinking more and more about his Jewishness. Technically, he was not a Jew because his mother was Christian. His Jewish father had been deported and killed when Karol was only two years old. He and his mother had survived in hiding. After the war his mother had remarried another Jew, and while Karol was not Jewish, his stepfather and the legend of his father gave him a sense of Jewishness. He had grown up thinking of his home as a Jewish household, but he had no understanding of Judaism being a religion. In the Dubček era he was one of many people in Prague who had started pursuing an interest in Judaism. But Sidon's interest did not wane with the normalization, and in 1978 he began studying under Viktor Feuerlicht. In time he had a symbolic, though legally dubious, conversion. His wife, and therefore his children, were already Jewish.

It was not a good time to be a Jew, but since Sidon was already a Charter 77 founder, he had little standing to lose. It seemed that one day soon he would be arrested and not released. And he could not work. The regime wanted it to be impossible for him to live in Czechoslovakia anymore. Other writers, such as Kohout, had been permitted to leave and then were not let back in. When in 1982 Sidon was offered a scholarship in Jewish studies at Heidelberg, he moved there with his wife and children. Someday, he reasoned, the regime would fall and he would go home.

In 1984, Tomás Kraus's jazz group was dissolved, and three of its members were sentenced to two-year prison terms. Kraus went on with life, marrying the following year, hoping for changes, not certain what to do. He did not think playing jazz was as dangerous as being active in the Jewish Community. People would be called in and interrogated for being seen at the synagogue: Why are you going to the synagogue? Who did you meet? Why? What did you talk about?

THE OVERTHROW of the government was almost an accident. By November 1989, it had already happened in Poland and Hungary. Then the wall had been torn open in Berlin, and people were selling chunks of it as souvenirs of the past. The unthinkable now seemed possible, even inevitable. But Czechoslovakians were still playing the game they had long played, pushing the limits—some jazz, some theater, an underground newspaper, a peaceful apolitical public event—going as far as they could without spending time in prison. Some miscalculated and really did go to prison.

The first mistake the regime made was on November 17, 1989. On that day fifty years before, nine Czech students had been executed and all Czech universities were shut down by the Germans. In 1989 a march was organized to commemorate the event. This was possible: It was politically correct to commemorate antifascist struggles, and the demonstration had been organized by the state-backed student union. But the regime seemed to panic when they saw this march attended by fifty thousand people, many of them young. Government leaders realized that this demonstration was against them. Having seen what happened to soft Communists in neighboring countries, the Czechoslovakian regime decided to

show toughness, and it unleashed the police with a violence seldom seen in Prague. More than seventy were injured, and an
unconfirmed rumor spread through Prague of four deaths.

Three days later, 200,000 people demonstrated. Every day, the
crowds grew bigger. From across the crook of the Vltava River in
the old Jewish quarter, Tomás Kraus saw police on the other side
massing on the high green slopes. They were waiting for orders to
move on the city in force. Kraus, like thousands of others, went
every day to Wenceslas Square, which is not really a square but a
wide boulevard with a grassy mall in the center. A half-mile long
and sixty yards wide, day after day it was filled with demonstrators.

One evening, a police car made its way up the street through the
crowd. Policeman were in both the front and back seats. Demonstrators jeered as the car forced its way through the crowd. Suddenly, it stopped and all four doors opened. Kraus braced
himself—this was going to be bad. The four policemen started
hurling something at the crowd. It was newspapers. It was illegally
printed underground newspapers. That was the moment when
Kraus realized that Communist Czechoslovakia, which was all he
had ever known, was about to come to an end.

HAVEL CALLED IT the Velvet Revolution. If a writer leads a revolution, it gets a good name. However soft and nonviolent it was, it
wasn't really as smooth as velvet. Lives changed very quickly and
kept changing for years. There was Karol Wassermann's favorite
playwright as president of the country, and his fellow dissident
writers in legislative and diplomatic positions. For that matter, Wassermann himself, the temperamental pharmacist in an ascot, an
outsider who showed up for Sabbath at the Old-New Synagogue
and never belonged to anything, was elected president of the Federation of Jewish Communities. Tomás Kraus became the director.
The former official Community leadership was removed immediately. Their collaboration with the regime would not be forgiven.
Some had cooperated with the secret police monitoring activities
from the station across the street from the Jewish town hall. Some
had cooperated in the persecution of their own Jewish Community
members.

Throughout the country there was a move to purge collaborators. Twenty new legislators were accused of having worked with
the state security and were told that if they did not resign, they

would be exposed. Ten refused, and they were not only exposed but their hearings were televised live. In the morning the public was convinced of their guilt. By the afternoon the accused had persuaded the public that they were innocent victims of the state security. The next day, it again appeared that they were guilty. The case was never settled, and most of the legislators kept their seats.

In post-Communist Central Europe, rifling through once-top-secret police files and exposing moles, snitches, collaborators, and secret agents became a public passion. Society had a psychological need for the sensation of a purge. But the state records were a bottomless maelstrom, because the system had tried to control people by compromising them. To get the right school, the right job, a good car, you had had to give something. In most cases, all the state wanted was to get your name in a file. All most people really wanted was to live their lives and contribute as little as possible to the state security apparatus. Martin Mandl wanted nothing more than to pursue his career as a scientist and live a modestly comfortable life in Brno with his wife and their two children. He said, "The worst thing about the Communist regime was that every few months you had to make a very hard moral decision on the degree of collaboration you would permit yourself, to get the things you needed for your life and your family."

The hunt for collaborators cost Czechoslovakia its only remaining rabbi. At a time when there had been no rabbi left in Czechoslovakia, Daniel Mayer had studied for six years at the rabbinical seminary in Budapest. He not only gave the Community a rabbi where there would have been none in the country, but he also helped keep Judaism alive by gathering around him the small group of people willing to practice. After the revolution his stubborn work was remembered, and he was asked to run for parliament in the 1990 elections. As with all candidates, his police files were searched, and it was found that before Mayer had been allowed to go to Budapest, he had had to sign a paper agreeing to cooperate with the secret police. According to the records, if he received any information detrimental to the state, he agreed to report it. There was no evidence that he ever did pass on information. The regime did not really care. The important thing was they had him in their files. He was theirs. He was compromised and therefore part of the system. He could be trusted because they had this on him. After the regime was overthrown, the Jewish Community in its antiregime zeal used the information exactly the way the regime would have—to discredit the community's leader. Mayer was told he could no longer be their rabbi. Mayer could have argued, as did Ilona Seifert in Budapest, that his compromise had made some measure of Jewish life possible. But Mayer did not argue. To the disappointment of some in the community who very much liked him, he left Czechoslovakia.

Karol Sidon said, "Daniel Mayer was chosen by the regime to do their work. And he was used by the regime. I can understand it. It is difficult to condemn someone when you are not in their situation." Sidon, who had been studying Jewish law for six years in Germany, always thought that this moment would come when Czechoslovakia would need a new rabbi. Now he went to Israel for an official conversion and to finish off his studies. He returned to Prague as rabbi in the fall of 1992, and with Viktor Feuerlicht's help, he began establishing a kosher system and other institutions of traditional Judaism. They even planned a *mikveh*, though few Czech Jews had ever seen one. Hebrew classes were offered, and 150 students came the first year. By the second year, enrollment had doubled.

Sidon no longer had time for writing, and in any event, being a writer in this new capitalist world seemed unappealing. "The greatest artistic freedom this country ever knew was from 1968 to 1970," said the screenwriter-turned-rabbi. "Now, after the revolution, what is important is money. The great influence is money."

The Krauses, on the other hand, had become what had been considered before the war a typical Czech Jewish family, like the families of Tomás's parents Alice and František. The children had religious training, and the parents were involved in the Community. But they were not religious. Tomás described it as "a typical Prague Jewish atmosphere, where we celebrate both Christmas and Hanukkah." He said he would like to attend Sabbath services, "but come the weekend, we have to get out of Prague. The kids need to breathe some fresh air."

Prague became the hot travel destination in the post-Communist world—in fact, it became the new place to go in Europe. While prices soared far beyond the grasp of Czechs, the city was a bargain for Germans, French, and Americans. The old stone architecture, with ornaments on everything from lampposts to drainpipes, was still stunning. The lantern-lit cobblestone streets, where shadows from the dark archways and the echo of footsteps once gave an air of mystery, were now the terrain of youths on noiseless sports shoes, hunched over maps, their backpacks casting enormous deformed shadows.

Since "Jewish" had been out under Communism, now it was in. Everybody loved Jewish things. A popular non-Jewish rock group was called Shalom. Sometimes they wore yarmulkes, and their emblem was a star of David. Czechoslovakian youths often sported a star of David, and it was hard to say if they were Jews or simply Shalom fans, but there were more Shalom fans than Jews in Czechoslovakia.

Bus tours to Theresienstadt, "an easy day trip from Prague," became popular. Viera Krulis, who was in Theresienstadt from December 1941 until Liberation, got on one of those buses. When the bus arrived, she stepped off, saw the gates to the old fortress city, and fainted. She was put back on the bus and taken home. Before the war, her marriage to a prominent non-Jewish banker might have saved her, except that the banker had realized that his career would not go well under the Germans if he was married to a Jew. He divorced her, and she was deported along with her parents and sister. The rest of the family was sent to Auschwitz and killed, but Viera, on the strength of a childhood first-aid course, spent the next four years trying to deal with epidemics of typhoid, encephalitis, and scarlet fever—the diseases that overtook the crowded camp. After being liberated, she returned to Prague and took her son— now her only living relative—back from her former husband. She never spoke to her husband again. Her son grew up to also marry a non-Jew, and their children have no Jewish identity. Viera went back to Theresienstadt on a second bus tour, and this time, she proudly announced, she made it through the tour, blending in with the rest of the tourists.

Prague's Old-New Synagogue, the oldest synagogue in Europe, became a star attraction listed in all the guidebooks. At first, the old guard minyan was so unprepared for the onslaught of tourists that there were not even extra yarmulkes. Male visitors would walk through the ancient synagogue bareheaded, camera in hand. The synagogue was open all week for tourists but closed to nonworshipers early Friday evening and Saturday morning so that a service could be held. The Saturday morning scene began not unlike it had seven hundred years ago, when this synagogue was new—with one small difference. In those days the men would mill around the high-ceilinged, stone-walled synagogue. Some would study Hebrew, others would pace and fidget with their prayer shawls. When the sun cleared the horizon, it would hit the amber glass in a small, bullet-shaped window concealed in the eastern wall, and a single ray of gold-tinted light would penetrate to the reading area in the middle of the synagogue, and the morning prayers would begin.

This window was a forgotten detail. Six-story turn-of-the-century art nouveau buildings now blocked the sun from entering that window until it was well over the horizon. But the men still paced around waiting—not for a ray of light, but for tourists. Stocky Viktor Feuerlicht, meticulous Karol Wassermann, and about five other aging stalwarts patiently waited for the Israeli, American, or Dutch Jewish tourists so that the cantor could begin.

Some of the tourists who filled out their ranks showed little interest in following the service. Others were genuinely religious. The women in this medieval synagogue are kept truly out of sight behind a thick stone wall. They can catch glimpses of the *bimah* through narrow windows that seem more like tunnels because they are several feet deep. When the time came to read the Torah, Pavel Erdos, who was younger and stronger, helped lift the heavy antique scroll. No one could recall Erdos having been Jewish until the tourists arrived. He made a profitable business booking tour arrangements for Israelis, although he understood no Hebrew, which may have been one of the reasons he looked so bored during the services. But with Feuerlicht's bad arm and Wassermann's heart condition, it was good to have him to help with the Torah. He always came late but on time for his part.

By the end of the Saturday morning service, the nonworshipping tourists would begin to arrive in a trickle, then more and more, armed with cameras, pushing their way in to see one of Prague's must-do attractions, while the aging locals struggled to explain in five languages that the synagogue was closed on the Sabbath. In 1993 the synagogue had to undergo major repairs, because the added vibration and humidity of the daily crowds was deteriorating the sandstone. The cemetery had twelve thousand ancient Hebrew-lettered tombstones, dating back to at least 1439, lined up to mark the layers of graves beneath the surface and had little room on its tiny plot for the thousands of tourists or for the few practicing Jews who still placed stones on graves, in the tradition of a desert people. Pathways were built in the cemetery in the hope of reducing the damage from the onslaught.

Among the Jews of the Community, the taboo words were sometimes whispered: "It makes me ill to see German tourists walking on Jewish graves."

"I know," Feuerlicht responded when the son of a Theresien-stadt survivor said this. "But tourism brings in money. It helps us." The only other synagogue, the elaborately decorated, dusty Moorish-style Jubilee, with its tiled arches and turn-of-the-century grandeur, did not get the tourists. Its congregation still prayed in an austere room off of the balcony, with plaster patches on the walls and a bare heating pipe protruding. In the late 1890s, when Jews were moving out of the ghetto and into more fashionable Prague neighborhoods, the Jubilee had been built in what seemed an excellent location. How could they have known that one day this synagogue would have difficulty finding minyans because it was just a few blocks off the tourist beat?

Tomás Kraus, as the new Community director, had inherited a painful problem in the form of the state-owned Jewish Museum, which included the cemetery, the Maisel Synagogue, and the rich collection of antique Judaica that Heydrich had stolen from deported Jews. The new Czechoslovakian state agreed to turn over to the Community the handsome sums now earned in tourist entry fees at each site. The government wanted to privatize and was selling off state industries to private small-scale investors. It would have been happy to turn over all Jewish property to the Community. And the Community would have liked to take it all over. It wanted to do things differently—broaden the displays and change the presentations to give more of an appreciation of living Judaism. As it was, it almost resembled Heydrich's dream, an exhibit of an extinct people, their unused ritual objects on display in the unused Maisel Synagogue. Kraus described the display of artifacts under the graceful, vaulted ceiling of the Maisel as, "breathing death on a shelf." It was difficult to look at the neat rows of silver Torah pointers and not think about booty stolen from deported Jews—an empty synagogue full of the relics of annihilated Jews.

The struggling Community with one thousand members could not afford to run all this, however. It had other priorities, such as the newly privatized Jewish hospital and a home for the elderly, which opened in the fall of 1993. But before the Community had even taken possession of all these treasures, it was bombarded with advice from Americans and Israelis. One Israeli group wanted to arrange to have the entire collection moved to Israel. The Community was furious. It had struggled to keep the collection together in this country, in spite of the willingness of the Communists to sell it off, a piece at a time, when there was a good offer. Like the old Communist regime, these Israelis had argued that Jewish things belonged in Israel, not in Czechoslovakia. Wassermann delivered so many angry tirades about American and Israeli Jewish organizations that in 1992 the board voted him out of the presidency. The Federation of Jewish Communities simply could not have a president who shouted at visiting Jews. "Why are American Jews always trying to tell us how things should be done?" Wassermann would shout. "What are you doing here? Why don't you leave? This is where we live! And the Israelis are even worse! They think they can tell us everything!"

Another infuriating experience, for those few who had managed to stay and at last had a chance to rebuild, was to be constantly told by foreign Jews that they should leave. The Israeli ambassador brought a group of Jewish students from Australia on a tour of Jewish Prague to meet Tomás Kraus. One of them asked, "Why don't you go to Israel?" Kraus had his standard answer prepared, but before he could say it, to his great satisfaction, the Israeli ambassador turned to the Australian and said, "Why don't you?"

THE COMMUNITY'S RECOGNIZED EXPERT on its historical treasures was Bedřich Nosek, who had been chief curator of the Jewish Museum until 1991, when he was able to start teaching Hebrew and Jewish studies at the university. His two sons, Marek and Michel, grew up around the Jewish community. Although their family wasn't Jewish, except for Bedřich's father's maternal grandmother, they did not eat pork and they read some of their father's books. Marek, who became a lawyer and worked with one of the big American corporate firms that came in with Western capitalism, wanted very much to marry a Jew. This would restart the Jewish line that had vanished in their family five generations before. He married Elena, an Odessa concert pianist who had come to Prague for a music festival in 1985, given up her career, and stayed. When Marek met her, she was teaching piano to Rabbi Mayer's wife. Elena and Marek married and had a daughter, Anna, whose Jewish education was placed in the hands of her grandfather, Professor Nosek.

In Odessa, Elena's sister Louba, 23, separated from her young husband and came to Prague in 1992 with her four-year-old daughter. She had no skills with which to support herself and her baby, but through the Jewish Community she found work with

Pavel Erdos, the Torah lifter from the Old-New Synagogue. The relationship was reminiscent of the old Soviet joke, "I pretend to work, and he pretends to pay me." Louba's job was to act as interpretor for Erdos, translating into English for Israeli and other Jewish tourists since Erdos spoke only Czech and Russian. Louba, pressed into iridescent stretch pants, her hair frosted and fluffed, would gamely meet Israelis at the airport with the brutish Mr. Erdos and try to figure out what they were saying, all the while hoping that Erdos, whose face showed more cunning than perception, did not notice that she actually didn't speak much English.

Erdos paid her as little as possible for this service, and when tourists threatened not to pay him because he really had very little to offer them as a tour operator, he would claim that it was all because of Louba's bad translation and threaten to withhold her pay. Louba tried to earn additional money giving walking tours of the Jewish quarter based on the knowledge she had acquired from Bedřich Nosek. But it was a hard life, this new capitalism, as her parents had warned her back in Odessa. Still, Louba would point out to her parents the fresh anti-Semitic graffiti that was appearing in Odessa, in the newly independent Ukraine, including a sign that said, "Kill the Jews." She was trying to convince them to leave, but they always replied that both of them had good pensions and would not have anything if they left.

Nosek's other son, Michel, went to a kibbutz in 1990. Then he began attending a yeshiva. He moved to Jerusalem and had himself circumcised and converted. Although he retained his Czechoslovakian citizenship, he stayed in Jerusalem, praying three times a day, keeping strictly kosher, living a traditional Jewish life. The Noseks, five generations later, had finally become Jewish again. But not that Jewish. Far from the shriek most assimilated Jewish parents would muffle at their sons' new hat and beard, far from Robert Altmann's criticism when Daniel had been married in the Pletzl, when Bedřich Nosek was asked how he felt about his son turning Orthodox, he simply said, "I'm very happy. I hope he will know more than I do."

THE GREATEST THREAT to the survival of Judaism in the Czech lands was intermarriage. Even if someone was determined to find a Jewish mate, unless they left the country the odds were against it. In addition to the one thousand Jews in the Prague community, there may have been another thousand in Prague who did not have a Jewish identity and a few thousand more in all of Bohemia and Moravia. The majority of the Prague community were elderly, and their children had left. The Feuerlichts were still a Jewish family, but their children were in Australia and Israel. Only Viktor Feuerlicht and his wife remained in Czechoslovakia. Some family lines were already ending. Karol Wassermann's wife was a Protestant, and they had no children.

Zuzana Skálová was skeptical about mixed marriages. Her sister Eva had married a non-Jew and to the distress of their parents was raising their children without any Jewish background. Zuzana was still hoping to find a Jew to marry. She estimated that there were about fifty Jews her age in Prague. The community was very heavily weighted with the war generation. But her world expanded in 1991 when she got a banking job that enabled her to travel frequently for the first time in her life. About mixed marriages she said, "I think that it's not a major problem. But I am sure that it's easier to have a Jewish partner because there are many problems that can arise in a mixed marriage." Breaking into an earthy laugh, she added, "I have to organize some competitions with foreign participants."

AFTER THE VELVET REVOLUTION, the name of Victory Street in Brno was once again changed back to Masaryk. In December 1990, eighty thousand people shoved into the little square at the head of the street to see their new president, Václav Havel.

Martin Mandl for the first time became active in the Brno Jewish Community, which was now down to three hundred people. He wanted to resuscitate Jewish life in his town, the Moravian capital where he would always live and to which he was passionately attached. He was now very happy that his parents had not settled in West Germany after 1968. "I wouldn't want to be a German," he said.

He liked showing people around his town. According to Mandl, when in Brno, there are two things that one must see. Next door to the music conservatory was a nineteenth-century house with eagles sculpted on the corners. It had been the home of Brno's great twentieth-century composer, Leoš Janáček. But what excited Mandl even more was a certain vacant lot that had been taken over by tall weeds. This was the garden where Gregor Mendel discovered the theory of genetics. The garden had spent years overgrown and forgotten because Trofim Lysenko, who with Stalin's backing had taken over scientific dialogue in the Soviet Union, had declared genetics "a bourgeois science." Wasn't the notion that innate qualities were coded into genes at birth a contradiction in the egalitarian society? Gregor Mendel was not to be honored in the Soviet era.

Mandl looked at the forgotten lot and marveled at the absurdity of being a scientist at all in such a system. He had wanted to be a doctor, but he could not get into medical school. His mother had limited his future when she resigned her party membership after the invasion. You had to choose your degree of collaboration. He had studied chemistry and biology in Bratislava, where he met his future wife.

Their home was filled with good music, the walls were covered with the work of Czech painters, and the shelves were filled with good books. Friends of Martin's sister, Milana, had smuggled Jewish books in German to her. But even several years after the Velvet Revolution there were still few books on Jewish subjects in the Czech language. It was a major event when, in 1989, the first Czech edition of Leon Uris's *Exodus* was published. The Mandl family read it together.

The three-hundred-person Jewish Community was held together by the cantor, Arnošt Neufeld, whose father had also been a cantor. Neufeld's face and thick, gray beard were so classically Semitic that his blue eyes seemed startling. His wife converted to Judaism, and their two daughters were raised to be Jewish, but only inside the home. Both daughters married non-Jews but kept a few customs such as separate meat and dairy dishes.

As cantor, Neufeld had drawn a salary from the Communist state that was continued after the revolution. But the Community had a double burden: the state had returned all its property but had cut all state subsidies. The theory was that the Community could earn its own money from the property. But the property included forty-six Jewish cemeteries scattered throughout southern Moravia and thirty buildings, most of which had either been abandoned or used for storage. Not only did the property not earn income, most of it would cost money to restore. The only income-earner was a building with a television station, which started paying rent. About thirty new people had become active Jews after the Velvet Revolution. Many of them were people like

Milana Mandl—in their forties and educated in the liberal days of Dubček.

Brno's discreet synagogue with its plain exterior was still operating on Friday nights and Saturday mornings. On a major holiday it could get thirty people. But this included non-Jews, more and more of whom had been showing up for services since the revolution. Some explained that they were Christians interested in the Jewish roots of their religion. Others seemed to think they were making an anti-Communist statement.

Neufeld restored the Jewish cemetery, and occasional mourners still turned up on the now well-trimmed tree-lined grounds to place a stone on a grave. The coffins were made from unstained, untreated wood, according to Jewish law. The dead were still buried in the traditional white smocks, with a small sachet of soil from Israel placed under the head. But it was getting increasingly difficult to find Jews for the funerals, and Jewish law states that the body must be prepared by Jews.

"I worry about what will happen when I am gone," Neufeld often confided to Martin Mandl. Mandl wondered, too, because neither he nor anyone else in town had the knowledge to take Neufeld's place. Two people from Brno went to study in Israel, and it was hoped they would be back in a few years.

In 1992, Brno had its first open Community Passover seder since Dubček. It was the first seder Martin Mandl had ever been to. With the same natural enthusiasm with which he dragged people to the Janáček house, he was trying to learn and teach his two children. Both he and his wife wanted their children to have a Jewish education, although they would have to convert if they wanted to be Jews. When their bright and serious daughter, Veronika, was 13, they sent her to Israel for one month. Before she went, she did not think of herself as Jewish, but after one month in summer camp she was not only ready to convert but, like her aunt twenty-four years earlier, was ready to move there. It was almost useless for Martin to talk to her about building Jewish life in Brno because there was only one other Jew of her age in town. "I like being Jewish," said Veronika, "And in Czechoslovakia there are not a lot of Jews. Jewish holidays are very sad here. In Israel they are a lot of fun."

"This is what the Israelis teach," said Martin with a tone of resignation. "You must leave here. You must go back to Israel. No matter what you are doing, Europe is only tragedy. For two thousand years it has been only tragedy for Jews. You must leave. That is what we keep hearing from Israel."

But Mandl did not think that way. Not now. Not after all those years of compromise and patience. "For twenty years a great source of information was the Voice of America in Czech," he said. "About fifteen years ago I heard a commentator say, 'During the next twenty or thirty years, all Jewish life in Czechoslovakia will die.' And I thought, yes, that's right. But since '89, it's not certain. It's a question. But we must help ourselves."

Even without conversions or a high birthrate the Jewish population has kept growing. New Jews seemed to get unearthed in the society. In 1992 there were officially one thousand Jews in Prague. By 1994, without any Jews moving to Prague, the official list had grown to thirteen hundred.

29

The
New Slovak
Republic

O NE OF THE MOST TRAVELED PATHS IN THE NEW SLOVAK
Republic must certainly have been the one between the
dining-room table and the coffee table in the Bratislava living
room of Zuzana Šimko Stern. This was the path she paced on
Thursday afternoons after reading that week's edition of *Zmena*.

Zmena means "change," and it was the name of one of the
many new Slovak newspapers born in post-Communist liberty.
When Juraj Stern came home on Thursdays, his wife had already read the weekly *Zmena* and was pacing, ready to report
that week's assortment of nebulous anti-Semitic innuendo.
Zmena was not one of those flagrant neo-Nazi-printed-in-the-
U.S.A. hate tabloids. It was respectable in appearance and tone,
with a staff of recognized journalists who wrote in Slovak, a
linguistic cousin of Czech, in a well-crafted style that appeared
to be targeting educated readers.

The Sterns were possibly the handsomest couple in Bratislava.
They both crackled with energy. She had obsidian black eyes that
glowed a wondrous anger as she told of the latest outrage she had
heard or seen in fast-changing Bratislava. Juraj was small, fit, fine-
featured and so charged that he could not seem to bear to be
motionless, in spite of a painful back ailment.

Their home was in an uninspired block of apartment buildings
surrounded by similar blocks on the edge of town, where there was

room to build and no costly old buildings in the way. But it was a pleasant home, full of paintings and books.

That Thursday, *Zmena* had published part two of a series called *"Vynútené Klamstvo"* which means something like "Lie under Duress." It did not actually say that the Holocaust didn't happen. It simply quoted others saying so. According to some people, *Zmena* reported, there were no gas chambers at Auschwitz, only refrigeration units.

Zmena could have been merely reporting on the phenomenon of revisionism. And it could have been merely because Slovak activist Peter Gall had a very classically Jewish face that the cartoonist portrayed him with a face that could have been a poster for the Nazi propaganda film *Der Ewige Jude*, The Eternal Jew. And what was to be made of an editorial complaining that such a fuss was made over a Jewish cemetery recently vandalized in the Slovak Republic, yet when the Israelis committed violence against Palestinians, nothing was said? Was it significant that when a foreign rabbi settled in the small Jewish community in Košice, *Zmena* referred to "internationalism going on there"?

The Sterns were concerned because the new Slovak Republic, the second attempt at Slovak nationhood, was under way. Juraj still remembered the first one, when he had hid in a bunker covered with potatoes. Someone shooting through the potatoes. Little thwacks around him as the bullets missed. All the good Slovaks who had hidden him. All the bad ones who had pursued him. He was thinking more and more about those times. And it seemed as if they had gone through so much—just to arrive back at Slovak nationalism.

AFTER THE INVASION came the "normalization." The way to live through the "normalization" was to stay out of trouble and concentrate on your career and the opportunities for your children. Children were a great tool for repression. You could risk prison and even feel good about yourself. But how could you destroy your child's future—only in grade school, and already there would be no possibility of a university education because you had opened your mouth once too often.

With Jewish life ended in Nitra in 1964, Zuzana had moved to Bratislava, where she worked as a teacher and met Juraj, who was a prominent economist and an expert on factory productivity—a major, if not *the* central issue for the government. They married and had two children. She became a research engineer. They built themselves a wooden cottage in the mountains for the weekends, where they could sip the powerful *slivovitz* made by their neighbors from local plums and recall their childhoods in the Slovak mountains.

Life was going well for them. Both their son and their daughter got into gymnasium, the upper-level secondary school that was the required track for university. Then in 1989, the very year that their son Tomás was about to apply for university, a student group approached Zuzana and asked her to sign a petition demanding academic freedom. She wanted to sign, but did she have the right to do this to Tomás? Whatever Tomás might think, her husband would certainly be furious. She told the students that she had to read the petition carefully and sent them away. She thought and talked with a friend and finally decided to sign. Then she went up to their mountain home to join Juraj for the weekend. He was there, pacing in that energetic way he always had when something was on his mind, and she had to confess immediately.

"Juraj, I know this is going to make you angry, but I signed a student petition—"

"Well, I know this will make you angry," he said mockingly, "but I signed it too."

Tomás was able to go on to university and medical school after all because that same year, in November 1989, the Communist regime fell in Czechoslovakia. After the fall both religion and nationalism reemerged. They had been linked before. Josef Tiso, the pro-Nazi nationalist, had been a priest, and most of his government had had Church ties. The supporters of an independent Slovak state had to seesaw between assurances that the new state would be nothing like the last Slovak state, and persistent efforts to rehabilitate Tiso because he was the only leader of a Slovak state they had.

Juraj Stern began to see things that he had not seen since his childhood. Walls in Bratislava occasionally had slogans on them such as "Jews go to Palestine" and "Gas the Jews." He went to a soccer game—Bratislava against Budapest. People shouted the old Slovak fascist cheer *"Na stráz,"* "Attention!" In the crowd, along with the occasional anti-Semitic sign, he saw two flags of the Guardists, the Slovak SS.

SILVIA KRAUS was still in high school in 1989. "November was the revolution," she said. "In January came the religion." Suddenly, students were required to attend lectures by clergy. When a Catholic priest came to the school and lectured on the greatness of Josef Tiso, Silvia stood up and said, "It's not true. All of my family died in the war because of Tiso, because of the Germans and because of the Slovaks." Most of the other students were angered by this outburst, and feeling isolated, Silvia walked out of the room.

In spite of such incidents, the Jews in Bratislava were seeing more Jewish life than at any time since 1968. There was a wide range of figures on how many Jews live in Bratislava—between five hundred and one thousand. More seemed to turn up all the time as Jewish activities increased. In 1990 a Jewish Forum started offering regular meetings that drew several hundred participants to hear speakers on subjects of Jewish interest.

The new freedom since the fall of Communism meant different things to different people. To some, it meant that they could say "Na stráz" again. To a few youths, it meant they could shave their heads, hang out near the university under a bridge across the Danube, and occasionally find someone to rough up. To some, it meant having a Jewish Forum and filling the largest hall in Bratislava, some eight hundred seats, for a Hanukkah program.

To Fero Alexander, it meant learning for the first time about his country. His parents were Auschwitz survivors. His grandparents had not survived. His older brother was born in Theresienstadt. But his parents did not talk about any of this very much. As he toured with his Slovak folk group in traditional costume, Fero never thought this was an odd thing for a Jew to be doing until after 1989, when he heard a historian speak on the history of the Slovak state at the Jewish Forum. Fero was shaken. "I didn't know. I didn't ask. Now the situation is that I know what happened during the Slovak state, and still I'm here."

He asked—and repeated the question as though speaking to himself—"Why am I here and playing folk music?"

The cry for Slovak independence was born out of post-Communist liberty. In the old days just talk of such a thing could have sent Soviet tank columns in from the Ukraine. But when the Slovak leadership that had come to power in fair elections began demanding independence, the democratically elected Czechoslovakian legislature had no democratic alternative but to dissolve the nation. The agreement in principle came in the spring of 1992, but it took three tries to get the breakup bill passed—not because of Czech opposition but because of Slovak hesitation. Finally, in January 1993, a new nation was born, as Czechoslovakia shed its poorest region. The new emblem of the Slovak Republic was a cross, and its new coins bore a crucifix.

The Slovak region had never produced enough to support its population and had been living like a poor relation off the earnings of the Czech lands. This was the root of the resentment Slovaks felt toward Czechoslovakia. It had been tempting to conclude that the Czechs were "holding the Slovaks down." But the new Slovak state instantly became an orphan in a hostile world. Not yet independent, it had already gotten into a major dispute with neighboring Hungary over a proposed dam on the Slovak Danube, a debate that played into the hands of Hungarian nationalists.

The elements of the situation were too familiar for any Jew to miss. Slovaks no longer had Czechs to blame. If their economy was a failure—and according to most economists, including Juraj Stern, it had little hope of success—who would they blame? The level of anti-Semitism that had driven Slovak Jews such as Karol Wassermann to Prague had remained. Before Czechoslovakia split, one survey of Central Europe showed the Czechs to be the least anti-Semitic people in the region and the Slovaks to be among the most. In May 1991 a poll by the Independent Institute of Social Analyses recorded only five percent of Czechs but 25 percent of Slovaks believing Jews had too much influence on society. Fifteen percent of Czechs and 30 percent of Slovaks said they did not like the idea of having Jews as neighbors, and four percent of Czechs and 20 percent of Slovaks thought Jews endangered political development.

In the early days of the new Slovak Republic, the anti-Semites, as these polls forecasted, were a minority, but a significant one. "We are worried about it, because the new government is doing nothing against them. They [the government] are occupied with the problems of building an independent state," said Juraj Stern. In fact, the government could not really afford to attack anti-Semites, since they also happened to be the ultranationalists who were the state's greatest enthusiasts. In the fall of 1993, with the government lacking enough votes to pass major legislation, including the 1994 budget, the extremist Slovak National party—which celebrated the memory of Tiso—was invited to join the ruling coalition. That coalition also failed. It was hard to build consensus with extreme nationalists.

The Slovaks began to swing to the left, and the nationalists were forced out of government. Throughout Central Europe nationalists and anti-Communists were being voted out and replaced by former Communists. Communists became the largest party in Poland and made gains in both the Slovak Republic and the eastern part of reunited Germany. In Hungary, Antall died in 1994 and a former Communist official, Gyula Horn, was elected Prime Minister. It was not so much nationalism that was alienating voters. Everywhere in Central Europe except the Czech Republic, a large part of the electorate was already disillusioned with capitalism.

But Slovak nationalists also had a public relations dilemma. If Slovaks started looking at the history of the last Slovak state, they would be afraid of the new one. So a little revisionism was needed to assuage public fear. But the new revisionism instead reinforced that fear.

Zuzana was at an office party talking to someone whose husband was involved in planning the new Slovak state. The woman assured Zuzana that there was no reason to be worried.

"I am afraid for my children," Zuzana explained.

The woman smiled and said, "Why are you afraid? I'm not afraid. Why are you afraid for your children?"

Zuzana said, "You are not worrying because your children are not Jews."

Without a moment's hesitation the woman answered, "It is not true about the Second World War. It's not true about the Holocaust. Why are you so afraid?"

This, of course, was exactly why Zuzana Stern was afraid.

For many Jews the issue was less what they would do than the future of their children. Silvia Kraus's father, Tomás Kraus, son of the Slovak Jew accused of burning his own shop to avoid nationalization in the late 1940s, thought both his daughters should leave. But he intended to stay. After the fall of Communism he dropped his career as a sports journalist to start an import-export business. He believed capitalism had a future in the Slovak Republic. He resigned as president of the Bratislava Jewish Community to give more time to his new business. But he was determined that his daughters leave as soon as they finished school. Silvia said that she would at least like to do some specialty work in Vienna. "Then I will see," she said. Vienna, which had been an impossible world away under Communism, turned out to be a half-hour commute from Bratislava. But no one on a Slovak salary could afford to go there. Economics replaced police controls as the isolating factor for Slovaks.

Still, travel did become a possibility. Summer trips to Israel were organized every year, and some fifteen Slovak Jews moved there permanently in the first three years after the Velvet Revolution. To Fero Alexander, the new possibilities became almost an obsession. He had always traveled with his folk group. Now, instead of finding his way through the labyrinth of Communist bureaucracy, there were airfares to be researched, compared, and quoted at length. He, his wife, and his three sons went to Israel. "I got a wonderful fare," he said, "$250 round trip. But here that is two months' salary."

So many Slovak Jews were visiting Israel that the community attempted to persuade El Al to offer twice-weekly flights from Bratislava to Tel Aviv. In Israel, Fero's second son, who had wanted to be bar mitzvahed several years earlier but could find no one in Bratislava to teach him, belatedly had the ceremony. His youngest son was bar mitzvahed in Bratislava in January 1993, the first Bratislava bar mitzvah in almost twenty years.

The Bratislava community searched world Jewry for a rabbi who would move to the new republic. Fero wanted to find someone in the American Conservative tradition, but no such rabbi could be found. Instead, they found a twenty-nine-year-old American Lubavitcher, Baruch Myer. To most Bratislava Jews, the Hasidic practices of Lubavitchers seemed extreme, but one of the things that made Lubavitchers different was the fact that they were willing to come. "They come. They settle anywhere," said Fero Alexander. If Baruch Myer did not exactly fit in with his dark clothes, beard, and hat, he made up for that difference by learning fluent Slovak before arriving. He immediately began a wide range of projects. He eagerly established a kosher chicken operation. He slaughtered the birds and trained women to clean them by hand under strictly observed religious law. But when Bratislava Jews discovered that kosher chickens were three times as expensive as regular chickens, they were not willing to buy them. Myer's kosher chickens were simply unaffordable.

A Jewish hotel was built next to a weedy lot, below the ramparts of the castle that once overlooked the old city and that now overlooked a highway. A kosher restaurant was established in the hotel, and a *mikveh* was built in the basement. But few people came. A lonely, hopeful desk clerk waited in the new pristine-white lobby underneath three clocks that gave the time in New York, Bratislava, and Tel Aviv.

The new Slovak Republic was frantically rebuilding hotels and fixing up monuments, preparing for a tourism boom that did not come. In fact, tourism, never an important industry, was now declining. The restless few from the crowds that pressed into Prague no longer drifted into Bratislava, because it was no longer in the same country. The new Slovak currency—much of it simply old Czechoslovakian bills with new Slovak stamps glued to them—did not immediately collapse as feared. Fero Alexander bought a new sound system before the new money was issued, because he feared that foreign products would be unaffordable once Slovak money hit the currency market and promptly sank. The money dropped a little, but it did not sink. The impending crisis of cutting loose state industry was put off. The chemical industry might struggle and survive, but the obsolete steel and textile mills were certain to fail, and the factories that had made heavy armaments such as tanks for the now-defunct Warsaw Pact would have to find a new product or die.

The Czech Republic was selling off its state industries by offering shares to the public. But the new Slovak state was deferring such decisions, because it was keeping the economy at least limping for the time being and besides, it was hard to imagine anyone buying into a Slovak steel mill. Life was, if not prosperous, at least peaceful in the new republic. The inevitable economic crisis had not yet hit, and while the government took a strident tone toward Czechs and gypsies, there were few problems for Jews. There were occasional incidents. In September 1993 the skinheads who based themselves by the bridge cornered Baruch Myer on a quiet street at midday and beat him. But most Slovaks were still honoring Jews, still thinking of this as an anti-Communist act.

In the flat plains east of Bratislava, where massive sugar-beet cooperatives were struggling to restructure, the town of Veča celebrated its 880th anniversary. It hadn't celebrated any previous anniversaries, and in fact, it had not even existed for about two decades. A chemical plant had been built in the newer, less historic town of Šala. Soon both towns looked the same, because their centers were torn up to build rows of block housing for the workers who relocated for the chemical plant. Then the town of Veča was eliminated, simply absorbed into Šala. There were many Slovak towns like this. Šala was more fortunate than many, because the factory for which the town had been destroyed had a chance at survival. Other towns were destroyed for steel and arms factories that might soon be closed.

In late 1993 the town government of Šala, to celebrate the new Slovak independence and defy the old Communist order, decided to observe the anniversary of the defunct town of Veča with a four-day celebration, including goulash stands, Slovak folk dancing, speeches, and brass bands. To kick off the event, a plaque was dedicated in the Jewish cemetery to 110 Veča families who had been deported to Auschwitz. Honoring the deported Jews would be a perfect rejection of the old regime. But the cemetery looked like a vacant lot in the center of a gargantuan housing project, and nothing was even done to groom the shaggy little spot for the ceremony. As the mayor finished his speech, a strong bony hand gripped the shoulder of a visitor. He was an elderly man, one of seven remaining Jews in the town. "Look at this place," he said, waving his hand at the akimbo tombstones obscured by tall weeds, the encroaching blocks of housing units that looked poised to swallow the little space. "After everything they have done to this place, do you think this ceremony makes a difference?"

Of all the towns in this region, the largest Jewish community was the seventy Jews, Orthodox and observant, in Galanta. Compared to Veča or even Nitra, this was a thriving community. In fact, these few Jews had preserved considerably more Jewish life than the hundreds of Jews in Bratislava. Before the war there had been fifteen hundred Jews in Galanta, but fourteen hundred had been deported to Auschwitz. The surviving population had stayed almost stable since the war.

Along with most of the town, the synagogue had been torn down to build workers' housing, but the community prayed in a fifteen-by-thirty-foot room with prewar Torahs. There were minyans every Friday night and Saturday morning. In the absence of any trained religious leader, Adolf Schultz, in his early seventies, kept the community functioning. He and most of the other Galanta Jews observed the kosher laws. Like Arnošt Neufeld in Brno, Schultz almost obsessively maintained the Jewish cemetery.

FERO ALEXANDER and his wife, an orthodontist, were still committed to Bratislava. The five-story building where they had an apartment, on the slope of the castle-topped hill, had been owned by his wife's family, who had built it in 1932. In the last Slovak state Jewish property had been "Aryanized." The "Aryans" who had been given this building were forced to turn it over to the Communist state in 1961. Now both the Alexanders and this "Aryan" family were trying to get their property back. It was one of hundreds of such cases.

The Sterns resisted emigration. Zuzana, who had visited her relatives in Israel in the 1960s and returned feeling that Czechoslovakia was her home, felt a little less certain about the Slovak Republic. But she said, "I think that it is very necessary that there are some communities in other countries." The Sterns have always been proud of the ancient Jewish history of Slovak towns, and even if they were among the few Jews left, they still felt they lived in a place with Jewish roots. They celebrated the major Jewish holidays with their closest friends, who happened to be Protestants. "It is a good thing to have some very good friends who have nothing against Jews and who are able to celebrate Jewish holidays too," she said.

Zuzana Stern believed that by deciding against emigration in 1968, when all of their Jewish friends had left, "we just deferred the decision to another generation." Soon their son and daughter would have to decide. To well-educated young Bratislava Jews, Israel was not nearly as tempting as such places as Vienna and Prague, which were culturally similar and close by.

Tomás Stern's father, the economics professor, was encouraging him to leave, predicting a dismal future for the new republic. But Juraj and Zuzana had no intention of leaving themselves. "This is an important place for Judaism. It had one of the great yeshivas of the 19th century," Juraj said.

"The greatest," argued Tomás. "But you can't have that now."

Juraj didn't hear his son and continued, "You can't let that disappear. Bratislava is a Jewish place."

"So you are going to sacrifice yourself for that?" Tomás asked.

Juraj did not answer.

30

In Antwerp

I T WAS FRIDAY AFTERNOON, AND YOUNG MEN AND BOYS were already appearing in the street in their Sabbath best—ever wider and furrier hats, and newer, shinier coats, and *peots* so exquisitely curled that they bounced with each step like party decorations. The clothing seemed to be a contest that no one was winning. At Seletsky's bookstore—where, in order of quantity, Yiddish, Hebrew, Dutch, French, German, and English books on Judaism were stacked so haphazardly that it was hard to get in the store—a Hasid was bartering with Seletsky for a set of commentaries. They were doing it in diamond-district style. Mechilem Silberman, a stout, well-fed, and happy father of five, called it "the diamond mentality." He never liked it, which is why he converted the storefront of the family home on Simonsstraat into a silver shop. The silver trade was at least a little more genteel.

His mother, Dwora Silberman, was never happy about this decision. She visited him from Israel, where she had been living since her husband Hershl died in 1985, and she cautioned him once again about going into silver. "You can't carry silver," she told him. If things get bad, "diamonds are a very easy thing to take with you when you flee."

Fleeing was increasingly on her mind. Again and again, she reviewed the way her parents, the last time she saw them, had told her and Hershl to flee because they were young. Her parents had assured her that they would not be touched because they were old. She had listened. Now she realized that they had not even been that old—only in their fifties, twenty years younger than she was now—and she knew that it was a mistake to have left them in Antwerp, left them there to die a horrible death at an early age. Over and over again, she reviewed the facts. Hershl hadn't let her turn back. She had tried. Over and over again, she examined every detail of her guilt. Why had she left them to the Nazis? Mechilem often pointed out to her that if she had stayed, she simply would have been sent to Auschwitz with them. "I could have hidden," she argued.

Mechilem knew that arguing with her was useless, but he had somehow to stop her from hurting herself. It was as though she felt guilty for living into old age, for outliving everyone, for living twenty years more than her parents had been allowed to. "I can't enjoy my life," Dwora insisted. "I eat, and I think of how my parents had nothing to eat."

Her first child, born when Antwerp was barely behind the combat lines, had married an English dentist and moved to Israel. The second had married a French doctor and moved to Israel. In all, four of her children had married professionals and moved to Israel. Mechilem was the only Silberman left in Europe.

That was how the Jewish population of Antwerp remained at about the same size—large families where most left but a few brought in a mate and stayed. Mechilem's wife came from England. The important thing was that traditional Orthodox Judaism remained in the world. Still, it was difficult for Antwerp Jews to see their children leave. Harry Biron was an Antwerp Jew who raised his two daughters to be Zionists. When they went to Israel, he said, "We gave them the idealistic education of Israel, the dream. So they followed the dream. The education was right, but I would like them in Antwerp, preferably in a house just down the street."

In 1986, Jozef Rottenberg sold his multimillion-dollar pharmaceutical company, which he had started after the war with a few employees, to an American multinational. The company had become large by Belgian standards, but he thought it would be too small to stand up to competition in a fully integrated European economy. His family's dark, handsome, high-ceilinged Flemish house had a coatroom always filled with the hats and wraps of a half-dozen visitors, and the elegant little garden was littered with the toys and tricycles of grandchildren. Mordechai, the first postwar

Rottenberg, whose birth was celebrated on the streets of the diamond district, grew up to have the Rottenberg good looks and charisma. He worked for his father's company, then after it was sold moved into cosmetics. He had one brother with an Antwerp diamond company, another in Vienna, one in Israel, two in New York, and a sister in England.

Mechilem Silberman was comfortable in the heart of the diamond district where they had always lived, with his shop full of antique silver that was too heavy and unsuitable for sudden flight. "If only he would do a little diamonds on the side," Dwora said.

Mechilem wore a vest and a yarmulke with a hat over it, shaved the top of his head, and wore a frizzy blond beard. He did not want to be like his father, Hershl, who had seemed afraid, stayed clean-shaven, and taken his hat off when gentiles came in. But for all Mechilem's apparent boldness, he confessed, "I'm not sure why, but I am not sure we are safe here." And he admitted that if he went to a doctor or lawyer or bank director, he still took his hat off. His doctor always laughed about it, because none of his other Jewish patients did that anymore. Removing the fear would take one more generation. His children would not take off a hat. "Kids today would never do that. They aren't ashamed of anything." But it was different for Mechilem. When they were traveling, away from the world of the diamond district, and his children started speaking Yiddish in loud voices, Mechilem felt embarrassed and would tell them to speak English, his wife's language—a good, neutral international language.

In 1988 a liberal synagogue, like those of the American Reform movement, was attempted in Antwerp, but it found few followers and soon died. Those who were not kosher or did not observe the Sabbath tried to keep it out of the sight of those who did. There were Jews in Antwerp who drove their cars on Saturday. But they would not drive down the Belgielei. It was believed that Jewish law made a distinction between nonobservance in private and flaunting in public.

"We've lost that golden middle way of my parents," said Mechilem. "Everyone is getting either nonpracticing and modernized or Hasidic." There was a consistent pattern. The survivor generation was clean-shaven and dressed normally but with a hat; the postwar generation wore vests and beards and their children were in full regalia. Sam Perl, an Orthodox Jew of the clean-shaven hat-wearing survivor generation, thought this impulse toward ever more exotic dress was driven by fear of assimilation. "They are afraid they will come reaching over the other side of the world and they will be lost. It's a weakness." He blamed religious leaders for trying to keep the young traditional. "I tell you, the spiritual leaders think all this clothing and everything will keep them back. Keep them away from the street. But unfortunately, they are putting this into their heads as though it were a great principle, and it's not true. Judaism is not just this. If you have to count only on the clothing, it's very sad and very bad. If you don't have a way to live life—Jews are becoming more and more extreme. I think there will be a reaction against this," he said.

But far more troubling things were looming on the gray Antwerp horizon. The VMO, Flemish Military Order, host to the extreme right at Diksmuide, had been banned in the early 1980s and renamed itself the Vlaams Blok, the Flemish Bloc. It played down the SS service records of some within its ranks, and it prudently avoided anti-Semitic rhetoric—unless of course you drank beer with its members at Diksmuide. Their public speeches, like those of the German Republicans, Dutch Centrum, and French National Front, concentrated on the "immigrant problem"—the claim that the quality of life in the nation was being eroded by the presence of Moroccans, Turks, and Arabs. This approach seemed to settle much better with the general population than attacking Jews, a polemic that was associated with Nazis and occupation. In the general election of November 1991 the Vlaams Blok won 25 percent of the vote in Antwerp. This was a shock in a city where they had won only 1.9 percent in the previous election four years earlier, and where there were few notable conflicts between the general population and the highly visible Jewish four percent. The strongest negative feeling commonly expressed about Jews was that they were dangerous to be around because they could be targets. A swimming instructor said that people shied away from the pool on Sundays when the Orthodox Jewish children were offered instruction, because they feared that someone might attack the pool.

Palestinian attacks seemed fresher in Antwerp memories than the Holocaust. The Jewish Community was spending considerable money on security operations against possible future incidents. But it did not expect those attacks to come from the extreme right. The Community was still focused on Arabs. On a few occasions North

African juvenile delinquents had singled out Jews for physical attacks. But the Jews were disturbingly passive about the fact that a quarter of their city had voted for a racist right-wing party. When Mechilem Silberman said he did not feel entirely safe in Antwerp, he could not even name a reason why he felt that way. Sam Perl pointed out that Antwerp Jews had not had any problems with the extreme right. "They say that they have nothing against Jews. We are glad to hear it, but we don't trust them." Aside from this sad lack of solidarity with other minority groups that were being attacked by the extreme right—partly influenced by difficult relations between the Jews and some of the groups being victimized—there was a curious naive confidence among Antwerp Jews that the Flemish extremists would not dare turn against them. Perl said, "The Flemish are afraid to go out openly against us. If they go out openly against us, they will lose part of their votes."

Part of the problem was that the Jews had once again become a happy and prosperous community, and strolling down the Belgielei on a Shabbat, it was possible to forget that there ever had been a Holocaust. Survivors did not want to remember, but they knew they could not let the rest of the world forget, and for this reason in the 1990s Perl began speaking about his experiences. He was not able to dismiss the historical revisionists with the same optimism with which he shrugged at the Flemish nationalists. People were being published who said it was all a lie, that the Holocaust had never happened, and that meant that Perl could no longer keep his nightmares to himself. In February 1993 he spoke for the first time about his Holocaust experiences, torture, and his two escapes from deportation. This was not an intimate conversation in his home but a lecture to forty students. "I feel that we have to come out and witness now. My story is nothing compared to those of the people who have been in Auschwitz. Nevertheless, I have my part also."

Though he was born after the war, the Holocaust remained on Mechilem's mind also. If nothing else, his mother would have kept it there. After the fall of Communism an influx of illegal Poles came into Belgium. Everyone in Antwerp was hiring Polish cleaning women. Mechilem saw a television interview with a Belgian official who, asked about all the illegal Poles in Belgium, said, "What can I do if the Jews keep giving them work?"

Mechilem told his wife, "I will mop myself, but I don't want Poles in my house!" They hired a Yugoslavian. "I'm not sure if that's better," he said. People would come into his store with stories about the Poles, how they would switch dishes or slip *traif*, unkosher food, into the pot. They did not trust Poles because they thought they still hated Jews. "They call us all rich and greedy," someone said to Mechilem.

"And in Poland," it was pointed out, "there are only a few Jews that haven't been killed or driven off. And the Poles are still anti-Semites even without the Jews. They want to get those few."

"See," said Mechilem, "the Poles are greedy."

31

In Paris

ANDRÉ JOURNO FUMBLED IMPATIENTLY WITH HIS CIGAR-trimmer and snipped the tip of his long hand-rolled Havana. He thrust it into his mouth and then took it out as though too exasperated to even smoke. "It's shameful. Shameful, absolutely disgusting, no shame."

It was the tenth anniversary of the gun attack on Goldenberg's, a day that he had told countless reporters over the years, "We must always remember." The first few years, journalists would work Rue des Rosiers, and when they got to him, he liked to say something about how the day must always be remembered. But this year, they weren't even asking him. They had a television crew down at Goldenberg's filming some special, and that was all. "It's just shameful the way he's exploiting that tragedy to get himself publicity. That is all I have to say."

By 1990, the Marais had taken over the Pletzl. All that was left of the Pletzl was the Rue Pavée synagogue, a few *shtibls*, a center the Lubavitchers had set up on Rue des Rosiers, a few kosher butchers, some bookshops, Goldenberg's, the several shops of the Journo family, and the three bakeries of the Finkelsztajn-Korcarz family. And there was one old-time barbershop, whose owners, being the only non-Jews in the neighborhood, had witnessed the roundups and deportations throughout the occupation.

These remnants were surrounded by the chic, the trendy, and

the American. In the 1980s, just as the refurbishing of the Marais was largely completed and ready to sell and Paris real estate prices had become inaccessible to most, the dollar became strong against the franc and Americans felt that they were getting bargains. The Marais became a neighborhood of gay bars and fashionable restaurants, where the language lingered halfway between French and English. Signs went up for *"le Brunch de Dimanche,"* where no one had even eaten Sunday breakfast before. Lingerie and jewelry shops replaced old Pletzl shops.

The Journos had expanded. In 1989, André's father, Roger, died, and his mother decided to retire and sold the little grocery. André bought a bigger store, then expanded it into a store and restaurant. Another brother started a café across the street from Goldenberg's, and another sister had a food store. They all lived on Rue des Rosiers and raised their children there. On Friday nights André closed his restaurant and shoved all the tables together into one long table set with roasted peppers, pickled vegetables, and challahs. More than a dozen Journos with their teenage children sat around and said the blessing for the candles and the wine, the men putting their paper napkins on their heads for the blessing. That was their only religious concession before they settled into the family Friday-night couscous. Outside, Orthodox Jews were scurrying to their *shtibls*, and young couples were strolling, looking for the newest restaurant, wondering what sort of silly party they were passing with the men all putting paper napkins on their heads.

André also had an art gallery with paintings of behatted Orthodox life that did not seem to attract much interest from the Orthodox but drew some tourists, who expected this kind of thing in the Pletzl. The gallery was in Finkelsztajn's building, and the restaurant was directly across the street from Henri's store. Henri, who had never really wanted to be a baker, now had family and employees and was functioning largely as a host. He greeted people at his store, especially old-time customers. He gossiped. He would find a day-old challah and put it in a bag, silently drift out in the street, and hand it to a beggar without ceremony. He wandered.

He had bought back the old bakery with the blue tiles at the corner of Rue des Ecouffes, and it was now run by his son Sacha. They had the kind of working relationship that Henri had enjoyed with his own father. When Sacha was 12 he had gone to a summer camp, where he fell in love with a girl, Florence, from the twentieth arrondissement. She was from a Jewish family, and her mother's grandfather had owned a shop selling religious articles on Rue des Rosiers. But the grandfather had been deported and killed, and after the war the family had settled into a more affluent part of Paris. After summer camp ended, Florence and Sacha did not see each other again, because they lived too far away for twelve-year-olds to visit each other, and their parents wouldn't let them take the *métro*. That dewy, dry-throated, forever-and-ever twelve-year-old first love was left to fade.

Twelve years passed, and Florence happened to visit Rue des Rosiers and saw a bakery called Finkelsztajn's. She started asking questions. Sacha and Florence were married three years later, in 1985. In 1986 they had a daughter. While Sacha ran the store on Rue des Ecouffes, Florence ran Henri's store. In 1992 she had triplets, two girls and a boy. A long-range planner, when the children were still infants, Florence had already spoken to a rabbi about doing two bat mitzvahs and a bar mitzvah on the same Saturday.

Henri, with all this commerce and family, had taken on a contented look as he drifted between the cash register and the deli-counter in the bakery. Down the street, Sacha was in charge of non-bakery food—several kinds of herring and different dishes with cheese and spices, and liver, all with the old Yiddish names. As in Antwerp, the Poles who came to Paris after the fall of Communism headed straight for the Jewish neighborhood looking for work. Poles worked for Henri and Jo Goldenberg and any of the Ashkenazim still in the Pletzl. Henri was amused by the irony of it, but on the other hand, after a lifetime of being told he was from Poland, he was at last getting to observe some Poles first-hand.

Finkelsztajn's favorite thing was when new customers hovered uncertainly over the platters. He explained that they could buy by the gram or in a sandwich. But before they decided, he would tell them that they must try everything. Taking little pieces of bread, he would carefully spread samples on each, handing them one by one to the customer who tasted and moaned with approval while Finkelsztajn smiled his warm, easy smile, a happy man in his trade. He had never wanted to bake bread, but feeding people and listening to them purr was a trade for Henri.

Although everything American had become fashionable in the Marais, Americans were starting to annoy him. When they spoke Yiddish they always used the familiar form. Always *"Vos makhst du"* for "How are you" and never *"Vos makht ir?"* And in any language

Henri was tired of the line, "Just looking"—because they really were just looking. American Jews who had heard there was something Jewish on Rue des Rosiers went to have a look. They examined the small shop and stared up at the mid-nineteenth-century curlicues on the ceiling, and they walked out without buying anything, but what was worse to Henri, without saying anything. If he said something to them, they replied, "Just looking." Then they walked out, crossed the street, and standing in front of Journo's, they would snap a photograph of Henri's ocher-colored storefront with the scrapes and chips from trucks that tried to go up on the sidewalk to pass parked cars on the narrow street and didn't quite make it. "The Americans come here as though this is a museum and we are not real people," Henri complained.

He drifted out of the shop, into the narrow street, and found people to chat with or things to watch. If nothing else, he could watch the oversized trucks scraping away his paint. André Journo was often running nervously between his restaurant and his art gallery, a cigar clenched in his mouth. The spry, tightly wound Mediterranean would fly past the dreamy, heavyset Central European. Their paths crossed a few dozen times every day. But they seldom had as much as a nod for each other. It was not about the difference between Ashkenazim and Sephardim. It was about real estate.

In French law, owning a commercial space and owning the walls to that space are two separate transactions. Icchok Finkelsztajn, with the money loaned to him by friends in the Pletzl, had only been able to buy the space for his bakery. Henri had later tried to buy the walls, but by then the owner would not sell because he wanted to sell the entire building. The building was run-down, and the tenants were paying 80 francs for an apartment. When the Journo family lived there, they had paid 60 francs. The owner earned barely enough to maintain the building. In 1980 he happily unloaded the building to someone interested in the real estate market. The new owner slowly drove his tenants out and restored the building, selling off the apartments at more than $2,000 a square foot.

At this point Journo had seen an opportunity to get control of the building and asked Finkelsztajn to go into business with him. Henri, by instinct, could not imagine having nervous, fast-talking André Journo as a business partner and declined. Managing on his own, Journo got the art gallery on the ground floor and the Arab

café next to it when the owner retired and went back to North
Africa. Then, in the spring of 1992, to Henri Finkelsztajn's astonishment, he discovered that Journo now owned the walls to his
bakery and wanted him out.

The wall owner can evict the space owner at any time by buying
out his space. If Journo did this to Henri, he could renovate the
space and sell a luxury apartment "in the heart of the Marais."
Because the ground-floor storefront was not well-suited for an
apartment, Finkelsztajn was able to talk Journo into taking over
only the upper space where Henri had grown up. It was now
kitchen space, and losing it meant that he would have to go back to
baking in the basement. Almost a half-century after Icchok had
sealed up the basement, declaring, "Working in a basement is slavery," Henri had to reopen it and once again move the hot ovens
down below. The bakery ceiling had to be propped up with steel
while the work overhead shook the building. And then the Journos
moved into what the Rue des Rosiers gossip mill reputed to be the
most spectacular luxury apartment in the entire Marais.

EVEN PHYSICALLY DETERIORATING from Parkinson's disease,
Chaim Rottenberg poured enormous energy into building his Orthodox community. When Daniel Altmann joined the community,
his was one of fifty families. But by the 1990s, a decade later, more
than three hundred families were directly involved, and some thousand families followed the leadership of the Rue Pavée synagogue.
On a Saturday morning, the tall, elegant, art nouveau chamber was
filled with men wrapped in their white prayer shawls, swaying and
bobbing and bowing like frenetic bearded angels, periodically rest-
ing and gossiping with friends, the Hebrew chanting sometimes
barely audible over the conversations in French and Yiddish. Occasionally, a thumping noise from the *bimah* would uselessly try to
hush them, while their children ran and wrestled in the aisles and
the women chatted and prayed high up on the balcony. The children covered their heads with major league baseball caps and ran
playfully between the men's prayer shawls and took turns to see
who could jump high enough to touch the mezuzah on the doorway. It was a large, lively, noisy community.

To a great extent, this was the work of Rottenberg's own charisma and energy. But it continued to grow after he fell sick. There
seemed to be an increasing demand for this kind of old-fashioned

Orthodox community. Many of the people in it, both Sephardic and Ashkenazic, were, like Daniel Altmann, people who had turned away from a secular life. For Altmann it had to do with a need, in modern French society, to feel a sense of belonging, of not being alone. "You have this development in French society," he said. "People want to put themselves somewhere. You are linked, or you are not linked. But also, it's like a snowball. When you have a very strong center, things start to grow."

The community had a committee of elders , and Rottenberg got the idea of putting some younger men on the committee. He had built a diverse community with many younger people, and he wanted them represented too. Altmann became one of two younger men on the committee. Then he became the vice president, then the president died. "You be the president," declared Chaim Rottenberg to Daniel Altmann. Daniel tried to protest, said that he was too young, that he had young children to worry about, that he didn't want to get embroiled in "*shtibl* politics." But no one ever could say no to Rottenberg. Altmann became president. After this, he had Rottenberg to contend with on a daily basis. The telephone would ring at the Altmann house. It was the Rav. He had asked Daniel to raise some funds for a certain project, and a week had gone by and he had not done it. "You didn't do it because you have money and you think you don't have to do things because you are rich? You think it is some small thing? Not important! Here, I will put up fifty francs, and I want you to put up fifty francs! I don't understand! You are ruining this whole thing!"

Altmann spent years being shouted at by Rottenberg. But he also knew him as a compassionate man. He called him a dinosaur, "the last of the man alone who can hold together a whole community." And while Daniel pursued his religious life, his chemical trading business prospered. Like his grandfather, he found good opportunities in barter arrangements with a disintegrating Russia.

In 1990, Rottenberg's wife Rifka had a hip replacement operation and was hospitalized for two months. When she was released, Rottenberg's severe face smiled. "You're back," he said, and suggested they take a vacation together to Switzerland. He died while they were away, and their son Mordechai took over the community. "We went on vacation. Then he died," said Rifka with a laugh she had that seemed almost like crying. "That's life. But I found fifty years, because I was dead once already."

PARIS BECAME the fourth-largest Jewish community in the world and the most important in Europe. Although there were an increasing number of Daniel Altmanns, French Jews still tended to assimilate. About a third of Paris Jews considered themselves to be "religious," although many nonreligious Jews had strong Jewish identities. Florence Finkelsztajn said of her education plans for her four children, "I want them to learn the tradition, not the religion." But a third of French Jews were marrying non-Jews, although French society continued to point out the futility of assimilation. Mitterrand's first government contained a number of very assimilated Jews, including Laruent Fabius, who had a Catholic education and took communion. But when the government was announced, the French talked of the "Jewish government," and when Fabius later became prime minister, he was "that Jewish prime minister."

In 1987, René Sirat, the first modern sephardic Grand Rabbi of France, resigned. His successor was also from North Africa, from Tunisia. Sephardim or Ashkenazim was no longer an issue that interested many, although differences persisted. North Africans missed their countries. They spoke Arabic and listened to the free-spirited, whooping Arab music. But the Ashkenazim—the few who could remember—had no nostalgia for Poles or Poland. And some traditions remained different, such as the music of prayer chanting. The Sephardim made the Passover dish *charoset* with dates, while the Ashkenazim always made it with apples, and the Sephardim ate olives and didn't eat horseradish or chicken soup with *knadlech*, matzoh balls. And even in Paris Algerians still grilled lamb the night before Passover because they had each killed a lamb before Passover when they lived in Algeria and owned lambs. Sirat would confess to his family of his one great failing in rabbinical school: When he had studied *kashrut*, each student was required to slaughter a lamb in the ritual way, and he couldn't do it. He could not bring himself to kill the lamb.

But the Ashkenazim were no longer concerned about the Sephardim taking over; they respected the Sephardic rabbis. On the other hand, some Sephardim, despite their numerical superiority, were concerned about the new Orthodox Ashkenazim taking over. Many Sephardim who had strayed from religion in France were brought back by Rottenberg or the Lubavitchers. This was not in itself upsetting. But when they grew *peots*, put on broad black hats and long black coats, dressing like they were from a shtetl in

Poland, this was disturbing because it had nothing to do with North African Jewish tradition. Some Sephardim wondered why an Algerian would want to imitate the culture of poverty and oppression from Central Europe.

Sirat had resigned as Grand Rabbi because he wanted to return to his true avocation, teaching, and participate in the extensive Jewish educational structure that he had done much to establish. With his soft, compassionate almond-shaped eyes, his black frizzled beard, moving his yarmulke around his head as he searched for words, he looked like a professor. He had a clear message for modern Jews about God's covenant, the responsibility of "the chosen people." He warned Jews against self-imposed ghettos: "I think that we must also be a presence in the world, especially in the places where men are suffering or humanity is attacked. Every time that people suffer somewhere in the world, the Jews suffer with them, and they must not remain indifferent to the pain and suffering in the world—not in Yugoslavia, not in the former Soviet Union. We do not have the magic to solve all the world's problems, but we must not be indifferent. If we are indifferent to the suffering of other people, how can we ask others to be sensitive to our suffering? Because we must never forget that all people suffer, not only Jews."

EMMANUEL AND FANIA EWENCZYK were having coffee on a rococo table in their spacious, ornate sixteenth-arrondissement apartment. There was a time when they could not have dared hope that life would turn out this well. One of their teenage grandsons, a son of Lazare and Suzy, was there. The question came up, if Fania had ever regretted her decision in 1945 not to move to Israel. Emmanuel smiled at the question, but his smile was blunted by Fania's response. "Yes and no," she said.

The air between them in their gracious living room somehow seemed to stiffen.

"Yes and no." She insisted on making clear that the look Emmanuel was giving her would have no effect on what she had to say. "No, because I wouldn't have been married and all, but I do regret not having lived in Israel."

Emmanuel looked away. Their grandson was watching from a distant couch with bemused fascination.

"If he would agree right now," she continued, "I would move to Israel."

"And leave all our children here?" Emmanuel challenged.

"Ah, you see, there it is."

"You wouldn't want that."

"No?"

He shook his head.

"I am just more steadfast than you."

"One of my brothers once almost went to Israel . . . "

And the conversation safely passed on to the story of how Sam had left Poland.

32

In Amsterdam

MEIJER'S KOSHER BUTCHER AND SANDWICH SHOP WAS too new and uncluttered to have any kind of a look other than clean. It was in the Rivierenbuurt, one of those twentieth-century parts of Amsterdam where everything was built to show off a little extra space because it had been settled by people from the center in search of more room. Sal Meijer and his son complained of a declining business, but they were busy most of the time. It was a pleasant place to be—a place to meet other Jews, which was not that easy to do in Amsterdam anymore. "I come for the society, not the food," Victor Waterman, now in his nineties, would say to annoy Sal. In 1975 he had retired from the kosher chicken business in New Jersey and moved back to Amsterdam with this advice: "When you are from Europe, you have to go to America when you are young, make a lot of money, and then get out. *Don't die in America!*"

For years, when Waterman ran into people whom he had not seen since he left, he had this little joke he would try. They would say, "Where have you been?"

"In New Jersey," he would say, hoping they took the bait.

"What were you doing in New Jersey?"

He would lower his voice, turn his face sinister, and say, "I was a killer."

"A killer!"

Quickly he would shoot an index finger straight up and lighten his tone, "But kosher."

One of Waterman's sons had also moved back to Amsterdam and had a prosperous art dealership. The two were inseparable. But in 1991 the son died of a heart attack and Waterman quarreled with his grandchildren and was alone. He settled in the Rivierenbuurt and was a regular, a kind of local character in the sandwich shop part of Sal Meijer's. He never talked about his son, just as he had avoided the distant memories of his murdered family.

Sal Meijer was also a well-loved local character. People didn't know that in the same long, narrow, bay-windowed apartment he had found after the war, his nights were spent screaming. In quiet Holland, where people control themselves and don't carry on, where the story of Anne Frank was endlessly promoted instead of discussing the Dutch record under occupation, where Resistance heros increased their ranks in the popular mythology every decade, but collaborationists and deportees were not to be mentioned, more and more survivors and children of survivors were beginning to scream.

The Rivierenbuurt had been settled in the 1920s. The neighborhood sprawled with low buildings of handsome wooden art deco details and wide streets that told Amsterdamers that here there would be space to waste. The old Jodenbreestraat neighborhood never became Jewish again. There were not enough Jews. The synagogues of the neighborhood, except the Esnoga, remained in ruins. To the Jewish Community, they were ugly reminders of missing Jews. The Community gladly would have torn them down, but the city regarded them as historical landmarks and to save them bought them from the Community. The survivor generation was not interested in synagogues. They wanted to preserve the Hollandse Schouwburg, the theater that had been used to collect deportees. The Jewish Community fought furiously to prevent its being turned back into a theater. This was the past they wanted preserved.

The gutted old ghetto was torn down and replaced with tall new buildings on widened streets. Sal Meijer in 1964 had moved to Nieuwmarkt, an old commercial area near the Central Station. Enough Jews still lived in the center to support a kosher butcher, but in the 1960s a street life dominated by young people and drugs gradually drove Sal and most of his customers away. Ten years younger than Waterman, Sal no longer felt up to a full work schedule at the butcher shop, so his son and daughter-in-law ran the shop, making the third consecutive generation of kosher butchers. He still had the brass menorah on the wall that he had hidden during the war, and books and photos that he studied intensely. The screaming usually began at night, but he would be like that sometimes even during the day. Suddenly, in his eighties, he could no longer stay silent about the Holocaust and what had happened to his family. He also became obsessed with news, particularly focusing on wars. "God is busy!" he would angrily declare when the death toll from some distant conflict was reported on the television.

In recent years the Netherlands has seen a dramatic increase in World War II survivors of all kinds seeking psychiatric help. The 1940–1945 Foundation had been created in 1944 by Resistance members to help their people and Jewish survivors after the war. It was thought that the organization would disband sometime in the 1950s. But in the 1990s thousands still turned to it for help— Resistance veterans and camp survivors who were still trying to live secret lives, keeping their phone numbers unlisted, even trying to hoard unlicensed firearms.

Many Jewish survivors, recalling the compulsively efficient Dutch lists that had marked them for deportation, still shied away from official records, refusing to answer census questionnaires, asking Jewish organizations to use unmarked envelopes when sending them mail. Many Jews refused to state their religion when they checked into a hospital. Psychiatrists found many patients with problems from their childhood in hiding, including some who had been sexually abused by their protectors. Jitschak Storosum, a psychiatrist with a Jewish agency, said that he often had patients who were sexually abused while in hiding as children. Jewish social services reported that about three thousand people each year—10 percent of the Jewish population of the Netherlands—sought help from them. Most of those cases were war-related.

It is tempting to see this as a Dutch phenomenon, a product of a repressed society that, unlike France, never exploded the myth of a valiant Resistance. The emphasis in Holland was always on how the Anne Frank family had been hidden from the Nazis; the fact that they were also betrayed by Dutch collaborators—possibly for 7.5 guilders—was overlooked. No one wanted to hear the stories of deportees, and survivors kept their stories to themselves. The facts that Holland had its own neo-Nazi movement and that a racist, far-right political party had won legislative seats were ignored as aberrations without precedent. When these subjects were brought up, the usual response was, "It is shocking. This is very un-Dutch. We have always been a tolerant people." *Tolerant*, which is the same word in the Dutch language, was an obsessively overworked term. The Dutch frequently spoke of their tolerance of minorities, as though Jews, blacks, and Asians were an unpleasant burden that they were able to bear because they, the Dutch, were a strong and stoic people.

But there was another factor. The Dutch health system encouraged people to seek psychiatric help. Someone who could show psychological problems as a result of wartime experiences was entitled to a special pension. Unfortunately, none of this had been available in the years immediately following the war, when these people could have been most helped by it. The mental health profession was strongly influenced in the 1970s and 1980s by the work done in America on traumatized Vietnam war veterans.

The noticeable increase in war-related traumas was frequently attributed to retirement. People who had kept busy all their lives were suddenly faced with inescapable free time. "They hold it down," explained Jitschak Storosum, "but very suddenly something very specific, often very small, sets them off, and they can no longer cope. Sometimes it is just a normal illness, or a picture of Auschwitz on television. My mother could never look at a train without getting a flashback. Many don't sleep because they want to avoid the dreams they have. When they have a bad dream, it can take them weeks to recover."

Seeing what had happened to others, some survivors, like Marian Turski in Warsaw, avoided retirement. Joseph de Groot was a tailor, and even in his late seventies he kept working out of his house. He smiled and laughed easily, he loved to gossip with his clients, and he pointed with pride to his well-fed pot belly. He also pointed with pride to the numbers tattooed on his forearm. An elderly widower with no children, he lived in his large-windowed, spacious home. A ring at the door, and he would leap to his feet, then painfully remember that his back hurt. Down the hall was the fitting room, and a helper worked in the basement. After one customer left, de Groot studied him through the window. "Ah, he is a millionaire. I'm going to make him pay. If you are poor, you pay very little If you are rich, I get you. That's how this operation works," he said, chuckling.

He seemed a happy man. His face of deep-set eyes and strong

nose bore a look of contentment, and he had bad dreams only about once every five months. "I have good work. When I want. I don't want. I have worked enough in my life. In the concentration camps. I am seventy-eight. On the weekends I have a lady friend, I have many people over, we drink coffee. I have a good life. I live well. I am in good health. I am content. But I do not look at concentration camp films. When there is a film about a concentration camp on television, I never watch it. I do not want to look back too much at the concentration camps. And that is good for me. I will talk about it a little bit. But I have friends who talk about the concentration camp every day. I say I don't want to think about the concentration camp every day. That is good. I live well."

De Groot only recently started talking about his camp experiences. The story would come out in disjointed segments. He would often say that tailoring had saved his life at Auschwitz. But sometimes he would talk of how he did manual labor for I.G. Farben, the chemical manufacturer. Sometimes he would explain that tailoring hadn't really been his work there, but that he got food and money by making clothes for prisoners who attempted to escape. He also described how the prisoners would be forced to stand for hours in the cold, looking at the people in his clothes that the guards had hanged for trying to escape. Then his voice would break, and he would change the subject.

During those executions a band would be forced to play. When visitors go to Auschwitz, they can see a photograph of the band by the front gate. De Groot's friend Lex Van Weren played trumpet in that band. He survived and followed a trumpet career in Holland until he was too old to play. Then he also had to face retirement. A pension was available—not for camp survivors, but for Resistance veterans, and Van Weren had been in the Resistance. He had been originally arrested as a Resistance operative, not as a Jew. When he applied for his Resistance pension, he was required to see a psychiatrist, who told him that his habit of talking openly about his experiences was healthy. That was what he decided to do with his retirement, write books and articles and give talks on his experiences as "the trumpet player of Auschwitz."

"I was always able to speak out about my memories," Van Weren said. "People like Joopie de Groot, they have their memories and they can speak out with some acquaintances. But I have had the chance to speak out to people all over Holland. To millions, and that's good for a person. I am lucky that every thought inside has come out. I have had the opportunity to speak about it. That is the pity for all the hundreds and hundreds who are living now. They have had no chance to speak about it."

He seemed very pleased with his life, in his flat modern house in the flat modern Buitenveldert in the expanding south, where many affluent Jews settled. He sat on his patio looking across his small lawn at the rosebushes that edged the canal. "This is a very expensive neighborhood. My neighbors are rich. I'm just a musician. It was hard for me to get the money. But every time I look out at my roses, I feel happy."

Behind his blustery optimism was a voice of isolation like that often heard from camp survivors. "I don't trust people. I don't want to need anyone, but that is very difficult to achieve. You do need people. But I am ninety percent there. I don't believe in friends."

Mauritz Auerhaan, who never married, retired to a Jewish home for the elderly and made a similar observation, "To make friends is very difficult. To make a real friend, I couldn't find one. Everybody looks after his own life and to make money without caring."

Some remained fixated on their memories, like the woman who had a larger-than-life-size photo of her friend who had been with her in Auschwitz and had not survived. The photo was on the inside of the kitchen cabinet door, staring mournfully at her every time she opened the cabinet.

To de Groot, not thinking about the Holocaust was a prerequisite of living well. "I want to live. When you think about the concentration camp, you don't live. If I start thinking about my friends in the concentration camps, how they died—the more you see of the concentration camp on the television, the more it is in your dreams. I watch football. That is my hobby."

Somewhere in the 1980s it started to get increasingly difficult for those who wanted to avoid reminders. Both television and publishing rained Holland with information about World War II and the Holocaust. Most of it was general. Sometimes it dealt with the Dutch past. Survivors found Auschwitz images coming into their peripheral vision regularly. Some survivors feared turning on the television, and random channel flipping was not to be risked.

THE GHOSTLY PRESENCE of World War II was part of Dutch life. Political careers were still being ruined by revelations of dubious wartime activities. The underground Resistance tabloids, notably

Het Parool, had become the press establishment. In crowded, cosmopolitan Amsterdam, a city of northern Renaissance architecture along a maze of interconnecting canals, tourists could ask directions in any Western language but German. Most Amsterdamers were multilingual, but they always said that German, which has the same roots as Dutch, was too difficult. Amsterdamers deliberately gave German tourists wrong directions. Some would respond to a question from a lost German, "First give me back my bicycle," as though the mass deportation of bicycles to Germany was the most remembered atrocity.

Even de Groot's hobby, soccer, was a reminder of the war. When the Netherlands' soccer team played Germany, signs saying "Give me back my bicycle" were held up in the Dutch crowd. De Groot was a fan of the Ajax team, as many Jews had been before the war. In those days, when Holland still had a large Jewish population, a number of Jewish soccer stars played for Ajax. De Groot said, "I have three Jewish places: *shul,* the Jewish cemetery, and Ajax." In modern times Ajax has Surinamers but not Jews on the team. But that does not stop people from referring to it as the *Jodeclub,* the Jewish team. Fans of opposing teams show up at Ajax games with swastikas and have at times chanted, *"Jodeclub, sieg heil,* gas them!" The Jewish community is assured that these are just tasteless, overzealous soccer fans. Soccer fans are notoriously excessive. The police have interrogated some of these fans who shout "Gas them" and reported that they appear to know nothing about World War II. Do they not watch television?

Lody van de Kamp grew up in a family that talked about the war. He learned about his father in Auschwitz, where his first family had been killed, and about his mother's life in hiding. In 1965, Lody went to school in England, and when he returned as a rabbi, to his surprise he was spending much of his time helping people with war-related problems. "When I came back in 1981 from England, I did not realize that in Holland there is such a thing as a war syndrome. Now I know differently. Some become depressed, some show a spirit of fighting and survival. Some people show an attitude toward children of overcaring and overprotection. There are things of guilt. Very often a wife dies, a husband dies, and then they have to face not only the tragedy of what has just happened but the tragedy of years back."

Every year that Lody was back, he found that people talked about the war more and more. But not all their problems were psychological. Scores still remained to be settled. In 1990, Van de Kamp organized a committee to try to get back property that had been stolen from deported Jews and that was still in the hands of Dutch Nazis or their children. The most bizarre case was in a small town named Winschoten, where there had been a synagogue before the war and a committee was formed to raise money to restore it. One of three surviving members of the prewar Winschoten Jewish community lived in Amsterdam, and while visiting his hometown to raise money for the restoration, he stumbled across something called the Siemens Foundation.

Willem Siemens was not a name that he would forget. Siemens had been a Dutch policeman in Winschoten who deported Jews to the death camps and then stole their property. He had personally placed 440 Jews on trains for Westerbork. Only nine survived, but those survivors told how he threatened them, forced them to give him their money, or sometimes took it in exchange for a promise to help them. In 1943, Siemens volunteered for the Waffen SS and fought on the Eastern Front. When he returned in 1945, he was arrested and served eight years in prison. Upon his release he returned to the same little town and lived in almost total seclusion. When he died in 1985, he left a large amount of money for an animal shelter that would bear his name. He loved animals. But when people learned that an animal shelter would be subsidized by the Siemens Foundation, since everyone in the area suspected how Siemens had gotten so much money, there was general opposition. The notary who was in charge of the Siemens money came up with another idea. Siemens's money could be used to quietly subsidize the cremation of pets. There was a nearby animal crematorium, and it was arranged that when a pet owner called to arrange the cremation of his dog, he would simply be told, "Oh, you get a fifty percent discount."

THE BIEDERMANNS raised their two sons with a Jewish education. Sieg took them to the synagogue until they were bar mitzvahed, and then told them that they had to decide if they wanted to continue going or not. But after the second bar mitzvah, he himself never went again. His wife, Evelyne, would never talk about her camp experiences and had her tattooed numbers surgically removed. When Sieg's sons asked about the numbers on his arm, Sieg would always say he wrote his phone number there so he wouldn't forget it. On vacation at the beach the boys would notice that their father's back was covered with perfectly round scars, each the size of a very large coin. "What's that?" they would always ask. But he wouldn't answer. Then one day, in an unemotional voice, he told them. There had been something missing, and the SS had decided to take three prisoners and hang them upside down by their feet. After they hung for about four hours, the SS stuck them repeatedly with rifle bayonets. They would stick the bayonet in and twist it around.

One of the sons, Barry, became a very aggressive child. He was a sturdy little boy, and he believed that the best response to any comment about Jews was a fist in the mouth. For several years Sieg was regularly paying for the repair of other children's teeth. On Barry's seventh birthday, Sieg and Evelyne gave him a cowboy outfit. He wore it to school, and the teacher pointed at the sheriff's badge and said, "There was a time when your parents had to wear those stars." Having no idea what this could mean, he asked his parents and they explained about the stars. Barry stopped hitting people and grew up to be an active man in community affairs, but one thing never changed—he always hated that schoolteacher.

Sieg and Evelyne's goal was to build a normal life for their family, and they succeeded, even though neither of them ever regained their health. Barry could not remember a year of his childhood when at least one of his parents did not spend time in the hospital. When Sieg was 65, under pressure from his family, he reluctantly retired. The Biedermanns bought a house in Tel Aviv and moved back and forth trying to relax, enjoy life, and not think about the past. Two years later, Sieg died. Evelyne, who was eleven years younger, also died in her mid-sixties.

Once his mother died, Barry felt completely alone. He did not know how to deal with the loss of both his parents. He had never lost anyone. All his other relatives had been killed before he was born. It had always been just the four of them. His brother moved to New York, but Barry stayed in Amsterdam and married an Aruban Jew whose family had no Holocaust experiences. They had two children, whom they named after Barry's parents.

Barry's wife came from a religious family and they took up a traditional Jewish life. He began to wear a yarmulke and a beard. They were one of an estimated three hundred kosher households in the Netherlands. Barry believed it was important to have a religious background. "If you have to get knowledge starting from the age of eighteen, you will never be at the top. It is a free choice in a way, but on the other hand it is not free choice because what you learn in your very first years, you can never make up later. You will never *dovin* in a natural way."

Dovining—the bowing, bobbing, dipping, and other ecstatic moves of traditional Jewish prayer—was something he grew up seeing, but because he was not encouraged to participate, he was not sure that he completely fit in during prayer. He was not sure if he dovined in a natural way. "I can't *shuvel* in a natural way. You know, I can't be in a *kdans*. I can pretend to. But my three-year-old boy—it's not forced. He's just got it!"

If Barry Biedermann had one friend who he was certain would never dovin in a natural way, it was Theo Meijer. A small, fit-looking man with close-cropped hair and beard who almost always wore his rhinestone star of David neck chain, Theo, in his own way, was also a war victim. His mother was Catholic, and his father, as he suddenly discovered at age 14, had been Jewish. The father had survived in hiding. After the war he decided he was no longer Jewish and never discussed it again. Theo did not know exactly what had happened to his father during the war. He was not even sure if there were surviving relatives, except for a grandmother whom he met briefly on only two occasions. Living on a shady canal near the Nieuwmarkt, Theo was raised Catholic like his mother. Then one day a neighbor told him, in a not unpleasant way, that he was a Jew. To everyone but Theo, this was not surprising, since *Meijer* is often a Jewish name and the family lived in a somewhat Jewish neighborhood. It had been very Jewish before the war, and Theo could remember as a child how survivors would show up from time to time and claim a house and try to force the people there out, almost always leading to an angry legal battle. Someone came back from Russia and demanded the house next to theirs. Theo liked to joke with Sal Meijer, the butcher, about being a distant relative. Sal, whose shop was then nearby in the Nieuwmarkt, joked that Theo was from the wealthy side of the Meijer family, although no doubt Sal had more money than Theo's father, who was a ship rigger in the nearby docks.

Theo had grown up around Jews, and then he discovered that he was one. The only problem with this new idea that so struck Theo was that it was really not true. He wasn't a Jew—not by Jewish law, since his mother was not Jewish, and not by culture, since he knew nothing about Judaism. He was a generally well-adjusted man. But he became the reverse of his father, who had worked so hard at being a non-Jew—Theo tried hard to be a Jew, even though no one in the Jewish community thought of him as one. He tried to learn, but the Orthodox would not have him. The liberals were more accepting, but he didn't like liberal Judaism. It lacked that exotic other-world kind of feel. "It's all or nothing," Theo would say.

Theo went his own way, insisting that he "felt Jewish" regardless of what anyone said. "People say I am not Jewish, but I think I am." On Jewish holidays he stubbornly went to the Esnoga. His father did not discuss Jewish issues except to object to his son's preference for German cars. Theo loved expensive cars and drove around in a Mercedes, always interrupting conversations to point out cars he admired. He would stop in midsentence and say, "Oh, nice Bentley." When his father asked how he could drive a German car, Theo would point at the three-pronged hood insignia on his Mercedes and say, "That's the star the Germans have made *my* generation wear," and laugh.

Theo became a social worker of tremendous energy and talent, a man with an instinct for working with people and a genuine sense of dedication. In 1970 he started working at Wallenberg, a homeless shelter in his old neighborhood. He roamed the streets looking for people in trouble to take to the shelter, and he especially sought Jews.

He kept a pile of yarmulkes and Hebrew books in a corner of his office and tried to teach people of Jewish background and offer them Hanukkah and other Jewish holidays. If they died, he would say kaddish for them.

"Look at this," he said, springing from behind his cluttered desk in his cramped Wallenberg office. "Hanukkah—I can do this part," and he picked up a prayer book, opened it, and began reciting Hebrew and dovining, bending and nodding and swaying. It was exactly what his friend Barry Biedermann called "not dovining in a natural way." Still, it was impressive that he could read Hebrew that well. He moved his finger along the page and occasionally stumbled over a word, but it was generally good reading.

"Naw," he said with a big smile. "I memorized that passage from transliterated Dutch. I can't read Hebrew."

"Theo," said Barry, "is a perfect example of why, if you have a mixed marriage, you should make clear to the children that they are not Jewish. It's just confusion."

WALLENBERG WAS LOCATED near the tight ancient waterways on the east side of Amsterdam's center city—a picturesque area so cramped that the stairways in houses had to be as steep as in a ship cabin.

The Dutch don't like the word *homeless* or the word *shelter*. Probably none of the people living on the streets of Amsterdam lacked an alternative, because the government guaranteed all citizens an income and, if necessary, a home. The Wallenberg shelter was a government program consisting of two houses and a series of additional apartments, which in total gave private rooms to six hundred people who did not fit into society. There were no dangerous barracks with rows of beds. Seasoned drifters preferred Wallenberg because of the private rooms, whereas in the other Amsterdam homes you might be assigned a roommate. The state subsidized the home by charging residents $420 monthly from the social pensions paid them by the state. This still left them with spending money and enough extra for the annual May vacation at off-season rates in Palma de Mallorca, Spain, a package-tour spot popular with the Dutch.

On his rounds Theo found Aaron, sleeping in the Central Station. It took several visits to gain his confidence, but Aaron eventually moved to Wallenberg and lived there for years. A small man with pronounced Semitic features, he was nervous and given to unprovoked fits of laughter, and like many of the residents, he had strong emotional ties to Theo. According to Theo, "He is a very nice man, but he will steal anything."

Aaron was a kleptomaniac. His elderly mother said he started stealing and acting oddly at age 12. When Aaron was one year old, she was deported to a concentration camp and saved her son by throwing him off the train. One thing that life in Wallenberg had in common with "normal" life in the rest of Amsterdam was that the society was still haunted by World War II.

"There are many people here who still have problems with the war," said Theo Meijer. "I have one who is Jewish but denies it. If you say, 'You are Jewish,' he says no. His problem is that he thinks the troubles might come back and that he won't be recognized." This man lived a secret life, rarely talking to anyone except when the horror of his dreams awakened him and Theo spent the night comforting him. In those long late-night sessions he told Theo that he had been in the camps, but he never explained the long thick scars that covered his body.

Another Wallenberg resident could not find his way in society because he bore the psychological burden that his father was a well-known Dutch Nazi. And there were others who themselves had been Nazis or collaborators. In Holland, once you are labeled as having been "wrong in the war," you are an outcast. Of the several Nazis he had looked after, Meijer could recall only one who expressed remorse. Most of them were simply unhappy with their sense of isolation. "But I take care of them, too," said Meijer. "It's my job."

Barry Biedermann and Lody van de Kamp helped Theo celebrate holidays. For Hanukkah in 1991 the three were having a dinner in Theo's office with four Wallenberg Jews wearing the yarmulkes that Theo distributed. Van de Kamp blessed the wine, said another blessing, lit the menorah, and while they were sipping the wine, a pleasant man with a childlike openness named Bobby de Vries started telling Van de Kamp that he couldn't get circumcised because he had been born during the war. The troubled people of Wallenberg tend to have these disjointed conversations, stringing together nonsequiturs while normal people smile and nod politely, which was what Van de Kamp did. The conversation moved on, but then Bobby repeated his statement about being circumcised and added, "I was born during the war. My twin was sick, so we both had to be in an incubator."

The conversation moved on again, but Bobby persisted, asking the rabbi, "Do you think you could do it?" Van de Kamp realized that Bobby meant what he was saying. The rabbi frequently got requests for circumcisions from people who had been born during the war. He explained to Bobby how it was done in a hospital in the presence of a surgeon. "It would round things off," Bobby said, and then became embarrassed at the inadvertent pun.

De Vries was circumcised at an Amsterdam hospital by a surgeon with a local anesthetic, supervised by Van de Kamp and with the good-natured but slightly nutty crowd from Wallenberg enthusiastically attending the ceremony. These were De Vries's friends, and Wallenberg was their home. In fact, Bobby called Wallenberg the only real home he had ever had. When his parents were deported to the camps, they had managed to find hiding places for their sons. Suddenly the small child Bobby had been underground and alone. Only his father survived, and the children seemed an unwelcome reminder to him. Both Bobby and his twin brother had spent most of their lives in a kind of homeless limbo, never marrying, never holding down jobs for long. Asked why he and his brother were that way, he said, "I think it was from the war. We never saw my mother. Three years in hiding." His brother died in a fluke biking accident, and Bobby lived alone in a sunny, one-room Wallenberg apartment with a view of a canal. His only early childhood memory was of living in a basement. If he thought hard about it, he could remember this one thing: "'Playing outside. Happiness outside from other children. But that's all I can remember."

THE ESNOGA remained Amsterdam's most famous synagogue, but on the five hundredth anniversary of the Spanish expulsion, the Sephardic community was down to only five hundred Jews, and the younger ones were rapidly intermarrying with Ashkenazim. None of Leo Palache's three children married a Sephardi. But Palache and others worked hard to preserve their traditions. Sephardim still wore top hats in the Esnoga, but the front row was no longer their proud and exclusive reserve. They were now happy to have any Jew who would learn and follow their rites. There were Iraqis, Turks, Surinamers from the Sephardic community in Paramaribo, even a Russian Jew from an atheist background who learned of Judaism after emigrating to Amsterdam. Some of the Moroccan families who went to Israel instead of France and sent back unfavorable reports later emigrated to Amsterdam and were active in the Esnoga. Originally, the old-line Sephardim were very upset about this influx, fearing that North African rituals would overtake their traditions, as has happened to the Salonikans in Paris. But in time they learned that if they were conscientious enough, their own tradition would prevail. If someone made an error while chanting in a service, others would immediately correct him. Palache searched his memory for tunes and chants from his childhood to reintroduce to the service. Everything had to be conserved.

A Turkish Jew who grew up in Amsterdam was training thirteen boys to take over as the next generation. One of these young men, wearing his top hat, was showing Israeli visitors around the synagogue. He mentioned that he had learned some of the rites from Israelis. "See," said one of the Israelis, "the only future for Judaism is Israel." The comment seemed to lie there for an instant like an hors d'oeuvre that had just dropped onto someone's shoe. Then the young man said, "But I was born in Israel." The Israelis did not want to discuss this phenomenon of people leaving Israel to return to Europe.

Amsterdam, like Antwerp and Paris, had an ever-increasing Israeli population. Like Moishe Waks and Ron Zuriel, these were people who found that material life was better in Europe than in Israel. But what was more embarrassing to Israelis, some of these new emigrants were not even European-born. They were Israelis or North Africans who had chosen to forget the Zionist dream and live in Europe, where they could earn a good living. In Amsterdam they often opened little carry-out restaurants featuring falafel and other Middle Eastern specialties. As in other European cities, most of the Israelis in Amsterdam were neither religious nor involved with the Jewish Community.

Leo Palache worked for Israel for forty years as the Dutch director of the United Israel Appeal. He noted, not with unhappiness, that Holland had one of the highest percentages of Jews who emigrated to Israel. He called the ones who had left "the best of us." But in all those years he never was tempted to make the move himself. "It's very interesting. I worked forty years for Israel. I have visited Israel privately and in my job many many times. I have traveled up and down. I have a lot of friends. Israelis are my life. But looking at my background and my roots, my social contacts and my friends are in Holland and the language and the climate and the food, and the total picture. Living there is a different story, I think, if you are very young."

ISAAC LIPSCHITS'S brother Alex, for whom Isaac had taken so many risks to get to Israel, stayed there, changed his name to David, became a civil servant living near Haifa, and had three children and grandchildren in Israel. But every now and then, Isaac still had a recurring nightmare that he was in Israel and something had happened to his brother. Most of Isaac's friends from the orphanage did not stay in Israel and ended up living in many different countries. They remained a family to each other and continued to visit each other regularly.

Isaac became a noted Jewish historian, married, and raised two children in Groningen. The synagogue there had been converted into a dry cleaner after the war, then an Episcopal church. In the 1970s it was restored as a synagogue, only to lack enough Jews to fill it. So it was rented out for lectures and exhibitions.

Isaac did not give his children a religious upbringing, but he did give them a Jewish identity. And he seemed almost driven to assert that he was no longer in hiding: "I am known as a Jew throughout the Netherlands. I'm on TV as a Jew. I'm writing in the newspaper as a Jew. I'm always writing on Jewish problems. I'm a Jew."

Isaac was a successful and well-adjusted man. The great irony of his life was that if his world had not been torn up by a Holocaust, he would have spent his life selling bananas in the Rotterdam market. When he turned 50, he completely broke down and sought psychiatric help. "You start looking back. I have reached things my parents couldn't dream of. My father was a poor man working in the market. My brothers worked in the market. All my uncles, as far as I know, worked in the market. Without a war I would have, too. Without any doubt. I worked so hard that I became a professor. I studied so hard. I was from such poor surroundings that I would never have gone to a secondary school. But I worked so hard, when I came home at quarter past five and I asked my wife when we would have dinner and she would say ten minutes, I would go to my study and work for ten minutes. Later, with the help of a psychiatrist, I found out that I didn't want to give myself the leisure to think. To sit and think, to sit and listen to music. I was frightened. If you are fifty, you can't stand it anymore. You have to sit down and think over what you have done in your life. And then the war comes. The memories. The problems."

THE PAIN did not vanish. It passed to another generation. Barry Biedermann contemplated how he had grown up with no surviving relatives but his parents, and how hard it had been for him when they died. And he often reflected on the fact that it would be much the same for his children. Because the camps had ruined his parents' health and they had died young, the Holocaust that deprived him of grandparents had also deprived his two children of them. They, too, had no extended family and had a sense of being raised in isolation, with the sometimes-spoken subject always looming somewhere. "I wonder when it ends?" he asked.

Most survivors said they saw little future for Jews except in Israel. But whatever they said, they were still Dutch, and Holland was their home, and many of them never left. In the 1970s their children started taking over the Community. To this new generation there was more than the Holocaust to Dutch history. They wanted to preserve the Jodenbreestraat synagogues in Amsterdam and turned the four that had been saved by the government into an elaborate museum of Dutch Jewish history.

The old generation with its terrible memories was dying off. Mauritz Auerhaan retired from business and was alone. He moved into the Jewish home for the elderly in the south. As Amsterdam moved farther south, the architecture became more stripped down and less ornate. Far in the south it was just blocks of apartments and shopping centers. Beth Shalom, where Auerhaan lived, seemed to be the latest in homes-for-the-elderly, the optimal artificial environment that maintained the perfect temperature and healthiest air for elderly people—the human parallel to Dutch computerized greenhouses with their six-foot-tall hydroponic tomato vines. At Beth Shalom a central patio with comfortable chairs had a glass roof that assured that it was at once light, airy, and warm. In the hallways the elderly sat in silence. Auerhaan's room was not unpleasant, with its balcony and little kitchenette, but neither was it quite up to what Bobby de Vries had in Wallenberg.

Auerhaan looked around his small tidy room. "If you are young, you are young, and you see all from your young eyes, and you don't believe that one day you will live here. No. You can't believe it." He held out his arm. "Do you see the number? That is the only proof that I have been there. Sometimes I think it was a bad dream. I can't believe it."

AMONG YOUNGER DUTCH JEWS, as in Paris, there was a trend toward more Orthodox practices. This, too, had its roots in the Holocaust—the conviction that assimilation did not work. One Orthodox rabbi said, "In my own family, directly after the war I had an uncle who said the only solution was to assimilate. But this was not true. Even Jews who were baptized—they found them."

Jewish culture remained ingrained in Dutch life, especially in Amsterdam, where Yiddish words belong to the popular slang in much the same way as they do in New York. *Mazzel* is luck, a crowd or gang is a *miesjpoge*, they speak of *shlmeils*. Amsterdam ended up with ten working synagogues and even four *shtibls*. Most of them had to struggle for a minyan, because so many of the Jews had moved to the flatland in the south and were no longer within walking distance for the Sabbath. Even the

Esnoga began experimenting with offering a service in the south once a month.

The five-hundred-year history of Dutch Jewry was not over. In the 1990s only thirty thousand Jews remained in all of Holland — just slightly more than the population immediately after the survivors returned in the late 1940s. Survivors wanted the past to be remembered by others, but they did not want to look back on it themselves. Leo Palache said about watching television, "If I know there is something about the war, I switch off because I don't want to test myself. Where is the limit of what I can stand? I don't want to test myself. And I say if I want to know about the war, the concentration camps, I just close my eyes."

33

In Berlin
and the
New Bananerepublik

IN NOVEMBER 1989, WHEN THE WALL OPENED UP FOLLOW-
ing a surprise announcement, Sophie Marum, the daughter of
a rabbi and a longtime Communist party member in the East, was
asked if she wanted to join the thousands who were rushing across
to the West for a four-decade-delayed shopping spree. "I didn't go
there. I am not interested in eating something special. I don't think
the things here were so bad. I like apples. I don't know why I must
eat bananas."

For a long time the Westerners had been talking about how the
poor East Germans had no bananas. Their Germany was such a
failure that it could not even offer its population bananas. Such
was the religion of consumerism that West Germany had embraced. A society that offered bananas was better than a society that
didn't. When the Wall opened, a curious rumor circulated that
parts of West Berlin had become strewn with banana peels. West
Germans, Helmut Kohl, and probably most of the Western alliance
wanted this moment to be their dramatic triumph, with the down-
trodden East Germans, in hysterical joy, bursting into the West,
basking in freedom. The cameras were there to record it.

There were people who seriously believed the *Ossis* would be
flooding in to buy bananas. They did flood in. The West German
government gave each of them one hundred marks to spend (about
fifty-five dollars at the time), a small price for a government to pay

to assure its own version of history. According to West Berlin Mayor Walter Momper, Germans were now "the happiest people in the world."

Ron Zuriel was happy. Still a photography enthusiast and still a Berliner, he went daily to the Wall to take pictures of the *Ossis* coming through. "I was happy for them. To see those faces when they came into the West and saw all those lights and the shops and all that. They came into a different world. For them it was a fantasy."

After forty years of separation the visual differences were dazzling. The *Wessis* were throwing the party, and the *Ossis* came Irene Runge, now a teacher of cultural anthropology at East Berlin's Humboldt University, heard that the Wall had opened, and her first thought was, "What fun!" You could just cross over and back anytime you wanted. The first night she went over, she turned around and went back. As a privileged Communist academic, she had often crossed over before. There was nothing in the West that she wanted, other than the thrill of walking through without being stopped.

"I was not very happy," said Sophie Marum. "I did not think it was good that we had gifts from the other side. I didn't think so. Things for nothing. And I thought, 'In time it will become difficult.' I had no illusions."

In not much time at all it became very difficult, and the staged moment faded. But for the first week Westerners were willing to go to great lengths to make it all seem the way they thought it should be. An American television crew asked Irene Runge, since she spoke American English, if they could film her shopping for food in the West. Irene never shopped anywhere but in Prenzlauer Berg. But they insisted, and she liked being on television. The gourmet floor of West Germany's most deluxe department store, the Ka De We on the Ku'damm, was chosen.

"I would never go there. It's too expensive," she said.

But they argued that the Ka De We was where they had made all their filming arrangements, so for this one time she went shopping on the famous *Feinschmeckeretage*. Ka De We is the popular abbreviation for *Kaufhaus des Westens*, or Western Department Store, so called because when it opened in 1907, the city center was the part of East Berlin where Irene's Kulturverein was located, and this was the far western suburb. Bombed into little more than a brick pile, the rebuilding of the Ka De We in the 1950s was seen as a symbol of the progress of West Berlin. Now it was being used as a symbol again, and Irene Runge, who lived in a badly lit world of pockmarked surfaces, was taken to this smooth, perfectly lit sixty-thousand-square-foot gourmet display on the sixth floor. The *Feinschmeckeretage* alone boasted more than one million dollars in weekly sales and claimed to be the largest luxury food store "outside of Tokyo."

This was more than bananas. There was Irene in her habitual baggy plaid, followed by a film crew, careening through an alleged 25,000 food items, including fruit and vegetables from around the world, 1,200 varieties of sausage, 1,500 varieties of cheese, and twenty aquariums for salt- and freshwater fish. Was not West Berlin a fun place to shop, now that there was no Wall? Irene did look as if she were having fun. In Prenzlauer Berg where she usually shopped, there were a few apples, a few kinds of cheese, and some smoked fish. Here, the stands were full of things that she had never seen before, things that she could pick up and poke at—like a ten-mark piece of fruit from Asia. The only problem was that she had never seen prices like this in Prenzlauer Berg. Even most West Berliners didn't normally pay Ka De We prices, and once the television crew turned off its floodlights and left, she could never afford to shop there again.

Soon, most East Berliners began to realize that the change was not going to be quite what it seemed at first. "This euphoric feeling disappeared very quickly because they expected too much," said Ron Zuriel. "They expected to be on the same footing as the West tomorrow. Not in a few days, but tomorrow. So their expectation was too high, and the German government promoted this."

West German Chancellor Helmut Kohl had rushed to assure East Germans that their future would be decided democratically by their own choice. Then he proceeded to lure their votes, bribe them with promises, guarantee them that in a united Germany they would get all the bananas and other goodies that the successful Federal Republic, the Bundesrepublik, had to offer. Factory workers were promised that their pay would be brought up to West German standards by 1994. Later, in the spring of 1993, they were told that the economic situation had changed and that their scheduled 26 percent pay raise was just not possible. When workers responded with the first industrial strike since before the Third Reich, West Germans expressed surprise at the depth of bitterness the *Ossis* were showing. What had happened to those radiant faces that Zuriel had photographed coming through the Wall and the happy woman in the oversize coat shopping at the Ka De We?

Irene had been naive about the changes that were taking place. Walking over to the West, she did not at first realize that her country was about to vanish. "I never thought that the GDR would be lost," she frequently said. "I think I just didn't want to believe it. Now I can't believe that I didn't believe it." She always referred to the unification as "the beginning of the not-the-GDR time."

"I thought this would be the time for the better East Germany." But soon there were elections, and the right-of-center parties backing Helmut Kohl won 48 percent of the vote. The Communists, who were offering the kind of program to reform the GDR that Irene had hoped for, only won 16 percent, and in October 1990, Irene's country ceased to exist.

The Stasi, the GDR's state security police or Staatssicherheitsdienst, died with its state, and now its secrets were left unguarded. The Stasi had wanted to compromise everybody. According to Stasi records, it had deployed 100,000 agents and another 400,000 "unofficial agents," its euphemism for informers. Some East Germans had spied for the Stasi. Others had fed it information. Others had simply been duped into an association. It had reputedly operated one of the world's finest espionage networks. It even stole the underwear of suspects, filing it in jars so that later they could be tracked down by sniffer dogs. Before it covered up the graffiti on its walls, it would analyze the lettering and brushstrokes. It collected minute details of peoples' lives, such as what time they went to bed. But it also did an excellent job of monitoring popular sentiment. Stasi files showed that there had been a growing disenchantment with the regime.

Once the Stasi files became accessible, people started finding that their friend Irene had talked about them. "You know, I gossip with everyone, and I gossiped with them. That was the problem," Irene explained without a hint of embarrassment. Someone found a postcard they had sent Irene years ago stored in a Stasi file with a notation that Irene had turned it over. On the other hand, someone else found a letter Irene had written them, apparently turned over by someone else and filed by the Stasi, with the notation "This must be the Irene who teaches at Humboldt." She had signed only with her first name.

Irene had used her bilingual skills to show journalists and other foreigners around and then report to the Stasi on their activities.

She was frequently questioned on her colleagues' attitudes about the regime, and later on about people she knew in Jewish circles. But Irene tended to see everyone in her circle as loving the GDR. By 1985 the Stasi were convinced that she was untrustworthy and were having others inform on her.

After the collapse Irene was the one compromised German who seemed to like talking about the Stasi and who often mentioned it. Certainly the many parliamentarians from the former East Germany who were involved with Stasi never mentioned it, because it would have destroyed their new political careers. All three new political parties in the East lost their leaders when they were ruined by Stasi revelations. Even the staff of the Committee to Dismantle the Stasi was found to include some with Stasi links.

Irene had thought that since everyone wanted to start talking about this Stasi business, she should come forward. She and a friend made a joint announcement that they had been Stasi informants. It seemed like the civic-minded thing to do at this point. Other colleagues at the university could come forward as well, she reasoned, and they could discuss this Stasi issue. "Everyone said we have to talk about it. We have to talk about the past," Irene explained. It was the old Communist way of doing things—have a meeting and discuss it. The new German way, however, was to fire both of them immediately. "All our former colleagues who we never knew were so antisocialist only turned out to be that way after the unification," said Irene angrily. "I still think it is stupid what they are doing to marginalize people like us, but technically I agree. If they win the war, they will dictate the conditions."

A Canadian journalist interested in Jews in the former East wanted to speak with her, and he brought along an interpreter from the German government press office. Irene explained that there was no need for the interpreter since she was completely fluent in English. But the interpreter sat in on the interview and wrote careful notes in a little book. Suddenly Irene turned to him and in a loud, good-natured voice said, "I know what you're doing. I used to do the same thing for the Stasi!"

Stasi scandals ruined many of the most productive people from the East, including not only political leaders but important writers and scientists. Most of these people were not agents but simply people who wanted to do things and had been compromised by a conversation—or a series of conversations. Where was the line to be drawn in a society where, as Martin Mandl in Brno said, you had to make decisions every day about what degree of collaboration was acceptable? When Polish General Jaruzelski offered to release Adam Michnik from prison if he would be willing to accept exile and forgo a trial, Michnik angrily responded, "To believe that I could accept such a proposal is to imagine that everyone is a police collaborator." That was exactly what the system wanted to imagine.

After unification the West Germans, who had never purged the Nazis from their ranks, who had lived for forty-five years with Nazis in government, Nazi judges, teachers, and policemen, now wanted to disenfranchise, fire, and disgrace all half-million East Germans on file at the Stasi, if they could find them. Not all of them made it as easy as Irene.

Moritz Mebel, after years as an outsider because of his Soviet Army record, managed to become head of the urology department at the Charité Hospital. He built a reputation for the department, starting its kidney transplant program, and always felt that the West Germans showed great interest in his work. But once Germany was unified, the same West German professionals suddenly looked down at the work at Charité, somehow implying it was second rate. "I think that all things that were good in the GDR must be put down," he said. In 1988 he had retired from both the hospital and the university. Under the GDR he got a pension of 5,600 marks monthly, but once the GDR was dissolved, his pension, like many of those that had been paid by the GDR, was reduced by the German government to 2,010 marks.

"When the Wall came down," said his wife Sonja, the microbiologist, "it was already clear that the GDR was over."

"But that it would come in the way it came, that we would be a colony," said Moritz, pointing toward Sonja. "She saw it better than I did. I thought they were more intelligent than that, the Western politicians." The Mebels' daughter, Anna, lost her job as a paralegal working for a city service. Most of the East German civil service was fired. But Anna's husband knew how to adapt to the new Germany. In 1990, when he lost his job as a lawyer in the Ministry of Trade, he started retraining as a tax lawyer.

THE FIRST THING Mia Lehmann did to prepare for unification was to reinforce the thin wooden door that had served her Prenzlauer Berg apartment since 1946, with new thick steel plating. She thought the steel very ugly and covered it with her grandchildren's drawings, but you could not live in this West German society without a strong door. She was not the only one who thought that. At the time of unification East Berlin experienced a run on locks.

In the last years of the GDR, Mia Lehmann had seen dissident meetings in her neighborhood broken up by the police. "I found it horrible. They had a different meeting, and they were persecuted just for that."

But asked if she was surprised, she laughed, "No. It has happened before." The years of the exciting new democratic socialist Germany had been weighted with disappointments. But to Mia, the new united Germany was even more horrible.

"Horrible. There are about two million people out of work. The factories are gone. The teachers are changed because they were GDR people and had to teach people what the party said. The doctors are changed. Everything is gone. Everything that was good in our system—And they are so awful. They think they know everything—everything was good in the Bundesrepublik, and here everything was bad."

Mia's figure of two million thrown out of work in the East was the often-quoted conservative estimate. Among those thrown out of work was her daughter, who had worked at a state-owned communications center that was eliminated after unification. Nor was Mia's criticism of the West unusually harsh. A good-natured new television comedy about Wessis and Ossis was popular, but in real life to most Berliners, the differences were more heartfelt than amusing. Ossis sometimes called the West Berliners Besserwessis, a play on the word Besserwisser—someone who thinks they know better.

Even time was different in the East and West. In the East there was always time to sit and discuss, to schmooze in both senses of the word, according to popular mythology. Easterners were even reputed to have better sex. The Westerners, from the Eastern point of view, were always in a hurry, always cold and insincere. They did not have true friendships. All they seemed to value was money.

To the Wessis, the Ossis seemed lazy, unproductive, backward, and parasitic. They had promised the East Germans everything to make them happy about unification, and then they became irritated because the Easterners expected them to deliver on their promises, as though Ossis should have been grateful that they got promises.

As time went on, East Berliners grew increasingly nostalgic about things that reminded them of the GDR. Not agents and informants or guard dogs. But they liked their neighborhood stores with their limited choice of second-rate food. They, in fact, were willing to continue their bananaless lifestyle. The once official party organ, *Neues Deutschland*, still maintained about 95,000 circulation. Club Cola, the East German Coca-Cola substitute, also maintained a following. Sales were greatly boosted with an advertising campaign that used a 1970s slogan "Hooray, I'm still alive," with clips of excited crowds from the early Erich Honecker days.

There was the right-turn on red debate. After unification the green arrows next to East Berlin stoplights, which indicated that a right-turn-on-red was permitted, were taken down because there was no such traffic rule in the West. East Germans began painting green arrows next to stoplights. So many East Germans demanded their right-turn-on-red back that a government commission was set up to study it. In East Berlin, where the rhetoric of Communism was still in the vocabulary, this produced the headline, "Green Arrows Rehabilitated." Local elections in 1994 showed that the Communist party was also being rehabilitated in East German cities.

Berlin remained a divided city, with most Berliners keeping to their own side. Only the tourist map changed, because what had never been mentioned when the Wall was there was that most of historic Berlin was in East Berlin. West Berlin made no sense as a European city. It was a city only in the way that new American cities are—a series of ingrown suburbs that pass for a city because of a critical mass of population and economic and cultural activity. A map of Berlin from before the late nineteenth century does not even include present-day West Berlin. Once the city was divided, people in the West did not like to mention to tourists that the historic European capital called Berlin was actually in the East. That was where the Spree River was, on which the city was built. The old city center was there, along with the working class districts that had grown up around industrialization. The old Jewish neighborhood, the streets of theaters, cabarets, and museums, the historic government buildings were all in the East.

Now you could walk through the once walled off Brandenburg Gate. Only buses and taxis were permitted to drive through because it was feared that the eighty-five-foot-high pillars that were supposed to recall the entrance to the Acropolis would not withstand the traffic. On top was a bronze Victory statue with four horses charging east. Victory had originally been charging West. Napoleon stole the statue, and when the Germans got it back after his demise, they remounted Victory charging East, which, curiously, was the direction of the Napoleonic victory. Through the old unified Germany, the Third Reich, the Soviets, East Germany, and now the new unified Germany, Victory has remained charging East.

The East—the people, the streets, the buildings—was not manicured in that tidy way that Westerners think of as German. Buildings were dilapidated, and exposed steel rods made pedestrians think twice about walking under balconies. Almost fifty years after the street-fighting ended, bullet holes were still splattered across buildings in dense and irregular patterns, cornices were still in their rearranged shapes from incoming shells, and the scars of flying shrapnel still showed.

HEADING NORTH from the gate through a dark, shot-up neighborhood, there was something shiny on the horizon resembling a gilded and egg, too shiny and new to fit in. It was the newly reconstructed dome of the Oranienburgerstrasse synagogue, which had been damaged by the Nazis to kick off their extermination of Judaism on *Kristallnacht* in 1938 and later had been damaged far worse by Allied bombs. Now it was being restored for use as a museum. The few East Berlin Jews did not need another large synagogue. They had the one not far away on Rykestrasse, and they generally used a small side room because the handsome main synagogue was too large for the dozen or so worshipers.

Just as West Germany had taken over and dissolved the East German nation, the West German Jewish Community had taken over and dissolved the East German Jewish Community. In both cases the *Wessis* had dissolved the Eastern institutions, simply eliminated jobs and positions and superimposed their own institutions, which they assumed to be superior in all ways. In 1991, according to the West Berlin Jewish Community, the two Berlin Jewish Communities were "combined." Irene Runge called it a "hostile takeover." In reality, the Eastern one was eliminated. A West German Jewish welfare organization that was principally concerned with the problems of Jewish immigrants moved into what had been the offices of the East Berlin Community on the Oranienburgerstrasse. It became a center for Russians. There was no longer any place for

East Berlin Jews. Peter Kirchner, who had miraculously survived the Holocaust in Berlin and had served as both *mohel* and Community leader since 1971, was simply dismissed from service.

The West Berlin Community recognized that some East Berliners should be involved in their governing body. Some West Berliners, however, said they did not want Kirchner because they preferred someone with a less forceful personality, someone who, in effect, would sit quietly in meetings. But they also were genuinely troubled by Kirchner's relationship with the Stasi, even though his files showed that at times, such as during the Yom Kippur War, he had showed a fair amount of independence from official GDR policy. Rather than simply snubbing him, the West Berlin Community finessed Kirchner out of his position by exploiting the economic hardships that unification was causing for East Berliners. At a time when East Germans, especially East Germans with Stasi links, had little hope of employment, the West Berlin Jewish Community offered Kirchner's wife a good job. But once she signed the contract, it was pointed out that the families of employees were barred from participating in Community politics. Kirchner had been eliminated. That was how the *Wessis* operated.

In 1993 a man who had had a history of heart attacks died on the floor of the Kulturverein. He was divorced, and had lived alone near the Rykestrasse synagogue, and while not a religious man, he always made himself available when a minyan was needed. But when Irene called the Jewish Community to make arrangements for a Jewish burial, she was told that they did not know that the man was Jewish. There was only one Jewish Community now, and this man had not been a member.

The West Germans showed so little interest in the Jews of East Berlin that some Easterners began to suspect their primary interest was in the property. This suspicion was fueled by the fact that so many of the West German Jewish leaders were involved in real estate. Most of the historic Jewish property, including the Oranienburgerstrasse synagogue, was in the East. That was where the Jewish history was. And it was an area with a tremendous potential for development.

The "united" Berlin Community invited more Russians than East Germans into its ruling institutions. Mark Aizikovitch was invited to join a cultural committee. Recognizing the emerging importance of the Kulturverein, some Westerners, including Moishe Waks, thought that Irene Runge should be offered a similar position. "We have a problem with her past," said Moishe. "But I don't want to judge these people, because I don't know what I would have done in a totalitarian state." Most of the Community leadership was opposed to giving any position to Irene. But Waks, who was often a dissident in their ranks, argued for her until it was agreed that they would examine her Stasi files, and as long as they found no strong evidence that she had harmed Jews, they would give her a position. It was still not a simple matter to gain access to Stasi files, but they were able to see what the Stasi had on Irene Runge and it turned out to be quite a lot. When the Community became convinced that she had been informing on Jews in the late 1970s, even Moishe Waks backed down.

Since there was no longer a Community for East Berlin, Irene's Kulturverein became the place to contact the Eastern community, because in reality, even if not on paper, it remained a separate community. There were only an estimated two hundred Jewish East Berliners and another two hundred Jews in all of the former East Germany. Few East Berliners signed up as members of the West Berlin Community. West Berliners were rarely seen at the Kulturverein.

The Kulturverein became a refuge for lost and searching East Berlin Jews. It didn't really matter what they were searching for. Irene did not model the Kulturverein on the old East German Community. It resembled more her memories of her father's bookshop in Times Square. It was a place to come and relax and meet other Jews and talk. It clearly operated on East and not West German time. Irene's description of it reveals the stereotypical East Berlin view of the difference between *Ossis* and *Wessis*. "Everybody is on first name. Nobody is into money. It's much simpler. People come here to talk to each other. There's coffee. In the West you have all these millionaires, and you know, it's a different atmosphere. Here people aren't drinking, they're drinking coffee and tea and standing, arguing, and people don't dress up."

Irene, like many East Berliners, did not like rich people and did not like people who dressed expensively. She liked her neighborhood in Prenzlauer Berg where she lived with her husband, a non-Jewish opera director. She had little need for West Berlin other than the popcorn and the sushi.

The Kulturverein had a kitchen, and there was always food. A jar in the main room asked for contributions, but most people didn't pay. They just drank the coffee and ate the cakes. It was like the old GDR. No one had to pay, yet everything ran somehow. There were still a large number of non-Jews that came. But there were also confused people from the GDR who had lost their country and had suddenly started thinking about being Jewish. They would drift in to see what this place was about. Some would become regulars. Others would drift out again.

A lean, tall man in a French beret wandered in one day, cautiously saying his name was Fred. He had the look of an old-time American Communist, which was what he was. He said he was from Texas, but his English had so many accents layered on it that it sounded unidentifiable. On the other hand, when he spoke German, he sounded like he was from Texas. His father had been a Silesian Jew and had been arrested by the Germans during World War I for agitating against the war. Fred was born in El Paso, Texas, in 1926, where his father, an active Communist, had raised him not to ask questions and to follow the lead of the Young Communist League. Fred had served in Europe in the Army Corps of Engineers during World War II. In 1950 he was called up again to serve in Korea. Since Austria was under partial Soviet control, he considered fleeing there. But a friend advised him that the Communists were going to lose Austria and he would be better off in East Germany, "It was good advice," said Fred in his sad-eyed way. "I would have only gotten five years. In Germany I got forty."

He did not really know what to do in the new Germany. It seemed as if he had wandered into the Kulturverein looking for ideas, and he spent most of an afternoon sipping coffee and talking to whoever was around. "I never thought it would end up like this," he said. "I thought Communism was the model for the future and everyone would move toward it." Before he left he said that he had been thinking a lot about El Paso of late. "If I applied for U.S. citizenship, I'm pretty sure I could get it. But I would have to bow my head and say it was the biggest mistake of my life. It was all wrong. And doing that would offend my sense of dignity.

"Well," he said, adjusting the jaunty angle of his beret, "nice talking to y'all." And he sadly sauntered to the door, down the dark and tattered stairway, and disappeared into the streets of the former East Berlin.

THE DISTANCE between *Ossis* and *Wessis* was even greater in the case of Jews than non-Jews. While Mia Lehmann and Werner

Händler had returned to East Germany out of a sense of idealism, the West Berlin Jews had returned to make money or to enjoy middle-class German materialism. Ron Zuriel had come back to help his father set up a lucrative law practice handling reparation claims. He had never really made a decision to stay in Germany. He had never thought he was capable of living permanently in Germany: "It came about. My son was born here. In my profession you cannot go back and start again where you started. You climb to a perch. And here I had a job morning until night. I worked sixteen hours a day at least. Saturday and Sunday." Zuriel was making money and had no illusions that he was doing anything else. Asked if he had come back to help Jews, he said, "Well, I was helping Jews, and I was helping myself. A lawyer who says he is in the Red Cross is a liar." The law firm became more and more profitable. In the 1970s the reparation claim business under the West German *Wiedergutmachung* law started slowing down, and he switched to general civil law. In time his own son became a lawyer and joined the firm.

In 1990 the firm began specializing in the section of the unification law dealing with restitution of nationalized property. According to this law, if a Jew had property confiscated by the Nazis and then the "Aryan" who received the property had it confiscated by the GDR state takeover of private property, the original Jewish claim would supersede that of the later owners. By 1993, there were about two million claims on confiscated GDR property. Zuriel's clients were Jewish and lived mostly in the United States and Canada but also in Israel and Western Europe. Virtually none of these Jews were interested in returning to Germany. They wanted to reclaim the property and then sell it at the plump prices of the postunification real estate market. "They never expected to get their property back," said Zuriel with an ironic chuckle. For them, it was "a gift from heaven."

Moishe Waks did come back to help German Jews. After living in Israel for seven years, in 1980 he was asked to run the youth center for the West Berlin Jewish Community. With a lifelong commitment to German Jews, he thought this would be a worthwhile project for a few years, and then he would go back to Israel. But he became involved in the profitable real estate market. "If you start to make a living here, if you try to set yourself up here, it is very hard to leave. There is no doubt that a good standard of living is much easier to get here than in Israel."

Before unification, however, Moishe had still considered returning to Israel. There was no opportunity to make money in real estate there, but he thought he might be able to get something going in import-export. He had made some contacts with Russia. Then Russia had collapsed, and the German real estate market exploded. At the same time things were getting very difficult in Israel. His friends in Israel and his brother Ruwen were growing increasingly frustrated with the right-wing Israeli government, and when Moishe talked of returning to Israel, they discouraged him.

The woman he lived with was born in Israel, but when she was three years old, her parents had returned to Germany to study and never left. Neither she nor Moishe was committed to living in Germany, but that was nevertheless where they lived. And since he lived there, he wanted to be active in the Jewish Community because that was how he had always lived. "As long as I am here, I think that I have to be active in Jewish life and try to do something for the Jewish community," he said. To him, part of that was a concern for the few Jews from the former East Germany. But he was almost alone in that view. Ron Zuriel visited the Jewish Community in the East "once or twice" when they were divided. Among Westerners, ironically, there was less interest in the East once it opened. Irene Runge complained that she knew people in West Berlin who always kept in contact with her until the Wall came down. After that, she never heard from them.

"I KNEW THEM from the thirties, and I can't believe they're back," said Mia Lehmann. Skinheads and neo-Nazis marched through Prenzlauer Berg with their white-laced boots, swastikas, and slogans of hate against Turks and Jews and foreigners. Mia, who had not participated in a Jewish organization since the German Communists in Belgium had side-tracked her plans to move to Palestine almost sixty years earlier, now became a regular participant at the Kulturverein. She had not found religion or forgotten how the synagogue in the Bucovina had closed its doors and made her mother cry. Mia probably never forgot anything. It was just that she thought she should be around Jews, that Jews should stick together, because Nazis seemed to be coming back.

It is widely believed that the fall of the GDR and the unification of Germany brought neo-Nazism to the East. According to the Western version, the GDR was too repressive for neo-Nazis to function, and now, because there was freedom of expression, neo-Nazis appeared. In the Eastern version, neo-Nazism was imported to Eastern Germany from the West.

Neither version is completely true. Neo-Nazism may have had a twenty-year headstart in the West, but by the 1980s, and probably earlier, there were neo-Nazi activities in the East. In 1987 neo-Nazis broke up a concert in Prenzlauer Berg shouting anti-Semitic slogans and *"Sieg heil."* This was known because for the first time the GDR media were allowed to report on the neo-Nazis' trial, at which the light sentences belied the legend of GDR severity toward Nazis. Neo-Nazi graffiti was seen on walls, carefully analyzed by the Stasi, and then painted over. Numerous neo-Nazis were brought to trial and imprisoned. The West German government had a practice of paying the GDR for East German "political prisoners." Curiously, a number of the prisoners they chose to rescue—for substantial fees—were neo-Nazis, who went on to become active in West German neo-Nazi groups. By the time of unification, the extreme right organization had become fairly sophisticated, with the Republicans and their former SS leader Schönhuber winning votes by staying above the fray, the neo-Nazi parties changing names as fast as they were banned, disseminating the propaganda, while the brutal young skinheads did the dirty work. The same pattern had emerged in other Western countries, including the United States, where orchestrated racist violence was also on the rise. But while the FBI and other law enforcement agencies were concerned about the degree of organization, even international organization, of racist attacks, German law enforcement continued to insist that these attacks were only random. In the face of overwhelming evidence to the contrary and a mounting international embarrassment, in 1994 they grudgingly conceded that there was some organization to skinhead violence. In Germany approximately five racist attacks occurred every day, usually against immigrants, with at least one person killed almost every month.

In 1992 there were an estimated 2,200 right-wing attacks, in which 17 people were killed. Yet in February 1993, Federal Prosecutor Alexander von Stahl said that neo-Nazis were under control and the real danger was left-wing terrorists. There had been only one death caused by a leftist that year. But von Stahl went on to explain that the leftists were organized while the neo-Nazis were just drunken kids.

The skinheads learned when arrested to always say they were drunk, and they consistently got lighter sentences than the leftists. Until 1994 law enforcement had tended to stand by passively and "let the young people blow off some steam."

The politicians were scrambling to master the winning Nazi issue, immigration. It was true that Germany had an extremely liberal immigration law and that the 450,000 asylum-seekers taken in by Germany in 1992 were twice as many as those taken by the rest of Western Europe combined. But it was also true that at the time of unification the foreign population of East Germany represented only 1.2 percent of the total. Yet "the foreigner problem" was given great credence there. When Hitler had first gained popular support by decrying "the Jewish problem," Jews had been only one percent of the German population. In reunited Germany, the growing antiforeign sentiment did not correspond to the presence of foreigners. Violence against foreigners increased even in East German cities, which foreigners had left after the fall of the GDR. While Magdeburg experienced a dramatic increase in antiforeigner violence, the number of foreigners there declined from 9,200 in May 1990 to 1,400 in January 1991.

The extreme right was able to get the government to treat the antiforeigner issue as though it had some validity. Once the right started winning voters, the establishment started talking as though there really were a foreigner problem. The Republican party, by watching their rhetoric and not talking too often about Jews, was able to give the Nazi agenda the appearance of a legitimate grievance, winning seats in municipal elections and respectable showings in state contests.

Helmut Kohl had been trying to gain the anti-immigrant vote for years by toughening the immigration law, but the Social Democrats had blocked him from gaining the two-thirds in Parliament required for a constitutional amendment. At the end of 1992, seeing where their votes were going, the Social Democrats were ready to cave in, and the German asylum law, a showpiece of the West German constitution that was supposed to demonstrate a new Germany open to foreigners, was curtailed. Three days later, skinheads set a fire in Solingen, near Düsseldorf, and killed five Turkish women and children.

Neo-Nazis liked to talk about making Germany "great again." This was a cause that was spirited by the unification, the anniversary of which has become a neo-Nazi holiday, like Hitler's birthday and the anniversary of Rudolf Hess's 1987 death. It was clear that after unification, many Germans wanted to see Germany's past treated more kindly. Helmut Kohl decided that the 1992 anniversary of reunification would be an appropriate occasion to celebrate the fiftieth anniversary of the first launching of a V-2 rocket, one of the stars of the Third Reich's arsenal. International protest forced him to cancel.

One of the first problems with making Germany "great again" was that it was still a nation in disrepute because of what it had done the last time it was great. For this reason a major part of the neo-Nazi agenda everywhere was to establish that the Holocaust did not happen. This was an oddly flawed argument that basically claimed both that the Holocaust never happened and furthermore that the Jews deserved it. Nowhere was this contradiction more succinctly stated than on the walls of a suburb north of Paris, where it was scrawled in matching penmanship both "Auschwitz is a lie" and "Gas the Jews."

The right was able to offer Germans not only the catharsis of racial hatred but also freedom from guilt. Germans who were born after 1945 had spent their lives with the guilt of Nazi Germany around their neck. Now the extreme right was freeing them. Republican leader Schönhuber was promising that there would no longer be "a television program of Dachau on channel one, Treblinka on two, and Auschwitz on three." He called for an end to all this examination of the past, presumably including an end to the examination of his own SS record—freedom at last from the legacy of guilt and at the same time Germans could blame all their current problems on foreigners. Auschwitz is a lie, and the Jews should be gassed.

After unification the issue inevitably arose, as it had in Poland, of what to do with the concentration camps that had been in the GDR, where the Communist version of history had been imposed on them. Two forms of revisionism were being attempted at East German camps. One was an attempt to ignore, banalize, and forget the sights. There was a cobblestone road leading up to the Ravensbrück camp, where 200,000 women had been imprisoned, of whom 90,000 had been beaten, tortured, starved, shot, or gassed to death. The road itself had been built by forced women's labor from the camp. At the entrance to the road was a stark black-and-white sign that said "Frauen-KZ Ravensbrück," Ravensbrück Women's Concentration Camp. Next to it was a red triangle, implying that it had been a camp for Communist political prisoners. That was one of the badges used in the camps. But the sign made no reference to other badges, such as the yellow triangle, which was used for Jewish prisoners.

Next to the sign was another one with a palm tree, which said "Sylvia's Fitness Center." There, at the camp entrance, a sauna and solarium were made available, in spite of protests. As a compromise, the fitness center sign was moved slightly away from the camp sign. Across the street was built a new but empty supermarket with a fresh unblemished blacktop parking lot, new windows, checkout lanes, and fresh wires hanging from the ceiling waiting for fixtures. That was as far as the supermarket got before international pressure stopped it from opening. A rival supermarket chain decided to try for one next to Sachsenhausen.

Sachsenhausen had been mostly leveled. One of the few remaining barracks had been burned down by neo-Nazis in 1992. The small triangular field where the camp had once been was now marked with various Soviet monuments. But a pathology laboratory for medical experiments, the remains of a gas chamber, and crematoriums with their iron racks were still there. Nearby, on the site of an SS barracks, the town of Oranienburg had plans to build a new housing project, complete with a fitness center.

But the other kind of revisionism was also in evidence. In addition to building new housing, there was a move for a new monument to the victims of Stalin. While the other Allies had also had prison camps in which many died of diseases, tens of thousands had died of illness and starvation in the Soviet camps. Sachsenhausen was one of a number of concentration camps that, after Liberation, the Red Army had used to imprison Nazis, black marketeers, prostitutes, and political opponents. But the proposed monument at Sachsenhausen would have honored them all equally as victims of Stalinism. This seemed to be part of a broader desire to equate Communist crimes with Nazi crimes. If it could be said that the GDR was as bad as the Third Reich, in time it could be said that the Third Reich—which had racial hatred as a founding premise and mass extermination as a stated goal, and which killed by the millions—was no worse than the GDR, which had egalitarianism as a founding premise but became a repressive dictatorship. Once the German Communists were established as the worst of all Germans, and once all Germany needed to do to purge itself was to chase down Stasi informers, once the German past started in 1945, Germany would be a country like other countries without a special guilt, and it would be free to be "great again." It was already written in *Die Welt* that former GDR leader Erich Honecker was "the greatest German murderer and war criminal."

Among the active Sachsenhausen survivors who were objecting to the proposed monument was Werner Händler. He still felt the obligation of the Sachsenhausen prisoners who had asked him, when he was leaving, to tell the world about what he had seen: "I think these men who said to me in the winter of 1938 look here, tell them that we are going in for a war, I feel that I have their vote." Using the same direct language with which he confronted people all his life, he said, "The original ovens are still standing there in the Fatherland, so anybody saying there's nothing to it, we can bring them there and lie them on the roaster."

THE NUMBER OF JEWS in Germany suddenly increased. After reunification there were 30,000, and then the German government approved permission for 25,000 Soviet Jews to be distributed in all the major areas of Germany, welcomed, offered temporary housing and language lessons, and given a home in Germany. But it was not always clear why these Russians had come. When asked their reasons, they consistently said that it was because Berlin had nice weather. No one else had ever thought so.

Boris Kruglikov, 33, had been a railroad engineer until Mikhail Gorbachev came to power. Realizing the opportunities presented by glasnost, he started selling radios and VCRs on the Russian black market. Soon this business became legal. In 1991, on an electronics-buying trip to Germany, he learned about the program for Jews and immigrated to Germany with his wife. He had originally hoped to move on to the United States, but decided to remain in Germany. "The social services are good. I was told they are not good in the United States," he explained.

Stanislava Mikhalskaia was born in Moscow in 1963. In 1990 she learned that her mother, who had been adopted by a Russian family, was originally the daughter of two Jews. Shortly after that a friend of hers went to Germany and told her about the new law. The Soviet Union had just survived a coup d'état attempt, and the future was looking uncertain and frightening. Since she now was Jewish, she applied, after first marrying her non-Jewish boyfriend. They both moved to Berlin. In Moscow they had both been successful professionals with large apartments, a car, and a country home. In Berlin they moved into a fifty-square-foot room in an immigrant hostel. Eventually, they were able to find a small apartment, and Stanislava hoped to resume her profession as architect in time. But Germany worried her. "Germans are against foreigners, and now I think it is not a good country for Jews." Still, like most Russian Jews in Germany, she planned to stay. Economic and political problems were steadily worsening in Russia.

Most of the Russian Jews arrived with excellent credentials but no skills. They were engineers, doctors, and scientists—but they somehow did not qualify for any work in the West. Their stories were not always convincing. One who spent time with coffee and cakes at the Kulturverein claimed to be a psychologist researching the creativity of left-handed people. He admitted that he did not exactly have a degree in psychology but he was, in fact, himself left-handed. Eugeni Elizatov, 34, from Turkmenia, claimed to be a matchmaker. In traditional Judaism marriages are arranged by a *shadkhan* whose business it was to know many families and bring together good matches. This looked to Elizatov to be a promising business in Berlin, because there were many Jews hoping to find Jewish mates. But he did not really know how to be a *shadkhan* according to Jewish law, because he didn't know Jewish law. He said that his parents had both been Jewish, but they had given him no Jewish education. To offer his services to East Berlin Jews, he simply took their names and then tried to find an eligible woman in Leningrad who wanted to move to Germany. Not surprisingly, his clients had little confidence in this process, and in his first two years in Germany he did not make a single match, not even one for himself. His wife had divorced him before he moved.

Whatever their motives for coming, the Jewish communities around Germany welcomed the Russian Jews, and most of them tried to participate in their communities. By 1994, 70 percent of the nine thousand members of the Berlin Jewish Community were Russian. Few of the Russians knew anything about Judaism, but Jewish communities offered them courses in religion and Hebrew that, like all Jewish programs offered in Germany, were widely attended by German non-Jews. In fact, they outnumbered the Russians.

German Jews suspected that not all of these Russian immigrants were Jewish. A rumored figure was that 30 percent were non-Jews who had lied for papers. Considering that there were still Jews wanting to leave the former Soviet Union and that the 25,000 quota was already filled, with no assurances that any more would be allowed in, the Community was deeply disturbed by this. But there was little they could do. They did not want to rigorously interrogate each applicant because they understood how difficult it would be for Soviet Jews to prove their Jewishness after seventy years of Communism.

When Mark Aizikovitch came to Berlin, he discovered to his surprise a great local interest in traditional Yiddish songs. He had grown up hearing Yiddish in the Ukrainian town of Poltava. The few religious Jews there had died off and been given traditional funerals, as had his father, but when his mother died in 1985, he did not know how to say kaddish for her. He went to the few elderly men left in the neighborhood, but none of them knew either. Aizikovitch had received formal theatrical training, played Chekhov, and sang opera. But when times changed, he learned that the money was in folk rock, and he performed with a Ukrainian rock group called the Philharmonica. When he immigrated to Berlin with a non-Jewish wife and two children to support, he could see that no one was interested in Russian folk rock. Speaking no German, he had few possibilities in theater. But this great interest in the Yiddish folk songs of his childhood gave him his opportunity.

"All the Germans are doing a big business with Yiddish," said an astonished Aizikovitch. "But the goyim don't speak the Yiddish right. They don't play the role. They don't play the soul. They play a Jew. I don't play a Jew. I learned those songs from my grandmother."

At concerts and festivals of Yiddish music in Germany, thin young Germans with long blond hair would strum a guitar and sing Yiddish songs. Aizikovitch would plant his feet on the stage, and with broad gestures and wild black eyes, he would sing Yiddish in a voice trained to fill a large house. The Germans would stare at him. He was not doing it right. He was not like the other Yiddish singers.

One night, Irene Runge, always in search of things Jewish, was in the audience. "I thought, 'Geez, this guy is unbelievable.' One song, and then they get him offstage. Then they try not to let him onstage too much. He can sing the little evenings when nobody comes."

Irene had been taking to some Western ways. She had a computer, a fax, a cordless telephone. She was getting really good at Western media. She cultivated relations with local reporters and foreign correspondents. She made herself available to local press as a "Jewish expert," then consulted by telephone with her rabbi in Jerusalem to see if what she had said was correct. She loved to show off what she knew, which may have been how the Stasi tricked her. But she was a die-hard *Ossi* who took to the pace of the West. And now she had another idea. She could sell Mark Aizikovitch. She could make his career happen. She knew how things worked in the West. She could be a New Yorker.

Carefully booking his appearances, she developed his image, telling him to avoid the gold chains and open shirts and keeping him away from the Yiddish programs with non-Jewish singers. Showing her fluency in both New York culture and Western-style marketing, she said, "He doesn't fit into their hippie thing. He's more Broadway, and they're somewhere in the Village. They're sitting in Washington Square singing, and he's onstage, and that's the problem. You know, they are all skinny and they don't have any voice and the guilt feeling. He comes onstage, he looks great. He's in a suit. Nobody wears a suit. They have some kind of rotten clothing . . . and he has a real trained voice and knows how to play with an audience, and you know that's it!"

IRENE RUNGE'S FATHER was in his nineties when Irene became an outspoken Jewish figure. He reacted to her open display of Jewishness the way others had reacted when she revealed her Stasi ties. He was so angry, *broygez*, that he refused to speak to her anymore.

Irene was virtually unemployable because of her Stasi record. Many of her friends were in the same situation. For the first two years they had temporary, state-funded jobs. After two years they went on unemployment compensation. Accidentally, the new Germany had provided them with the socialist society that the GDR had failed to provide. Now there was no Stasi to dole out privileges, and no elite. They were all earning the identical state-funded incomes. And when they wanted to do something, they all pooled their resources—"each according to his ability," just as Marx had said.

Irene's son, Stefan, wanted to marry a Jew and live a Jewish life. But a Jewish wife was hard to find, especially because he did not want a Westerner. Even Israelis were too Western for him. "I can't. In Germany I've tried. But I have no connection to the West." But in some ways Stefan was not all that different from a Westerner. He had a job as an accountant. When Germany reunited, he moved to Israel. There he lived on a kibbutz, but he was soon back in Berlin. "I don't like it, but I can live better here. I have more money. I have my own apartment. I have a company and friends. In Israel I have nothing."

And something else had changed for him. "I can go there anytime I want. Why should I move to Israel when I can go there anytime I want?"

Nor was Ron Zuriel leaving Berlin, where he had his law practice and his son and a married daughter with a child. But he did not exactly think of Germany as his homeland. Using the very German word *Heimat*, he said, "If you asked where is my home, my home, because everyone needs a home, I would say being Jewish is my home. It's a bit peculiar, but that is the only identity, the only point of identification I have, because I can't say I'm German. I have a German passport, I'm German by nationality, I'm German by culture, my mother tongue is German, but I wouldn't say that my *Heimat* is Germany. For me it is difficult to say."

He never forgot that he had saved himself once before by knowing when it was time to leave Germany, and he made this calculation: "I would say that the time to leave for a Jew, to pack the suitcases, is when the right extreme party—I would add the Republicans, for me they are also right extreme, although they try to keep up appearances—if they some way or another would be taken into a position of responsibility, join in some form a coalition or whatever, if the existing parties consider them as possible political partners, I think that would be the time a Jew should think twice if he should leave or not."

Helmut Kohl repeatedly said he would never accept a partnership with Republicans. Some of the local parties were less adamant. It almost happened in Hesse in the spring of 1993.

In that sense Zuriel was always prepared to leave Germany. "Wherever I go, I take my being Jewish with me, and if I ever at my age would leave, which I certainly don't think, first thing would be to search out a Jewish community that would be my point of contact."

Moishe Waks remained in Berlin, and his brother remained in Israel. Ruwen, like Moishe, had offers in Germany, but he never took them. He joked that his wife would kill him if he did.

Carmela had never lived in Germany and never had any interest in it. They raised their children to be Israelis. Ruwen lectured visiting Germans about the Holocaust, lectures that were included on the itinerary of many German vacation packages to Israel.

Looking back, Ruwen was disappointed in the German Zionist movement. "In my opinion it was a big failure," he said. "We couldn't persuade people. We could not bring to them the message. Everybody was very involved. It was very active all over Germany, but if you look at the numbers of how many went—"

He talked of how German Jews would support Zionism, "until the moment they had to go." His mother, Lea, still said she had no German friends and little contact with Germans, but she remained in Düsseldorf even after Aaron died. In 1991 both Lea and Moishe finally became German citizens. Nevertheless, Ruwen started shopping for an apartment to buy her in Israel. After all, she still said that she intended to move to Israel someday.

THE JEWISH COMMUNISTS who had returned from camps, hiding, and exile to build the GDR were now living in the Germany they never wanted to live in. One said, "Had I known in 1947 what would happen after forty years, I would definitely not have come back to Germany."

Werner Händler remained *broygez* with God and quite a few people. He busied himself with the Sachsenhausen committee and went to municipal hearings to try to stop the city from removing Communist names from streets. He was trying to organize survivors abroad to stop Berlin from reverting to Prussian street names. "What kind of a message does it give to these young gangsters when they see it is Wilhelmstrasse again?"

Werner would occasionally go to the Rykestrasse synagogue if they needed a tenth man, but he was not involved in religion. One of his daughters was interested in her Jewish background and sometimes went to the Kulturverein. The other had no interest. His wife Helle, a social worker, retired. Her program which had given money and help to pregnant women, ended with the GDR. Now Werner and Helle could travel, and they went to Israel. He was impressed by how nonreligious most Israelis were. "Even though there is the theocratic state," he said with wonder in his voice, "you find the same attitude as I have."

They also visited the United States, where Jews expressed

tremendous sympathy for their having endured the GDR. "Look here," Händler said to them. "The question is what I want to do with my life. If I think what I have to do is live decently with my family and raise my children, give them a good education and have a good living and get on in my life, then I must say I'm glad, I had a good life and I didn't commit any crimes. If I say that I want more in my life and look for a better future of mankind, then I must say that I feel sad that the first attempt at making an alternative society has failed. But I am not sorry that I participated in it."

SIXTY YEARS AFTER she set out for Palestine, Mia Lehmann got there with her friends from the Antifascist League. At last she could understand the vexing Palestinian problem with which the party had always sympathized. But she didn't really get to understand them, to listen to their troubles the way she did with everyone else, because the first Palestinian she and her friends found was throwing rocks at her bus. After the group of old-time Communists got back from Israel, they thought about what they had seen and they talked to Moti Lewy, the Israeli consul in Berlin. Israel was in peace negotiations at the time, and he explained that they might be willing to give up the Golan Heights. "No!" the antifascists muttered. They warned him not to give it up.

To Mia Lehmann, living in the reunified Germany was living in West Germany. "I don't like it now, and I didn't like it before. I came back to have a different Germany, not a Germany like this." But she was not despairing. She was too busy. There were two million unemployed East Germans with whom she could talk and give sympathy. And she was collecting money to send milk to Cuba, where children were going hungry because of the U.S. embargo.

"I am always an optimist," she said. "And I think there are enough people who don't like it. The way it is now, this country has no future. You see. The way people are so rich and other people are so poor. It can't go on forever." She smiled cheerfully, as though she had not lived through most of this fast-paced and terrible century that had been her life.

EPILOGUE

Freedom in the Marais

"And when, in time to come, your son asks you, saying, 'What does this mean?' you shall say to him, 'it was with a mighty hand that the Lord brought us from Egypt, the house of bondage.' "

EXODUS 13:14

Two very ordinary things happen at the same time on Friday nights in the fourth arrondissement of Paris. In the fashionable Marais young Parisians—and more than a few visiting young New Yorkers—dressed in exotically cut, brightly colored evening clothes, drift by shop windows to expensive restaurants that serve modern light fare. In the Pletzl religious men dressed in black wool suits—preferably pure wool, because the Torah forbids mixing wool with linen—and dark hats, sometimes large furry *shtreimels*, hurry to synagogues and *shtibls*.

This weekend, all this was also happening Saturday and Sunday nights because Passover began after the Sabbath ended. By Sunday, the second night of Passover, the bearded dark-suited men of the Pletzl were in a particular hurry to get home to their families. Since religious Jews cannot use transportation on a holiday, and most of them could no longer afford the Pletzl now that it was the Marais, they had a long way to walk from their home to the synagogue and back to the family seder.

A police van with several heavily armed patrolmen was stationed in front of the synagogue on Rue Pavée. Inside, men were gathering anxiously under the long thin columns with the art nouveau tulip-shaped lamps. Daniel Altmann was intently studying a passage of Hebrew, but others were pacing, anxiously looking at a spot under the balcony where an electric clock had been discreetly placed. A few bored children were playing in the aisles.

Finally, the cantor began chanting at 9:15 and the service was brief. Altmann could get home quickly because he could afford to live in the Marais. It was not that long ago that he had been a young affluent single man much like the young people enjoying their weekend night. But now he hurried by them to his apartment and his family to start the Passover seder. He was a typical Orthodox, part of the color of the neighborhood with his hat and beard. Only a weakness for expensive silk ties made him look slightly different from the others.

This seemingly gradual evolution from Pletzl to Marais in the sweep of history had taken place in the flick of an eyelid. As the Marais was modernized, a nearby ancient square was bulldozed to make a parking lot and sixty tombs were accidentally discovered from the long-forgotten Frankish dynasty that had ruled the neighborhood and much of France and Germany eleven hundred years ago. But even then, Passover had been two thousand years old.

Saturday night, the seder went on until four o'clock, but the five Altmann children had slept during the next day, and on Sunday night they were ready to do it all again. They were wound up and waiting for their father to get home. The Passover seder is for children—to teach them the meaning of freedom. To ask them questions. Challenge them. It is fun because it is a ritual in which they play a central role. They could hear their father stumbling down the long, dark hallway, which his religious observance would not permit him to light.

Lynda was dressed in a fashionable suit for the occasion and everything was ready—past ready because it was now ten o'clock at night. Daniel put on a white smock. Seders were messy at the Altmanns'. Four times the wineglass gets filled to the brim for blessings, and little six-year-old Ariel, with bright dark eyes like his mother, invariably kicked the table as he anxiously shifted around and the wine always spilled. Daniel drank each glass in a single long gulp, leaning on his left arm. "We drink on the left side because we are free men," he explained. When Jews were slaves in Egypt, it is supposed that they were cramped into small quarters and had to eat straight up. Now that they are free they can stretch out.

Everything on this night is about freedom. Daniel read from the Haggadah the story of Moses and the pharaoh, of slavery in Egypt and the struggle of the Jews some 3,200 years ago—the earliest known successful slave rebellion.

Ritual foods were placed on a platter, and before beginning, in accordance with the tradition in Lynda's native Morocco, the platter of foods was held over each person, one at a time, saying in Hebrew, "Last year we were slaves, this year we are free, next year we will be in Jerusalem."

The family took turns reading from the book in Hebrew, rapidly, fluently, often offering almost simultaneous translation in French. They could all read like that except one-year-old Nethen and three-year-old Naemi, who kept doing a disturbingly realistic pantomime of changing her dolls' diapers.

The Altmanns made their way through the prescribed ritual, each item of food a symbol of an aspect of the freedom struggle—a departure point for discussion of another aspect of the nature of freedom, God and man. The children were asked questions, and they asked other questions in response, and Daniel and Lynda tried to explain. It was a family discussion.

Breaking off a piece of matzoh—thin, black-edged, round, charcoally handmade matzoh, not the industrial squares, but something that seemed to resemble the handmade yeastless bread that Hebrew slaves might have hastily thrown together for their flight from Egypt—Daniel turned to nine-year-old Itshac and said, "This is made with nothing but flour and water. What is in challah?"

Itshac rubbed his yarmulke on his blond head. His fair looks came from the Ashkenazic side of the family. "Flour, water, yeast, eggs . . . " He was thinking.

"What else?" asked Daniel.

"Oil!" said Itshac.

"That's right. Now, which of these is the richer bread?"

"The challah."

"No," Daniel explained. "The matzoh is richer. It is only flour and water, but it is all a Jew needs. It can be taken anywhere. A Jew can go with only flour and water."

Itshac's eyes seemed to widen with an idea. "It's freedom!"

Lynda and Daniel expressed their pride in a quick glance at each other. "Yes, exactly!" said Daniel. "To not need anything else. Just flour and water. That is freedom. You are right!"

APPENDIX

===

Jewish Populations in Europe

Since not all Jews register with communities and many, especially nonpracticing Jews, do not declare their origin on any document, all estimates are educated guesses. These figures have been compiled from the works of Holocaust scholars, notably Raul Hilberg and Lucy Dawidowicz, and from the World Jewish Congress, and interviews with Jewish leaders in the various communities. Of the half dozen or so sources used there were rarely two in exact agreement on any of these figures, but there is agreement on the demographic developments that they indicate.

	1935	1945	1994
EUROPE	9,000,000	3,000,000	4,000,000
Germany	500,000	15,000	40,000
Poland	3,300,000	275,000	3,000–7,000?
Netherlands	140,000	30,000	30,000
Hungary	400,000	240,000	120,000
France	340,000	250,000	650,000
Czech lands	120,000	12,000	1,600–3,300?
Slovak	135,000	25,000	600–1,200?
Belgium	90,000	20,000	41,000
Antwerp	50,000	1,000?	20,000

BIBLIOGRAPHY

EUROPEAN HISTORY

LAQUEUR, WALTER. *Europe in Our Time: A History, 1945–1992*. New York: Viking, 1992.

THÉOLLEYRE, JEAN-MARC. *Les Néo-Nazis*. Paris: Temps Actuels, 1982.

WALTERS, E. GARRISON. *The Other Europe: Eastern Europe to 1945*. New York: Dorset Press, 1990.

ZEMAN, Z.A.B. *Pursued by a Bear: The Making of Eastern Europe*. London: Chatto & Windus, 1989.

THE END OF THE SOVIET BLOC

GOLDFARB, JEFFREY. *After the Fall: The Pursuit of Democracy in Central Europe*. New York: Basic Books, 1992.

GWERTZMAN, BERNARD, and MICHAEL T. KAUFMAN, ed. *The Collapse of Communism*. New York: Times Books, 1991 (an anthology of *New York Times* dispatches).

KONRÁD, GEORGE. *Antipolitics*. New York: Harcourt Brace Jovanovich, 1984 (an insightful look at East-West politics a few years before the fall).

TISMANEANU, VLADIMIR. *Reinventing Politics: Eastern Europe from Stalin to Havel*. New York: The Free Press, 1992.

JEWISH HISTORY

DAWIDOWICZ, LUCY S. *What Is the Use of Jewish History.* New York: Schocken Books, 1992 (collection of essays).

HOFFMAN, CHARLES. *Grey Dawn: The Jews of Eastern Europe in the Post-Communist Era.* New York: HarperCollins, 1992.

JOHNSON, PAUL. *A History of the Jews.* New York: Harper & Row, 1987.

SACHAR, ABRAM LEON. *A History of the Jews.* New York: Alfred A. Knopf, 1966 (originally published in 1930).

SACHAR, HOWARD M. *Diaspora: An Inquiry into the Contemporary Jewish World.* New York: Harper & Row, 1985.

JEWISH REFERENCE BOOKS

Encyclopaedia Judaica. 16 vols. Jerusalem: Keter, 1972.

Tanakh: The Holy Scriptures. New York: The Jewish Publication Society, 1988 (a new translation in modern idiom).

EPSTEIN, ISIDOR, ed. *The Babylonian Talmud.* 17 vols. London: Soncino Press, 1935.

KOLATCH, ALFRED J. *The Jewish Book of Why.* Middle Village, NY: Jonathan David, 1981.

PHILIPPE, BEATRICE. *Les Juifs dans le monde contemporain.* Paris: MA Editions, 1986.

RUNES, DAGOBERT D. *Concise Dictionary of Judaism.* New York: Philosophical Library, 1959.

UNTERMAN, ALAN. *Dictionary of Jewish Lore and Legend.* London: Thames & Hudson, 1991.

HOLOCAUST HISTORY

ARENDT, HANNAH. *Eichmann in Jerusalem: A Report on the Banality of Evil.* New York: Viking Press, 1965.

BREITMAN, RICHARD. *The Architect of Genocide: Himmler and the Final Solution.* New York: Alfred A. Knopf, 1991.

DAWIDOWICZ, LUCY S. *The War Against the Jews 1933–1945.* New York: Holt Rinehart and Winston, 1975.

HILBERG, RAUL. *The Destruction of the European Jews.* 3 vols. New York: Holmes and Meier, 1985.

———— *Perpetrators Victims Bystanders: The Jewish Catastrophe 1933–1945.* New York: HarperCollins, 1992.

SHIRER, WILLIAM L. *The Rise and Fall of the Third Reich: A History of Nazi Germany.* New York: Simon and Schuster, 1960.

SNYDER, LOUIS L. *Encyclopedia of the Third Reich.* New York: McGraw-Hill, 1976.

Speer, Albert. *Inside the Third Reich.* New York: Macmillan, 1970.
Taylor, James, and Warren Shaw. *The Third Reich Almanac.* New York: World Almanac, 1987.

By Country

Belgium

Dumont, Serge. *Les Brigades noires: L'extreme-droite en France et en Belgique francophone de 1944 à nos jours.* Berchem: Editions EPO, 1982.
Gutwirth, Jacques. *Vie juive traditionnelle: Ethnologie d'une communauté hassidique.* Paris: Les Editions de Minuit, 1970.
Kranzler, David, and Eliezer Gevirtz. *To Save a World: Profiles of Holocaust Rescue.* New York, London, Jerusalem: CIS Publishers, 1991. (With strong orthodox prejudices and awkward writing, this book describes among others, the story of Recha Rottenberg Sternbuch.)

Czechoslovakia

Chapman, Colin. *August 21st: The Rape of Czechoslovakia.* London: Cassell, 1968 (Sunday *Times* correspondent's account of the invasion).
Fiedler, Jiří. *Jewish Sights of Bohemia and Moravia.* Prague: Sefer, 1991.
Kusin, Vladimir V. *From Dubcek to Charter 77: A Study of "Normalization" in Czechoslovakia.* New York: St. Martin's Press, 1978.
Rybár, Ctibor. *Jewish Prague: Notes on History and Culture.* Prague, 1991.
Wolchik, Sharon L. *Czechoslovakia in Transition: Politics, Economics and Society.* London and New York: Pinter, 1991.

France

Bensiomon, Doris, and Sergio Della Pergola. *La Population juive de France: Socio-demographie et identité.* Paris: Hebrew University of Jerusalem and Centre National de la Recherche Scientifique, 1986.
Berg, Roger. *Histoire du rabbinat français (XVIe–XXe siècle).* Paris: Cerf, 1992.
Burns, Michael. *Dreyfus: A Family Affair—1789–1945.* New York: HarperCollins, 1991 (important insights into the nature, origin and development of twentieth-century French anti-Semitism).
Eskenazi, Frank, and Edouard Waintrop. *Le Talmud et la république: Enquête sur les juifs français à l'heure des renouveaux religieux.* Paris: Bernard Grasset, 1991.

GREEN, NANCY L. *The Pletzl of Paris: Jewish Immigrant Workers in the Belle Epoque.* New York: Holmes & Meier, 1986.

HARRIS, ANDRÉ, and ALAIN DE SÉDOUY. *Juifs et français.* Paris: Grasset & Fasquelle, 1979.

JOSEPHS, JEREMY. *Swastika Over Paris: The Fate of the French Jews.* London: Bloomsbury, 1989.

LACOUTURE, JEAN. *De Gaulle.* 3 vols. Paris: Le Seuil, 1985–86.

———— *Pierre Mèndes-France.* Paris: Le Seuil, 1981.

MORGAN, TED, *An Uncertain Hour: The French, the Germans, the Jews, the Klaus Barbie Trial and the City of Lyon, 1940–1945.* New York: William Morrow, 1990.

ROUSSO, HENRY, trans. by Arthur Goldhammer. *The Vichy Syndrome: History and Memory in France since 1944.* Cambridge: Harvard University Press, 1991.

SZAFRAN, MAURICE. *Les Juifs dans la politique française: De 1945 à nos jours.* Paris: Flammarion, 1990.

WINOCK, MICHEL. *Edouard Drumont et Cie: Antisémitisme et fascisme en France.* Paris, Seuil, 1982.

Germany

ASSHEUER, THOMAS, and HANS SARKOWICZ. *Rechtsradikale in Deutschland: Die alte und die neue Rechte.* Munich: Beck, 1990.

BORNEMAN, JOHN. *After the Wall: East Meets West in the New Berlin.* New York: Basic Books, 1991 (one of the first honest attempts in the West to give the *Ossi* viewpoint).

CRAIG, GORDON A. *The Germans.* New York: Penguin, 1991 (deservedly regarded as a classic study).

DEMETZ, PETER. *After the Fires: Recent Writing in the Germanies, Austria and Switzerland.* New York: Harcourt Brace Jovanovich, 1986.

FROHN, AXEL. *Holocaust and Shilumin: The Policy of Wiedergutmachung in the Early 1950s.* Washington, D.C.: German Historical Institute, 1991.

GELB, NORMAN. *The Berlin Wall.* New York: Dorset Press, 1990.

JASCHKE, HANS-GERD. *Die Republikaner: Profil einer Rechtsaussen-Partei.* Berlin: Dietz, 1990.

KRAMER, JANE. "Neo-Nazis: A Chaos in the Head." *The New Yorker,* June 14, 1993.

McELVOY, ANNE. *The Saddled Cow.* London: Faber and Faber, 1992.

MAÒR, HARRY. *Über den Wiederaufbau der jüdischen Gemeinden in Deutschland seit 1945.* Mainz: Universität zu Mainz, 1961.

MOREAU, PATRICK. *Les Héritiers du IIIe Reich: L'extrême droite allemande de 1945 à nos jours.* Paris: Seuil, 1994.

RAFF, DIETHER. *A History of Germany: From the Medieval Empire to the*

Present. Oxford: Berg, 1990. (A textbook for German studies courses, this is a German view of German history.)

RANGE, PETER ROSS. *German-Jewish Reconciliation? Facing the Past and Looking to the Future.* Washington, D.C.: American Institute for Contemporary German Studies, 1991.

REINHARZ, JEHUDA, and WALTER SCHATZBERG, ed. *The Jewish Response to German Culture: From the Enlightenment to the Second World War.* Hanover, N. H.: University Press of New England, 1985.

SCHMIDT, MICHAEL. *The New Reich: Violent Extremism in Unified Germany and Beyond.* New York: Pantheon Books, 1993.

SCHNEIDER, PETER. *The German Comedy: Scenes of Life After the Wall.* New York: Noonday Press, 1991.

Hungary

LUKACS, JOHN. *Budapest 1900: A Historical Portrait of a City and Its Culture.* New York: Grove Weidenfeld, 1988.

The Netherlands

Documents of the Persecution of the Dutch Jewry 1940–1945. Joods Historisch Museum, Amsterdam: Polak & Van Gennep, 1979.

HERS, J.F. PH., and J. L. TERPSTRA, ed. *Stress: Medical and Legal Analysis of Late Effects of World War II Suffering in The Netherlands.* The Hague: Gegevens Koninkluke Bibliotheek, 1988.

Poland

ABRAMSKY, CHIMEN, MACIEJ JACHIMCZYK, and ANTONY POLONSKY, eds. *The Jews of Poland.* Oxford: Basil Blackwell, 1986.

DAVIES, NORMAN. *Heart of Europe: A Short History of Poland.* Oxford: Oxford University Press, 1991. (The author is a British professor considered a leading authority on Polish history, but this book is appallingly anti-Semitic.)

DOBROSZYCKI, LUCJAN, ed. *The Chronicle of the Łódź Ghetto 1941–1944.* New Haven: Yale University Press, 1984.

GEBERT, KONSTANTY. "Anti-Semitism in the 1990 Polish Presidential Election," *Social Research,* vol. 58, no. 4 (Winter 1991).

GUTMAN, YISRAEL, EZRA MENDELSOHN, JEHUDA REINHARZ, and CHONE SHMERUK, eds. *The Jews of Poland Between Two World Wars.* Hanover, N.H.: University Press of New England, 1989.

HALKOWSKI, HENRYK. "Cracow, 'City and Mother to Israel,' " in *Cracow: Dialogue of Traditions.* Cracow: Znak, 1991.

HERTZ, ALEKSANDER. *The Jews in Polish Culture.* Evanston, Ill.: Northwestern University Press, 1988.

KLEIN, THEO. *L'Affaire du Carmel d'Auschwitz*. Paris: Jacques Bertoin, 1991.

KRALL, HANNA. *Shielding the Flame: An Intimate Conversation with Dr. Marek Edelman, the Last Surviving Leader of the Warsaw Ghetto Uprising*. New York: Henry Holt, 1986 (almost unbearably artsy approach, but Edelman is fascinating).

PEASE, NEAL. *Poland, the United States and the Stabilization of Europe, 1919–1933*. Oxford: Oxford University Press, 1986.

TOLLET, DANIEL. *Histoire des juifs en Pologne du XVIᵉ siècle à nos jours*. Paris: Presses Universitaires de Paris, 1992.

Soviet Union

GITELMAN, ZVI. *A Century of Ambivalence: The Jews of Russia and the Soviet Union—1881 to the Present*. New York: Schocken Books, 1988.

PINKUS, BENJAMIN. *The Jews of the Soviet Union: The History of a National Minority*. Cambridge: Cambridge University Press, 1988.

RAPOPORT, LOUIS. *Stalin's War Against the Jews: The Doctor's Plot and the Soviet Solution*. New York: The Free Press, 1990.

FICTION

KONRÁD, GEORGE. *A Feast in the Garden*. New York: Harcourt Brace Jovanovich, 1992 (semi-autobiographical novel of growing up in the Holocaust in Hungary through four decades of Hungarian Communism).

OZICK, CYNTHIA. *The Shawl*. New York: Alfred A. Knopf, 1989 (brilliant fictional portrayal of an anguished survivor).

WEIL, GRETE. *The Bride Price*, translated by John Barrett. Boston: David Godine, 1992 (a novel weaving the experiences of a German Jewish survivor with the biblical story of David).

WEIL, JIŘÍ. *Mendelssohn Is on the Roof*, translated by Marie Winn. New York: Farrar, Straus, and Giroux, 1992 (a sparkling tragicomic novel about Nazi-occupied Prague).

INDEX

ACKNOWLEDGMENTS

Thank you is not enough to say to some 150 Jewish people who gave up their time and their privacy and were often willing to stir up the worst of memories to help me understand. They all have my deep affection.

I cannot find the words to thank Christine Toomey, who put many hours into this book, for all her interest, generosity, uncompromising intelligence, and the integrity to tell me whenever I was wrong. At a hundred turns she made this book far better than it would have been.

Also thanks to: Rabbi Chaskel Besser for his advice; Rabbi Hershl Gluck for his help in the Czech and Slovak Republics; Hanna Kordowicz for her generous help, guidance, and friendship in Poland; Edith Kurzweil for her time, her thoughtful and well-informed advice, and her interest; the Mandls in Brno for their hospitality; Carol Mann who helped me through a couple of tough years; my agent Charlotte Sheedy for her wisdom and generosity; Eleanor Michael for her friendship and for sharing both her personal insights and the work of her father Harry Maór; Nancy Miller, my editor, for her clearheaded guidance and her steadfast vote of confidence; Jack and Rubye Monet, whose home was an oasis of warmth and humor; Linda Polman for her help and hospitality in Amsterdam; Daniel and Lynda Altmann for making me feel welcome in their home and community; Yale Reisner for both Russian and Hebrew translations; Irene Runge for her enthu-

A Chosen Few

Mark Kurlansky

A Reader's Guide

A Conversation with Mark Kurlansky

In November 2001, Mark Kurlansky and Philip Gourevitch sat down to discuss *A Chosen Few*. Gourevitch, a staff writer at *The New Yorker* and formerly an editor at *The Forward*, is the author of *We Wish to Inform You That Tomorrow We Will Be Killed With Our Families: Stories from Rwanda* and *A Cold Case*.

Philip Gourevitch: It's nearly ten years now since you traveled through Central and Eastern Europe gathering the material for this book. At that time, the region was still just emerging from half a century behind the Iron Curtain. Today the Communist period already seems a much more remote memory—at least from over here. What is your sense of how the Jewish communities you immersed yourself in for this book have experienced the intervening decade?

Mark Kurlansky: I did the reporting for this book in '92 and '93. I've been back to most of these places since anyway, but I specifically went recently to write a new introduction. The communities have not greatly changed, in part because I did my original reporting after the fall of the Soviet Union, which was a huge event. It is remarkable that the East Germans and the West Germans, both Jews and non-Jews, are no closer together now than they were ten years ago. They are so distinct that you could just walk into a bar or restaurant and pick out who's an Ossie and who's a Wessie. In the Jewish communities in Western Europe, there's a slight difference in atmosphere now because they went through a period, mostly in the '80s, of constant attacks, bombings, and machine gunnings by Palestinian groups. Sometimes neo-Nazi groups claimed the attack, but most of them turned out to be the work of Palestinian groups. This is all clearly remembered but the attacks have become less frequent.

PG: What made them taper off?

MK: I don't think anybody is really sure, since so little was done to apprehend the terrorists. What do you want to bet that some of these people who were doing that then are still very active attacking other places? It is interesting to note that those terrorism networks were not nearly as urgent to uncover and stop when they were just killing Jews. The climate in those places has somewhat changed, although you can still go to any city in Western Europe on Rosh Hashanah, or even on a Friday night, and if you are looking for a synagogue just look for a place where the armed guards are out in the street, and there you will find a synagogue. That has become a way of life for European Jews, just as I suspect it is going to become for American Jews.

PG: When you wrote this book, you were writing in a time of transition, and the transition was a time of hope. There was a sense of emergence and reconnection with the rest of the world—and for Jews with their Jewishness and with international Jewish life more broadly. So when you say that things haven't changed all that much in the intervening decade, I wonder do the people you visited at the time still feel that hope, or has it faded into discouragement?

MK: I would have to say a lot of that hope came from America, or from the world Jewish community. Especially in Central Europe. The Jews there were always a little dubious, kind of dazzled by the interest that the Jews in the rest of the world were taking, and fascinated by what was available to them and what they were learning. And now a lot of these people, a lot of their children, have spent a year or two in Israel—something that was unimaginable before—but it hasn't translated into a flowering of Judaism in Central Europe, partly because the numbers aren't really there, and partly because of the irony that while Communism often repressed Jews it also repressed anti-Semites, or at least right-wing anti-Semites. So now Jews are much freer, but anti-Semites are much freer too. It's extraordinary the kinds of debates that are going on in Poland, that would have been unthinkable under Communism.

PG: Like what? Is the Nazi past being reckoned with or denied, or both?

MK: It was recently discovered in Poland that some Poles actually were involved in the Holocaust. This was not very surprising news to you and me, but when it was revealed by a Polish Jewish writer, Jan Gross, it launched a debate in all of the major newspapers, with hundreds of articles. Some responses have been positive. The government for the first time actually issued an apology. According to a survey, only about 30 percent of the Poles approved of the apology and there is a lot of talk about how this is just a Jewish conspiracy to defame the Polish people. Things get said in these debates that are the kinds of things that you and I would just be appalled by. You have to really extend your imagination to understand why these Jews are there and why they are staying there. After all of the history they have been through and their families have been through and the kinds of things that are still said, you'd say, "Why don't you leave?" They don't leave because it's their home.

PG: Yes, people on the outside often look at people in tough spots and say, "Oh, I would just get out of there," but that really shows a failure of imagination, a failure to understand what it means to have a home, and even more what it means to be displaced from that home as a refugee. There are places in the book where you address this, and suggest that the continuation of European Jewish life after the Holocaust means, in an important way, that Hitler failed. I'm not so sure—but do you continue to feel that?

MK: Yes, in a certain symbolic sense, although I recognize that it isn't very easy to live your life as a metaphor. I went to a regular Friday-night service last week, which happened to be the sixty-third anniversary of Kristallnacht, and the Rabbi commented on the statement it made that we were still all there, a crowded synagogue with hundreds of Jews. You can feel good about that. But it's one thing to go on a Friday night for an anniversary and another to make it your life's work. I don't think that these people were largely motivated by symbolism. It's a thought they may have from time to time and feel good about, but they by-and-large went back and stayed for other reasons, often very pragmatic reasons, and there are a lot of people who really intended to leave someday but just never got it together to go to Israel or wherever it was they were planning on going. Or they came back and got involved with family things—all the things that happen to people that stop them from doing things they are planning on doing.

PG: My experience has been very much that Jewish life in Europe is vestigial—that, yes, there are Jews in Europe but not European Jewry, as it was before the Nazis, and that this reflects the sad fact that non-Jewish Europeans, as a whole, got what they wanted, or anyway lost what they didn't much mind losing. They didn't much care to have Jews around, and when Nazism created the opportunity, they succeeded pretty much in getting rid of them. I don't mean that all Europeans are guilty of banishing Jews, but that in the event, whether it was silently and passively or loudly and aggressively expressed, this was, alas, the sentiment that prevailed. And nowadays, you can certainly find more European Jewish culture in Tel Aviv or in New York or in Melbourne or in L.A., than you can in most European cities, even if there are Jews there. Of course, there's also a new, post-War generation in Europe that tries to act differently from its parents, and—I don't want to generalize—

certainly in Germany and elsewhere that you find the post-War generation feeling guilty, there is a kind of intellectual fetishization of Jews and of antique Jewish culture, which is not entirely comfortable to behold. I wonder if you've encountered this, and if you feel as I do that there is a form of demonstrative philo-Semitism that can smell a lot like anti-Semitism on account of its fascination with Jews as exotic "others."

MK: I think it is basically a modern, politically correct way of being an anti-Semite: Really, we love the Jews. Poles began to crave kosher vodka because the Jews really make it well. Everything Jewish in Poland is very sought after. And there is something clearly anti-Semitic about that but, I think that while you are right about European Judaism existing in Melbourne and in New York and L.A., I don't think that it will remain European in these places. You and I were raised with Europeans in our families. But I have a daughter and it amazes me to realize that she has three American-born grandparents. When I was growing up, somebody with three American grandparents was a WASP. She is growing up without knowing any European Jews. If European Judaism as a culture is going to survive, it won't be here. Here, it will evolve into something else—American Judaism. Only Europe can keep European Judaism alive, and the level of survival of the European Jewish culture tremendously varies from country to country. I would say that—and I have Jewish friends in Poland who are going to be upset with me for saying this—but I would say that it is really not surviving in Poland. There has to be a certain critical mass to have a Jewish community. That is the concept of a minyon. And really, it's not there in Poland. Plus the fact that people who grew up in a Communist society, just like the New York Jews who came from that kind of socialist background, are reflexively secular. Religion is alien. They encourage the religious rituals because they think they're nice, because of "culture," but they don't want to spend their weekend in schul. In Hungary, Budapest has a sizable Jewish community. Paris has a thriving Jewish community with a strong North African component to it. But a lot of the North African Jews were also of European culture.

PG: And do these thriving communities represent a Jewish renewal to you, rather than a vestigial manifestation of the presence of those who remained because they didn't want to or couldn't leave?

MK: I think that Judaism has been throughout its history, since A.D. 70, a diaspora culture that's all about being a minority. In fact, being a small minority. When I'm in Israel, I cannot get used to the notion that we're all Jewish. It doesn't seem to me that we're supposed to all be Jewish. I didn't grow up in a Jewish neighborhood. I'm just very used to the idea that Jews are a tiny group within a group, that functions in this larger country where things work well as part of a country, but it's never a huge force. So, I don't need to see huge Jewish communities throughout Europe to feel like European Judaism is surviving. If there is a Jewish community in most major cities, which there is, and if the Jew who chooses to live a Jewish life is able to, then there is.

PG: So what do you mean when you say Jewish life? When one speaks of a thriving Jewish presence in Europe before the war, it really falls into two categories. On the one hand there were the shtetls and ghettos, distinctively Jewish villages and neighborhoods, where Jews lived largely among themselves, where Yiddish was widely spoken, and religious tradition was strong. And then, on the other hand, there was the very cosmopolitan, assimilated form of Jewish interaction with the non-Jewish world, in the arts and culture, politics, intellectual life, and the sciences.

MK: And that is still there. It is very much there in France. It's there in the Czech Republic. It's there in Poland. I use to laugh at the fact that everybody I knew in Poland was Jewish because I used to go to Poland just to research this book. But subsequently I have gone to Poland researching other things and still almost everybody I know in Poland is Jewish. A lot of prominent people in intellectual life and cultural life and political life in Poland today are Jewish, which is incredible because there are only a few thousand Jews.

PG: Over the years, you've written a number of books about very different peoples and cultures around the world. But when you write, say, about the Basques, you are not a Basque, whereas you are a Jew, and it matters to you, and that comes through in this book. How do you feel that writing about your own people—however distant their experience may be from your own—affected your approach, either as a writer or a reporter? Did your Jewishness make this project closer to you or harder to get close to?

MK: There are two things. As a reporter it made it easier. People ask me, "How did you find these people?" I went to places and said, "I'm a Jew. I want to talk to some Jews." It's not very difficult. But emotionally, I think it was the hardest book I ever did. It was very hard. I would never have set out to write a book about the Holocaust. But in fact I've spent hundreds of hours talking to Holocaust survivors about their experiences, experiences that aren't in the book. But it's what they want to talk about. You can't get to 1945 until you've done the stuff before it. I remember there was one point at which I had done some work in Amsterdam. I was living in Paris and I was going to swing through Antwerp on my way back to Paris and do some research there. I started dreaming at night that I was in Auschwitz and instead I just took a couple of weeks off. It really gets to you. I never had such dreams of identification or connection with the Basques or Caribbeans. I've talked to Basque survivors of Guernica and the Civil War . . . and I could feel their pain but was still able to maintain my position as the objective observer. If you are Jewish you can't objectively talk—I'm not sure anybody can—to Holocaust survivors.

PG: You said you never set out to write a Holocaust book, but did you end up feeling that this is a Holocaust book?

MK: That's a tough question. Because I so wanted it not to be.

PG: But then the Holocaust permeates the territory you chose, and it comes to permeate you when you immerse yourself in that territory.

MK: It does. One of the truly horrible things about the Holocaust is that it doesn't end in 1945. It keeps affecting our lives in the way we think, and it will affect the way our children see the world. Sixty years later. And so yes, it is a Holocaust book. It is a book about survivors and how they dealt with being survivors. It taught me things that I will always remember. Listening to that CEO of Cantor Fitzgerald after the World Trade Center attack, I knew what was getting to him was the fact that he had all these people who died and he didn't. He survived. In *A Chosen Few* I spent hours and hours listening to the pain of people of who had survived wondering why they survived and what their life means and what right do they have to survive. Yeah, this has to be a Holocaust book, because for it not to be a Holocaust book you would have to have survivors in 1945 saying, "Oh, thank God that is over, and now onto something else."

PG: You write that if you want to find Jews in many parts of Central and Eastern Europe you go to the graveyard, because that's where they go—the three or four surviving Jews in the town—to be

with their people and meet visiting Jews from elsewhere. That is an extremely powerful image. So it's not a metaphor to call Europe a cemetery of Jews, even as Jews continue to live there. And I felt that the impetus for your book came from your desire to examine that tension: "How could any Jew want to live in Europe at this point? Let's find out. Let's see how they think about it." I wonder how you found attitudes toward the Holocaust past—and toward its continuing presence—to differ in the communities you visited from the attitudes one finds amongst American Jews, who have become so steeped in the legacy of the Holocaust that at times you almost feel like the extermination of European Jewry has come to be one of the cornerstones of Jewish identity.

MK: My big fear is that we will become—almost in a Christian way—a culture of martyrdom.

PG: Have you ever thought about writing another book on a subject that is as deeply personal to you?

MK: Personal issues, yes, but not necessarily so personal a setting. But I am working right now on a novel that is very Jewish. It's set in New York and as I write, it keeps getting more and more Jewish. In fact, in seven books from *Cod*, to my books about the Basques to the Caribbean, to *Salt*, I have never written a book that does not mention the Jews. It always comes up because it is part of my view of the world. I think when you are Jewish, your Jewish concerns have a life of their own and keep coming to the surface whether you want them to or not.

PG: At the same time, as you say, Jews have been a diasporic people for two thousand years, and the way that one's Jewish concerns surface and are expressed is distinctively colored by where you live. A French Jew and a Russian Jew may feel their common Jewishness strongly, and not only when Hitlerian push comes to Stalinist shove, but their national identities may exert at least an equal and opposite sense of difference between them. Consider how Primo Levi was acutely aware of and perceptive about the manifestations of national character among his fellow inmates at Auschwitz.

MK: A lot of Jews don't like to think about this, but the truth is that the nationalism is not an unimportant part of my book. That is why certain Jews wanted to go back to Germany—because they were Germans and they liked Germany. The Jews I know in Poland are a very special group of people not only because they came back but because they stayed through all the anti-Semitic campaigns. They were a small minority of the Jews who were there in 1945. After the pogrom in 1946, many left. Things kept happening and Jews kept leaving. These were the hardcore people who stayed. They stayed because Poland is their home and they love Poland. There is this tremendous tension between the Jews in Poland and Jews in the United States because Jews in the United States hate Poland, and they know it in Poland and both Jews and Poles there resent it.

PG: That makes sense, especially when you consider that among the Jews in Poland there must be a great many who were protected—or whose parents were protected—through the Holocaust and since by their Catholic neighbors. In fact, many who were hidden in this way as children are steeped in Polish Catholic culture, and a good many Jews have continued to live as Catholics, or at least as non-Jews. This is something one finds in the Czech republic and Hungary, unrecognized or unacknowledged Jews.

MK: Madeline Albright is a classic story.

PG: Yes, and it remains awfully hard to believe that she was as shocked as she claimed to be to learn of her Jewishness. I suspect that many Jews who were raised as Christians in Europe do know, at least vaguely, about their ancestry, and of course these days especially there are Jewish groups coming around seeking them out and trying to win them back.

MK: In a lot of these countries—Germany and Poland are two outstanding examples—it is practically a vocation to be a Jew. And not everyone wants to spend the rest of their lives in this vocation of being one of the 7,000 Jews in Poland. But in the time I was researching this book, the Jewish population of these places, especially in central Europe, was growing dramatically.

PG: You mean because Jews were coming out of the closet, so to speak?

MK: Yes, a lot of people, and this was very exciting.

PG: And now?

MK: I was back in Warsaw recently and some had gone much deeper into Judaism, but others say, "This was an interesting experience, but now I want to get on with my life." But sometimes their children have done a lot of Jewish studies there, and even in Israel, to the point where parents are getting concerned that perhaps they are doing too much.

PG: It's the eternal question for Jews: How Jewish—or assimilated—is it okay to be?

MK: Exactly. It's always too much or too little.

Reading Group Questions
and Topics for Discussions

1. The book both opens and closes with Passover. What is the significance of this holiday to this story?

2. What has been the impact of the Holocaust on subsequent generations of European Jews? How does this differ from the impact on subsequent generations of American Jews?

3. Was it reasonable for Jews to return after the war to the countries where they had been betrayed?

4. After the fall of Communism, very few Jews were left in Eastern Europe who had any experience with the practice of the religion. What does it mean to rebuild a Jewish community with secular Jews?

5. Explain the difference in motivation between those Jews who returned to East Germany and those who returned to West Germany after the war.

6. Should the Zionists who returned to postwar Europe have gone to Israel instead?

7. Would it have been easier to rebuild a religious community or an assimilated community in postwar Europe?

8. Has European Jewry since 1945 undergone a resurrection, as implied in the subtitle of this book, or is it something less than that?

9. What impact has the state of Israel had on European Jews?

10. What does it mean for American Jews that these communities in Europe still exist?

11. Throughout European history, France was always thought of as a haven for Jews, until the twentieth century. As the country with the largest Jewish population in Europe, will it be a haven or a dangerous place for Jews going forward into the twenty-first century?

12. Why is the survival of European Jewry so crucial to the Jewish people throughout the rest of the world?

A Reader's Guide

13. In countries with some of the worst records of treatment of Jews, it has become fashionable to embrace everything Jewish. Is this philo-Semitism another form of anti-Semitism, and is it dangerous?

14. Three million Polish Jews were killed in the Holocaust, and most of those who returned were subsequently driven out. In the current political climate of Poland, is there a future for Jews, and are there enough to build a real community?

15. Why do survivors in Holland appear to be in more pain than in most other countries? Is it because Holland never came to terms with its war history? Is it that as a society, Holland is more open to discussing psychological problems than other countries in Europe?

16. What has the impact of terrorism been on Jewish communities in Europe?

17. Russian Jews have been immigrating to Western Europe, especially Germany, most of them with very little knowledge of Judaism. What will be their impact?

18. What has been the role of the Hasidic movement in modern European Judaism?

19. Following the Six-Day War, the Soviet Union, Eastern Europe, and even deGaulle's France shifted their policies toward Israel. What was the impact on European Jewry?

20. Are the communities described in this book merely vestigial or is there a future for Jewry in Europe?

© Lisa Klausner

Mark Kurlansky is the author of *Salt*; *The Basque History of the World*; the *New York Times* bestseller *Cod: A Biography of the Fish that Changed the World*; *A Continent of Islands: Searching for the Carribean Destiny*; and a collection of stories, *The White Man in the Tree*. He is a regular contributor to the *Partisan Review*. He has also written for the *International Herald Tribune*, the *Chicago Tribune, Harper's*, and *The New York Times Magazine*, among other publications. He lives in New York City.